ABUSIR XI

THE ARCHITECTURE OF THE MASTABA OF PTAHSHEPSES

To my mother

Excavations of the Czech Institute of Egyptology

ABUSIR XI

THE ARCHITECTURE OF THE MASTABA OF PTAHSHEPSES

Jaromír Krejčí

Czech Institute of Egyptology,
Faculty of Arts,
Charles University in Prague
Academia,
Publishing House of the Academy of Science of the Czech Republic
Prague 2009

Reviewers: Peter Jánosi, Břetislav Vachala

Preparation and publication of this monograph was supported by the Czech Grant Agency by means of the Grant No. GAČR D404/99/D003, and by the Ministry of Education, Youth and Physical Education through the Research Projects No. MSM 11210006 and MSM 0021620826.

Photographs: Archives of the Czech Institute of Egyptology, Faculty of Arts, Charles University in Prague; Jaromír Krejčí, Jaroslav Novotný, Kamil Voděra, Milan Zemina; Sammlung des Ägyptologischen Instituts der Universität Heidelberg

Illustrations: Jaromír Krejčí, Jolana Malátková, Luděk Wellner, Vladimír Hamata; Griffith Institute, Oxford

ISBN 978-80-200-1728-4

Contents

Abbreviations, sources and bibliography

Abbreviations

ACER	Australian Centre for Egyptology Report, Sydney
ÄAT	Ägypten und Alten Testament, Wiesbaden
ÄgAbh.	Ägyptologische Abhandlungen, Wiesbaden
ÄF	Ägyptologische Forschungen, Glückstadt–Hamburg–New York–Brussels
Ä&L	Ägypten und Levante, Wien
AV	Archäologische Veröffentlichungen, Mainz
ArOr	Archiv orientální, Praha
ASAE	Annales du service des antiquités de l'Égypte, Le Caire
ASAW	Abhandlungen der Sächsischen Akademie der Wissenschaften zu Leipzig, Berlin
BAR	British Archaeological Reports, Oxford
BdE	Bibliothéque des études, Le Caire
Beiträge Bf.	Beiträge zur ägyptischen Bauforschung und Altertumskunde, Zürich, Wiesbaden
CASAE	Cahiers. Supplément aux Annales du Service des Antiquités de l'Égypte, Le Caire
CCE	Cahiers de la Céramique égyptienne, Le Caire
DAWW	Denkschrift der Kaiserlichen Akademie der Wissenschaften in Wien, Philosophisch-historische Klasse, Wien; see also: *DÖAW*
DE	Discussions in Egyptology, Oxford
DÖAW	Denkschriften der Österreichischen Akademie der Wissenschaften, Philosophisch-historische Klasse, Wien
EA	Egyptian Archaeology, London
GM	Göttinger Miszellen, Göttingen
GOF	Göttinger Orientforschungen, Wiesbaden
HÄB	Hildesheimer ägyptologische Beiträge, Hildesheim
Internationale Archäologie	Internationale Archäologie, Espelkamp
IBAES	Internet Beiträge zur Ägyptologie und Sudanarchäologie, Berlin
JEA	Journal of Egyptian Archaeology, London
JNES	Journal of Near Eastern Studies, Chicago
LÄ	Lexikon der Ägyptologie. Begründet von Wolfgang Helck und Eberhard Otto. Herausgegeben von Wolfgang Helck und Wolfhardt Westendorf, I–VII, Wiesbaden, 1975–1992
MÄS	Münchener ägyptologische Studien, München–Berlin
MÄU	Münchener ägyptologische Untersuchungen, Frankfurt
MDAIK	Mitteilungen des Deutschen Archäologischen Instituts, Abteilung Kairo, Augspurg, Wiesbaden, Mainz, Berlin–New York
MonAeg.	Monumenta Aegyptiaca, Bruxelles
NAWG	Nachrichten von der Akademie der Wissenschaften zu Göttingen, phil.-hist. Klasse, Göttingen
OBO	Orbis biblicus et orientalis, Fribourg–Göttingen
Or	Orientalia, Nova Series, Roma
OrMonsp.	Orientalia Monspeliensia, Montpellier

PASA	Publications of The Archaeological Society of Alexandria, Alexandria
Radiocarbon	Radiocarbon, New Haven
RevArch	Revue archéologique, Paris
RdE	Revue d'Égyptologie, Le Caire, Paris
SAK	Studien zur altägyptischen Kultur, Hamburg
SASAE	Supplément aux Annales du service des antiquités de l'Égypte, Le Caire
SDAIK	Sonderschrifte des Deutschen archäologischen Institut, Abt. Kairo, Mainz
STBMÄS	Staatliche Museen zu Berlin, Mitteilungen aus der Ägyptischen Sammlung
Výtvarné umění	Výtvarné umění, Praha
WVDOG	Wissenschaftliche Veröffentlichungen der Deutschen Orient-Geselschaft, Leipzig
WZKM	Wiener Zeitschrift für die Kunde des Morgendlandes, Wien
ZÄS	Zeitschrift für Ägyptische Sprache und Altertumskunde, Leipzig, Berlin

Sources

Midžiak, J., *Výkopový deník, rok 1968* [Excavation Notebook 1968], Archives of the Czech Institute of Egyptology

Váhala, F., *Zpráva o 10. misi Čs. egyptologického ústavu do Egypta ve dnech od 17. ledna až do 10. června 1974* [Report on the 10th expedition of the Czechoslovak Institute of Egyptology to Egypt from 17th January to 10th June 1974], Archives of the Czech Institute of Egyptology, qu. 32, V/67/1962

Žába, Z., *Zpráva o 2. expedici Čs. egyptologického ústavu KU do SAR (12. 4.–16. 12. 61)* [Report on the 2nd expedition of the Czechoslovak Institute of Egyptology of the Charles University to UAR (12/04–16/12/1961)], Archives of the Czech Institute of Egyptology, qu. 4, V/67/1962

Žába, Z., *Report on the state of the Clearance of the Mastaba of Ptahshepses at Abusir at the time of the second season of the work done by the Czechoslovak Institute of Egyptology of Charles University* (for the Director General of the Department of Antiquities. Anwar Shukri, Cairo), Giza, December 1961, Archives of the Czech Institute of Egyptology

Žába, Z., *Work in the Tomb of Ptahshepses, Abusir; third season* (for the Director General of the Department of Antiquities, Cairo), Giza, September 9, 1962, Archives of the Czech Institute of Egyptology

Žába, Z., *Zpráva o výsledcích předcházející, VII. výpravy (1966)* [Report on results of the previous, seventh expedition (1966)], Archives of the Czech Institute of Egyptology, qu. 19, V/6a/1968

Žába, Z., *Zpráva o VIII. vědecké výpravě ČsEÚ do SAR* [Report on the Eighth scientific expedition of the Czechoslovak Institute of Egyptology to UAR), Archives of the Czech Institute of Egyptology, qu. 19, V/19/1968

Žába, Z., *Zpráva o páté vědecké výpravě Čs. egyptologického ústavu UK do Abúsíru (SAR) – Výkop Ptahšepsesovy mastaby, 12. XII. 1969–18. VI. 1970* [Report on the fifth scientific expedition of the Czechoslovak Institute of Egyptology at the Charles University to Abusir (UAR) – Excavation of the mastaba of Ptahshepses, 12/12/1969–18.6.1970], Archives of the Czech Institute of Egyptology, qu. 19, V/31/70

Žába, Z., *Find of Columns in the Mastaba of Ptahshepses in Abusir*, unpublished and undated manuscript, Archives of the Czech Institute of Egyptology

Žába, Z., *Excavations Mastaba of Ptahshepses in Abusir*, unpublished and undated manuscript, Archives of the Czech Institute of Egyptology, Prague

Žába, Z., *The Mastaba of Ptahshepses at Abûsîr. A preliminary report on the excavation of the Mastaba of Ptahshepses at Abûsîr done by the Czechoslovak Institute of Egyptology of Charles University in the years 1960–1, 1966, 1968 and 1970*, unpublished and undated manuscript Archives of the Czech Institute of Egyptology, Prague

Monographs and miscellanea bands

Abusir and Saqqara 2000 – M. Bárta, J. Krejčí (eds.), *Abusir and Saqqara in the Year 2000, Archiv Orientální Supplementa IX*, Prague 2001

Abusir and Saqqara 2001 – F. Coppens (ed.), *Abusir and Saqqara in the Year 2001. Proceedings of the Symposium (Prague, September 25th–27th, 2001), ArOr* 70/3 (2002)

Abusir and Saqqara 2005 – M. Bárta, F. Coppens, J. Krejčí (eds.), *Abusir and Saqqara in the Year 2005*, Prague 2006

L'acqua – A. Amenta, M. M. Luiselli, M. N. Sordi (eds.), *Proceedings of the First International Conference for Young Egyptologists, L'acqua nell'antico Egitto, Egitto Antico*, Vol. III/1, Roma 2005

Ägyptische Tempel – R. Gundlach, M. Rochholz (eds.), *Ägyptische Tempel – Struktur, Funktion und Programm (Akten der Ägyptologischen Tempeltagungen in Gosen 1990 und in Mainz 1992), HÄB 37* (1994)

Alexanian, *Netjer-aperef* – N. Alexanian, *Dahschur II. Das Grab des Prinzen Netjer-aperef. Die Mastaba II/1 in Dahschur, AV* 56 (1999)

Altenmüller, *Begräbnisritual* – H. Altenmüller, *Zum Begräbnisritual in den Pyramiden des Alten Reiches. ÄgAbh.* 24 (1972)

Archäologie und Korrespondenzanalyse – J. Müller, A. Zimmermann (eds.), *Archäologie und Korrespondenzanalyse. Beispiele, Fragen, Perspektiven. Internationale Archäologie* 23 (1997)

Arnold, *Building* – Di. Arnold, *The Building in Egypt. Pharaonic Stone Masonry*, New York 1991

Arnold, *Baulexikon* – Di. Arnold, *Lexikon der ägyptischen Baukunst*, Zürich 1994

Arnold, *Architecture* – Di. Arnold, *The Encyclopedia of Ancient Egyptian Architecture*, Cairo 2003

L'art égyptienne – Do. Arnold, K. Grzymski, Ch. Ziegler (eds.), *L'art égyptien au temps des pyramides*, Paris 1999

Aspects of Early Egypt – J. Spencer, *Aspects of Early Egypt*, London 1996

Aufrère, *Univers minéral* – S. H. Aufrère, L'univers minéral dans la pensée égyptienne, Vols. 1–2, BdÉ 105/1–2 (1992)

Badawy, *Egyptian Architecture* – A. Badawy, *History of Egyptian Architecture I, From the Earliest Times to the End of Old Kingdom*, Giza 1954

Badawy, *ʿAnkhmʿahor* – A. Badawy, *Tomb of Nyhetep-Ptah at Giza and the Tomb of ʿAnkhmʿahor at Saqqara, University in California Publications, Occasional Papers* 11, Berkeley–Los Angeles–London 1978

Baer, *Rank and Title* – K. Baer, *Rank and Title in the Old Kingdom*, Chicago 1960

Balík, *Mastaba* – M. Balík, *Mastaba. Objevování a rekonstrukce staroegyptské hrobky* [A Mastaba. Unearthing and reconstruction of an ancient Egyptian tomb], Praha 2002

Bárta *et al.*, *Qar* – M. Bárta *et al.*, *Abusir XIII. The Tomb complex of the vizier Qar and his sons. Part I: Tombs of the vizier Qar, Qar Junior and Senedjemib*, Prague (2009)

Baud, *Famille royal* – M. Baud, *Famille royale et pouvoir sous l'Ancien Empire égyptien*, *BiEtud* 126 (1999)

Begelsbacher-Fischer, *Götterwelt* – B. L. Begelsbacher-Fischer, *Untersuchungen zur Götterwelt des Alten Reiches, OBO* 37 (1981)

Bissing, *Gem-ni-kai* – F. W. von Bissing, *Die Mastaba des Gem-ni-kai*, I–II, Berlin 1905–1911

Bolshakov, *Man and his Double* – A. Bolshakov, *Man and his Double in Egyptian Ideology of the Old Kingdom, ÄAT* 37 (1997)

Bonnet, *Reallexikon* – H. Bonnet, *Reallexikon der ägyptischen Religionsgeschichte*, Berlin 1952

Borchardt, *Denkmäller* II – L. Borchardt, *Denkmäller des Alten Reiches im Museum von Kairo, Nr. 1295-1808, Teil II*, Le Caire 1964

Borchardt, *Pflanzensäule* – L. Borchardt, *Die aegyptische Pflanzensäule*, Berlin 1897

Borchardt, *Re-Heiligtum* I – L. Borchardt, *Das Reʿ-Heiligtum des Königs Ne-woser-reʿ (Rathures). Herausg. von F. H. F. von Bissing. Band I, Der Bau*, Berlin 1905

Borchardt, *Neferirkare* – L. Borchardt, *Das Grabdenkmal des Königs Nefer-ír-keꜣ-reʿ*, *WVDOG* 11, Leipzig 1909

Borchardt, *Neuserre* – L. Borchardt, *Das Grabdenkmal des Königs Ne-user-reʿ*, *WVDOG* 7 (1907)

Borchardt, *Sahure* I – L. Borchardt, *Das Grabdenkmal des Königs Śaꜣḥu-reʿ*, *Band I – Bau*, *WVDOG* 14 (1910)

Borchardt, *Sahure* II – L. Borchardt, *Das Grabdenkmal des Königs Śaꜣḥu-reʿ*, *Band II – Die Wandbilder*, *WVDOG* 26 (1913)

Boulos, *Flora* I – L. Boulos, *Flora of Egypt, Volume One, Azollaceae-Oxalidaceae*, Cairo 1999

Brinks, *Grabanlagen* – J. Brinks, *Die Entwicklung der königlichen Grabanlagen des Alten Reiches*, *HÄB* 10 (1979)

Brovarski, *Senedjemib* – E. Brovarski, *Giza Mastabas Volume 7, The Senedjemib Complex, Part I, The Mastabas of Senedjemib Inti (G2370), Khnumenti (G 2374), and Senedjemib Mehi (G 2378)*, Boston 2001

Brunner, *Felsgräber* – H. Brunner, *Die Anglagen der ägyptischen Felsgräber bis zum Mittleren Reich*, *ÄF* 3 (1936)

Brunner-Traut, *Seschemnofer* – E. Brunner-Traut, *Die altägyptische Grabkammer Seschemnofers III. aus Gîsa*, Mainz 1993

Capart, *Rue de tombeaux* – J. Capart, *Une rue de tombeaux à Saqqarah*, I–II, Bruxelles 1907

CEAEM[2] – S. Clark, R. Engelbach, R. – *Ancient Egyptian Masonry. The Building Craft.* (Oxford 1930) – 2nd edition – *Ancient Egyptian Construction and Architecture*, New York 1992

Cherpion, *Mastabas* – N. Cherpion, *Mastabas et hypogées d'Ancien Empire. Le probleme de la datation*, Bruxelles 1989

Critères de datation – N. Grimal (ed.), *Les critères de datation stylistiques à l'Ancien Empire*, *BiEtud* 120 (1998)

Charvát, *Pottery* – P. Charvát, *The Mastaba of Ptahshepses, The Pottery*, Prague 1981

Davies, *Ptahhetep* – N. de Garis Davies, *The Mastaba of Ptahhetep and Akhethetep at Saqqareh* I–II, London 1900–1901

Duel, *Mereruka* – P. Duell, *The Mastaba of Mereruka* I–II, Chicago 1938

Edel, Wenig, *Jahreszeitenreliefs* – E. Edel, S. Wenig, *Die Jahreszeitenreliefs aus dem Sonnenheligtum des Königs Ne-user-Re*, *STBMÄS* 7 (1974)

Eigner, *Grabbauten* – D. Eigner, *Die monumentalen Grabbauten der Spätzeit in der thebanischer Nekropole* 1, *DÖAW* 8 (1984)

Egyptian Museum Collection – M. Eldamaty, M. Trad (eds.), *Egyptian Museum Collection around the World*, Cairo 2002

Épron, Daumas, *Le tombeau de Ti I* – L. Épron, F. Daumas, *Le tombeau de Ti. Fascicule I. Les approches de la chapelle.* Le Caire 1939 (see also Wild, *Le tombeau de Ti* III)

Firth, Gunn, *TPC* – C. M. Firth, B. Gunn, *Excavations at Saqqara. Teti Pyramid Cemeteries*, Vol. 1–2, Cairo 1926

Fitzenreiter, *Statue und Kult* – M. Fitzenreiter, *Statue und Kult, Eine Studie der funerären Praxis an nichtköniglichen Grabanlagen der Residenz im Alten Reich*, *IBAES* 3 (2001)

Feucht, *Vom Nil zum Neckar* – E. Feucht, *Vom Nil zum Neckar, Kunstschätze Ägyptens aus pharaonischer und koptischer Zeit an der Universität Heidelberg*, Berlin–Heidelberg–New York 1986

Foucart, *L'ordre lotiforme* – G. Foucart, *Histoire de l'Ordre lotiforme*, Paris 1897

Fritz, *Typologie* – U. Fritz, *Typologie der Mastabagräber des Alten Reiches*, *Achet* 5 (2004)

Fs Petráček – P. Zemánek (ed.), *Studies in Near Eastern Languages and Literatures, Memorial Volume of Karel Petráček*, Praha 1996

Fs Sawi – K. Daoud, S. Abd el-Fatah (eds.), *The World of Ancient Egypt. Essays in Honor of Ahmed Abd el-Qader el-Sawi*, *SASAE* 35 (2006), 159–165

Fs Schott – W. Helck (ed.), *Festschrift für Siegfried Schott zu seinem 70. Geburtstag*, Wiesbaden 1968

Germer, *Flora* – R. Germer, *Flora des pharaonischen Ägypten*, *SDAIK* 14 (1985)

Grab und Totenkult – H. Guksch, E. Hoffmann, M. Bommas (eds.), *Grab und Totenkult im alten Ägypten*, München 2003

HWB Äg.-Deutsch – R. Hannig, *Die Sprache der Pharaonen. Großes Handwörterbuch Ägyptisch-Deutsch (2800– 950 v.Chr.)*, *Lexica 1*. Mainz 1995

Harpur, *Decoration* – Y. Harpur, *Decoration in Egyptian Tombs of the Old Kingdom. Studies in orientation and scene content*, London 1987

Hassan, *Gîza* – S. Hassan, *Excavations at Gîza*, Vols. I–X, Oxford, Cairo 1929–1960

Hassan-Iskander, *Hemet-Rᶜ*– S. Hassan, Z. Iskander, *Mastabas of Princess Hemet-Rᶜ and Others, Excavations in Saqqara, 1937–1938*, Volume II, Cairo 1975

Hassan, Iskander, *Neb-Kaw-Her* – S. Hassan, Z. Iskander, *The Mastaba of Neb-Kaw-Her, Excavations at Saqqara, 1937–1938, Vol. I*, Cairo 1975

Hassan, Iskander, *Ny-ᶜankh-Pepy* – S. Hassan, Z. Iskander, *Mastabas of Ny-ᶜankh-Pepy and Others, Excavations in Saqqara, 1937–1938 Vol. II*, Cairo 1975

Helck, *Beamtentitel* – Helck, W., *Untersuchungen zu den Beamtentiteln des ägyptischen Alten Reiches, ÄF 18* (1954)

Hölscher, *Chephren* – U. Hölscher, *Das Grabdenkmal des Königs Chephren*, Leipzig 1912

Homm. Leclant – C. Berger, G. Clerc, N. Grimal (eds.), *Hommages à Jean Leclant*. I–IV, *BdE* 106/1 (1994)

Homm. Lauer – C. Berger, B. Mathieu (eds.), *Études sur l'Ancienne Empire et la nécropole de Saqqâra dédiées à Jean-Philippe Lauer*, *OrMonsp*. IX (1997)

James, Apted, *Khentika* – T. G. H. James, M. R. Apted, *The Mastaba of Khentika called Ikhekhi*, London 1953

Jánosi, *Pyramidenanlagen* – P. Jánosi, *Die Pyramidenanlagen der Königinnen. Untersuchungen zu einem Grabtyp des Alten un Mittleren Reiches*, *DÖAW* 13 (1996)

Jánosi, *Giza* – P. Jánosi, *Giza in der 4. Dynastie, Band I: Die Mastabas der Kernfriedhöfe und die Felsgräber*, *DÖAW* 30 (2005)

Jánosi, *Gräberwelt* – P. Jánosi, *Die Gräberwelt der Pyramidenzeit*, Mainz 2006

Jéquier, *Manuel* – G. Jéquier, *Manuel d'archéologie égyptienne. Les élements de l'architecture*, Paris 1924

Jéquier, *Mastabat Faraoun* – G. Jéquier, *Fouilles à Saqqarah, Le Mastabat Faraoun*, Le Caire 1928

Jéquier, *Neit et Apouit* – Jéquier, G., *Fouilles à Saqqarah. Les pyramides des reines Neit et Apouit*, Le Caire 1933

Jéquier, *Oudjebten* – G. Jéquier, *Fouilles à Saqqarah. La pyramide d'Oudjebten*, Le Caire 1928

Jéquier, *Tombeaux* – G. Jéquier, *Tombeaux des particuliers contemporains de Pepi II*, Le Caire 1929

Jéquiér, *Pepi II* – G. Jéquier, *Le monument funéraire de Pepi II. I–III*, Le Caire 1936–1940

Jones, *Titles* – D. Jones, *An Index of Ancient Egyptian Titles, Epithets and Phrases of the Old Kingdom*, *BAR* 866 (2000)

Junker, *Gîza* – H. Junker, *Bericht über die von der Akademie der Wissenschaften in Wien auf gemeinsame Kosten mit Dr. Wilhelm Pelizaeus unternommenen Grabungen auf dem Friedhof des Alten Reiches bei den Pyramiden von Gîza*. I–XII, *DAWW* 69–75 (1929–1953)

Kanawati, *Governmental Reforms* – N. Kanawati, *Governmental Reforms in Old Kingdom*, Warminster 1980

Kanawati, *el-Hawawish* 4 – N. Kanawati, *The Rock Tombs of el-Hawawish, Vol. 4*, Sydney 1987

Kanawati, Abder-Raziq, *Meryteti* – N. Kanawati, M. Abder-Raziq, *Mereruka and His Family. Part I. The Tomb of Meryteti, ACER* 21 (2005)

Kanawati, Abder-Raziq, *Neferseshemre* – N. Kanawati, M. Abder-Raziq, *The Teti Cemetery at Saqqara, Vol. III, The tombs of Neferseshemre and Seankhuiptah, ACER* 11 (1998)

Kanawati, Abder-Raziq, *Nikauisesi* – N. Kanawati, M. Abder-Raziq, *The Teti Cemetery at Saqqara, Vol. VI, The Tomb of Nikauisesi, ACER* 14 (2000)

Kanawati, Abder-Raziq, *Iyneferet* – N. Kanawati, M. Abder-Raziq, *The Unis Cemetery at Saqqara, Vol. II, The Tombs of Iyneferet and Ihy (reused by Idut), ACER* 19 (2003)

Kanawati, Hassan, *Nedjetempet* – N. Kanawati, A. Hassan, *Teti Cemetery at Saqqara* I, *ACER* 8 (1996)

Kees, *Re-Heiligtum* III – H. Kees, *Das Reᶜ-Heiligtum des Königs Ne-woser-reᶜ (Rathures). Herausg. von F. H. F. von Bissing, Band III, Die Grosse Festdarstellung*, Leipzig 1928

Kees, *Totenglauben* – H. Kees, *Totenglauben und Jenseitsvorstellungen der Alten Ägypter. Grundlagen und Entwicklung bis zum Ende des Mittleren Reiches*, Berlin 1956

el-Khouli, Kanawati, *el-Hammamiya* – A. el-Khouli, N. Kanawati, *The Old Kingdom Tombs of el-Hammamiya, ACER* 2 (1990)

Klemm, Klemm, *Steinbrüche* – R. Klemm, D. D. Klemm, *Steine- und Steinbrüche im Alten Ägypten*, Berlin–Heidelberg 1993

Korecký, *Objevy* – M. Korecký, *Objevy pod pyramidami* [Discoveries below the pyramids] Praha 1983

Krejčí, *Stavebně-historický vývoj* – J. Krejčí, *Stavebně-historický vývoj abúsírské královské nekropole v době Staré říše* [Building and historical development of the Abusir royal necropolis during the Old Kingdom], unpublished Ph.D. thesis, Charles University in Prague 1999

Labrousse, *L'architecture à textes* I – A. Labrousse, *L'architecture des pyramides à textes* I. *Mission archéologique de Saqqara* III, *BdE* 114/I (1996)

Labrousse, Lauer, Leclant, *Le temple haute du roi Ounas* – A. Labrousse, J.-Ph. Lauer, J. Leclant, *Le temple haut du complexe funéraire du roi Ounas. Mission archéologique de Saqqarah* II, *BdE* 73 (1977)

Labrousse, Lauer, *Ouserkaf* – A. Labrousse, J.-Ph. Lauer, *Les complexes funéraires d'Ouserkaf et de Néferhétepès, BdE* 130 (2000)

Lauer, *Pyr. à degrés* – J.-Ph. Lauer, *La Pyramide à degrés* I, Le Caire 1936

Lauer, *Hist. mon.* I – J. Ph. Lauer, *Histoire monumentale des pyramides d'Egypte, Vol. 1, Les Pyramides à degrés (IIIᵉ Dynastie)*, Le Caire 1962

Lauer, Leclant, *Teti* – J.-Ph. Lauer, J. Leclant, *Le temple haut du complexe funéraire du roi Téti* I, Le Caire 1972

LD – K. R. Lepsius, *Denkmäler aus Aegypten und Aethiopien*, Berlin 1849

LD, Text I – K. R. Lepsius, *Denkmäler aus Aegypten und Aethiopien. Text.* Eduard Naville (ed.), Lepzig 1897

Leclant, *Pépi I* – J. Leclant, *Recherches dans la pyramide et au temple du pharaon Pépi Ier à Saqqarah*, Leiden 1979

Lehmann, *Serdab* – K. Lehmann, *Der Serdab in den Privatgräbern des Alten Reiches*, Ph.D. thesis, University of Heidelberg, Heidelberg 2000 (http://www.ub.uni-heidelberg.de/archiv/2863)

Lehner, *Complete Pyramids* – M. Lehner, *The Complete Pyramids*, Cairo 1997

Macramallah, *Idout* – R. Macramallah, *Le mastaba d'Idout*, Le Caire 1935

Mariette, *Mastabas* – A. Mariette, *Les mastaba de l'ancienne empire. Fragment du dernier ouvrage de A. Mariette, publié d'après le manuscrit de l'auteur par G. Maspero. Livraison 1– 8*, Paris 1882–1885

Martin, *Garantsymbol* – K. Martin, *Ein Garantsymbol des Lebens: Untersuchung zu Ursprung und Geschichte der altägyptischen Obelisken bis zum Ende des Neuen Reiches, HÄB* 3 (1977)

Martin, *Horemheb* – G. Martin, *The Memphite tomb of Horemheb, commander-in-chief of Tut'ankhamun, 1., The reliefs, inscriptions, and commentary*, London 1989

de Morgan, *Carte de la nécropole memphite* – J. de Morgan, *Carte de la nécropole memphite. Dahschour, Sakkarah, Abou-Sir*, Le Caire 1897

de Morgan, *Souvenirs* – A. Jaunay, *Mémoires de Jacques de Morgan. Souvenirs d'un archéologue*, Paris 1997

Mostafa, *Opfertafeln* – M. M. F. Mostafa, *Untersuchungen zu Opfertafeln im Alten Reich, HÄB* 17 (1982)

Moursi, *Hohenpriester des Sonnengottes* – M. I. Moursi, *Die Hohenpriester des Sonnengottes von der Frühzeit Ägyptens bis zum Ende des Neuen Reiches, MÄS* 26 (1972)

Moussa, Altenmüller, *Nianchchnum und Chnumhotep* – A. M. Moussa, H. Altenmüller, *Nianchchnum und Chnumhotep, Old Kingdom Tombs at the Causeway of King Unas at Saqqara Excavated by the Department of Antiquities, AV* 21, 1977

MRA – V. Maragioglio, C. Rinaldi, *L'architettura delle piramidi menfite* II–VII, Rapallo–Torino 1963–1977

Munro, *Unas-Friedhof* – P. Munro, *Der Unas Friedhof Nord-West* I, *Topographisch-historische Einteilung. Das Doppelgrab der Königinnen Nebet und Khenut*, Mainz 1993

Murray, *Saq. Mast.* – M. A. Murray, *Saqqara mastabas* I, London 1905

Naggar, *Voûtes* – S. el-Naggar, *Les voûtes dans l'architecture de l'Égypte ancienne, BdE* 128/1–2 (1999)

OHAE – I. Shaw (ed.), *The Oxford History of Ancient Egypt*, Oxford 2000

OKAA – M. Bárta (ed.), *Old Kingdom Art and Archaeology*, Prague 2004

Patočková, *Fragmenty soch* – B. Patočková, *Fragmenty soch z Ptahšepsesovy mastaby v Abúsíru* [Fragments of the statues from the Mastaba of Ptahshepses in Abusir], unpublished M.A. Thesis, Charles University in Prague 1994

Perring, Vyse, *Appendix* – J. S. Perring, H. Vyse, *Appendix to Operations Carried on at the Pyramids of Gizeh in 1837*, London 1842

Petrie, *Architecture* – W. M. F. Petrie, *Egyptian Architecture*, London 1938

Petrie, *Deshasheh* – W. M. F. Petrie, *Deshasheh*, London 1898

Petrie, *Royal Tombs* – W. M. F. Petrie, *The Royal Tombs of the Earliest Dynasties* I-II, London 1900–1901

Petrie, *Antaeopolis* – W. M. F. Petrie, *Antaeopolis. The tombs of Qau*, London 1930

Petrie, Mackay, Wainwright, *Meydum and Memphis* – W. M. F. Petrie, E. Mackay, G. Wainwright, *Meydum and Memphis, Vol. III*, London, 1910

Petrie, Murray, *Seven Memphite tomb chapels* – H. F. Petrie, M. A. Murray, *Seven Memphite tomb chapels*, London 1952

Phillips, *Columns* – J. P. Phillips, *The Columns of Egypt*, Manchester 2002

PM – B. Porter, R. L. B. Moss, *Topographical Bibliography of Ancient Egyptian Hieroglyphic Texts, Reliefs and Paintings. 7 vol.*, Oxford 1927–52, 2nd ed. since 1960, revised and augmented by J. Malek

Posener-Kriéger, de Cenival, *Abu Sir Papyri* – P. Posener-Kriéger, J. L. de Cenival, *Hieratic Papyri in the British Museum. Fifth Series. The Abu Sir Papyri*, London 1968

Posener-Kriéger, *Les papyrus d'Abousir* – P. Posener-Kriéger, *Les archives du temple funéraire de Néferirkare*ᶜ*-Kakai (Les papyrus d'Abousir), Traduction et commentaire I–II. BdE* 65 (1976)

Preliminary Report – Verner, M. *et al.*, *Preliminary Report on Czechoslovak Excavations in the Mastaba of Ptahshepses at Abusir*, Prague 1976

Pyramid studies – J. Baines, T. G. H. James, A. Leahy, A. F. Shore (eds.), *Pyramid studies and other essays presented to I. E. S. Edwards*, London 1988

Ranke, *PN* – H. Ranke, *Die ägyptischen Personennamen*, Glückstadt 1935

Reisner, *Mycerinus* – G. A. Reisner, *Mycerinus. The Temples of the Third Pyramid at Giza*, Cambridge, Mass. 1931

Reisner, *Tomb Development* – G. A. Reisner, *The Development of the Egyptian Tomb to the Accession of Cheops*, Cambridge, Mass. 1936

Reisner, *Giza Necropolis* – G. A. Reisner, *A History of the Gîza Necropolis, Volume I*, Oxford 1942

Ricke, *Bemerkungen AR* I–II – H. Ricke, *Bemerkungen zur ägyptischen Baukunst des Alten Reichs* I-II, *Beiträge Bf.* 4–5 (1944, 1950)

Roik *Längenmaßsystem* – E. Roik, *Das Längenmaßsystem im alten Ägypten*, Hamburg 1993

Saad, *Helwan* – Z. Y. Saad, *Royal Excavations at Helwan (1945–1947), SASAE* 14 (1951)

Schäfer, *Priestergräber* – H. Schäfer, *Priestergräber und andere Grabfunde vom Ende des Alten Reiches bis zur Griechischen Zeit vom Totentempel des Ne-user-Re*ʿ, *WVDOG* 8 (1908)

Schmitz, *Königssohn* – B. Schmitz, *Untersuchungen zum Titel S3-NJŚWT „Königssohn"*. Bonn 1976

Simpson, *Qar and Idu* – W. K. Simpson, *The Mastabas of Qar and Idu. G 7101 and 7102. Giza Mastabas* 2, Boston 1976

Smith, *Sculpture* – W. S. Smith, *A History of Egyptian Sculpture and Painting in the Old Kingdom*, Oxford 1946

Smith, *Art and Architecture* – W. S. Smith, *The Art and Architecture of Ancient Egypt*, Harmondsworth 1958

Spencer, *Brick Architecture* – A. J. Spencer, *Brick Architecture in Ancient Egypt*, Warminster 1979

Stadelmann, *Pyramiden* – R. Stadelmann, *Die ägyptischen Pyramiden – vom Ziegelbau zum Weltwunder*, 2nd ed., Mainz 1991

Stationen – H. Guksch, D. Polz (eds.), *Stationen. Beiträge zur Kulturgeschichte Ägyptens. Rainer Stadelmann gewidmet*, Mainz 1998

Steckweh, *Qâw* – H. Steckweh, *Die Fürstengräber von Qâw, Verröffentlichungen der Ernst von Sieglin-Expedition Sechster Band*, Leipzig 1936

Steindorff, *Grab des Ti* – G. Steindorff, *Das Grab des Ti*, Leipzig 1913

Strouhal, Bareš, *Secondary Cemetery* – E. Strouhal, L. Bareš, *Secondary Cemetery in Mastaba of Ptahshepses at Abusir*, Praha 1993

Structure and Significance – P. Jánosi (ed.), *Structure and Significance. Thoughts on ancient Egyptian architecture, DÖAW* 33 (2005)

Strudwick, *Administration* – N. Strudwick, *Administration of Egypt in the Old Kingdom*, London 1986

Studies Simpson – P. der Manuelian (ed.), *Studies in Honor of William Kelly Simpson*, Boston 1996

Temple in Ancient Egypt – S. Quirke (ed.), *The Temple in Ancient Egypt*, London 1997

Temples of Ancient Egypt – B. E. Shafer, *Temples of Ancient Egypt*, London–New York 1997

Unearthing – M. Verner *et al.*, *Objevování starého Egypta. Unearthing Ancient Egypt 1958–1988*, Prague 1990

Userkaf-SH I/II – H. Ricke (ed.), *Das Sonnenheiligtum des Königs Userkaf*, *Beiträge Bf.* 7–8 (1965, 1969)

Urk. I – K. Sethe, *Urkunden des aegyptischen Altertums (begr. von Georg Steindorff). Urkunden des Alten Reichs. Erster Band*, Leipzig 1933

Vachala, *Literární texty* – B. Vachala, *Nejstarší literární texty v nekrálovských hrobkách egyptské Staré říše* [The Oldest Literary Texts in Non-Royal Tombs of the Egyptian Old Kingdom], Brno 2000

Vachala, *Relieffragmente* – B. Vachala, *Abusir VIII. Die Relieffragmente aus der Mastaba des Ptahschepses in Abusir*, Prag 2004

Verner, *Reliefs* – M. Verner, *Abusir I. The Mastaba of Ptahshepses. Reliefs I/1*, Prague 1986

Verner, *Baugraffiti* – M. Verner, *Abusir II. Baugraffiti der Ptahschepses Mastaba*, Prague 1992

Verner, *Forgotten Pharaohs* – M. Verner, *Forgotten Pharaohs, Lost Pyramids. Abusir*, Prague 1994.
Verner, *Khentkaus* – M. Verner, *Abusir III. The Pyramid Complex of Khentkaus*, Prague 1995
Verner, *Pyramids* – M. Verner, *Pyramids. The Mystery, Culture, and Science of Egypt's Great Monuments*, New York 2001
Verner, *Realm of Osiris* – M. Verner, *Abusir. Realm of Osiris*, Cairo 2003
Verner, Callender, *Djedkare's Cemetery* – M. Verner, V. G. Callender, *Abusir VI. Djedkare's Family Cemetery*, Prague 2002
Verner *et al.*, *Raneferef* – M. Verner *et al.*, *Abusir IX. The Pyramid Complex of Raneferef. The Archaeology*, Prague 2006
Wb – A. Erman, H. Grapow (eds.), *Wörterbuch ägyptische Sprache*, I–VI, Berlin–Leipzig 1926–1961
Weeks, *Cemetery G 6000* – K. R. Weeks, *Mastabas of Cemetery G 6000, Including G 6010 (Neferbauptah); G 6020 (Iymery); G 6030 (Ity); G 6040 (Shepseskafankh), Giza Mastabas* 5, Boston 1994
Wege öffnen – M. Schade-Busch, *Wege öffnen*. Festschrift für Rolf Gundlach zum 65. Geburtstag, *ÄAT* 35 (1996)
Wiebach, *Scheintür* – S. Wiebach, *Die ägyptische Scheintür. Morphologischen Studien zur Entwicklung und Bedeutung der Hauptkultstelle in den Privat-Gräbern des Alten Reiches*, PhD. Diss. University of Hamburg, Hamburg 1981
Wild, *Le tombeau de Ti* III – H. Wild, *Le tombeau de Ti. Fascicule III. La chapelle (deuxième partie)*, Le Caire 1966 (see also Épron, Daumas, *Le tombeau de Ti* I)

Articles

Alexanian, N.,
- 'Ritualrelikte an Mastabagräbern des Alten Reiches', in: *Stationen*, 3–22
- 'Himmelstreppen und Himmelsaufstieg. Zur Interpretation von Ritualen auf Grabdächern im Alten Reich', in: *Grab und Totenkult*, 27–40

Altenmüller, H.,
- 'Zu Isis und Osiris', in: *Wege öffnen*, 1–17
- 'Der Grabherr des Alten Reiches in seinem Palast des Jenseits, Bemerkungen zur sog. Prunkscheintür des Alten Reiches', in: *Homm. Lauer*, 11–19
- 'Die Nachtfahrt des Grabherrn im Alten Ägypten. Zur Frage der Schiffe mit Igelkopf', *SÄK* 28 (2000), 1–27
- 'Der Himmelsaufstieg des Grabherrn. Zu den Szenen des *zšš w3ḏ* in den Gräbern des Alten Reiches', *SÄK* 30 (2002), 1–42
- 'Funerary Boats and Boat Pits of the Old Kingdom', in: *Abusir and Saqqara 2001*, 269–290

Arnold, Di.,
- 'Rituale und Pyramidentempel', *MDAIK* 33 (1977), 1–14
- 'Zur Zestörungsgeschichte der Pyramiden', *MDAIK* 47 (1991), 21–27
- 'Royal cult complexes of the Old and Middle Kingdoms', in: *Temples of Ancient Egypt*, 31–85

Balík, M., Vachala, B.,
- 'The scientific restitution of the Ptahshepses' mastaba at Abusir – an ideal reconstruction', in: *Abusir and Saqqara 2000*, 317–330

Bard, K. A.,
- 'The Emergence of the Egyptian State (c. 3200–2868 BC)', *OHAE*, 61–88

Barker, H., Burleigh, R., Meek, N.,
- 'British Museum Natural Radiocarbon Measurements VII', *Radiocarbon* 13 (1971), 157–188

Bárta, M.,
- 'Serdab and Statue Placement in the Private Tombs down to the Fourth Dynasty', *MDAIK* 54 (1998), 65–75
- 'The Mastaba of Ptahshepses Junior II at Abusir', *Ä&L* 10 (2000)

– 'Architectural Innovations in the Development of the Non-Royal Tomb During the Reign of Nyuserra', in: *Structure and Significance*, 105–125
Bonnet, H.,
– *'Ägyptische Baukunst und Pyramidenkult'*, *JNES* 12 (No. 4) (1953), 257–273
Brescianni, E,
– *'Serdab'*, in: *LÄ* V, 874–879
Daressy, D.,
– 'Inscription hiératique d'un mastaba d'Abousir', *BIE* III, Sér. 5, 1894, 109
Edel, E.,
– 'Zu den Inschriften auf den Jahreszeitenreliefs der „Weltkammer" aus den Sonnenheligtum des Niuserre', *NAWG* 8 (1961), 209–255
– 'Zu den Inschriften auf den Jahreszeitenreliefs der „Weltkammer" aus den Sonnenheligtum des Niuserre. II. Teil', *NAWG* 5 (1963), 89–217
Firth, C. M.,
– 'Excavations of the Department of Antiquities at Saqqara (October 1928 to March 1929)', *ASAE* 29 (1929), 64–70
Haeny, G.,
– 'Dach', *LÄ* I, 974–976
Hassan, S.,
– 'Les Fouilles', *CdE* 13 (1938), 68–70
Helck, W.,
– 'Treppe', *LÄ* VI, 755–756
Hoffmeier, J. K.,
– 'The Use of the Basalt in Floors of Old Kingdom Pyramid Temples', *JARCE* 30 (1993), 117–123
Hölzl, R.,
– 'Libation Basins from the Old to the New Kingdom: Practical Use and Religious Significance', in: *L'acqua*, 309–317
Jánosi, P.,
– 'Die Pyramidenanlage der »anonymen Königin« des Djedkare-Isesi', *MDAIK* 45 (1989), 187–202
– 'Die Entwicklung und Deutung des Totenopferraumes in den Pyramidentempeln des Alten Reiches', in: *Ägyptische Tempel*, 143–163
– 'Les tombes privées »des maisons d'éternité«', in: *L'art égyptien*, 56–63
– '„Im Schatten" der Pyramiden – Die Mastabas in Abusir. Einige Beobachtungen zum Grabbau der 5. Dynastie', in: *Abusir and Saqqara 2000*, 445–466
– 'Aspects of Mastaba Development: The Position of Shafts and the Identification of Tomb Owners', in: *Abusir and Saqqara 2001*, 337–350
Jéquier, G.,
– 'Rapport préliminaire sur les fouilles exécutées en 1924–1925 dans la partie méridionale de la nécropole Memphite', *ASAE* 25 (1925), 55–75
Junker, H.,
– 'Bedeutung und Symbolik der steinernen Becken in den Gräbern des Alten Reiches', *ArOr* 20 (1952),185–189
Kaiser, W.,
– 'Zu den Sonnenheligtümmer der 5. Dynastie', *MDAIK* 14 (1956), 104–116
Kanawati, N.,
– 'The Financial Resources of the Viziers of the Old Kingdom and the Historical Implications', *PASA* 5 (1974), 1–20
Korecký, M.,
– *Výtvarné umění*, 9–10 (1962), 482
Krejčí, J.,
– 'The origins and development of the royal necropolis at Abusir during the Old Kingdom', in: *Abusir and Saqqara 2000*, 467–484
Krejčí, J., Magdolen, D.,
– 'Research into Fifth Dynasty sun temples – past, present and future', in: *OKAA*

Krejčí, J., Verner, M.,
– 'Die „Zwillingspyramide" L 25 in Abusir', *Sokar* 8/1 (2004), 20–22
– 'Twin Pyramid Complex "Lepsius no. XXV" in Abusir', *Fs Sawy*

Labrousse, A.,
– 'Discovery of the Pyramid of Queen Ankhesenpepy II', *EA* 13 (1998), 9–11

Magdolen, D.,
– 'Some Notes on One Graffito from the Mastaba of Ptahshepses at Abusir', *GM* 182 (2001), 87–96

Malek, J.,
– 'The 'altar' in the pillared court of Teti's pyramid-temple at Saqqara', in: *Pyramid studies*, 23–34

Martin-Pardey, E.,
– 'Ptahwasch', *LÄ* IV, 1181–1182
– 'Ptahhotep (*Ptḥ-ḥtp(w)*)', *LÄ* IV, 1181

Meader, J., Demeter, B.,
– 'On closer Inspection. The Egyptian Blue Water Lily', *Kmt* 15:2, Summer 2004, 59–63

de Morgan, J. J.,
– 'Découverte du mastaba de Ptah-chepsés dans la nécropole d'Abou-Sir', *RevArch* 24 (3e série), 1894, 18–33

O'Connor, D.,
– 'Boat Graves and Pyramids Origin', *Expedition* 33/3 (1991), 5–17
– 'The Interpretation of the Old Kingdom Pyramid Complex', in: *Stationen*, 135–144

Patočková, B.,
– 'Fragments de statues découverts dans le mastaba de Ptahchepses à Abousir', in: *Critères de datation*, 227–233

Radwan, A.,
– 'Ein Treppengrab der 1. Dynastie aus Abusir', *MDAIK* 47 (1991), 305–308
– 'Recent Excavations of the Cairo University at Abusir. "A Cemetery of the 1st Dynasty"', *MÄU* 4 (1995), 311–314
– 'Mastaba XVII at Abusir (First Dynasty): preliminary results and general remarks', in: *Abusir and Saqqara 2000*, 509–514

el Raziq, M. A., Krekeler, A.,
– '1. Vorbericht über die Arbeiten des Ägyptischen Antikendienstes im nördlichen Teti-Friedhof in Saqqara im Jahre 1986', MDAIK 43 (1986), 215–224

Reisner, G. A.,
– 'The History of the Egyptian Mastaba', in: *Mell. Maspero* I, 579–584

Rochholz, M.,
– 'Sedfest, Sonnenheiligtum und Pyramidenbezirk. Zur Deutung der Grabanlagen der 5. un 6. Dynastie', in: *Ägyptische Tempel*, 255–285
– 'Statuen und Statuendarstellungen im Grab des *Ptḥ-šps*', *SÄK* 21 (1994), 259–273

Roth, A. M.,
– 'The Absent Spouse: Patterns and Taboos in Egyptian Tomb Decoration', *JARCE* 36 (1999), 37–53

Rzeuska, T. I.,
– 'The Pottery from the Funerary Complex of Vizier Merefnebef (West Saqqara). The Evidence of a Burial and Cult of the Dead in the Old Kingdom', in: J. Popielska-Grzybowska (ed.), *Proceedings of the First Central European Conference of Young Egyptologists, Egypt 1999: Perspectives of Research, Warsaw, 7–9 June 1999, Świantowit Supplement Series E: Egyptology*, vol. 1, *Warsaw Egyptological Studies* III, Warsaw 2001
– 'The Necropolis at West Saqqara: The Late Old Kingdom Shafts with No Burial Chamber. Were they False, Dummy, Unfinished or Intentional, in: *Abusir and Saqqara 2001*, 377–402

Schmitz, B.,
- 'Königssohn', *LÄ* III, 626–630

Seidlmayer, S. J.,
- 'Stil und Statistik, Die Datierung dekorierter Gräber des Alten Reiches – ein Problem der Methode', in: *Archäologie und Korrespondenzanalyse*, 17–51

Soukiasian, G.,
- 'A Governers' Palace at ʿAyn Asil, Dakhla Oasis', *EA* 11 (1997), 15–17

Stadelmann, R.,
- 'Rampe', *LÄ* V, 100

Stadelmann, R., Alexanian, N.,
- 'Die Friedhöfe des Alten und Mittleren Reiches in Dahschur', *MDAIK* 54 (1998), 293–315

Vachala, B.,
- 'Ein weiterer Beleg für die Königin Repewetnebu?', *ZÄS* 106 (1979), 176
- 'Literarische Texte aus der Mastaba des Ptahschepses in Abusir', in: *Fs. Petráček*, 581–587

te Velde, H.,
- 'Ptah', *LÄ* IV, 1177–1180

Verner, M.,
- 'Discovery of an Obelisk at Abusir', *RdE* 28 (1976), 111–118
- 'Excavations at Abusir. Season 1976 – Preliminary Report', *ZÄS* 105 (1978), 155–157
- 'Excavations at Abusir. Season 1978/1979 – Preliminary Report', *ZÄS* 107 (1980), 158–164
- '*Ṯbt* – Ein bisher unbekanntes altägyptisches Maß?', *MDAIK* 49 (1981), 479–481
- 'Eine zweite unvollendete Pyramide in Abusir', *ZÄS* 109 (1982), 75–78
- 'Excavations at Abusir. Season 1980/1981 – Preliminary Report', *ZÄS* 109 (1982), 157–166
- 'Excavations at Abusir. Season 1982 – Preliminary Report', *ZÄS* 111 (1984), 70–78
- 'Ein entfallener und ein neuer Beleg zur Geschichte der achtstengligen Lotossäule', *BSE* 9–10 (1984–1985), 323–336
- 'Les statuettes de prisonniers en bois d'Abousir', *RdE* 36 (1985), 145–152
- 'Les sculptures de Rêneferef découvertes à Abousir', *BIFAO* 85 (1985), 267–280
- 'Un roi de la Ve Dynastie: Rêneferef ou Rênefer?', *BIFAO* 85 (1985), 281–284
- 'Zu den «Baugraffiti mit Datumsangaben» aus dem Alten Reich', in: *Mell. Mokhtar*, 339–346
- 'Excavations at Abusir. Season 1984/85 – Preliminary Report', *ZÄS* 113 (1986), 154–163
- 'A Slaughterhouse from the Old Kingdom', *MDAIK* 42 (1986), 181–189
- 'Supplément aux sculptures de Rêneferef découvertes à Abousir', *BIFAO* 86 (1986), 361–366
- 'Remarque sur le temple solaire *Ḥtp-Rʿ* et la date du mastaba de Ti', *BIFAO* 87 (1987), 293–297
- 'Excavations at Abusir. Season 1985/1986 – Preliminary Report', *ZÄS* 115 (1988), 77–84
- 'Excavations at Abusir. Season 1987 – Preliminary Report', *ZÄS* 115 (1988), 163–171
- 'A Late Dynasty 5 Cemetery at Abusir', *ZÄS* 117 (1990), 72–78
- 'Remarks on the Pyramid of Neferirkare', *MDAIK* 47 (1991), 411–418
- 'Archaeological Survey of Abusir', *ZÄS* 119 (1992), 116–124
- 'Excavations at Abusir. Seasons of 1994/95 and 1995/96', *ZÄS* 124 (1997), 71–85
- 'Newly Disovered royal sarcophagi from Abusir', in: *Abusir and Saqqara 2000*, 561–580

– 'Archaeological Remarks on the 4th and 5th Dynasty Chronology', *ArOr* 69 (2001), 363–418
– 'Once more to Niuserre's dyad', in: *Egyptian Museum Collection*, 1195–1203
– 'The Columns of Abusir', in: *OKAA*, 343–356

Wartke, R.,
– 'Zum Alabaster-Altar des Königs Sahu-Rē', *ZÄS* 104 (1977), 145–156

Winter, E.,
– 'Zur Deutung der Sonnenheiligtümer der 5. Dynastie', *WZKM* 54 (1957), 222–233

List of ilustrations

(authors of photographs were: *JK* – Jaromír Krejčí, *JN* – Jaroslav Novotný, *VM* – Vladimír Martinák, *KV* – Kamil Voděra, *MZ* – Milan Zemina)

Plates

Chapter 1

Chapter 2

Chapter 3

Chapter 4.1

Chapter 4.2

Chapter 4.3

Chapter 4.4

Chapter 5

Acknowledgements

In the first place I would like to thank Prof. Miroslav Verner for his entrusting to me the investigation into the architecture of the Ptahshepses mastaba in Abusir, and for his valuable help and advice during the preparation of the book. However, my thanks also go to Doz. Peter Jánosi (Vienna) for his sound and frank advice, which has been invaluable in shaping this present manuscript. Very special thank goes to Dr. Vivienne Gae Callender (Sydney), who not only discussed with me a number of problems connected with the mastaba, but also took an active role in helping me to determine probable family relationships between the tomb's owner and members of the royal family. I am also very indebted to her for reading of the final version of the manuscript. Special thank goes to Dr. Robert Anderson (London) for his assistance in obtaining the Robert Anderson Charitable Fund grant, which enabled me to work in London's Egyptological libraries. I am also indebted to him for his generous hospitality and companionship whilst I was in London and thank him sincerely.

In addition to these friends, I would also like to thank Prof. Hartwig Altenmüller (Hamburg), Prof. Dieter Arnold (New York), Dr. Tarek El-Awady, M.A., (Cairo), Prof. Ladislav Bareš (Prague), Prof. Erika Feucht (Heidelberg), Dr. Eva Pardey (Löweste), Mgr. Barbora Patočková-Krumphanzlová (Prague), and Prof. Eugen Strouhal (Prague) for discussions concerning various facets of individual problems described in this book.

I would like to express my gratitude to those who made important contributions to this publication, namely to Ing. Luděk Wellner for his co-operation in connection of the pen-and-ink drawings, to Ing. Vladimír Hamata for his time and expertise freely given in the preparation of the computer three-dimensional visualisations of the mastaba's architecture, to Ing. Jolana Malátková for her work on the colour reconstruction of the palace-façade decoration in Room no. 26, to Ing. Marta Štrachová for scanning the majority of the photographs used and for the typesetting of the book. I would also like to add my appreciation to Mesdames Malátková and Štrachová for their valuable help during the proof-reading of the book, and to Mr. Philip McIntosh for an earlier reading of the first version of the manuscript.

For the entire period of preparation of the manuscript, I very appreciated the personal support and ongoing encouragement given to me by Dr. Dušan Magdolen (Bratislava).

Last but not least, I wish to thank my family: first of all, my parents Blanka and Pavel for their encouragement of my work and tolerance during many absences whilst the work was in progress. And, to my sister Hana and all her family, I give my heartfelt thanks for their constant support.

Motto:

'In English the word "architecture" can mean either a process – the thoughts and acts of designing and erecting a large artefact – or its product – a building, a bridge, a defensive wall, a ship. Viewing buildings from a distance over time, we tend naturally to focus our attention on the finished product. We try to "read" it much as we do works of art, music, and literature. We ask what a building has to say, or how it resonated among its contemporaries and later generations. We trace the influence of styles and ideas. ... Buildings have a functional importance in life quite apart from aesthetics. They do not carry a "subject matter," such as a mythological narrative or a moral message, in the same straightforward way as other artistic genres. Yet it was understood that architecture was full of meaning, and every effort was made to exploit its expressive and communicative potential...'

Rabun Taylor, *Roman Builders. A Study in Architectural Process* (Cambridge, 2003), 9.

Introduction

The Mastaba of Ptahshepses is one of the most important monuments in the Abusir necropolis. It is both one of the largest and probably the most complicated non-royal tomb of the Old Kingdom. It has, therefore, an important place in the development of ancient Egyptian architecture during the time of the pyramid builders. Its extraordinary appearance was influenced by the unusual course of the life of its owner. He became not only the highest official in the country, but also a direct member of the royal family. Because of his high rank in the royal court and direct connections with the royal family, Ptahshepses was able to use in his own mastaba architectural elements that had previously been exclusive to royal mortuary monuments.

The building development of the mastaba shows the increasing importance of the already significant social position of Ptahshepses towards the end of his life. In addition to that, the mastaba presented in its final building stage a large construction which in some respects came close to the dimensions of a royal mortuary temple. These features possibly reflect the key role which may have been played by Ptahshepses in connection with Niuserre's ascent to royal power. The complexity of the tomb's ground plan and its size hint at the introduction of changes in ancient Egyptian society during Niuserre's reign. These processes, which started in the second half of the Fifth Dynasty and peaked during the Sixth Dynasty, include among others, the gradual weakening of the state administration system and of the slowly declining power of the king. This resulted at the end of the Sixth Dynasty in the overall decline of the Egyptian state.

The Mastaba of Ptahshepses is one of a group of large mastabas built during this period. These tombs incorporated some of the same or similar elements of architecture. Moreover, they are set apart from other non-royal tombs built in the Memphite area by their impressive dimensions. In this way, they clearly show how prestigious the construction of a tomb was for the nobility of the time and, that as already N. Kanawati has shown,[1] tomb construction was one of the main indicators of their social status.

The above mentioned facts underline the importance of the need for a thorough examination of the development of the building that is the Mastaba of Ptahshepses. They also define the questions connected to this monument. Answering these questions is, apart from other issues raised, the main task of this monograph. This mission is not easy. As is the case with other stone monuments in the Abusir Pyramid Necropolis, the Mastaba of Ptahshepses was badly destroyed by stone robbers and other intrusive activities and only parts of the original architecture have remained *in situ*.

This present monograph is aimed at describing, evaluating and attempting the reconstruction of the mastaba's architecture. In addition to these aims, the monograph discusses the place of the mastaba not only in the development of non-royal funerary architecture, but also in connection with the development of royal architecture in the middle of the Fifth Dynasty. Tracing the forms and elements used in ancient Egyptian architecture formed an important segment in the investigation of our attempt to evaluate the function of the separate mastaba's rooms and spaces. Another important question, closely associated with the architectural elements used, has to deal with the dating of the mastaba's construction. These are some of the lines of investigation that the reader will encounter in this volume.

---

[1] N. Kanawati, 'The Financial Resources of the Viziers of the Old Kingdom and the Historical Implications', *PASA* 5 (1974), 1–20.

For Czech Egyptology, the work undertaken in the Mastaba of Ptahshepses has a very special importance. It was the first archaeological location excavated by the team from the Charles University in the Abusir Pyramid Necropolis. In its turn, the work provided a sound basis for further activities conducted by the Charles University of Prague on this site. In this monograph, not only the results of the Czech (formerly, Czechoslovak) excavations in the area of Ptahshepses' mastaba, but also other contributions concerning the tomb, such as its architecture and archaeology will be presented and discussed. As is clear from the title of the present volume, *The Architecture of the Mastaba of Ptahshepses*, this monograph will not include separate finds (such as the fragments of statues and relief decoration, stone vessels or Late Period burials) unearthed during the archaeological excavations; only data relevant to the description of the mastaba's architecture and its development will be incorporated here.

In the first chapter, the history of the research of the mastaba is described on the basis of the documents housed in the Archives of the Czech Institute of Egyptology, at the Faculty of Arts at the Charles University in Prague; this includes previous accounts concerning the excavation of the mastaba (for which see the chapter *History of the research*). The second chapter is dedicated to elucidating what we know about the tomb owner, Vizier Ptahshepses, his social status and his role within the royal court at that time. In addition to him, other members of his family (in particular, his known wife, Princess Khamerernebty) will be introduced (*Ptahshepses and his family*). The archaeological and epigraphic material concerning these persons will be discussed at this point. The special place of the mastaba in the development of the Abusir pyramid field is discussed in the third chapter (*The location of the mastaba*). The topographical placement of the tomb might have been influenced by several factors which will be noted in this chapter.

The largest part of the monograph, however, is represented by the fourth chapter, which is dedicated to the description of the individual building stages of the mastaba (*The building and architectural development of the mastaba*). Besides the description of the remaining masonry and the architectural elements, possible reconstructions of the original appearance of the mastaba's respective parts are presented as well. The fifth chapter (*Architectural and functional analysis of the mastaba*) emphasises some features of the mastaba's architecture which are discussed in the broader context of the development of ancient Egyptian architecture during the Third Millennium B.C. This chapter also includes a discussion on the spatial and functional analysis of the mastaba. One also tries here to put the architecture of the Ptahshepses mastaba and its individual elements into the broader context of both non-royal and royal architecture of the period. The sixth chapter, the *Conclusions*, will sum up the previously mentioned topics and the place of the tomb and its owner in the framework of the development of the Old Kingdom. The first part of this chapter is devoted to an analysis of the dating of the mastaba's construction, based on the study of the written sources concerning Vizier Ptahshepses and on investigations into the architecture of the mastaba of this powerful man from the middle of the Fifth Dynasty.

During the work, which is a result of the post-doctoral Grant Project GAČR D404/99/D003, Research Project MSM 11210006 and a consequent result of the Research Project MSM 0021620826, the author of the present monograph has not only been able to use the plan, the archaeological records and architectural and photographic documentation held in the Archives of the Czech Institute of Egyptology, but has also had the opportunity to study the architecture and the masonry of the Ptahshepses mastaba on site. The author is most grateful to previous colleagues who dealt with the tomb of Ptahshepses and, above all, to the Charles University and the Government of the Czech Republic who funded this work. This exhaustive survey was mainly carried out in the years 2000–2001, and at this time the author produced the photographs and plans which are presented in this volume. During subsequent years, this data was evaluated and has now become part of the *Abusir* series published by the Czech Institute of Egyptology.

Note 1: Main building stages of the Mastaba of Ptahshepses

In trying to describe, analyse and evaluate the architecture of the mastaba, it is very important that the complex nature of its development should be taken into consideration. With this aim in mind, it becomes crucial for a valid analysis of the monument's function and its architecture for the author to provide a chronological approach to the monument. For this reason, the description and evaluation of the tomb's architecture, phase by phase, has been seen as essential. In order to prevent any misunderstanding of terms, a summary of the separate building phases can be found in the following lines.

The first building stage covers the north-west part of the mastaba (Room nos. 21–31, see *chapter 4.1*). The basic architectural layout of the mastaba during this phase is fully comparable with the standard non-royal tomb of its times – it represents a rectangular, north-west oriented mastaba with the entrance in its eastern outer wall. Despite the fact that, at this stage, the mastaba could be classed as being typical for its time, this building stage still incorporated some features exceptional for the architecture of a non-royal tomb (of especial note is the saddle roof in the burial chamber). As this building phase created the nucleus of the future vast temple tomb of the vizier, the modern denomination "Initial Mastaba" for this building stage has been used throughout the text of this monograph. An annex (Room nos. 3–10, see *chapter 4.2*) was then built to the east of the Initial Mastaba, but this new addition only occupied the northern half of the eastern façade of the Initial Mastaba. This new annex presents the next, or *second building stage* and it included beside the storerooms and an extraordinary chapel with a triple altar for statues, also a grand new entrance to the mastaba with a pair of lotus bundle columns (this is the area now called the Old Portico). During the final major building phase of the tomb, here marked as *the third building stage*, the south-eastern and south-western parts of the Mastaba of Ptahshepses were built (Room nos. 1, 3, 11–20, 32–39, see *chapter 4.3*). During this construction phase, the mastaba became a vast construction and one of the largest non-royal buildings and very probably the most complicated non-royal tombs of its time. Moreover, its complicated ground plan, with a large pillared courtyard and tens of rooms and spaces, implies the performance of complicated rituals also connected with statues of the tomb owner (and other members of his family) erected in the monument's rooms and spaces. There is also the fact that a large amount of offerings and ritual instruments must have been housed in this vast building. Some minor adjustments were made after the completion of the third building stage, more than likely, after the death of Ptahshepses (see *chapter 4.4*). One has also to mention the construction of the mighty mud brick enclosure wall which was the last major building change in the development of the Ptahshepses mastaba.

The extent of the separate building phases can be traced because of the still existing casing blocks of the mastaba's outer walls, as well as by their imprints within the remaining construction. The courses of these casings have been thoroughly studied and documented in order to reconstruct the extent of the mastaba in its individual building stages (*cf.* respective discussions in chapter 4).

Note 2: The numbering of the rooms

The numbering of the tomb's rooms and spaces in this book follows numbers used in the *Preliminary Report* volume published in 1976 (for further information about this volume, see *chapter 1*). This numbering was also used in previous monographs relating to the Mastaba of Ptahshepses. For the numbers of individual rooms and spaces, see the plan in *fig. 1.9*. All spaces in the mastaba, regardless of whether they were roofed or open, are named as "rooms" combined with the number given to the individual space by Z. Žába. In some instances, other denominations ("Boat-room"– Room no. 40, "Old Portico" – Room no. 3, "Chapel with Three Niches" – Room no. 4) are also utilised because they were used more frequently than the room numbers themselves – even during the excavations and in subsequent studies on the tomb's masonry, epigraphy, relief decoration, *etc.*

1. History of the research

The Ptahshepses mastaba, lying in the central part of the Abusir Pyramid Necropolis necropolis, was not studied until 1840s. It is well known that *Karl Richard Lepsius*, during his exploration in the area of the Memphite necropolis, also visited Abusir (*fig. 1.1*). Aside from his investigation of the monuments in the royal

Fig. 1.1 Overall plan of the Abusir necropolis made by K. R. Lepsius

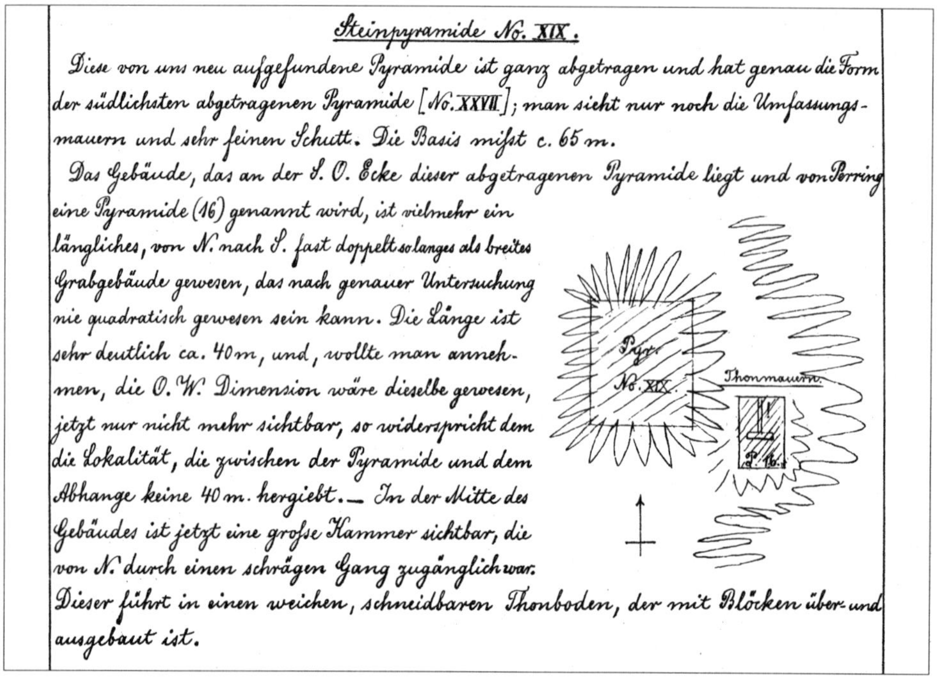

Steinpyramide No. XIX.

Diese von uns neu aufgefundene Pyramide ist ganz abgetragen und hat genau die Form der südlichsten abgetragenen Pyramide [No. XXVII]; man sieht nur noch die Umfassungsmauern und sehr feinen Schutt. Die Basis mißt c. 65 m.

Das Gebäude, das an der S. O. Ecke dieser abgetragenen Pyramide liegt und von Perring eine Pyramide (16) genannt wird, ist vielmehr ein längliches, von N. nach S. fast doppelt so langes als breites Grabgebäude gewesen, das nach genauer Untersuchung nie quadratisch gewesen sein kann. Die Länge ist sehr deutlich ca. 40 m, und, wollte man annehmen, die O. W. Dimension wäre dieselbe gewesen, jetzt nur nicht mehr sichtbar, so widerspricht dem die Lokalität, die zwischen der Pyramide und dem Abhange keine 40 m. hergiebt. — In der Mitte des Gebäudes ist jetzt eine große Kammer sichtbar, die von N. durch einen schrägen Gang zugänglich war. Dieser führt in einen weichen, schneidbaren Thonboden, der mit Blöcken über- und ausgebaut ist.

Fig. 1.2 Sketch plan of the area of the Mastaba of Ptahshepses – Lepsius' Pyramid no. XIX – by K. R. Lepsius

necropolis, he also paid some attention to the tomb of Ptahshepses. He marked the monument – wrongly, as it turned out – as a pyramid. This rather common sort of Lepsius's error was mainly due to the dimensions and the appearance of the destroyed monument.[1] Therefore, the mastaba was given the number XIX in Lepsius's list of the pyramids in the Memphite necropolis (see *fig. 1.2*).[2] Lepsius did

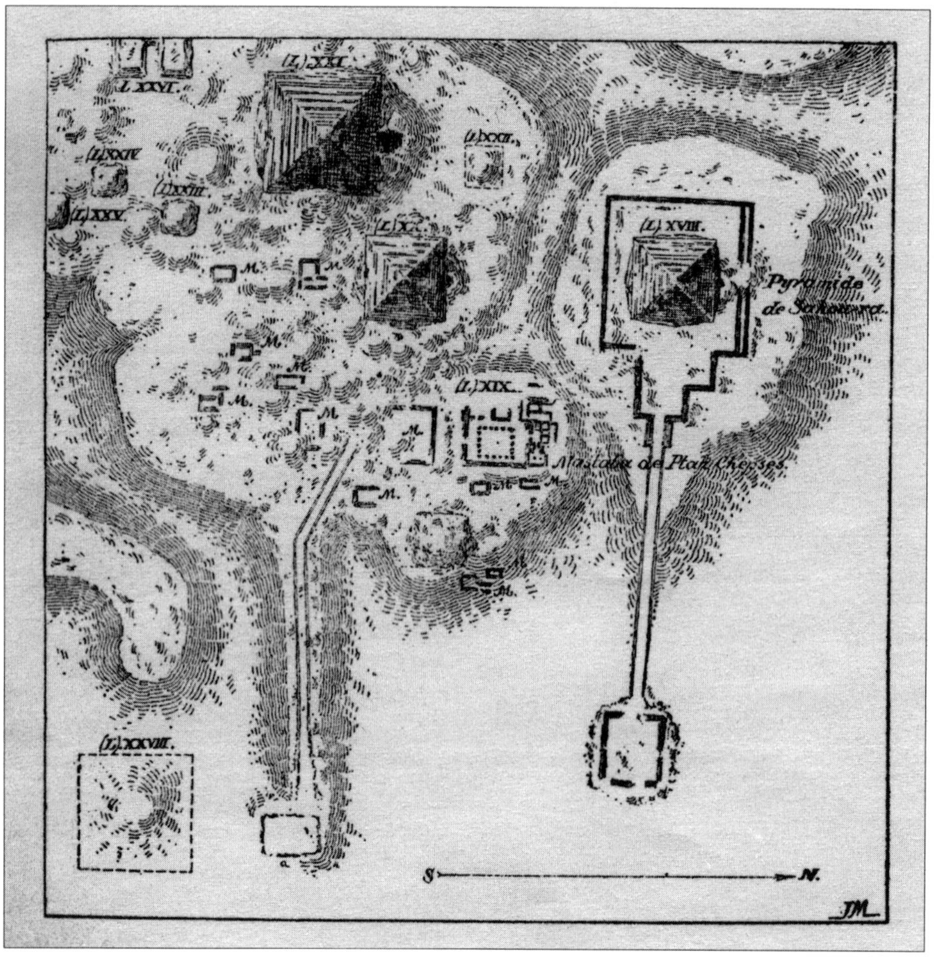

Fig. 1.3 Overall plan of the Abusir necropolis by J. de Morgan

[1] Lepsius states that the side of this "pyramid" was about 65 m.

[2] *LD* Text, 134.

not examine the monument. He only remarked that the area of the mastaba was covered by stone débris and sand and it was in a bad state of preservation.

None else took any serious interest in the tomb of Ptahshepses until the year 1893, when *Jacques de Morgan* made some diggings in Abusir that included the Mastaba of Ptahshepses.[3] Results of these works were also included in de Morgan's map of the Memphite area, published four years later, in 1897 (see *fig. 1.3*). De Morgan worked in the area of the mastaba from July till September 1893. His work represented the most important contribution to knowledge about the mastaba, its decoration and architecture before the excavation undertaken by *Zbyněk Žába* in the 1960s. De Morgan describes the ruined state of the mastaba before his excavations as the remains of a royal monument. Prior to de Morgan's initial work, the surface of the area was covered by drift sand, blocks of limestone, granite, diorite, dolerite, and fragments of statues scattered on the surfaces of an oblong mound with a depression in its middle.[4] J. de Morgan examined only a part of the tomb – his proper excavation confined to the present day Room nos. 3, 4, 5, 7, 8 (see *figs. 1.4–1.6*). The space nos. 21, 22, 25–27, 10, 11, 12 and 13–15 (the open courtyard) were only partially dug out, as may be noticed by the erosion marks on the surface of the mastaba's masonry and on the

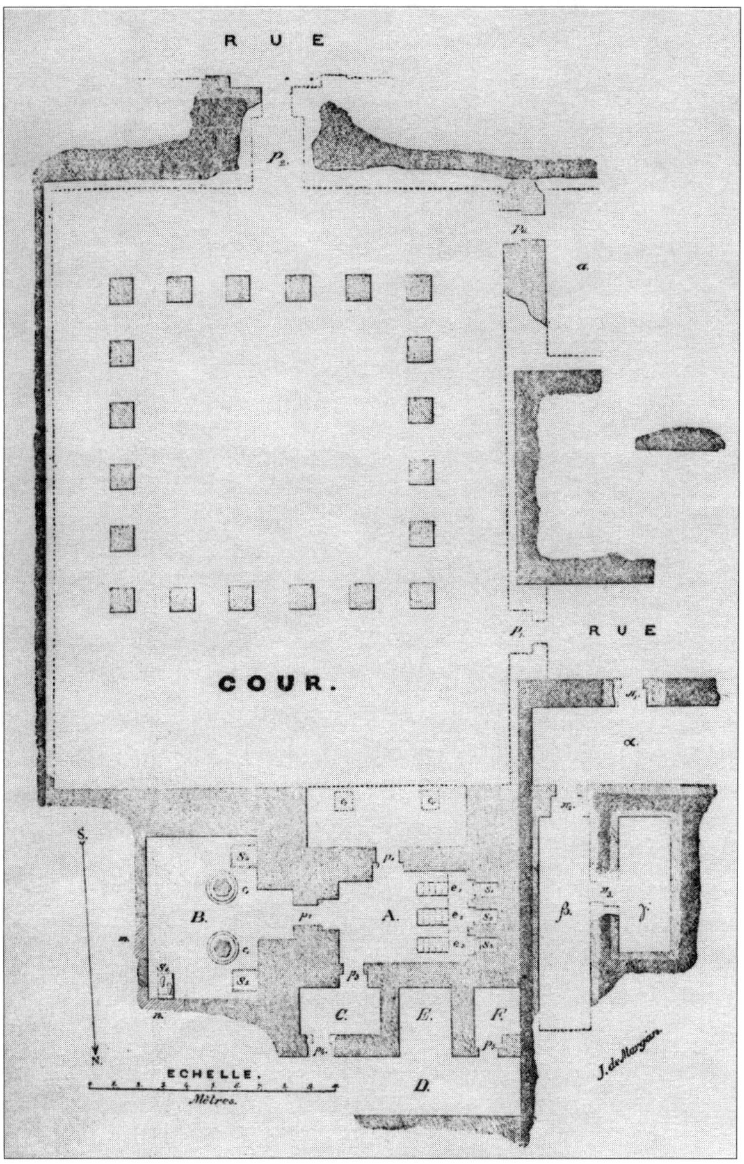

Fig. 1.4 Plan of the part of the Mastaba of Ptahshepses excavated by J. de Morgan

[3] J. de Morgan, 'Découverte du mastaba de Ptah-chepsés dans la nécropole d'Abou-Sir', *RevArch* 24 (1894) 18–33.
[4] *Op. cit.*, 18–19.

pillars. Unfortunately, de Morgan left the pillars in the courtyard unprotected, and this fact caused the deterioration of their upper parts. Because of financial problems and the extraordinarily large dimensions of the tomb, de Morgan failed to excavate the whole monument.

As clearly follows from his archaeological report, due to the extent and complexity of the internal layout of the mastaba, de Morgan also misunderstood the nature of these ruins. In his opinion, the excavated stonework belonged to a group of *several* mastabas.[5] It is possible to show this misunderstanding on his plan of the excavated area (see *fig. 1.4*); here, de Morgan even marked Rooms no. 22 and no. 16 as "streets" between the mastabas. The publication of de Morgan's work on the mastaba is quite sketchy and it represents only a short description of the separate rooms and their state of preservation. With regard to the columns of the Old Portico, however, he gave this analysis a wider scope and he emphasized their importance in the history of Egyptian architecture.[6] Another critical source of information on Ptahshepses prior to the excavations of Z. Žába were the finds of architraves with the magnate's

Fig. 1.5 View of the west wall of the Chapel with Three Niches

titulatury.[7] De Morgan also mentions fragments of Ptahshepses' statues, which were unearthed during his excavation.[8] He was not able to date the mastaba any more precisely than by making a general remark that the construction of the mastaba took place in the period of the Fifth Dynasty. A published photograph[9] shows clearly that relief decoration of the Southern Portico, contrary to the present state, at that time bore well preserved polychromy.

It seems that in his archives, now located in Marseilles, no further data other than those published in the aforementioned archaeological report concerning excavations in the mastaba are available.[10] Unfortunately, the Archives of the SCA say nothing

---

[5] De Morgan, *RevArch* 24 (1894), 22, 32–33.
[6] *Op. cit.*, 27–29, 31, figs. 5–6, 8–9.
[7] *Op. cit.*, 22, 24.
[8] *Op. cit.*, 31, fig. 9.
[9] *Op. cit.*, Pl. 1.
[10] Personal communication from Mme Andrée Jaunay, Marseilles, March 2002. See further A. Jaunay, *Mémoires de Jacques de Morgan. Souvenirs d'un archéologue*, Paris 1997.

about the restoration work done during and after de Morgan's diggings, either.[11] Reliefs in Room nos. 3 and 4 do not show signs of long exposure to the effects of the weather. As Z. Žába in his report on the work of the second season in the Mastaba of Ptahshepses quotes, this restoration work was done by de Morgan.[12] We can therefore speculate that the delay between the conclusion of the excavation and beginning of the conservation work was not long. This can be also attested by the reference made by Z. Žába in his unpublished account concerning the columns found in the Mastaba of Ptahshepses. Following his sources of information, which are not verifiable now, the work connected with the restoration of column bases in the Old Portico were either made by J. de Morgan or *Alessandro Barsanti*.[13] In connection with the construction of the wooden roof, remoulding of simple shaft above the lower original parts in the Old Portico was also carried out. Whenever these restoration works were made, they involved the construction of a wooden roof above both the excavated rooms and the moulding of the new column shafts in the Old Portico (Room no. 3). In addition to these measures, a partial re-assembly

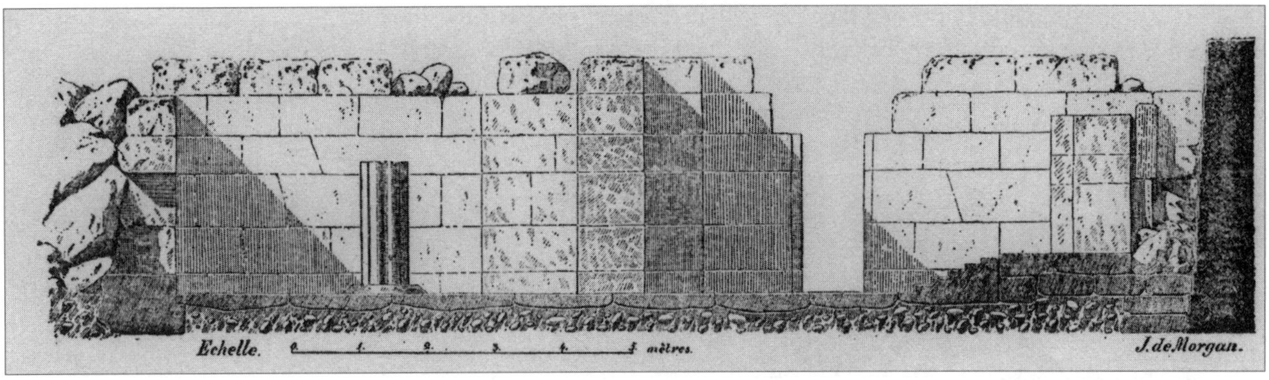

Fig. 1.6 Section through the Old Portico and the Chapel with Three Niches

of loose blocks with polychrome relief decoration found during the excavations was also carried out. Unfortunately, this intervention was not done properly and several blocks with relief decoration were not inserted accurately into the masonry. Their faces do not match with the face of the walls. In some places, restoration work even obscured some parts of the masonry and made the study of the mastaba's architecture more difficult.

Following data mentioned by *Georges Foucart*, the preserved part of the capital of one of the six-stemmed lotus bundle columns once erected in the Old Portico (see p. 85) was joined and completed in gypsum by A. Barsanti not long after the excavation of the mastaba.[14] This object was then exhibited in the Egyptian Museum (C 1748). Moreover, it became the base for an important account to the study of the columns of the Old Portico made by G. Foucart. He devoted, in his monograph on

---

[11] Following the statement of the officials of the Supreme Council of Antiquities, there is no piece of information in the Archives of the SCA, neither at the Saqqara Inspectorate, nor at the Documentation Centre in Zamalek, Cairo. On the other hand, the contents of the report on the works of the Czechoslovak Expedition in Abusir shows that at the beginning of 1960s it was possible to find the additional pieces of information relating to this question (Z. Žába, *Report on the state of the Clearance of the Mastaba of Ptahshepses at Abusir during the second season of the work done by the Czechoslovak Institute of Egyptology of Charles University*, Giza, December 1961, Archives of the Czech Institute of Egyptology).

[12] Žába in his 2nd report about the works of the Czechoslovak Expedition to Egypt (Žába, *op. cit.*, 2–3) adds to this problem, because the restoration and reconstruction works in the area of the Rooms no. 3, 4 and 10, the construction of the roof above Rooms no. 3 and 4 and the bricking up of the door between Rooms no. 4 and 5 were all executed by J. de Morgan, or following his orders; *cf.* de Morgan, *RevArch* 24 (1894), 20.

[13] Foucart, *L'ordre lotiforme*, 94. The same fact was mentioned by Z. Žába (*Find of Columns in the Mastaba of Ptahshepses in Abusir*, unpublished manuscript, Archives of the Czech Institute of Egyptology, 4, 22).

[14] *Op. cit.*, 20.

the lotiform order in the Egyptian art, the whole chapter only on these examples of the lotiform columns.[15]

Visitor's graffiti scratched or painted on the walls had already been mentioned by de Morgan in his article about the mastaba in *Révue archéologique*. *Georges Daressy*, who worked together with de Morgan (and who was also in charge of the documentation of relief decoration in the mastaba), also paid attention to these graffiti and published an article about them in the year 1894, only one year after de Morgan's report.[16] Ten years later, W. Spiegelberg discussed the same topic.[17] The longest inscription mentions two scribes who were going to make offerings in the pyramid complex of Sahure during the rule of Ramesses II. Importantly, the graffiti documents that Room numbers 3 and 4 were still accessible during the reign of this king and were not fully filled by the blown sand.

Despite the fact that *Ludwig Borchardt* was primarily occupied by the excavation of the royal pyramid necropolis and neighbouring tombs, he also worked briefly in the area of the Mastaba of Ptahshepses. While he was still at work in the nearby pyramid complex of Sahure, he partially cleared the minor offering room (Room no. 28) in Ptahshepses' mastaba and deposited there more than 2500 objects.[18] He also took his attention to fragments of lotiform columns – see chapter 4.2 in this monograph.

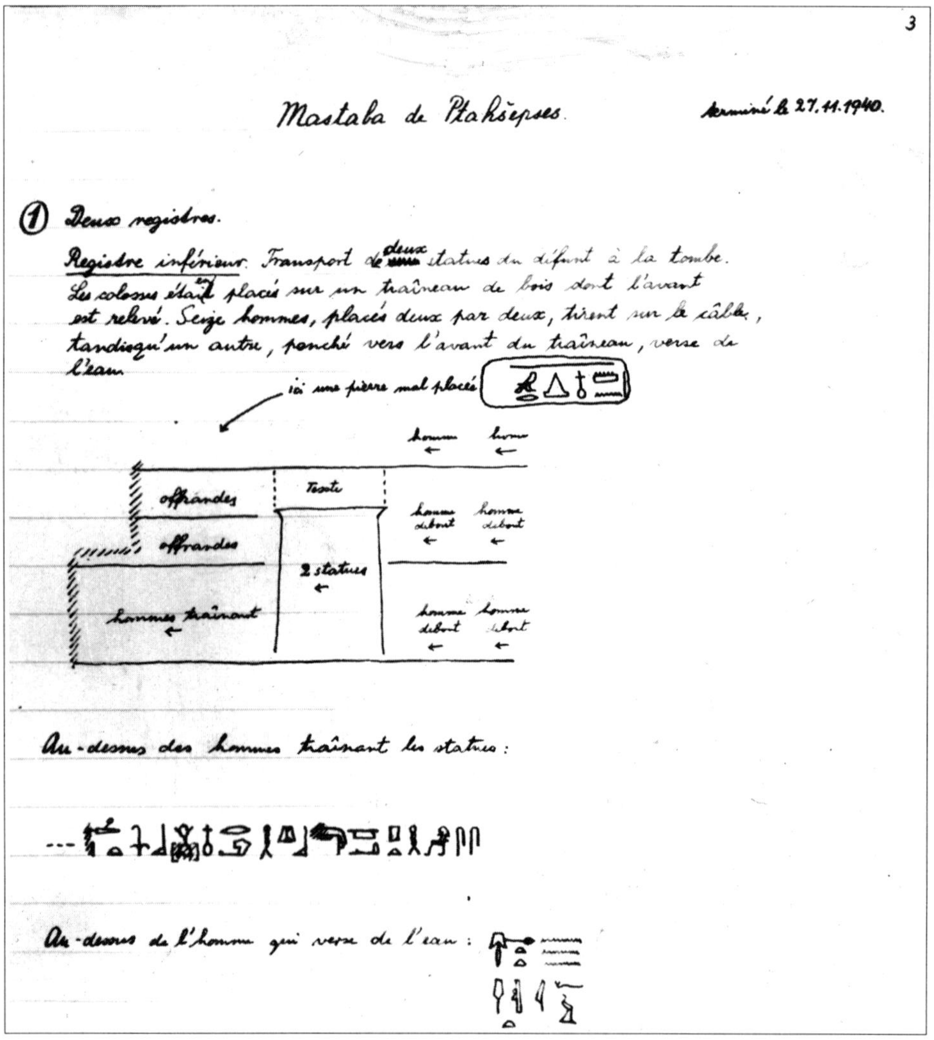
3

Mastaba de Ptahšepses. terminé le 27.11.1940.

① Deux registres.

Registre inférieur. Transport de deux statues du défunt à la tombe. Les colosses étaient placés sur un traîneau de bois dont l'avant est relevé. Seize hommes, placés deux par deux, tirent sur le câble, tandisqu'un autre, penché vers l'avant du traîneau, verse de l'eau.

Au-dessus des hommes traînant les statues:

Au-dessus de l'homme qui verse de l'eau :

Fig. 1.7 First page of J. Černý's notes concerning the Mastaba of Ptahshepses

---

[15] Foucart, *L'ordre lotiforme*, 90–117.

[16] G. Daressy, 'Inscription hiératique d'un mastaba d'Abousir', *BIE* III, Sér. 5 (1894), 109.

[17] W. Spiegelberg, 'Die hieratischen Graffiti der Mastaba des Ptahschepses zu Abusir', *RT* 26 (1904), 152–154.

[18] Z. Žába, *Zpráva o VIII. vědecké výpravě ČsEÚ do SAR* [Report on the Eighth scientific expedition of the Czechoslovak Institute of Egyptology to UAR], Archives of the Czech Institute of Egyptology, qu. 19, V/19/1968, p. 2; *idem*, in: *Preliminary Report*, 27–28.

Following the account of Z. Žába, the Mastaba of Ptahshepses did not long avoid the interest of the officials of the Antiquities Department. In the year 1924, the roof constructed by de Morgan above Rooms no. 3 and 4 was reconstructed under the direction of *Cecil Firth*.[19] He also saw to the repair of windows above these two rooms in the year 1924.[20] Unfortunately, C. Firth was not able to build a pent roof above the space of the Southern Portico (Room no. 10) as was proposed; one might suppose that this was due mainly to financial reasons.[21] The works were not finished fully, despite the fact that the side walls had been raised in order to install the roof.

During the Second World War, *Jaroslav Černý* worked inside the mastaba and made copies of inscriptions in the excavated rooms of the tomb (see *fig. 1.7*). Unfortunately, his notes, currently housed in the Griffith Institute, Oxford, have remained unpublished.[22] The period shortly after the end of the Second World War did not mean the end of the interest in the mastaba. As was mentioned by Z. Žába, *Abd es-Sallam Hussein* carried out the restoration on the polychrome relief decoration in Rooms no. 3 and 4. His main intention was to prevent the relief decoration from disintegrating in the ever-present humidity.[23]

Jaroslav Černý had great influence on his former student, Z. Žába, at a time when the latter was choosing the place for his first archaeological work in Egypt, at the

Fig. 1.8 The mastaba at the start of Žába's archaeological works

end of the 1950s. Černý's advice persuaded Žába and the archaeological team of the Charles University to settle on Abusir,[24] and they made the Mastaba of Ptahshepses their initial focus (see *figs. 1.8, 1.9*). At the turn of 1950s and 1960s the Mastaba of Ptahshepses represented a forgotten structure, mostly covered over by blown sand, limestone and mud brick debris. Pillars of the large courtyard were partially left uncovered and the southern entrance to the Room no. 4 was filled with sand.[25] Despite all the work done during the 60 years from de Morgan's excavations, no roofing of the Southern Portico had been made. This fact led to the almost total

---

[19] Žába, *Report on the state of the Clearance*, 3; *idem*, *The Mastaba of Ptahshepses at Abūsīr*, 8.
[20] *Idem*, *Report on the state of the Clearance*, 3.
[21] *Idem*, *The Mastaba of Ptahshepses at Abūsīr*, 8.
[22] Cerny MSS 17.118.1–20.
[23] Žába, *Report on the state of the Clearance*, 3.
[24] M. Verner, *Realm of Osiris*.
[25] This fact lead to the corrosion of their tops. It is noticeable even in our time.

annihilation of the colouring of the reliefs and to their partial corrosion in this space.[26] Adding to the declining condition of the reliefs, over by the north-east corner of the mastaba, there was a small hut erected for the Department of Antiquities guards; numbers of relief fragments were built into the masonry of this shed.[27]

Fig. 1.9 Pillared courtyard during the archaeological excavations made by Z. Žába

Z. Žába directed several archaeological excavations of the mastaba for the archaeological seasons from 1960 until his death in 1971.[28] Progress of work in the mastaba influenced the work of the Czechoslovak Expedition in its concessions in Nubia until the year 1965. Unfortunately, Žába did not succeed in publishing either the planned monographs concerning the mastaba, nor his remarks on its develop-

---

[26] *Cf.* De Morgan,'Découverte du mastaba de Ptah-chepsés dans la nécropole d'Abou-Sir', *RevArch* 24 (1894), Pl. 2. The photograph clearly documents that at the time of the excavation, the relief decoration of the Southern Portico was covered by the original, bright colours.

[27] These relief fragments and in some cases also fragments of statues came from L. Borchardt's excavations of Sahure's pyramid complex, see: Žába, *The Mastaba of Ptahshepses at Abūsīr*, 20–21.

[28] Work in the Mastaba of Ptahshepses was undertaken in the years 1960, 1961, 1962, 1966, 1968 and 1970. In the first half of the 1960s, this excavation was combined with the Czechoslovak archaeological survey project in the concession granted in Nubia. This fact also influenced the progress of works in the Mastaba of Ptahshepses. Z. Žába's reports on the archaeological excavations of Ptahshepses' tomb in the years 1960–1971 are published in *Preliminary Report*, 17–32. Czech versions of Žába's reports are now housed in the Archives of the Czech Institute of Egyptology (Z. Žába, *Zpráva o 2. expedici Čs. egyptologického ústavu KU do SAR (12.4.-16.12.61)* [Report on the 2nd expedition of the Czechoslovak Institute of Egyptology of the Charles University to UAR (12/04–16/12/1961)], qu. 4, V/67/1962; *idem, Report on the state of the Clearance of the Mastaba of Ptahshepses at Abusir at the time of the second season of the work done by the Czechoslovak Institute of Egyptology of Charles University* (for the Director General of the Department of Antiquities Anwar Shukri, Cairo), Giza, December 1961, Archives of the Czech Institute of Egyptology; *idem, Work in the Tomb of Ptahshepses, Abusir; third season* (for the Director General of the Department of Antiquities, Cairo), Giza, September 9, 1962, Archives of the Czech Institute of Egyptology; *idem, Zpráva o výsledcích předcházející, VII. výpravy (1966)* [Report on results of the previous, seventh expedition »

ment and its interpretation.[29] Under Žába's direction, however, almost the whole of the hitherto unexcavated part of the mastaba had been unearthed, including the burial chamber, the open courtyard, the south-eastern, the south-western and the northern complexes of storerooms, the "Boat-room" and the New Portico. The outer

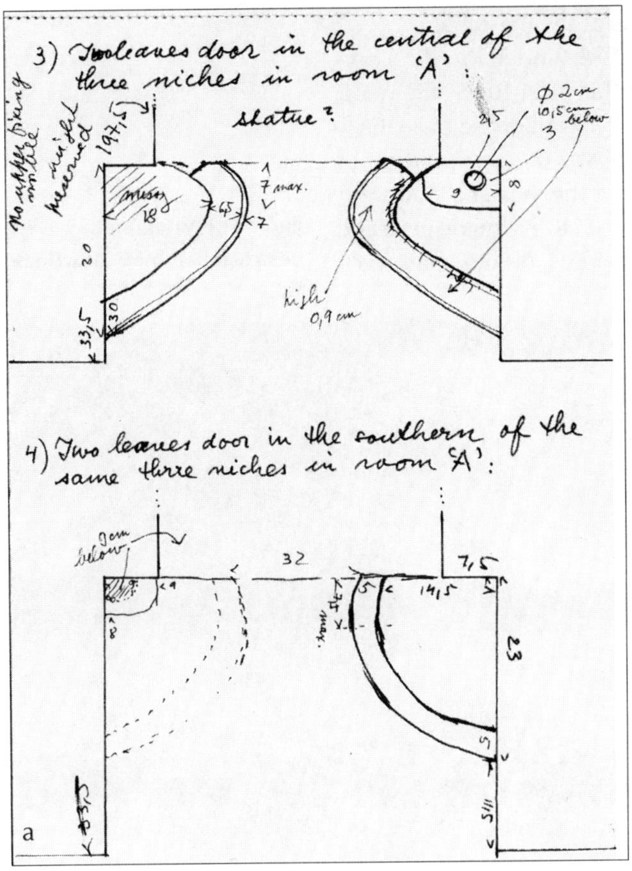

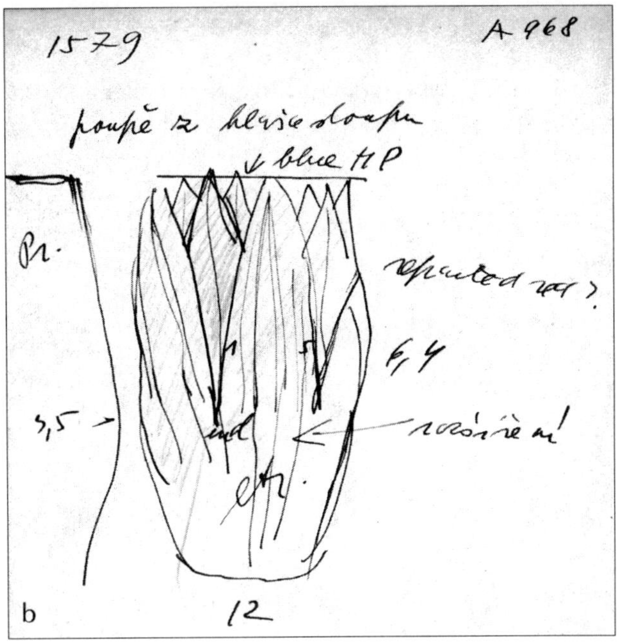

Fig. 1.10a–b Copies of Žába's field notebooks

faces of the tomb were also exposed. Large collections of fragments of statues, reliefs, pottery sherds, fragments of stone vases, wooden artefacts and other objects were also found during these excavations. It is a great pity that Žába's documentation, especially his records concerning the archaeology and architecture of the mastaba, is incomplete and therefore inadequate (see *fig. 1.10a, b*), and this makes the study and interpretation of the architecture of the mastaba more difficult. Apart from a few minor exceptions, records now held in the Archives of the Czech Institute of Egyptology mostly pertain to the loose blocks which contain relief decoration, fragments of statues, and other individual finds. Indeed the archaeological and architectural records made during the excavation are very limited. It seems very probable that a part of the documentation was lost after Žába's premature death in 1971. Žába's death also halted the excavation of the mastaba until the year 1974. One can only regret, that only remnants of Žába's planned monographs on Ptahshepses' mastaba were saved in the Archives of the Czech Institute of Egyptology.[30]

During the archaeological work conducted in the mastaba during 1960s, some architectural features of the Mastaba of Ptahshepses were studied by *Miroslav*

» (1966)], qu. 19, V/6a/1968; *idem, Zpráva o VIII. vědecké výpravě ČsEÚ do SAR* [Report on the Eighth scientific expedition of the Czechoslovak Institute of Egyptology to UAR], qu. 19, V/19/1968; *idem, Zpráva o páté vědecké výpravě Čs. egyptologického ústavu UK do Abúsíru (SAR) – Výkop Ptahšepsesovy mastaby, 12.XII.1969–18.VI.1970* [Report on the fifth scientific expedition of the Czechoslovak Institute of Egyptology at the Charles University to Abusir (UAR) – Excavation of the Mastaba of Ptahshepses, 12/12/1969–18.6.1970], qu. 19, V/31/70.

[29] On many occasions, Žába declared his intention of publishing the entire material concerning the mastaba (personal communication from M. Verner), but his intentions were never realised.

[30] Z. Žába, *The Mastaba of Ptahshepses at Abūsīr. A preliminary report on the excavation of the Mastaba of Ptahshepses at Abūsīr done by the Czechoslovak Institute of Egyptology of Charles University in the years 1960–1, 1966, 198 and 1970*, undated and unpublished manuscript, Archives of the Czech Institute of Egyptology, Prague; Z. Žába, *Find of Columns in the Mastaba of Ptahshepses in Abusir*, undated and unpublished manuscript, Archives of the Czech Institute of Egyptology.

Korecký who, in the year 1962, prepared a Czech article concerning columns found in the New Portico of the mastaba.[31] Some twenty years later he also published a monograph on Egyptian architecture which partly included results of his survey of the architecture of the mastaba.[32] Similarly, the work of the Czech surveyors, *J. Tlustý* and *O. Vosika*, should also be mentioned here. Among other documentation, they produced drawings of the columns and created plans of the mastaba.

Further work in the mastaba was resumed only in 1974, under the direction of *František Váhala*, the next director of the expedition. In his brief time, this work focused mostly on the excavation outside the southern outer wall of the mastaba.[33] Possibly the most important find made during this season was of a pyramidion of an obelisk found to the south of the south-western corner of the mastaba.[34] Among others who took part in the work this year, was *Vladimír Martinák*. He made geodetic measurements and he also took photogrammetric exposures of the mastaba's

Fig. 1.11 Photogrammetric exposure taken by V. Martinák

masonry (see *fig. 1.11*).[35] In the same year, *Vladimír Fiala* studied the remains of the mastaba's masonry and worked out the first evaluation of the architecture and the

[31] M. Korecký, *Výtvarné umění*, 9–10 (1962).
[32] *Idem, Objevy pod pyramidami* [Discoveries under the pyramids], Praha 1983.
[33] For the report on this season, see: F. Váhala, *Zpráva o 10. misi Čs. egyptologického ústavu do Egypta ve dnech od 17. března až do 10. června 1974* [Report on the 10th expedition of the Czechoslovak Institute of Egyptology to Egypt from the 17th January to the 10th June 1974], Archives of the Czech Institute of Egyptology, qu. 32, V/67/1962; M. Verner, in: *Preliminary Report*, 33–37.
[34] See M. Verner, 'Discovery of an Obelisk at Abusir', *RdE* 28 (1976), 111–118.
[35] Unfortunately, during the work, the stereometric camera was damaged, so that the use of the photogrammetric shots was limited, as was mentioned by V. Martinák in a personal communication, spring 2002.

archaeological plan of the mastaba (see *fig. 1.12*), two studies which were published two years later in the preliminary report. He also prepared the first project for the restoration and reconstruction of the mastaba.

In the year 1976, after the conclusion of the archaeological excavations in the area of the mastaba, the preliminary report concerning the archaeological work in the Mastaba of Ptahshepses was published under the direction of *Miroslav Verner*. This volume[36] includes the first summarising essays concerning separate problems, features and finds (architecture, masons' marks, pottery, *etc.*) connected with the tomb. Chapters on architecture (by V. Fiala),[37] and especially that concerning the pillared courtyard and the eight-stemmed columns in the New Portico – both by M. Korecký[38] – are the most important for the topic of the present monograph. Apart from these observations, V. Fiala paid attention to the building materials used for the construction of the mastaba. Included in the *Report* were also essays concerning

Fig. 1.12 Archaeological plan of the mastaba made by V. Fiala

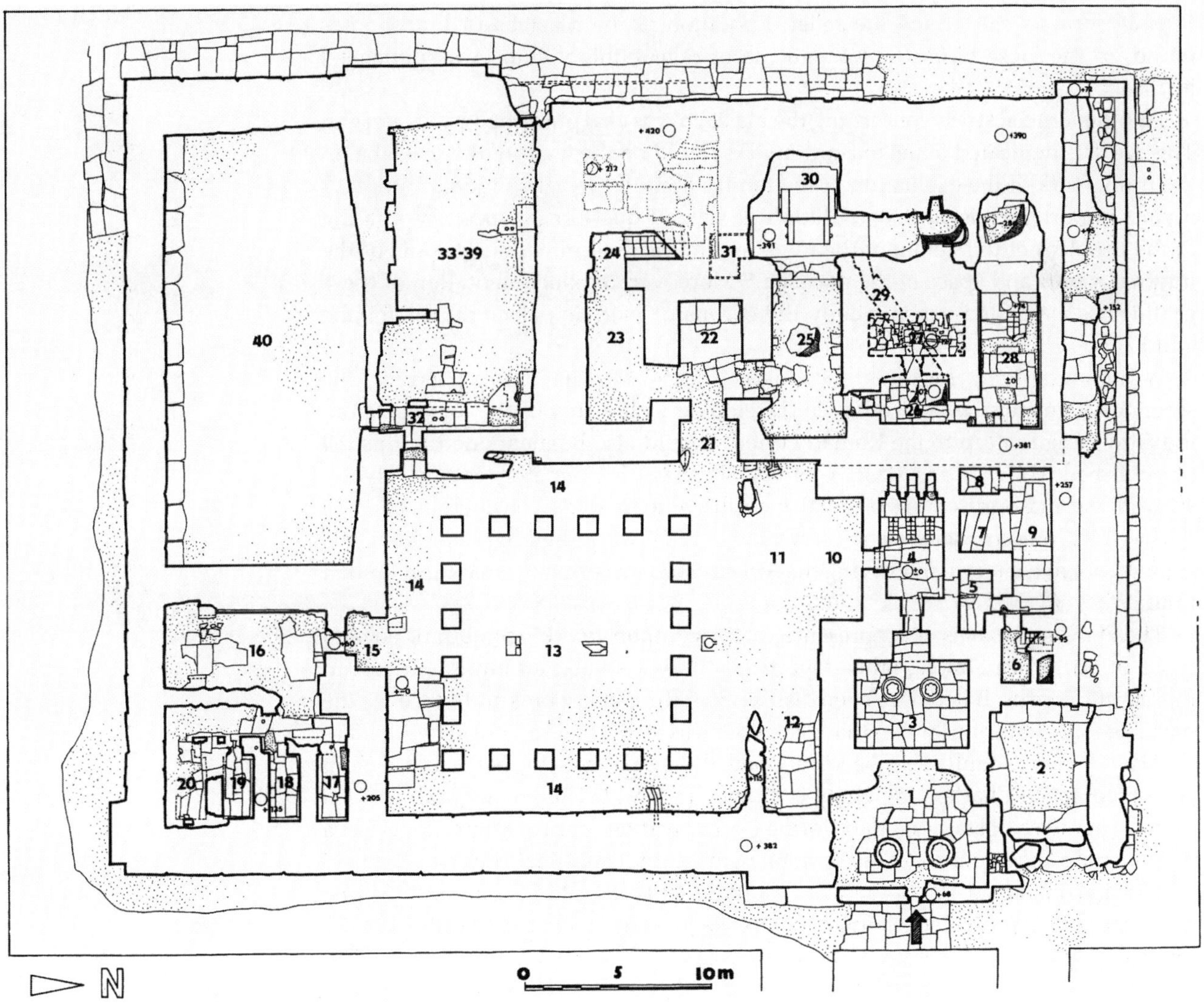

the relief decoration and masons' marks in the mastaba (M. Verner), pottery finds from the area of the mastaba (P. Charvát) and the secondary cemetery in and around the mastaba (E. Strouhal and L. Bareš).

---

[36] M. Verner (ed.), *Preliminary Report on Czechoslovak Excavations in the Mastaba of Ptahshepses at Abusir*, Prague 1976.

[37] V. Fiala, 'The Architecture of the Mastaba of Ptahshepses', in: *Preliminary Report*, 47–60.

[38] M. Korecký, 'The Pillar System of the Pillar Court of the Mastaba of Ptahshepses', 'The Eight-Stem Columns of the East Portico of the Mastaba of Ptahshepses', in: *Preliminary Report*, 117–124.

In the course of time, separate monographs concerning subjects related to the Mastaba of Ptahshepses began to be published. In the main they followed on from the separate essays in the *Preliminary Report*. The first was a monograph published in 1981 by *Petr Charvát* on pottery found in the mastaba.[39] Charvát studied the pottery in its entirety as it is recorded in the mastaba, from the period of the Old Kingdom to the Arab Period.

The Mastaba of Ptahshepses was once a splendidly decorated tomb. Unfortunately, the stone robbers and inhabitants of neighbouring villages, who transformed the area of the mastaba into a secondary cemetery during the Graeco-Roman Period, damaged the tomb to a very high degree. Only some 5% of the tomb's original decoration is now known, so Verner's description and analysis of the mastaba's reliefs which still remain *in situ*[40] represents a very important contribution concerning the mastaba, its decoration and also the personality of Ptahshepses. An important complement to this work is a monograph by *Břetislav Vachala* concerning the relief decoration of the Mastaba of Ptahshepses found on the loose blocks and fragments of reliefs: this volume was published in 2004.[41]

Another crucial study concerning the mastaba was also published by M. Verner. This work is dedicated to the masons' marks found on the walls of the mastaba. In the framework of the evaluation of the tomb's architecture, the monograph plays a very important role in the resolution of several questions, especially relating to the problem of the dating of the tomb and in the determination of some of the internal rooms and space of the mastaba.[42] Moreover, the documentation of these graffiti has expanded exponentially the corpus of hieratic palaeography for the Old Kingdom.

A monograph by *Eugen Strouhal* and *Ladislav Bareš* (1993), concerning the secondary cemetery which had been developing in the area of the mastaba from the New Kingdom up to the Roman Period, should also be mentioned in this list of published works on the Mastaba of Ptahshepses. This cemetery extensively destroyed the masonry of the original mastaba and to some considerable degree affected its present state of preservation.[43] This work highlighted again the significance of the population living the Abusir-Saqqara region in Greek and Roman times.

The Ptahshepses mastaba represented a "Gesamtkunstwerk", combining several types of art forms. Among other aspects, statuary assumed an important role in this artistic corpus. It had once been displayed in the cultic rooms and spaces of the mastaba. The first contribution that dealt with this statuary is an article by *Matthias Rochholz*.[44] Here should also be mentioned the MA thesis by *Barbora Patočková* presented at the Charles University in Prague in 1994.[45] This monograph focuses on the fragments of statues found during the excavation of the mastaba. Patočková demonstrated how important the position of the statue collection from Ptahshepses' tomb is in comparison with other collections dated to the Old Kingdom. A résumé of the thesis was presented during a conference concerning the dating criteria in the Old Kingdom art held in Cairo in the year 1998.[46]

---

[39] P. Charvát, *The Mastaba of Ptahshepses, The Pottery*, Prague 1981.

[40] M. Verner, *Abusir I, The Mastaba of Ptahshepses. Reliefs I/1*, Prague 1986.

[41] B. Vachala, *Abusir VIII, Die Relieffragmente aus der Mastaba des Ptahschepses in Abusir*, Prag 2004. The author concentrated on sorting and describing the fragments and also provided the translation and interpretation of the texts as preserved on the fragments.

[42] M. Verner, *Abusir II, Baugraffiti der Ptahschepses Mastaba*, Prague 1992.

[43] E. Strouhal, L. Bareš, *Secondary Cemetery in Mastaba of Ptahshepses at Abusir*, Praha 1993.

[44] M. Rochholz, 'Statuen und Statuendarstellungen im Grab des *Ptḥ-šps*', *SÄK* 21 (1994), 259–273.

[45] B. Patočková, *Fragmenty soch z Ptahšepsesovy mastaby v Abúsíru* (Fragments of the statues from the Mastaba of Ptahshepses in Abusir), unpublished M.A. Thesis, Charles University in Prague 1994.

[46] B. Patočková, 'Fragments de statues découverts dans le mastaba de Ptahchepses à Abousir', in: *Critéres de datation*, 227–233.

Fig. 1.13 Pillared courtyard during the documentation of its architecture and masonry

Two articles by *Peter Jánosi* concerning the private tombs dated to the Old Kingdom should also be noted here.[47] Jánosi's articles present an indispensable account of the architecture from the Mastaba of Ptahshepses and a discussion on the function of the separate rooms. These two articles were based on his study concerning the masonry of Ptahshepses' mastaba which was made by their author at the beginning of 1990s. In his articles, Jánosi placed Ptahshepses' tomb in the broader framework of the development of non-royal architecture during the second half of the Old Kingdom. He emphasised the importance of the cult of statues for the architecture of the mastaba as well.

The final contribution to these studies of the architecture of the mastaba is a popular book by *Michael Balík*, published in Czech in 2002. This book has two *foci*: providing a popular account of the architecture of the mastaba for the general public, and making a record of the stabilization of the masonry and reconstruction works carried out by that date in the area of the mastaba.[48]

In the years 2000–2001, a building, archaeological and photographic survey of the mastaba masonry was made by author of this monograph (*fig. 1.13*). This present monograph summarises the main outcome of this survey.

[47] P. Jánosi, 'Les tombes privées »des maisons d'éternité«', in: *L'art égyptien*, 60–63; *idem*, '„Im Schatten" der Pyramiden – Die Mastabas in Abusir. Einige Beobachtungen zum Grabbau der 5. Dynastie', in: *Abusir and Saqqara 2000*, 445–466. One sho uld also mention here a shorter account in the article of M. Bárta, 'The Mastaba of Ptahshepses Junior II at Abusir', *Ä&L* 10 (2000), 45–66.

[48] M. Balík, *Mastaba. Objevování a rekonstrukce staroegyptské hrobky* (A Mastaba. Unearthing and reconstruction of an ancient Egyptian tomb), Prague 2002.

2. Ptahshepses and his family

2.1 Ptahshepses

Ptahshepses' social status was undoubtedly reflected in the size and architectural appearance of his tomb. Apart from these indirect sources of evidence, we do not have any piece of knowledge regarding Ptahshepses' family origins and it should be underlined that it is not possible to find out more about his descent, his parents or his siblings.[49] The size of the Initial Mastaba and some parts of its architecture beyond doubt reflect the high rank and fortune of Ptahshepses already at the start of his career. Besides the dimensions of the first building stage of the mastaba, the presence of two large red granite sarcophagi in the burial chamber of the Initial Mastaba and the use of the saddle roof in the same chamber (see *chapter 4.1*) also indicate the important status Ptahshepses already possessed during that early period.

The inscriptions recovered from his tomb and especially from the relief decoration of the third building stage attest his wide-ranging titulary and clearly show that not only had the owner of this tomb made a very successful career for himself, but that he had achieved the highest peak of nobility by the time that his tomb construction and decoration came to a stop (see *pl. 1*). Unfortunately, only small fragments of the semi-biographical inscription, which once formed part of the tomb's relief decoration, survived. For the most part, these fragmentary texts focus on his provision of food supplies for the builders of his tomb. The texts also contain references regarding rituals for the "blessed" and "provided" Ptahshepses – as well as warnings to prospective depredators of the tomb. These fragments of his biographic inscriptions had the typical structure and form common in his time. The owner's actual deeds and a description of his career, however, were out of the scope of these texts and they are therefore not helpful in any discussion concerning the personality of Ptahshepses.[50]

Needless to say, Ptahshepses' gradually increasing social status very much influenced the development and final appearance of his vast tomb. The titulary of Ptahshepses included at least 37 titles and epithets[51] which survived mainly in the relief decoration (see fig. 2.1), but also in the masons' marks documented on the mastaba's masonry. Some of these items seem to be important for discussion concerning the social status of Ptahshepses. We should mention here those which were connected with the question of whether or not Ptahshepses took part in the king's daily toilet. Zbyněk Žába believed that Ptahshepses began his career as a Royal Hairdresser – *irw-šnj nśwt*.[52] In his titulatury, there is no direct attestation of the vizier's possession of such title, however, he owned the title *ḫrp irw-šnj* – Director of Hairdressers.[53] It is probable that Ptahshepses also possessed the similar title of *ḫrp irw-šnj Pr-ˁ3*, Director of the Barbers of the Great House.[54] It is hard to say,

---

[49] The name – Ptahshepses – was very popular in the period of the Fifth Dynasty, (*Cf.* Ranke, *PN*, 326), especially in the region of Memphis. Therefore, in the present state of our knowledge concerning individual persons and their families of that time, we are not able to find any further family clues that would help us trace the network of relationships that undoubtedly existed around Ptahshepses of Abusir.

[50] Vachala, *Literární texty*, 22; *idem*, in: *Fs. Petráček*, 581–587; *idem*, *Relieffragmente*, 40–43. For a discussion on the "real" and "ideal" biographies see: Kloth, *Biographische Inschriften*, 227–239.

[51] See Verner, *Reliefs*, 124–129. One should add one title – *irj Pjw* [*nb*], Mouth of all Inhabitans of Buto – which was documented on a fragment of relief decoration, see: Vachala, *Relieffragmente*, 17.

[52] Personal communication M. Verner. For this title, see: Jones, *Index*, 311.

[53] Vachala, *Relieffragmente*, 204; Jones, *Index*, 699.

[54] Vachala, *Relieffragmente*, 16; Jones, *Index*, 699; Goelet, *Two Aspects*, 611.

what the real meaning of these two similar prestigious titles might have been, i.e., whether their possessors also virtually attended to the daily toilet of the king. But, as it has been already suggested by O. Goelet,[55] it is not clear whether this title was connected directly with the king himself. As there are attestations of hairdressers, manicurists and barbers who show their direct access to the king by using of the epithet *nśwt* in their titulaturies, it seems more probable, that the title *ḫrp irw-šnj Pr-ꜥꜣ* does not include such a direct link. As has been already discussed,[56] touching the

Fig. 2.1 Pillared courtyard, one of the preserved architraves with the series of Ptahshepses' titles

ruler's – i.e. divine – body, which had had to be connected with performing these offices, may have influenced the social ascent of Ptahshepses and this might account for his receipt of his high-ranking offices later during his lifetime.

Among these titles there is one which is connected with personal service to the king: *irj nfr-ḥꜣt* – Keeper of the Headdress.[57] The fact that Ptahshepses was more connected with personal services to the king and in the royal court seems to endorse the extraordinary attestation of three *ir(w) šn (Pr-ꜥꜣ)*, Hairdressers (of the Great House),[58] among the officials depicted in the relief decoration of his mastaba.[59] These three men took part in the mortuary cult of Ptahshepses, which is very unusual in the framework of a non-royal mortuary cult.[60] Ptahshepses was also holder of another title connected with the *Alltag* of the king – that of *ḫrp-ꜥḥ* – Director of the palace *ꜥḥ*.[61] This title also connects its holder directly with the Egyptian king.[62]

Among the titles which are attested for Ptahshepses, one has to mention the executive titles. A very important one here was the title of *imj-rꜣ kꜣ(w)t nbt nt nśwt*.[63] As a consequence of our knowledge of the material coming from the Abusir Pyramid Necropolis, it is very probable that Ptahshepses was the person who was responsible for the large-scale construction works which were being carried out in Abusir during the reign of King Niuserre. In this connection, the occurrence of Ptahshepses' name and titles attested in the form of mason's marks detected in other

[55] Goelet, *Two Aspects*, 638–639.
[56] Verner, *Realm of Osiris*, 172.
[57] Verner, *Reliefs*, 125–127; Vachala, *Relieffragmente*, 20, 24, 26, 36, 142, 146, 204; Jones, *Index*, 321–322.
[58] Jones, *Index*, 309–310.
[59] Verner, *Reliefs*, 95, pl. 51, photos 87–88; Vachala, *Relieffragmente*, 74.
[60] See Speidel, *Friseure*, 25.
[61] Verner, *Reliefs*, 107, 119; Vachala, *Relieffragmente*, 18, 36, 204.
[62] Ptahshepses was also *ḥrj-sšꜣt n pr dwꜣt* – see Verner, *Reliefs*, 34, 41, 106, 107, 118–119.
[63] Verner, *Reliefs*, 34, 35, 41, 42, 118, 119; Vachala, *Relieffragmente*, 18, 22, 24, 26, 36, 180.

constructions in the Abusir pyramid plateau is important.[64] Among the titles which were connected with the performance of this function[65] we can mention here the title of *imj-r3 prwj nbw*, Overseer of the Two Houses of Gold.[66] This title might have made easier the access of its holder to the financial resources in connection with his duties as the director of large building projects. Moreover, Ptahshepses could have used his knowledge, the power of his offices, as well as his organizational skills in efforts to carry out the large-scale constructional project as his tomb was. Apparently, Ptahshepses, thanks to his duties concerning the construction of the king's pyramid complex, was able to use some left-over material originally intended for use in the ruler's monumental tomb.

As is well known, Ptahshepses became the highest official in the country as he obtained the title of Vizier, *t3jtj ṯ3tj n s3b*.[67] He was also *sš md3t nṯr*. This high social position certainly influenced the dimensions and architectural forms of his tomb. He was also *ḥrj-sšt3 n mdw-nṯr*,[68] *ḥrj-sšt3 m mdw ššt3 nw mdw-nṯr*,[69] *ḥrj-ššt3 n nb.f*,[70] *ḥrj-ššt3 n nśwt m św t.f nb(t)*,[71] *ḥrj-tp Nḫb*,[72] *ḫrp imjw nṯrw*[73] and *s3w Nḫn*.[74] Also these titles and epithets show an elevated social position for the tomb owner.

Beside these administrative titles, Ptahshepses also obtained titles of religious importance. He was *imj-ḫt Wr*,[75] *imj-ḫt Ḥ3(?)*,[76] *ḥm-nṯr Nḫbt nbt ꜥḥ-nṯr Šmꜥw*[77], *ḫrj-ḥb*[78] and *ḫrj-ḥb ḥrj-tp*.[79]

The high social status of Ptahshepses may also be documented in his possession of ranking titles. As the attestations of the title *śmr-wꜥtj*[80] show, he was a member of the elite level of Egyptian society[81] already during the construction of the first building stage – the Initial Mastaba.[82] Another high ranking title – that of *ḥ3tj-ꜥ*[83] has been attested many times in the relief decoration of the mastaba.[84] The receipt of these two titles are of especial chronological importance, as is discussed in the concluding chapter.

Ptahshepses also received from Niuserre the most important ranking titles of his time: *s3-nśwt* and even *s3-nśwt n ẖt.f*. Both these titles are recorded in the titulary incised on the pillars in the open courtyard, built during the third building stage (see *fig.* 2.2).[85] The receipt of these titles could be possibly connected with the duties of Ptahshepses concerning the Overseer of the all the King's works and

Fig. 2.2 Pillared courtyard, a fragment of a pillar with the title *s3-nśwt*

[64] Because they are important from the point of view of the mastaba's dating, they will be discussed in the concluding chapter.
[65] For further discussion on the title of Overseer of all the King's works and titles connected with it see: Strudwick, *Administration*, 89–90; Krejčí, *Ä&L* 10 (2000) 67–76.
[66] Vachala, *Relieffragmente*, 18, 20; Jones, *Index*, 132; Helck, *Beamtentitel*, 61.
[67] Verner, *Reliefs*, 34, 35, 41, 42, 118; Vachala, *Relieffragmente* 18, 22, 36, 152; Jones, *Index*, 1000–1001.
[68] Verner, *Reliefs*, 119.
[69] *Op. cit.*, 34, 41, 42.
[70] *Op. cit.*, 42.
[71] *Op. cit.*, 118.
[72] *Op. cit.*, 34– 35, 41, 44, 106–107, 109, 118–119.
[73] *Op. cit.*, 107.
[74] *Op. cit.*, 118.

duties of Ptahshepses concerning the Overseer of the all the King's works and also of Vizier as was mentioned by B. Schmitz.[86] We cannot exclude the possibility that Ptahshepses obtained some of his higher titles during the construction of the second building stage of the mastaba, since these titles are not attested among the masons' marks from the oldest part of the tomb. One can document them in the relief decoration of the third building stage. It is no doubt due to the destruction of the relief decoration in the Initial Mastaba that we have so little knowledge about the progress of this magnate's titulatury in the same period. It is likewise impossible to refute or ascertain the possibility that Ptahshepses' decision to enlarge his mastaba (in the form of the second and then of the third building stage) coincided with the bestowal of these high titles – especially that of *t3jtj ṯ3tj n s3b* – on his person. It is important to note that Ptahshepses was, together with Minnefer, one of only two viziers who could be identified as belonging to the reign of Niuserre.[87] It is only in the position of vizier that Ptahshepses became powerful enough to be able to build such a vast building as that which his mastaba became during the third building stage. It is obvious that he obtained the title of *s3-nśwt* and *s3-nśwt n ẖt.f* only during the construction of the third building stage, since these titles only appear in the relief decoration of the peripheral pillars of the courtyard (see *chapter 4.3*).

Needless to say, Ptahshepses was able not only to supply the builders of his tomb (see above), but he, as a person in the top echelons of the Egyptian society, also certainly established a large number of funerary domains for the provisioning of his own funerary cult. Fragments of the relief decoration found during the excavation works in the mastaba bear the names of only several domains[88] – among them, three incorporating the magnate's name – *P3ḳ Ptḥ-špśś* and *Wꜥḥ [Ptḥ-špś]ś*.[89] Besides these domains, one can also mention the fragments of the relief decoration with domains incorporating the names of Kings Khafre and Niuserre.[90]

It should be added that the name of a certain Ptahshepses is attested in the relief decoration of Sahure's mortuary temple.[91] As has been clearly shown by Ludwig

---

75 Vachala, *Relieffragmente*, 28.
76 *Op. cit.*, 28, 32.
77 Verner, *Reliefs*, 118.
78 *Op. cit.*, 34, 35, 41, 42, 106, 107, 109, 118, 119.
79 *Op. cit.*, 118.
80 *Op. cit.*, 34, 35, 41, 42, 44, 91, 94–95, 107, 109, 118–119; Vachala, *Relieffragmente*, 16, 18, 22, 24, 26, 28, 30, 32, 34, 36, 40, 146, 204; Jones, *Index*, 892.
81 Helck, *Beamtentitel*, 108, 111–114.
82 Verner, *Baugraffiti*, 190–191.
83 Helck, *Beamtentitel*, 110, 113.
84 Verner, *Reliefs*, 34, 35, 41, 42, 106, 107, 118, 119; Vachala, *Relieffragmente*, 16, 18, 22, 32, 40; Jones, *Index*, 496–467.
85 The owners of the titles *s3-nśwt, s3-nśwt n ẖt.f* were not only accorded to king's actual sons, but could also be given to persons of non-royal origin who worked in the highest offices of the Egyptian state during the period of the Fifth and the Sixth Dynasties. For further discussion concerning the titles, see: Schmitz, *Königssohn, passim.* 78–79; Baud, *Famille royal*, 171–172; Jánosi, *Giza*, 48.
86 Schmitz, *Königssohn*, 86, 88–90.
87 Helck, *Beamtentitel*, 136. In Verner's opinion he functioned as vizier after Minnefer (Verner, *Baugraffiti*, 191). Contradicting this proposal are the dates given to both men by Baer (*Rank and Title*, 76, 290) dating them to a time later than that of Niuserre, respectively in Baer's period V D (which coincides with the reign of Djedkare) and by Strudwick (*Administration*, 90) to the period from the end of reign of Niuserre to the early years of Djedkare. Minnefer is, 764, dated to the reign of Niuserre in *PM* III. Strudwick (*Administration*, 92) postulates that the early and middle parts of Niuserre's reign are dated slightly differently. In this way, it is not possible to fully ascertain Helck's suggestion.
88 Vachala, *Relieffragmente*, 244–250.
89 *Op. cit.*, 246; the name of another domain: .... *Ptḥ-śpśś* (Vachala, *Relieffragmente*, 244) has been also detected among the fragments of the mastaba's relief decoration.
90 *Ḥwt-[Rꜥ]-ẖꜥ.f* – *op. cit.*, 244. Among these fragments names of three other domains containing only parts of Niuserre's cartouches also survived: *op. cit.*, 248.
91 Borchardt, *Sahure* II, 118–120, 122, 124, Bl. 49–50, 54.

Borchardt,[92] and more recently by Nigel Strudwick,[93] this man is certainly not to be identified with later Vizier Ptahshepses. In Niuserre's mortuary temple a certain *śmr-wˁtj irj-nfr-ḥ3t Ptḥ-*[*špśś*] is mentioned.[94] Unfortunately, it is not possible to ascertain beyond doubt whether this attestation should be connected with the Vizier Ptahshepses (Senior) or rather with his son Ptahshepses Junior II, as suggested by M. Bárta.[95] Since Ptahshepses Senior also possessed these two titles,[96] the possibility that he was depicted in Niuserre's mortuary temple (for instance, at the beginning of his professional career at the court) cannot be ruled out. A masons' mark with the same combination of titles ([*śmr*]-*wˁtj, irj-nfr*-[*ḥ3t*]) was found on a loose block in the Ptahshepses mastaba, but without the addition of any personal name,[97] so it cannot be used in the discussion on this problem.

Generally speaking, and according to the data collected in the Mastaba of Ptahshepses, it appears that Ptahshepses lived roughly at the same period as King Niuserre (for further discussion concerning the dating of mastaba's construction which is connected with this question, see the concluding chapter). Ptahshepses was also personally connected with the king, as he was married to Princess Khamerernebty, a fact that is certainly contributed to the successful career of this man and *vice versa*. Needless to say, Ptahshepses' gradually increasing social status very likely influenced the development and final appearance of his vast tomb.

2.2 Ptahshepses' family

The pieces of information regarding other members of Ptahshepses' family are not very clear. In the relief decoration of the mastaba, the depictions and attestations of the titulatury and name of his wife and children survived until the present day.[98] One may mention in connection with the places of burial of other members of the magnate's family that there are many lacunae in our knowledge about the family

During his life, Ptahshepses became the husband of Princess Khamerernebty, a member of the royal family,[99] elevating in the process his own social status. Unfortunately, there is no direct attestation as to which king was the father of Khamerernebty. We can – only indirectly – suppose that she was a daughter of Niuserre. On the other hand, there is not enough data available in order to be able to fully solve this question.[100] Initially, Khamerernebty's burial apartment and a chapel with a false door were constructed in the Mastaba of Princesses built in the third line of the Cemetery of Nobles (see *fig.* 2.3).[101] In his report on the archaeological excavations of the mastaba, Ludwig Borchardt stated that she was unlikely to have been buried in the mastaba.[102] However, as it follows from his descriptions in the report, several components of the burial equipment were found in the sarcophagus chamber. Hypothetically, her burial may have been used secondarily for another person. In addition to that, her false door was very probably erected in the mastaba and her burial chamber was equipped with a large limestone sarcophagus.

Khamerernebty – as a daughter of the king – gained high titles and epithets (see also *fig.* 2.4).[103] It is interesting that her epithet *im3ḫt ḫr it.s* was not found in the

---

[92] Borchardt, *Neuserre*, 122.
[93] Strudwick, *Administration*, 90.
[94] Borchardt, *Neuserre*, 71.
[95] Bárta, *Ä&L* 10 (2000) 59; *cf.* Verner, *Reliefs*, 65.
[96] Verner, *Reliefs*, 125, 128.
[97] Verner, *Baugraffiti*, 70.
[98] Verner, *Reliefs*, 43–45, pls. 24–25, photos 38–40.
[99] See Baud, *Famille royale*, 534–535.
[100] *Cf.* Schmitz, *Königssohn*, 27–28, and especially 124, who thinks that Khamerernebty could be also a titular princess, not a real member of the nuclear royal family.
[101] Borchardt, *Neuserre*, 126–129.
[102] *Op. cit.*, 129.

Fig. 2.3 Mastaba of Princesses, burial chambers from the southeast

Fig. 2.4 Princess Khamerernebty kneeling in front of her husband

[103] *Sꜣt-nśwt, sꜣt-nśwt n ẖt.f, ḥm.t Ḥwt-Ḥr nb(.t) nht m śwt.s nbt, imꜣḫt ḫr it.s – op. cit.*, 127–128, fig. 107; Verner, *Reliefs*, 35–36, pl. 16, 41–42, pl. 22, 130.

Mastaba of Ptahshepses; on the other hand, her titles *ḫkrt nśwt wꜥtt* and *ḥmt.f mrt.f imꜣḫt.f* are not attested in the Mastaba of Princesses.[104] Khamerernebty's name was also recorded in three masons' inscriptions unearthed during the excavation of the oldest part of the Mastaba of Ptahshepses, the Initial Mastaba.[105] On the other hand, masons' inscriptions with the name and Ptahshepses' title of *ḥꜣtj-ꜥ* were recorded by Borchardt in the Mastaba of Princesses. They represent another document illustrating an early and close relationship of Khamerernebty and Ptahshepses (for further discussion, see concluding chapter).

Nevertheless, there is a hypothetical possibility, that Ptahshepses was engaged already before his marriage with Khamerernebty. Miroslav Verner[106] has pointed out that the name, the titles and the figure of Ptahshepses' son, Khafini, were removed and that the sequence of Ptahshepses' sons was changed in the relief decoration of the doorway between Room no. 3 and 4. The remaining decoration clearly shows a shift of the title Oldest Son from Khafini to Ptahshepses Junior II and a modification in the sequence of Ptahshepses' children. Following Verner's hypothesis, these changes to the relief decoration are of a great importance since they might indicate that Ptahshepses was married before his matrimony with Khamerernebty. The identity of this other woman is not known.[107] We do not know even, whether this lady should be buried in the Mastaba of Ptahshepses, or in another tomb, built exclusively for her. The location of this tomb is simply not known. This woman perhaps could have been the mother of Khafini. Unfortunately, due to the lack of any evidence, this matter remains for the time being problematic.

As was already mentioned, Ptahshepses was the father of eight known children: beside Khafini and Ptahshepses Junior II, the Vizier had altogether five sons (Ptahshepses Junior I, Nisuked, Kahotep, Hemakhti, Khenu) and two daughters.[108] Only tombs for two of the sons are known, and only one for his daughter, Meretites.

The tomb of Ptahshepses Junior II was excavated by the then Egyptian Antiquities Organisation under the direction of Inspector Muhammad Sughayar and subsequently studied by Miroslav Bárta.[109] This tomb was built in the immediate vicinity of Ptahshepses' mastaba, directly opposite the Vizier's portico (see *fig. 2.5*). Apparently, the endeavour of Ptahshepses' son to emulate his father is indicated by the position of his tomb and its architectural layout. Ptahshepses Junior II also possessed several identical titles to those held by his father; these titles put Ptahshepses Junior II among those of high status within the society.[110]

The tomb of another of Ptahshepses' sons – Kahotep – is located in the southernmost part of the Mastaba of Princesses (see *fig. 2.3*). During the excavations of his burial chamber, a great number of objects originating from his burial equipment were found.[111] Among these finds was also a reserve head.[112] In the same tomb, a daughter of Ptahshepses, Meretites was very probably entombed, too.[113] Beside this burial place, Meretites has been attested in the relief decoration of Ptahshepses' mastaba.[114] The location of the burial of other members of Ptahshepses Senior's family are not known.

---

[104] This fact might be connected with the gender hierarchy of men and women during the Old Kingdom. This problem has been discussed by A. M. Roth in *JARCE* 36 (1999) 37–53.
[105] Verner, *Baugraffiti*, 65, 66, 96.
[106] Verner, *Reliefs*, 45.
[107] As was demonstrated by M. Verner (Verner, *Reliefs*, 44f.; *idem*, *Baugraffiti*, 189).
[108] See Verner, *Reliefs*, 92–93, 102–103.
[109] Bárta, *Ä&L* 10 (2000) 45–66.
[110] These high ranking titles are: *ḥꜣtj-ꜥ*, *śmr-wꜥtj* and *ḫrj-ḥbt*. Better evidence on the deeds of its holder seems to borne out by the titles *imj-rꜣ Šmꜥw*, *irj-nfr-ḥꜣt* and *ḥm-śt*. For the titles of Ptahshepses Junior II see Bárta, *Ä&L* 10 (2000) 57–59.
[111] Borchardt, *Neuserre*, 128–132, Abb. 108–112, Bl. 25–27.
[112] *Op. cit.*, 133, Abb. 114.
[113] *Op. cit.*, 128; her burial chamber was located to the south of that of Princess Khamerernebty.
[114] Verner, *Reliefs*, 93; Vachala, *Relieffragmente*, 50.

Fig. 2.5 The area in front of the New Portico and the western part of the Ptahshepses Junior II tomb with a screening wall – as seen from the south

The social status of all known children of Ptahshepses Senior was high. The documented titularies of his sons[115] are predominated by the ranking titles *śmr-wˁtj*, *ẖrj-ḥbt* and *ḥm-śt*.[116] The high social rank one may observe also by Meretites. As was the case of her probable mother, Princess Khamerernebty, she was also entitled *ẖkrt nśwt wˁtt* and *irjt-iẖt-nśwt*.[117] The titles of Ptahshepses' children show, as was already mentioned in the case of Ptahshepses Junior II, that their owners were part of officialdom at the royal court. Moreover, the appearance of these titles in the relief decoration show that the incoming of these persons to the higher layers of the Egyptian society might have been rather early during their lives.

Hypothetically, one may suppose that also the burial chamber constructed between those of Meretites and Kahotep in the Mastaba of Princesses[118] was originally intended for the burial of another daughter or son of Ptahshepses. This burial chamber was found free of evidence of a burial and following the opinion of Ludwig Borchardt, the stone sarcophagus in it was not ever used.[119] Whether this burial chamber was planned for a female (a princess), as is indicated by Borchardt,[120] or for a male, one cannot decide and this question has to be left open.

2.3 The role of Ptahshepses in Egyptian history

The titulary of Ptahshepses Senior, his vast tomb and engagement with a royal princess represent pieces of evidence of importance concerning this magnate of King Niuserre's court. Apparently, Ptahshepses was an important player in the scene of the Fifth Dynasty. It is thought that Niuserre may have demonstrated his pleasure with Ptahshepses (and perhaps acknowledged Ptahshepses' hypothetical help at the beginning of his rule, after the abrupt deaths of Raneferef and Shepseskare).[121] There is a possibility that Niuserre's uncle, Netjerinenre,[122] who bore the title *s3 nśwt śmśw* and who thus may have had the right to succeed to the throne, might

---

[115] Khafini: *śmr-wˁtj, ẖrj-ḥbt*; Kahotep: *śmr-wˁtj, ẖrj-ḥbt, ḥm-śt* , Ptahshepses Junior I: *śmr-wˁtj, ẖrj-ḥbt, ḥm-śt*, Ptahshepses Junior II: *ḥ3tj-ˁ, śmr-wˁtj, ẖrj-ḥbt, ḥm-śt, irj-nfr-ḥ3t, imj-r3 Šmˁw*, Hemakhti: *śmr-wˁtj, ẖrj-ḥbt, ḥrj-śšt3 n nb.f, ḥm-śt, ẖrp-ˁḥ*, Khenu: *śmr-wˁtj, ḥrj-śšt3 n nb.f, ẖrj-ḥbt, ḥm-śt*, Nisuked: *śmr-wˁtj, ẖrj-ḥbt, ḥm-śt* (Borchardt, *Neuserre*, 128; Verner, *Reliefs*, 44, 65, 76; Bárta, *Ä&L* 10 [2000] 57).

[116] The title *ḥm-śt* is also carried by Ptahshepses Senior – Verner, *Reliefs*, 34, 41–42.

[117] *Irjt-iẖt-nśwt* and *ẖkrt nśwt wˁtt*: Borchardt, *Neuserre*, 128; Verner, *Reliefs*, 93).

[118] Borchardt, *Neuserre*, Bl. 25–27.

[119] *Op. cit.*, 129.

[120] *Op. cit.*, on Bl. 25 and 27: "Sargkammer einer unbekannter Prinzessin".

[121] Verner, *Forgotten Pharaohs*, 192; *cf.* Bárta, *Ä&L* 10 (2000) 65.

[122] Borchardt, *Sahure* II, 112, 115, 119, Bl. 33, 44, 49.

have still been alive at the time when Niuserre came to the throne. The time span between the death of Sahure and the beginning of Niuserre's reign may have been no more than about 12–14 years, therefore, Netjerienre might have been capable of holding the office of ruler of Egypt. For this reason, Niuserre might have had to struggle for the succession. In such a scenario, it is not unlikely that Ptahshepses put his weight behind the son of Neferirkare. Any help of this nature might well have been rewarded by the young king. Such help may have consisted of permitting Ptahshepses to use royal sources of material, permission to apply non-standard architectural forms in the building of his unusual tomb in the Cemetery of Nobles in Abusir, and giving him a burial site close to the king's pyramid complex. In this way, Ptahshepses was able to be with his Lord during his life in the next world.

3. The location of the mastaba

3.1 The Abusir Pyramid Necropolis

The pyramid necropolis at Abusir was founded near the present-day village of Abusir at the beginning of the Fifth Dynasty. It became the burial ground for at least four rulers of the early and mid Fifth Dynasty, namely Sahure, Neferirkare, Raneferef and Niuserre (and hypothetically, perhaps Shepseskare as well; for the overall maps of the necropolis, see *fig. 3.1* and *fig. 3.3*). Beside these vast complexes, the area of Abusir and its vicinity is usually associated with the sun temples of Userkaf and Niuserre, but the area may also have been the site of other, so-far undiscovered sun temples, too.

The reasons for the necropolis being founded right at this place are not clear, but, among the main reasons, we should consider the construction of the sun temple of Userkaf at the beginning of the Fifth Dynasty.[123] Following the realisation of this building project, the area belonging later to the royal necropolis was evidently "sanctified" by this initial monument. In addition to these reasons, we might also mention the proximity of limestone quarries with their easily accessible layers of building stone. Besides this explanation, we should take account of the geomorphological situation in other places and the shortage of free space in the older pyramid cemeteries within the Memphite necropolis. Some or indeed all of these reasons could have played an important role in the choice of Abusir as a royal necropolis.[124]

It is apparent that the pyramid complexes at Abusir also provided the basic framework for other monuments there, including the Mastaba of Ptahshepses. The oldest pyramid complex on the site belonged to King Sahure, who *de facto* founded the royal necropolis in Abusir.[125] His complex is situated on the finest location in the necropolis, on the northernmost promontory of the plateau. Among all the pyramids of the Old Kingdom, Sahure's pyramid is the one that is closest to the edge of the Nile valley.

The second ruler of the Fifth Dynasty who decided to build his mortuary complex in Abusir was Neferirkare.[126] For his monument, he picked out the highest point of the plateau, some distance away from the pyramid complex of his predecessor. In the light of new evidence, the view that he wished to distance himself from Sahure now seems unlikely.[127] The fact that Neferirkare was the son of Sahure – not his brother, as has so frequently been assumed – has only recently been attested by the find of a large block during the excavations of Sahure's causeway in Abusir.[128] A scene on this block shows not only the relationships within Sahure's family, but also the fact that Neferirkare was one of the "eldest sons" of Sahure.[129]

---

[123] J. Krejčí, 'The origins and development of the royal necropolis at Abusir during the Old Kingdom', in: *Abusir and Saqqara 2000*, 471.

[124] For further discussion on this topic, see: Krejčí, in: *Abusir and Saqqara 2000*, 468–474. However, the existence of the actual royal palace which has been extensively discussed has not been satisfactorily detected.

[125] Borchardt, *Sahure* I, II. The reasons behind the foundation of the necropolis on this particular spot are not fully clear, see: Krejčí, in: *Abusir and Saqqara in 2000*, 471–475. One of the reasons could be the foundation and construction of Userkaf's sun temple nearby.

[126] Borchardt, *Neferirkare*.

[127] As M. Verner recently mentioned in *Realm of Osiris*, 59. It seems improbable that Neferirkare used this spot because of his wish to distance himself from Sahure due to possible dynastic problems.

[128] I would like to express my thanks to Tarek El Awady for allowing me to publish here this piece of information.

[129] Personal communication T. El Awady, spring 2005; *cf.* T. El Awady, 'The Royal Family of Sahure: New Evidence', in: *Abusir and Saqqara 2005*.

Neferirkare's choice of site was due to the fact that it was the first convenient area to the south of Sahure's pyramid complex available for the construction of a pyramid complex, with advantageous conditions for the work of the constructional teams, as well as for the transportation and storage of building material. This choice of position was almost certainly influenced by the existence of a slope in this area, *i.e.*, between Sahure's and Neferirkare's pyramid (*cf. fig. 3.1*).[130] As a matter of course, this slope might have made the construction of such a large project as the pyramid complex very difficult, or even impossible.[131]

It seems that, after Neferirkare's death, the royal necropolis developed further to the north, as is shown by the unfinished construction of a monument, which is sometimes referred to as the pyramid platform of the possible successor to Neferirkare, Shepseskare.[132]

Nevertheless, Raneferef,[133] the possible successor to Shepseskare, commenced his pyramid further to the south of Neferirkare's pyramid.

Another son of Neferirkare was Niuserre; he established his pyramid complex in the close vicinity of Neferirkare's pyramid complex as well. However, as it was located to the north-east of Neferirkare's complex, it formed the western border of the Cemetery of Nobles. This cemetery, possibly, already existed in that moment of time and it was the area in which the Mastaba of Ptahshepses had been built. Niuserre also completed several older royal complexes: Neferirkare's mortuary temple, Raneferef's mortuary complex (the proposed pyramid of this pharaoh had not been finished prior to his death),[134] and the pyramid complex of Queen Khentkaus II, on the southern side of Neferirkare's pyramid.[135]

The development of the pyramid necropolis within the area south and south-east from Neferirkare's pyramid also played an important part in the further development of the private cemeteries. These royal cemeteries featured the pyramids and tombs of the royal consorts (tomb complexes Lepsius No. 24 and 25)[136] and further tombs for members of the royal family were constructed in this area (*e.g.* the line of mastabas to the south of Raneferef's mortuary temple, the tomb of Nebtiemneferes,[137] and the Eastern Field of mastabas for members of Djedkare's family[138]).

Not far away the pyramid complexes, there is Userkaf's sun temple,[139] as has already been mentioned, but there are also (in some cases older) tombs of royal

---

[130] *Cf.* Krejčí, in: *Abusir and Saqqara in 2000*, 477.

[131] However, this slope did not represent a problem for the construction of the small tombs which, still unexcavated, are clearly visible on the surface of desert in this sector of the Abusir Pyramid Necropolis.

[132] It is questionable for whom this partially started construction should be assigned. For further information and the most recent discussion concerning the problem of ascribing this complex to the ephemeral king Shepseskare, see: M. Verner, 'Who was Shepseskara, and when did he reign?', in: *Abusir Saqqara 2000*, 581–602; a further bibliography on this topic can be found in the article.

[133] Nevertheless, M. Verner (in: *Abusir and Saqqara 2000*, 597) argues that Shepseskare was the successor of Raneferef and not *vice versa*.

[134] See Verner *et al.*, *Raneferef.*

[135] Verner, *Khentkaus.*

[136] See Verner, 'Excavations at Abusir. Season 1982 – Preliminary Report', *ZÄS* 111 (1984) 11–12; Verner, 'Excavations at Abusir. Seasons of 1994/95 and 1995/96', *ZÄS* 124 (1997) 71–76; Verner, *Pyramids* 98–99, 319–321; Krejčí, Verner, 'Die „Zwillingspyramide" L 25 in Abusir', *Sokar* 8/1 (2004) 20–22; Krejčí, Verner, 'Twin Pyramid Complex "Lepsius no. XXV" in Abusir', *Fs Sawi*, 159–165.

[137] Verner, *ZÄS* 115, 1988, 167–168; ground plan published in: Verner, *Abusir*, plan on p. 84.

[138] Verner, Callender, *Djedkare's Cemetery.*

[139] Only two of the six known sun temples have been revealed – those of Userkaf and Niuserre (Ricke, *SH Userkaf* I–II; Borchardt, *Re-Heiligtum* I; von Bissing, Kees, *Re-Heiligtum* II). In this respect, it is difficult to establish whether other sun temples – which are known from the epigraphic material – were ever finished. For the resume of the archaeological excavations and previous investigations of the sun temples of the Fifth Dynasty see: Krejčí, Magdolen, 'Research into Fifth Dynasty sun temples – past, present and future', in: *OKAA*, 185–191.

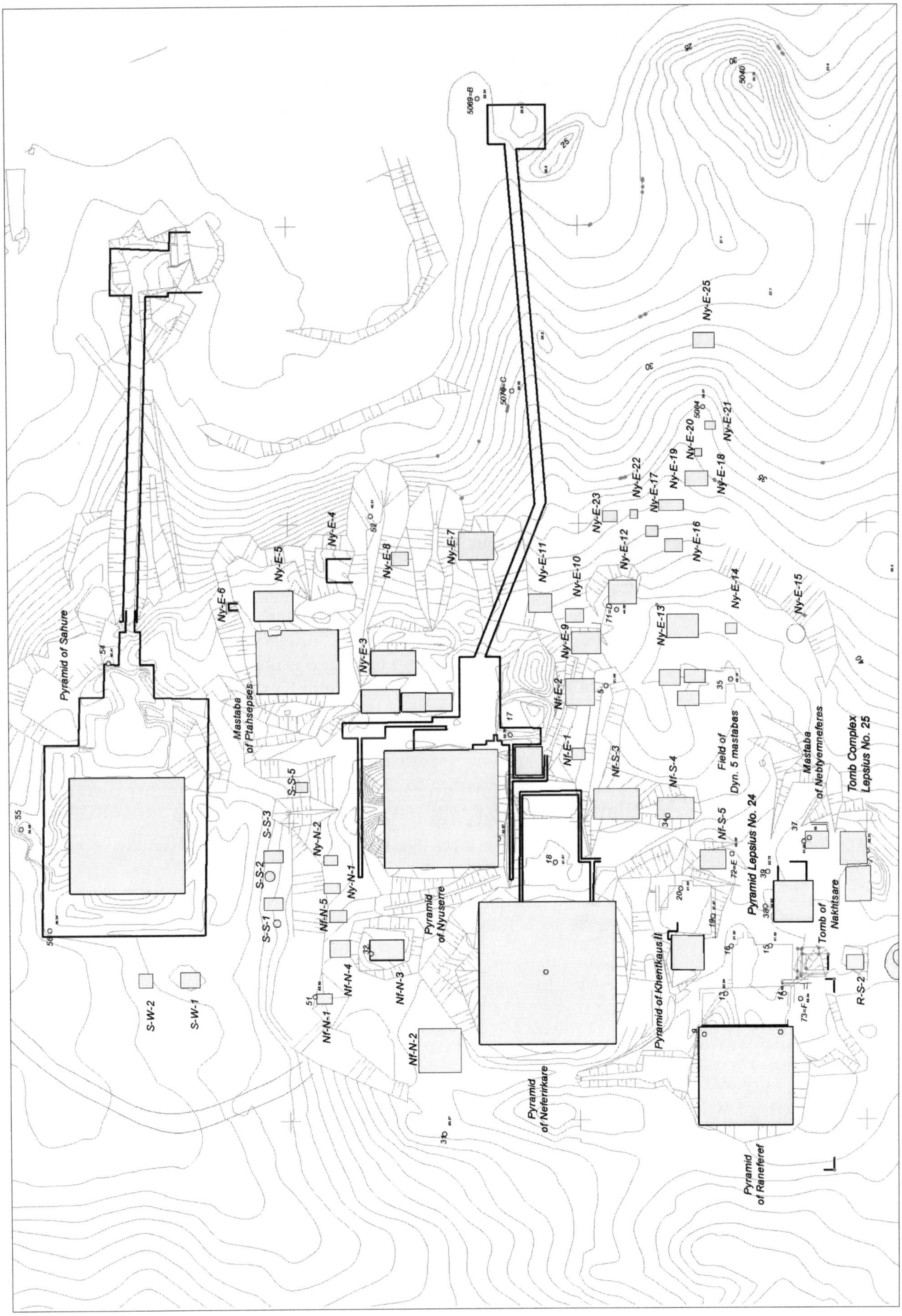

Fig. 3.1 Schematic plan of the Abusir Pyramid Necropolis

consorts and children, high officials, priests and their relatives. These can be dated to different periods of time:[140] those from the Old Kingdom cover the period from the first half of the Fifth Dynasty till the end of the Sixth Dynasty. However, the existence of tombs older than those of the Fifth Dynasty should also be noted: there are various finds from older periods which have been found in the areas between the private cemeteries around the pyramids, but also in the areas of the royal complexes themselves.[141] Nevertheless, the stratigraphical situation in this area is so complex and so badly damaged by later activities of stone robbers and *sabbakhin*, as well as by activities connected with the foundation and development of secondary cemeteries, that further observation concerning the earliest tombs on the spot is as yet not possible.

3.2 The Cemetery of Nobles and the Ptahshepses mastaba

The most prominent place in the Abusir cemetery is occupied by the Cemetery of Nobles, with large mastabas lying to the north-east of Niuserre's mortuary complex.[142] Some nobles of Niuserre's time,[143] as well as members of the royal family, were buried there. As was already mentioned, the Mastaba of Ptahshepses is located in this cemetery (*fig. 3.1* and *3.2*, *pl. 2* and *3*). In central Abusir, in contrast to private cemeteries in Dahshur,[144] or Giza,[145] there is no perceptible uniform pattern for the location of the tombs. In the case of the tombs to the south of Raneferef's mortuary complex, it is possible to see a more regular distribution pattern.[146] They are likely to be the tombs belonging to members of the royal family. Due to its location, these would most probably be Raneferef's closest relatives.

In the Cemetery of the Nobles, it is hard to work out the arrangement of the individual tombs. We can, at least, establish that the westernmost tombs (that of Userkafankh and Djadjaemankh and the Anonymous Tomb) of this cemetery were distributed in the "first line", running along the eastern enclosure wall of the pyramid complex of Niuserre. The Mastaba of Ptahshepses, forming a sort of a "second line", was located in between the first and the "third line", in which

---

[140] For the basic analysis of the distribution of the cemeteries across the entire Abusir necropolis and their dating see: M. Verner, *ZÄS* 119 (1992) 116–124.

[141] The most important among these finds is the discovery of a cylindrical seal with the Horus name of Khafre in the area to the east of Userkafankh's mastaba (Borchardt, *Neuserre*, 138, Abb. 118). Unfortunately, it is a find without any archaeological context and it does not permit us to assess the building activity on the spot. The excavations of the Cairo University to the north-west of the Abusir necropolis should also be taken into the consideration. In this area the expedition unearthed a tomb dated to the Early Dynastic Period (see: Radwan, 'Ein Treppengrab der 1. Dynastie aus Abusir', *MDAIK* 47 (1991) 305–308; *idem*, 'Recent Excavations of the Cairo University at Abusir. A Cemetery of the 1st Dynasty', in: *Gedenkschrift Barta*, 311–314; *idem*, 'Mastaba XVII at Abusir (First Dynasty) preliminary results and general remarks', in: *Abusir and Saqqara 2000*, 509–514). It is hard to date the masonry found by Borchardt during his work in Neferirkare's mortuary temple – Borchardt, *Neferirkare*, Abb. 8. Borchardt's dating of this construction to the Archaic Period – on the basis of Archaic pallets built into these mud brick walls – is not tenable. This masonry more likely represents the foundation for the construction of the king's mortuary temple. On the other hand, these pallets seem to indirectly document the existence of the monuments dated to the Archaic Period in the area of the Abusir pyramid field.

[142] See Borchardt, *Neuserre*, 25–33, 109–134.

[143] Userkafankh, Djadjaemankh, an unknown official and the children – members of the broader royal family – were among those who were buried in this cemetery.

[144] "Dahchshur-Mitte" Cemetery: Alexanian, *Netjer-aperef*, 15–17; Abb. 1 and 2.

[145] For the most recent account on these cemeteries see: Jánosi, *Giza*: such geometrical arrangement is obvious there, especially in the case of the large part of the Cemetery G 7000 (see p. 83 and the discussion regarding the development of the cemetery layout, Abb. 3) and of Cemetery G 4000 (Jánosi, *Giza*, 124–127, Abb. 8).

[146] For further information on the archaeological excavations of the northernmost tomb, see Verner, 'Excavations at Abusir. Seasons of 1994/95 and 1995/96', *ZÄS* 124 (1997) 76–77, Abb. 3.

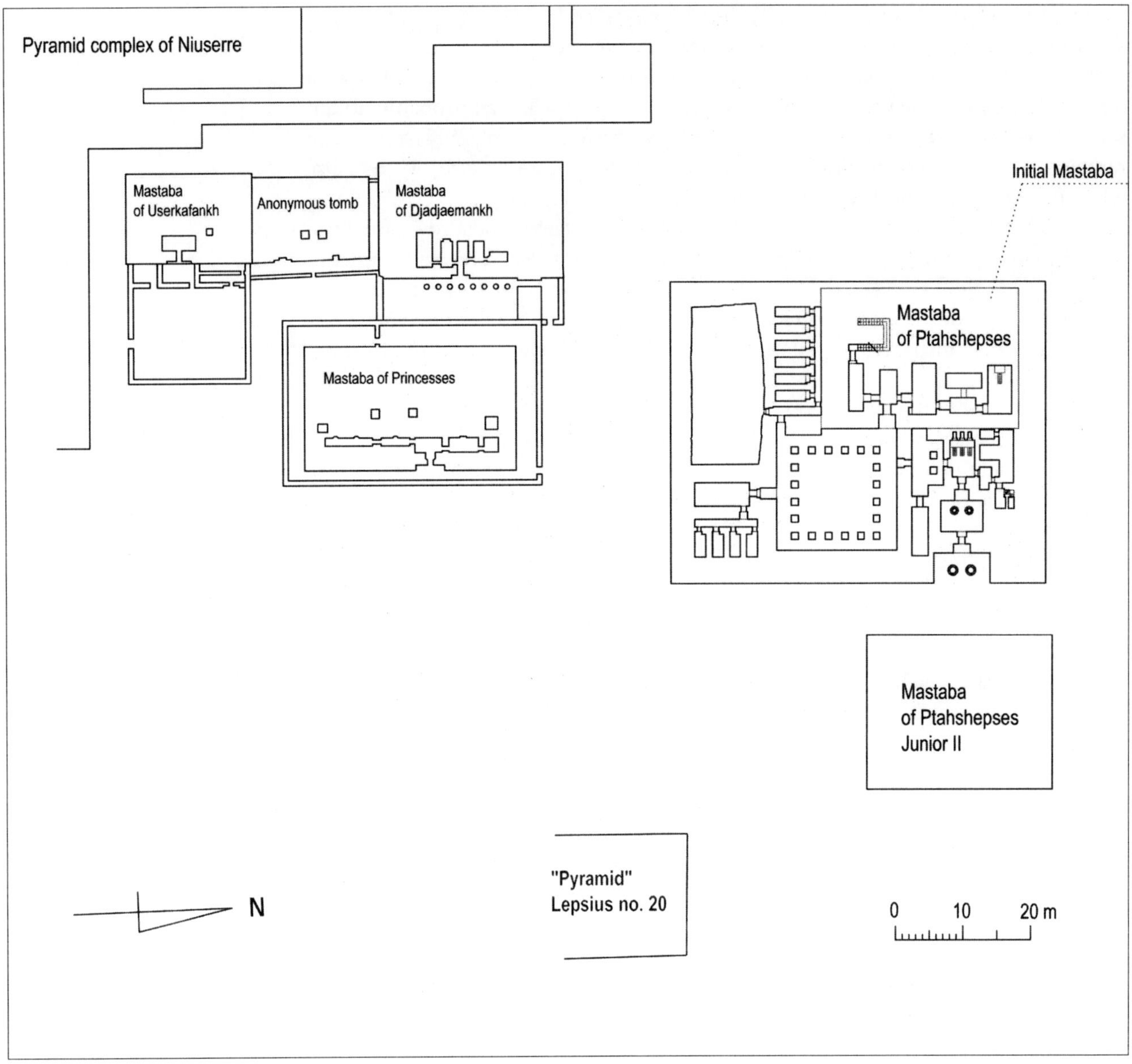

Fig. 3.2 Plan of the Abusir Cemetery of Nobles

the Mastaba of the Princesses is located. The tomb of Ptahshepses Junior II creates the "fourth line". From the easternmost part of the cemetery we know of only one tomb, Lepsius' "pyramid" No. 20, which is in fact a mastaba.[147] This tomb could create the "fifth line" for the Cemetery of the Nobles (for the overall plan of the Cemetery of Nobles, see *fig. 3.2*). One has to underline that this conspectus of the Cemetery of Nobles is only superficial, due to the fact that the major parts have not been excavated as yet.

One of the reasons for this lack of general uniformity regarding the distribution of non-royal tombs is the morphology of the terrain in this area. The Abusir Pyramid Necropolis was not established on a large flat plateau as was the case with other important Old Kingdom pyramid necropoleis, especially the one at Giza. There was not enough space in the area of the Abusir necropolis for a similar type of development,.

Interestingly, the long axes of Userkafankh's, and Djadjaemankh's mastabas, the Anonymous Tomb and the Mastaba of Princesses slightly differ in their orientation from the long axis of the Mastaba of Ptahshepses. The axis of the former tombs is

[147] See: Vyse, Perring, *Pyramids* III, 21–22, *MRA VIII–Testo*, 54–57, *VIII–Tavole*, Tav. 8. Further discussion of this monument can be found in: Bárta, 'The Mastaba of Ptahshepses Junior II at Abusir', *Ä&L* (2000) 64–65.

slightly shifted to the east (see *fig. 3.3*). The reasons behind this change in orientation are difficult to explain. One of the reasons might have been the high social status of Ptahshepses at the commencement of construction of his tomb, for he had, among other titles, that of the Overseer of all the King's works. He was probably able to set out his own tomb precisely in line with the cardinal points.[148] The question remains whether other nobles buried in the cemetery were able to do the same when founding and constructing their tombs.

The Mastaba of Ptahshepses was established off the westernmost row of the first line of tombs, in a second line of its own but, finally, by the time of its completion in the third building stage, it covered the space of two rows between the first and the fourth rows of the other tombs.[149] Had the Cemetery of Nobles developed in a standard way, Ptahshepses' Initial Mastaba would have had to be adjacent to one of the neighbouring tombs – or else would have been built only a few meters off it, in the easternmost row of the tombs, and not at a distance of 25 m from the nearest tomb, that of Djadjaemankh (measuring from the southwest corner of the Initial Mastaba).

The explanation of this arrangement is difficult to explain, primarily due to our limited knowledge of the original situation around the Mastaba of Ptahshepses and other mastabas in the Cemetery of Nobles. The most probable explanation seems to lie in the character of the terrain in the area where the mastaba was built. The mastaba was founded in a depression, five metres below the level of the base of the Mastaba of Djadjaemankh. The soil of the depression (as is also the case for the entire area neighbouring that of the Ptahshepses mastaba) consists of layers of gravel and sand which belong to the lowermost terrace of the Nile.[150] The terrain below the mastaba slopes from the west to the east. Because of this fact, a terrace consisting of limestone rubble had to be raised below the south-eastern corner of the future mastaba.[151]

We would expect that Ptahshepses, being a very prestigious official,[152] would have wanted to build his tomb as close as possible to the ruler's pyramid. The best location, however, was already occupied by other private tombs – those of Userkafankh and Djadjaemankh. This assumption might then help us with the relative dating of the mastaba, which seems to be later than these two tombs.[153] For

---

[148] For this complex problem, see Magdolen, *K zameriavaniu*, *passim*; *idem*, 'On the Orientation of the Old Kingdom Royal Tombs', in: *Abusir and Saqqara 2000*, 491–498.

[149] See *fig. 3.2*. At the end of its development, the south-east corner of the mastaba was 1.15 m to the east and 3.97 m to the north of the north-east corner of the Mastaba of Djadjaemankh. In the beginning, however, the situation looked rather different. The distance between the southwest corner of the Initial Mastaba – the first building stage of the Mastaba of Ptahshepses – and Djadjaemankh's tomb is 25 m in a north-south direction and 2.15 m in the east-west direction.

[150] During the works of the Czechoslovak archaeological expedition to Abusir, it was detected that such layers below the Mastaba of Ptahshepses extended to about three or four meters (F. Váhala, *Zpráva o 10. misi Čs. egyptologického ústavu do Egypta ve dnech od 17. až do 10. června 1974* [Report on the 10th expedition of the Czechoslovak Institute of Egyptology to Egypt from 17th January to 10th June 1974], Archives of the Czech Institute of Egyptology, qu. 32, V/67/1962, p. 2; unfortunately, no further documentation, other than this report, has survived in the archive of the institute.

[151] See p. 43 and Váhala, *Zpráva*, p. 2.

[152] We do not know precisely when he obtained his highest titles (*ṯ3jtj ṯ3tj n s3b, imj-r3 k3wt nbt nt nśwt, etc.*). Nevertheless, if we take into consideration the dimensions and the surface covered by the first building stage of the mastaba, we can see that in comparison with the other tombs of the Cemetery of Nobles: the Mastaba of Ptahshepses was even at that stage the largest mastaba in that cemetery. The comparison with the Mastaba of the Princesses is interesting, since this latter tomb was smaller, despite the fact that it was assigned to at least one member of the royal family. One can add to this fact that the tombs of women were usually smaller, than those of male counterparts.

[153] In the case of the Mastaba of the Princesses, the stratigraphical connection to the Mastaba of Ptahshepses is, unlike the case with other tombs in the Cemetery of the Nobles, not very clear. However, as at least three persons who were (or should be) buried there were directly connected to Ptahshepses and on the basis of several masons' marks, one can conclude that the mastaba of this noble was commenced *after* the beginning of the construction of the Mastaba of the Princesses.

the aforementioned reasons, the construction of the tomb of Ptahshepses was started at a greater distance from the ruler's mortuary complex than would otherwise have been the case – despite the significance of its owner to the king.

There is a possibility that Ptahshepses' career had already begun during the reign of King Neferirkare. During the time of this ruler, Userkafankh and Djadjaemankh might have been more mighty and of higher rank than Ptahshepes was at that time. Therefore, they were allowed to build their tombs a little closer to the pyramid of their lord. On the other hand, the unfinished construction of Neferirkare's pyramid complex, might have prevented their construction from being erected closer to that king's monument. During the reign of Niuserre, these tombs might have prevented this king from constructing his mortuary temple in the standard pattern. Niuserre might have respected these tombs because he respected his father in his decision to elevate them. Perhaps, too, these officials may have been instrumental in assisting Niuserre in the early days of his accession (which might have been also the case of Ptahshepses). For further discussion concerning the date of life of Ptahshepses and of the whole mastaba, see the conclusion chapter.

Just as interestingly, the Initial Mastaba was not only built at a greater distance from the king's pyramid complex than were the Mastabas of Djadjaemankh, Userkafankh and also the Anonymous Tomb, but it was also positioned at some distance from these tombs. One would normally assume that the Initial Mastaba would have lain closer to the aforementioned tombs. What could have been the reasons for this fact? Let us go through the possible explanations for this situation:

1) The Mastaba of Ptahshepses was built in a period later than these tombs, therefore the most convenient place for the construction of his tomb had already been used.

2) The place where the mastaba was built lies in a depression. At the time when the Initial Mastaba was built the depression could have been smaller in its surface than it is now. Therefore, it might not have allowed the construction of the Initial Mastaba any closer to the Mastaba of Djadjaemankh. During the following building stages, the slope of this depression could have been hypothetically – and this should be underlined here – shaped in order to permit the enlargements of the Mastaba of Ptahshepses to take place (therefore, the original shape of this depression before these hypothetical works could have been rather different). In the case of such a powerful official as Ptahshepses, we cannot rule out such large-scale levelling works on the south-west, for they were for that matter able to be documented in the south-eastern sector of the Mastaba of Ptahshepses (see above).

3) Another reason for the placement could have been the hypothetical existence of older buildings in the area between Ptahshepses' Initial Mastaba and the tomb of Djadjaemankh.[154] During the enlargements of the mastaba, such buildings as these could have been pulled down.

4) The hypothetical transport roads, which could have existed or remained in the area around the tomb, might also have influenced the location of the tomb. These roads could have served primarily for the construction of the pyramid complex of Niuserre, but might also have been used for the construction of the tomb itself.[155]

---

[154] We do not have any direct attestations of older constructions in the Abusir royal necropolis.

[155] Beside the main transport ramp, which followed the line of a wadi running northwards and north-westwards from the Abusir pyramids (see Verner, 'Archaeological Survey of Abusir', *ZÄS* 119 (1992) 117, Fig. 1; Krejčí, *Stavebně-historický vývoj*, 160), we should not completely exclude the existence of separate small transport ramps, which could be used not only for the transportation of the building material used for the royal complexes, but also for the construction of private mastabas.

5) The choice of place for the construction of the Mastaba of Ptahshepses might have been limited by already existing buildings in the area to the north and the north-east of the pyramid complex of Niuserre. Unfortunately, this space is now covered by debris, Borchardt's dumps and drift sand, so that it is not possible to survey it in sufficient detail. In this respect, neither does the satellite image of the necropolis (*fig. 3.3*) help very much.

Fig. 3.3 Satellite image of the Abusir Pyramid Necropolis

According to the satellite image of the necropolis, a large rectangular construction once seems to have existed in this area. However, this "structure" is almost certainly Borchardt's dump, made during his excavations of Niuserre's pyramid complex, and not another tomb. On the other hand, the existence of another tomb construction *was* detected during Žába's excavations[156] (this tomb is not visible on the satellite image), in the area north-west of the north-west corner of the Mastaba of Ptahshepses. It was a largely damaged mastaba, built of fine white limestone with a columned (!) portico.[157] This find clearly suggests that some tombs and constructions once existed in the area between Sahure's pyramid complex and the Cemetery of Nobles.

In this regard it should be also mentioned that the sun temple of King Sahure, *Śḫt-Rˁ*, might have been located in the area to the south-west of the Mastaba of Ptahshepses.[158] This suggestion was made on the basis of masons' marks[159] bearing its

[156] Unfortunately, the results of these clearing works have not been published, nor documented sufficiently. It is thus not possible to answer one important question regarding the problem of the location of the Mastaba of Ptahshepses – that of the dating and the relative chronological stratigraphy of this area.
[157] Personal communication from M. Verner.
[158] The area on which, hypothetically, the temple *Sḫt-Rˁ* was built, was later used by Niuserre for construction of his pyramid complex. Any such building blocks might have provided materials that were later utilized in Niuserre's construction.
[159] Borchardt, *Neferirkare*, 54–55.

name, which were found on limestone blocks which had been built into the masonry of Niuserre's pyramid complex.[160] The discovery of the quartzite pyramidion of an obelisk to the south-west of the Mastaba of Ptahshepses[161] and of heaps of quartzite fragments beside the northern *Eckbau* of Niuserre's pyramid complex,[162] also seem to suggest the existence of such a temple.[163] If this surmise is correct, this monument may have somehow influenced the location of the Mastaba of Ptahshepses.

6) It is not likely that the position of the tomb was chosen in regard to the pyramid complexes of Sahure and Niuserre as it was supposed by V. Fiala. The distance of the Mastaba of Ptahshepses from the pyramid of Sahure should be the same as that from the pyramid of Niuserre. In Fiala's opinion, this fact enables an approximate *post quem* dating of the mastaba's construction.[164] M. Verner also assumes that the location of the mastaba was deliberately chosen in relation to the royal pyramids in order to "round off the monumental architectonic composition" of the necropolis.[165] Such an explanation using the aesthetic criteria, however, could not be documented. Although the status of Ptahshepses was nonetheless high, he was only an official and not the king – the only god living on the earth – and it is hard to assume that the tomb of Ptahshepses would have been included into the overall building plan of the *royal* necropolis.[166]

7) At first glance, another factor seems to be important in elucidating the reasons why the Mastaba of Ptahshepses was located in its place – *i.e.* its prominence in the necropolis as viewed from the valley floor.[167] However, we have to recall that, in the beginning of its building history, the Mastaba of Ptahshepses was not so monumental as it was at its conclusion. The Initial Mastaba was ca 5.20 m high (see p. 41) and the abovementioned depression was 5 m deep. These readings rather exclude this "sight-prominence" explanation. The Initial Mastaba would not be high enough to be prominent in the line of sight from the valley floor. However, this does not mean that Ptahshepses did not make any effort regarding the display of his monument. It is apparent that by the execution of the later building additions to the Initial Mastaba he tried make his tomb much more prominent by raising the height of the roof above the area of the vestibule and other parts of the mastaba and by ensuring that the enclosure wall was clearly visible in the eyes of the viewers from the valley below. In this way he certainly stressed his importance, his high social ranking and authority.

It is hard to choose between these possible explanations for the location of the Mastaba of Ptahshepses. As was shown, many causes might have impacted the choice of the location for Ptahshepses' tomb. Among these causes we can enumerate the geomorphological situation on the site, the existence of older buildings, the social rank of the tomb owner and the fact that Abusir was a building site with transport roads, workshops and piles of building materials and rubbish during the middle of the Fifth Dynasty. Nevertheless, on the basis of our knowledge, we can suggest that the most important influence was connected with the terrain in the

---

160 Kaiser, 'Zu den Sonnenheligtümmer der 5. Dynastie', *MDAIK* 14 (1956), 112, note 2
161 Verner, *RdE* 28, 1976
162 Borchardt, *Neuserre*, Blatt 28.
163 Verner, *Pyramids*, 277–279; Verner, *Sokar* 10, 1 (2005), 42–43. Dieter Arnold however supposes that the *Eckbauten* were adorned by large monolithic obelisks (Arnold, in: *Temples of ancient Egypt, 63*), a summit of one of which was found by the Archaeological expedition of the Charles University.
164 Fiala, in: *Preliminary Report*, 58.
165 Verner, *Realm of Osiris*, 155–158.
166 Moreover, looking at *fig. 3.1*, we can see that the Mastaba of Ptahshepses is located a little bit closer to the pyramid of Niuserre than that of Sahure.
167 V. G. Callender, 'Reflections on Princess Khamerernebty of Abusir', in press. I would like to thank Dr. Callender for discussion concerning this problem.

area of the Mastaba of Ptahshepses and the period of time when the Initial Mastaba was started. The difference between the level of the Mastaba of Djadjaemankh and that of Ptahshepses is really remarkable and it prevented the construction of the Initial Mastaba closer to the former tomb. As previously stressed, the tombs built in the westernmost line of the Cemetery of the Nobles were built first, using the most suitable – and also the most prestigious – area. The Mastaba of the Princesses was built later to the east of these tombs, but still very close to Niuserre's pyramid, and thus it occupied another very favourable place for the construction of a mastaba. Ptahshepses then obviously did not have any better choice for his tomb than the aforementioned depression. Though the depression did not lie close to the pyramid of his lord, it had one great advantage – it enabled the construction of a large mastaba, and even from the very beginning, such was the Mastaba of Ptahshepses.

In comparison with the difficulties encountered in examining the reasons for the founding of the Mastaba of Ptahshepses in its specific place, the circumstance to the east of this monument are clear. In that area, there was space enough to build a large mastaba belonging to Ptahshepses' son, Ptahshepses Junior II,[168] perhaps as early as during the second, but more probably during/or after the third building stage of Ptahshepses Senior's tomb.

As has been shown by the above analysis, the reasons for the siting of the Mastaba of Ptahshepses are not easy to discern. Whilst logic can provide a selection of reasons for the original foundation, we have no concrete evidence to back up these hypotheses. As there are no viable historical records offering an explanation, we have to think mainly about the practical reasons (the lack of another, socially more appropriate, place nearer to the pyramid, *etc.*) for the explanation of why this magnificent tomb was built in this precise location.

---

168 See Bárta, 'The Mastaba of Ptahshepses Junior II at Abusir', *Ä&L* 10 (2000) 45–66.

4. The building and architectural development of the mastaba

4.1 The first building stage (the Initial Mastaba)

The first building stage of the Mastaba of Ptahshepses, named by Zbyněk Žába as the Initial Mastaba, was a rather monumental tomb. It can be said that this north-south oriented mastaba tomb with the entrance in its eastern façade surpassed in its dimensions many of the other large non-royal tombs in the Memphite necropolis. Nevertheless, it should be remarked here that in the Abusir pyramid plateau some other large tombs seem to exist – but they have yet to be excavated.[169]

4.1.1 Casing of the Initial Mastaba

For the evaluation of the Initial Mastaba's dimensions it is essential to try to reconstruct the original course of the mastaba's casing, which originally covered the core masonry of the tomb. The Mastaba of Ptahshepses – and thus the Initial Mastaba itself – was damaged by stone robbers many times during its later history, therefore, the state of preservation of its masonry is not good. The mastaba underwent a complicated process of development as well, so that some parts of the original masonry of the Initial Mastaba are now covered by later additions. In many sections, the casing of the mastaba was completely or almost completely removed. However, some parts of the casing of the Initial Mastaba still remain *in situ*. The best preserved part of the casing runs along the northern part of the eastern face of the Initial Mastaba. Here the annex of the second main building stage of mastaba, with its Rooms nos. 4 and 3 and the "Northern Storerooms" (especially Rooms nos. 8 and 9), was attached directly to the casing of the Initial Mastaba (see *chapter 4.2* for further information). The casing of the Initial Mastaba is most conspicuous in the area where the casing of the northern wall joins that of Room no. 11 (the Southern Portico, enlarged during the third building stage). In this case, the eastern outer wall of the Initial Mastaba created the western wall of this room (see *fig. 4.1.1*).[170]

Fig. 4.1.1 Join in the casing of the Initial Mastaba and of the second building stage in the north wall of Room no. 11

At this place, one can document the way in which the casing of the Initial Mastaba in this area (and also along the whole eastern façade?) was made. Contrary to the situation along the southern face of the Initial Mastaba (see further), the casing was constructed by means of interchanging blocks of white limestone in two formats: the first format used tall blocks (in section their dimensions were 0.46–0.60 × 0.12–0.15 m), whereas the second format used flat blocks (in

---

[169] *Cf.* Verner, 'Archaeological Survey of Abusir', *ZÄS* (1991), 178. For our understanding of the architectural development of large tombs in the time of the Fifth Dynasty, the archaeological excavations of tombs located to the north and southeast of the pyramids of Niuserre and Neferirkare will be highly important.

[170] This is not an extraordinary example; we can see similar designs in many other private tombs in the residential cemeteries, *cf.* Room no. IV belonging to Meriteti Meri's part of Mereruka's family tomb complex – *PM* III, 536; Duell, *Mereruka* I, plan facing pl. 2.

Fig. 4.1.2 Floor pavement of the area to the east of the entrance to the Initial Mastaba

Fig. 4.1.3 Backing and casing stones built in the southern outer wall of the Initial Mastaba

Fig. 4.1.4 South-west corner of the casing belonging to the Initial Mastaba

section: 0.31–0.33 × 0.18 m). As one can observe in Rooms no. 8 and 9, the length of the blocks might have reached a length of up to 1.05 m. The outer faces of the casing blocks were finely polished and their faces were set at an oblique angle, in order to create the slope of outer faces of the mastaba.

The imprints of the casing are preserved on the paving and under-paving blocks found in the area of the doorway to the Initial Mastaba (both to the north and to the south – see *fig. 4.1.2*). From the existence of these imprints, it follows that the face of the casing ran about 0.38–0.40 m in front of the foot of the core masonry along the eastern outer wall of the Initial Mastaba.

Along the southern core wall of the Initial Mastaba we can observe the remains of the casing which once covered the mastaba. The north wall of corridor No. 39, connecting magazines Nos. 33–38 (which in fact belonged to the third building stage), also has several casing blocks still lying *in situ*; the slope of their outer faces was 82°. This wall represented the southern façade of the Initial Mastaba and the architect of the third building stage of the mastaba used it as the northern wall of the corridor (as was the case with the western wall of Room no. 11). This is more obvious in the case of the block located in the north-eastern corner of corridor Room no. 39.

In the south-east corner of the Initial Mastaba, the distance between the face of the casing and the face of the core masonry varies from 0.73 to 0.83 m – the difference between these distances is caused by the fact that the core masonry of the outer wall of the mastaba was built from rather large, irregular greyish limestone blocks which were not carefully joined. The casing of the Initial Mastaba is well preserved in the area of its south-west corner. At this spot, the casing was constructed by means of large (0.48–0.53 × 0.60–0.80 × 0.57–0.88 m) white, well worked limestone blocks. As a matter of course, the outer faces of these casing blocks was carefully polished. The blocks were cemented with a quality mortar. The free spaces between the casing blocks and the core masonry were filled with the backing masonry, consisting of smaller fragments of local limestone (see *fig. 4.1.4*).

The other place in which the face of the Initial Mastaba's casing has been documented, is the space along the western outer wall of the mastaba. On the layer made of polished blocks of white limestone, which was laid down around the mastaba as the base for the casing but also serving as the pavement, the remains of lines indicating the course of the casing were found. These lines were documented by V. Fiala in 1974.[171] The width between the face of the casing and the core masonry measures about 0.45–0.50 m, or nearly one cubit (0.52 m).

In the southern part of this area, a second line of casing imprint, very probably belonging to the casing face has also been documented (see plan *fig. 4.1.5*). This second line was running in parallel 12 cm to the west of the first line. It is not possible to properly interpret this information – it might be that the second, western line represents a secondary imprint made during the positioning of the casing blocks or during their transportation to their final position. This question could not be solved satisfactorily. The main reason for ascribing these imprints to the casing of the first building stage is that the inner imprint line relates to the face of one casing block still lying *in situ* in the north-western corner of the Initial Mastaba (see *pl. 5*). This block is an original part of the casing of this building stage. This assumption has been based above all on the angle of the slope (82° 30′) of the northern face of this block: it is the same angle as that found on the faces of the already attested casing blocks. An important fact is that this block of stone is of a different colour from the other blocks, which were added to this block during the third building stage. The block lies directly on top of the pavement block which is also made from white limestone. Its northern face is carefully worked. Only a very small part of the block's northern face is accessible through the junction between this block and

[171] Today, due to the fact that this space has again been filled by deep layers of blown sand and rubble, it is not now feasible to re-excavate this space.

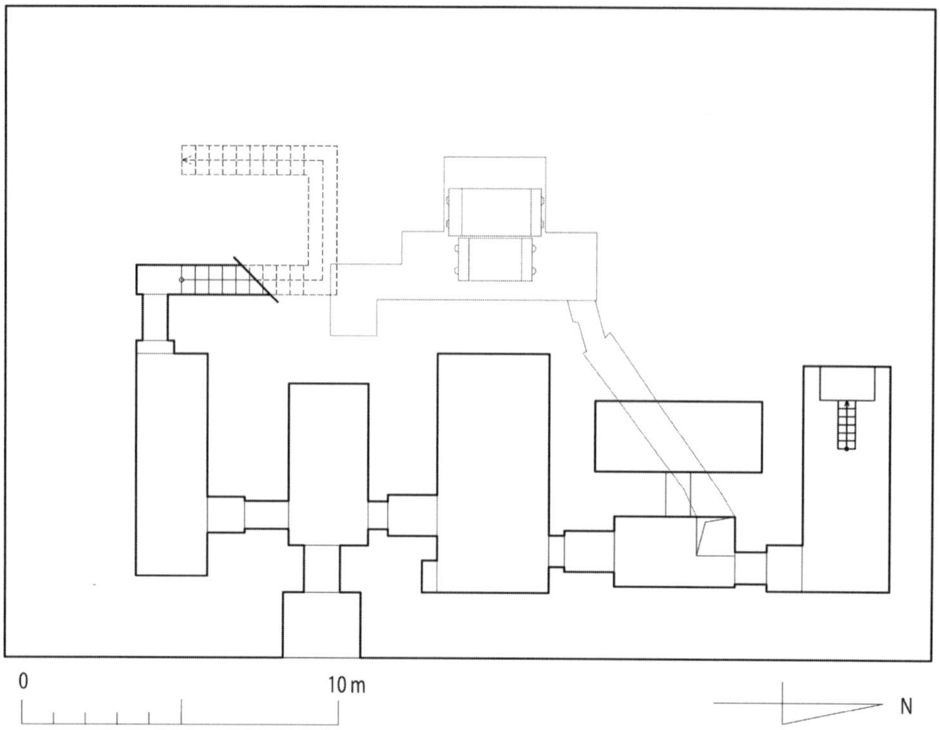

Fig. 4.1.5 Overall plan of the Initial Mastaba

another casing block which was added during the later building stages when the mastaba was extended to the north.

The measurement of the slopes of the preserved casing blocks show that the angle of the casing slope in the first building stage varied between 82° and 82° 30′ – as in the case of the eastern façade – and around 82° 30′ in the northern façade of the mastaba. The ratio of the slope was 1 to 7 1/5 palms, respectively 1 to 7 2/3 palms.

4.1.2 Dimensions of the Initial Mastaba

The remains of the casing discussed above allow us to calculate the dimensions of the Initial Mastaba. The mastaba was 29.35 (or 30.25 m) long and 19.85 m wide (*i.e.* the dimensions were 56.44 [58.17] × 38 cubits), therefore, the area, which the mastaba covered at that stage was 582.60 m² – 600.46 m². From these values it follows that the Initial Mastaba was already the most spacious tomb in the Cemetery of the Nobles. As was already mentioned, the size of the Initial Mastaba represents one of the indicators for the fact that its owner had a high social status (see also *chapter 2*). This statement can be supported by the simple comparison with other large tombs built on the Abusir pyramid plateau:

Mastaba of Userkafankh – 18.48 × 12.87 m,[172] *i.e.* 237.84 m² (with the brick extension to the east measuring 3.18 × 17.50 m, 293.49 m²),

Anonymous Tomb – 16.9 × 11.81–12.27 m,[173] *i.e.* 199.59–207.36 m²,

Mastaba of Djadjaemankh – 26.81 × 16.67 m (h. 5.295 m),[174] *i.e.* 446.92 m²,

Mastaba of Princesses – 32.04 × 16.44 m,[175] *i.e.* 526.75 m².

As has been convincingly shown by Naguib Kanawati, the total area which the tombs occupied was one of the indicators of social rank of officials during the Old Kingdom, especially in its second half.[176]

The height of the Initial Mastaba can only be estimated – its masonry was destroyed to such a large extent that the task of calculating its height is very difficult.

---

172 Borchardt, *Neuserre*, Bl. 20.
173 *Op. cit.*, Bl. 21.
174 *Op. cit.*, Bl. 22.
175 *Op. cit.*, Bl. 25.
176 Kanawati, 'The Financial Resources of the Viziers of the Old Kingdom and the Historical Implications', *PASA* 5 (1974), 1–20; see also: Alexanian, *Netjer-aperef*, 33.

The highest point in the masonry which has survived in the Initial Mastaba is the crown of the stonework located to the south of its burial chamber. This point is at a height of 4.20 m above the level of the pavement in Room no. 22.[177] Unfortunately, we do not know the precise height of the masonry above this surviving masonry. If we speculate that the height of the Initial Mastaba was about 10 cubits (*i.e.* ca 5.20 m),[178] then we should add about 1.00 m of masonry above the highest point in the surviving masonry. However, more accurate estimates can be apparently gained by the analysis of architectural features added during the later stages of the mastaba's building development. *i.e.* by the height of pillars in the open courtyard, which were erected during the third building stage (see p. 122–126). Their remains, found during the archaeological excavations of the mastaba, have allowed us to reconstruct their original height in respect of the level at which the ceiling of the ambulatory around the court was built.[179] From such calculations, it follows that the height of the masonry of the Initial Mastaba was at least 5.06 m. Blocks of the ambulatory ceiling had to be partly built into the masonry of the upper parts of the Initial Mastaba, which, therefore, supported them. Indirectly, this fact enables us to reconstruct the height of the mastaba as being at a level of at least 5.06 m.

There is, however, no piece of confirmed evidence concerning the way the original roof terrace of the Initial Mastaba was constructed. We can only speculate whether or not the roof terrace was slightly inclined in the direction of the outer walls of the mastaba (as is noticeable, *e.g.*, in the case of mastabas located in the Western Field in Giza)[180] in order to drain rain water from the roof. Such a strategy would prevent the accumulation of water upon the terrace. Nevertheless, there is a possibility that the roof was not constructed on one level, but on several different levels. The levels of these individual roofing terraces were dependent upon the height of the each room which they were covering. In this instance, the mastaba might have been topped by a wall encircling the upper rim of the mastaba's side walls. This wall then might have bound the separate roofs of the mastaba into a single unity in the eye of the spectator.[181] As a matter of fact, we have no idea how high such a wall might have been. In this case, however, the height of the crown of the mastaba should be also assumed to be at a level of ca 5.20 m. To date, no such remains, either blocks or imprints, which could attest to such a construction have been found during archaeological excavations.

4.1.3 The ground plan of the Initial Mastaba (see *pls. 6–8*)

In respect of its ground plan, the Initial Mastaba can be primarily compared with some of the tombs built in the Abusir necropolis, especially that of Djadjaemankh in the Cemetery of Nobles. A high degree of similarity can be found also in the case of the tombs which were labelled by M. Verner as Type-I tombs[182], *i.e.* Hedjetnebu's, Khekeretnebty's (in this latter case, we refer to the original appearance of each tomb), Neserkauhor's mastabas and of the anonymous tomb L – all of which were excavated in Djedkare's family cemetery.[183] In all these instances, the entrance to each tomb – located in its eastern façade – was followed by a vestibule. The vestibule

---

[177] The pavement of this room was taken as the mean level point in this part of the mastaba during the surveying of the tomb. The main reason for doing so was the fact that the original pavement in this room is better preserved than in other rooms of the Initial Mastaba.

[178] In fact, the figure of 10 cubits cannot be in reality confirmed. Converting readings in the modern units into cubits, their rounding and automatic supposing that they were important for the ancient Egyptians is only a modern construct.

[179] See: Balík, Vachala, 'The scientific restitution of the Ptahshepses' mastaba at Abusir – an ideal reconstruction', in: *Abusir and Saqqara 2000*, fig. 6.

[180] For example tomb G 5230, Reisner, *Gîza Necropolis*, fig. 153.

[181] Such a wall was constructed in the case of tomb on G6000 cemetery in Giza: Weeks, *Cemetery G 6000*, fig. 4–5.

[182] Verner, Callender, *Djedkare's Cemetery*, 109–117.

[183] Borchardt, *Neuserre*, Bl. 22; Jánosi, '„Im Schatten" der Pyramiden – Die Mastabas in Abusir. Einige Beobachtungen zum Grabbau der 5. Dynastie', in: *Abusir and Saqqara 2000*, 451; Verner, Callender, *Djedkare's Cemetery*, 113.

gave access to other rooms located to the north and south of it. A similar pattern can also be observed in the Initial Mastaba. Another similarity is represented by the form of the offering rooms in both Ptahshepses and Djadjaemankh's tombs. In these two instances, the tomb-substructures had a rectangular ground plan oriented in an east-west direction.

Nonetheless, there are several differences between these tombs which have been mentioned and the Initial Mastaba of Ptahshepses. Unlike Djadjaemankh's mastaba, the serdab of the Initial Mastaba is not located in the southern part of the mastaba, but in the northern part of the tomb, above the entrance to the descending corridor leading to the burial chamber (in Room no. 26). This room, which is located to the north of the vestibule in Djadjaemankh's mastaba, was used as a chapel. Why the serdab in Ptahshepses' tomb was not located in the same position as it was in the case of Djadjaemankh's tomb, but instead placed behind the western wall of Room no. 26, it is not fully clear (for further discussion on this topic, see hereafter). When comparing the Initial Mastaba with other Abusir tombs, another major difference can be seen in the existence of a further offering hall in the northern part of the Initial Mastaba. The existence of a stairway leading to the roof terrace of the Initial Mastaba represents another deviation. This feature offers a parallel between the Initial Mastaba and the most complex of the non-royal tombs in the Memphite area, as well as a connection with the royal mortuary temples. All this adumbrates further development of the Ptahshepses mastaba into a kind of analogy of a royal mortuary temple. Apart from the stairway, the existence of a descending corridor with the opening not in the façade of the mastaba, but in a room that is inside the tomb, represents another distinctly different element of architecture. These exceptional architectural elements permit us to emphasise the remarkable position of the Mastaba of Ptahshepses within the development of ancient Egyptian mortuary architecture.

Unlike the Type I tombs of the Djedkare Family Cemetery and the example in the tomb of Ptahshepses Junior II[184], *etc.*, it seems that no false shaft was located in the south-west corner of the masonry of the Mastaba of Ptahshepses. These shafts apparently functioned as depots for remnants of the mummification and/or of the funerary repast.[185] Moreover, as was mentioned by Bárta,[186] they may have been intended to misdirect the tomb robbers away from the real burial chamber. This feature of tomb architecture might not have been yet settled at the time of the construction of the Ptahshepses mastaba. The other reason for its non-existence could have been due to the construction of the complicated masonry for the staircase (Room no. 24) in the south-western sector of the mastaba's superstructure.

4.1.4 Core masonry in the western part of the Initial Mastaba

Following thorough research into the building materials of the Initial Mastaba, it is possible to reconstruct the way in which the mastaba's masonry was constructed. It is very probable that the building work started with the construction of the core masonry that created the western part of the Initial Mastaba. The masonry was built of large, rather regular, though roughly worked blocks of local limestone. Their dimensions differ and the blocks measure up to 3.27 m in length, and up to 0.85 m in height. Unfortunately, due to the poor stability of the masonry and because of the danger of the masonry's collapse, it was not possible to make a probe in order to obtain an idea of how the foundation of this masonry was constructed. Nevertheless, as it indirectly follows from the soundings made in 1974 (in a different

---

184 Bárta, 'The Mastaba of Ptahshepses Junior II at Abusir', *Ä&L* 10 (2001), 55, fig. 2.

185 Both M. Verner and T. I. Rzeuska came to the same conclusions: see Rzeuska, 'The Necropolis at West Saqqara: The Late Old Kingdom Shafts with no Burial Chamber. Were they False, Dummy, Unfinished or Intentional, in: *Abusir and Saqqara 2001*, 402. M. Verner in his account concerning tombs belonging to the members of Djedkare's family called these elements of architecture "subsidiary shafts": Verner, Callender, *Djedkare's Cemetery*, 115–116.

186 Bárta, *Ä&L* 10 (2000), 61.

part of Ptahshepses' vast tomb), the mastaba was built on a layer of stone blocks, which was about 1 m high. This layer formed a kind of platform for the construction of the tomb's masonry. Regrettably, we do not have direct attestation for such a layer for the area of the Initial Mastaba. It was only partially documented during the excavations of the area of this western core masonry (see the east-west section through the area of the burial chamber in *fig. 4.1.32*).

Fig. 4.1.6 Core masonry of the south-western corner of the Initial Mastaba

Here it should be mentioned that, as is also the case with the whole of the Abusir Pyramid Necropolis, the Mastaba of Ptahshepses was built on subsoil of inferior quality that had once been a terrace of the ancient Nile. This terrace of the Libyan Desert consists in its upper levels of layers of gravel, interchanged with silt sediments mixed with sand. Such a sequence was documented by soundings in the entrance to Room no. 16, in the area of a deep niche – "Room no. 15".[187] Unfortunately, this ca 5 m deep dig was not documented during its excavation.

The poor quality of the subsoil influenced the way in which the underground parts of the Abusir pyramids, and also of private tombs, were constructed. The burial apartments of both the royal pyramids and of the non-royal tombs (at least those which were erected in the area of the royal necropolis) were started in constructional pits which could be quite easily dug out in the soft subsoil of the Abusir plateau.[188] Masonry of the above-ground parts of the pyramids was erected on platforms made from layers of stone blocks.[189] Ptahshepses, well experienced in the construction of the Abusir royal pyramid complexes, was certainly able to use this method in his own tomb.

The supposed foundation trench of the western core masonry was very probably dug out at the same time as the construction pit for the burial apartment of the mastaba. This core masonry incorporates the entire western outer wall and the greater part of the southern outer wall of the Initial Mastaba,[190] as well as part of the north wall of the Initial Mastaba. An interesting fact is that the masonry of the neighbouring Mastaba of Djadjaemankh is very similar to this part of the core masonry of the Initial Mastaba (see *fig. 4.1.6*).[191] This fact could have at least two

[187] Personal communication, Ladislav Bareš, spring 2000.
[188] For discussion concerning the low quality of subsoil on Abusir plateau, see Krejčí, 'The origins and development of the royal necropolis at Abusir during the Old Kingdom', in: *Abusir and Saqqara 2000*, 473.
[189] Such a platform, about 1.5 m high, was constructed under Raneferef's planned pyramid – see Verner *et al.*, *Raneferef*.
[190] See Verner, *Baugraffiti*, E – Plan Nr. 8, Room 33, and north wall.
[191] See Borchardt, *Neuserre*, Bl. 22.

Fig. 4.1.7 Basalt hinge holder in the entrance to the Initial Mastaba

explanations: both of the tombs might have been built by one crew at different times, or, the tombs may have been built in the same period of time, however it would not be possible to ascertain whether by one, or more crews.

The core masonry of the eastern part of the Initial Mastaba has different parameters and these shall be discussed later.

4.1.5 Room no. 21 – the entrance to the Initial Mastaba

The entrance to the first building stage was located in the southern half of the eastern façade of the Initial Mastaba. As the casing was almost completely destroyed, it is hard to reconstruct the precise course of the wall face. However, the face of the southern wall of the entrance-niche is traceable. The previously discussed imprint of the mastaba casing in the south-eastern corner of the entrance to the Initial Mastaba documents the fact that the face of the entrance niche also ran 0.38 m in front of the face of the core masonry. Therefore, it is possible to ascertain that the depth of the entrance niche was about 1.98 m and its width was about 2.52 m. We cannot reconstruct the height of the entrance, because the entire casing of the doorway niche has been removed and no trace of any join for bonding the casing into the core masonry was found.

It does not seem probable that the niche came with a pair of pillars (or columns). Firstly no parts or imprints of such supports were found, secondly, the niche was too small for such a design, especially if we take into consideration the existence of the wooden leafs in the doorway. Only the basalt hinge holder was found (see *fig. 4.1.7*): this was located 0.42 m from the core masonry of the southern wall of the doorway and 0.10 m to the east from the western end of the same wall. While the presence of this hinge does not allow to us reconstruct the exact width of the doorway, it can be estimated to have been 1.2 m. The layout of the doorway allows us almost certainly to deduce that the doorway opened towards the exterior of the tomb.

4.1.6 Room no. 22 (*figs. 4.1.8–4.1.11*)

The entrance niche was followed by a rectangular, east-west oriented room. In this room some imprints of its side walls remaining on the pavement of the room and the building lines on the core masonry of the room allow us to reconstruct the dimensions of the room as being 4.50 m in length and 2.58 in width (= 8.65 × 4.96 cubits). In the western part, a kind of podium, or base has survived *in situ*. An important detail is that the surrounding core masonry of the room's side walls is built on to it. On the cores of the side walls, a net of masons' vertical and horizontal

Fig. 4.1.8 Room no. 22 from the west

Fig. 4.1.9 Room no. 22 from the south-east

lines has survived until modern times.[192] From these lines, it follows that this podium was originally one cubit (*i.e.* 0.52 m) high. Another, vertical, line indicates the eastern face of this base. If we investigate the base more thoroughly, we can see that it does not represent the face of the masonry itself. The base was apparently covered by casing blocks. Therefore, the above mentioned vertical line does not indicate the real face of this podium, but it certainly indicates the position of the face of this base core.

The base, tentatively ascribed by Miroslav Verner to be a base for an altar, is connected with the original function of the room. Previously, the room was interpreted as being an offering room.[193] As it was recently satisfactorily shown by Peter Jánosi, this room served as the location for the statue(s) of the tombs owner (*cf.* p. 134). The aforementioned base might have created the base not for an altar, but for the free standing statue. This arrangement then would imply that this room might functioned for a kind of a ritual connected with the statue.

Despite the fact that the there is no trace of a join between the ceiling slabs and the core masonry of the side walls, it is possible to reconstruct the height of the room. For this purpose, one of the horizontal masons' lines surviving on the core masonry of the room can be used. This line suggests that the ceiling would be at a level of 2.71 m above the base and 3.32 m above the pavement of the room.[194] If we take into consideration the estimated height of the Initial Mastaba (5.20 m) and the hypothesis that the roofing terrace of the Initial Mastaba was constructed in one level, the roofing masonry above Room no. 22 would have been 1.88 m thick. It is thus questionable whether the height of the filling masonry above the ceiling

---

[192] Verner, *Baugraffiti*, loose plan C – Room 22, north and south walls.

[193] Fiala, in: *Preliminary Report*, 52.

[194] *Cf.* Verner, *Baugraffiti*, loose plan C – Room 22, north and south walls.

of the room was really so high. Such a thick layer of the filling masonry (of course, without the casing of the roof terrace itself, supposedly another 1 cubit high) might have reached a height of circa 1.20 m. As was already discussed, there is a question whether or not the roofing terrace was constructed on one level, or on several levels. The example of Room no. 22 clearly shows that it is more probable that the roof of the mastaba was designed to have several different levels. We do not have direct evidence how the roofing masonry might have been high.

As follows from the partially preserved limestone beam above the entrance to Room no. 23 which had an east-west orientation (and was laid on top of the casing of the room's side walls), the ceiling beams of the room itself must have been laid crosswise (in a north-south direction) to it. Such an arrangement represented the standard construction method for ceiling beams in the ancient Egyptian constructions.

The room had two doorways – one placed in the south wall and leading to Room no. 23 and another in the north wall, opening into Room no. 25.

Fig. 4.1.10 Doorway between Room no. 22 and 23 from the south

Fig. 4.1.11 Doorway between Room no. 22 and 23 from the north. On the southern wall of Room no. 23 the building join of the first and second sub-phase of the first building stage is visible

4.1.7 Room no. 23

The entrance to this room is the only one in the Initial Mastaba, in which a fragment of a block above the doorway itself still survives *in situ* (*fig. 4.1.10–4.1.11*). This fact enables us to estimate the original height of the doorway. Considering the fact that the block is made of local limestone, it seems that it was part of the filling masonry above the doorway, *i.e.*, that it was covered from by the doorway architrave underneath. The lower side of this block is 2.54 m above the level of the pavement. Therefore, the height of this doorway was less than this reading – and it could be estimated at about 2.10 m. The width of the entrance was 0.95 m, a figure which we can compute from the imprints of its side walls.

Room no. 23 was an oblong room oriented in an east-west direction. It had completely lost its casing and pavement and its ceiling had also been removed.

Fig. 4.1.12 Roofing slabs found lying on the floor of Room no. 23

Nonetheless, the dimensions of this room can be estimated by using the *in situ* masons' lines, documented during the excavation of the room: its length was 6.43 m.[195] In the case of the width, the masons' lines on the east wall of the room show two numerical measures, 2.16 and 2.56 m.[196] Nevertheless, it seems that the smaller value was the right one, as is shown by a small arrow on one of the vertical lines and this indicates that this line marked the face of the southern wall of the room. The height of this room is not possible to calculate; however, we can guess that it was the same as in Room no. 22, *i.e.* about 3.32 m.

The roofing of the rooms in this part of the mastaba was made by means of large flat limestone beams, some of which were found during the excavation. The two largest of them – with dimensions 3.15–3.21 × 0.90–1.12 × 0.50–0.52 and 3.12–3.19 × 0.93–1.30 × 0.50–0.53 m – were excavated and still lie on the floor of Room no. 23 (see *fig. 4.1.12*). Having in mind the length of the room, it is very probable that the ceiling slabs were laid in a north-south direction.

Room no. 23 provides access to the stairway (Room no. 24) leading onto the roof terrace of the mastaba. The room, therefore, served in a practical way as a kind of a corridor connecting the staircase with other rooms of the Initial Mastaba. On the other hand, Room no. 23 might have had another function. In the ground plan of the Initial Mastaba, there was no space which could serve as a magazine. Such a room was a standard part of ground-plans of Djadjaemankh's tomb[197] and of other tombs dated to the period. Needless to say, a storeroom was very important from the point of view of the functioning of the tomb. Therefore it is highly probable that Room no. 23 was used additionally as a storage room.[198]

It cannot be, however, discounted that such a tomb magazine, or magazines, could have been located in (brick) buildings constructed in front of the eastern face of the mastaba as we can see in the case of Userkafankh's and Djadjaemankh's tombs,[199] having in mind only the tombs in the Abusir necropolis as examples here. One of the reasons for assuming this possibility is the confined space of Room 23.

---

[195] Verner, *Baugraffiti*, D – Plan Nr. 8, Room 25, and north wall, in regard to the imprints still remaining on the side walls; from these impressions the length of the room can be calculated quite precisely.

[196] Verner, *Baugraffiti*, D – Plan Nr. 8, room 25, east wall.

[197] Borchardt, *Neuserre*, Bl. 22.

[198] See also Fritz, *Mastabagräber*, 78–79, Abb. 29.

[199] *Cf.* Borchardt, *Neuserre*, Bl. 20 and Bl. 22 – and Khekeretnebty's mud brick magazines outside her tomb, too (Verner, Callender, *Djedkare's Cemetery*, fig. G1).

This hypothetical building could have preceded the construction of the annex to the eastern façade of the Initial Mastaba during the second building stage (in which several storerooms are incorporated). It is a fact though, that such a hypothetical building could not have survived all the alterations, which the space to the east of the Initial Mastaba went through during the following building stages of the tomb.

4.1.8 Room no. 24 – staircase to the mastaba's roof terrace

This room in fact consisted of two spaces – the staircase itself, leading to the roof of the mastaba, and a small vestibule at the bottom of the staircase, forming a kind of a landing.

The preserved casing of the stair vestibule attests to the fact that the width of this space was 0.72 m (which is similar to the width of the steps in the stairway). It is possible to estimate the length of the vestibule as 0.76 m. Following the state of preservation of the masonry in the area between the vestibule and the staircase, a pilaster might have stood here, by the western wall of the vestibule, where there is a fragment of limestone and mortar with the imprints of several stones. Unfortunately, because the restoration work done after the excavation of this part of the mastaba resulted in the construction of the block of masonry supporting the surviving part of the room's ceiling, the situation is clouded to such a degree that no definitive conclusions can be made concerning the pilaster. In the main, it is not possible to discern whether the mortar which is visible here is ancient, or modern. If such a pilaster really existed between the vestibule and the stairway, then it might have been 0.52 m (one cubit) long and about 0.10 m wide.

Fig. 4.1.13 Room no. 24, south-west corner of the vestibule to the staircase with the single remaining roofing slab *in situ*

Such a pilaster would have been necessary because of the construction of the ceiling of the staircase vestibule and also because of the ceiling of the staircase itself. The area of the vestibule is the only section where a part of the original ceiling has survived in the above ground part of the entire Mastaba of Ptahshepses. This small fragment of the room's ceiling remained in the south-western corner of the vestibule (see *fig. 4.1.13*). From the position of the fragment it follows that the ceiling of the room must have been at a height of 2.15 m above the pavement of the vestibule. The pavement is also partially preserved in the south-western corner of the room. The thickness of the ceiling limestone slab is 0.24 m and it was placed onto the top of the casing of the side walls. It seems that the ceiling of the room consisted only of one larger slab of fine limestone which was carefully worked. Above it, there was a filling, consisting of non-quality masonry (fragments of stones and mud bricks). This layer apparently filled the free space between the ceiling of the vestibule beneath and masonry of the stairway westwards and the roofing terrace above. The staircase itself is one of the most interesting features of the architecture of the Initial Mastaba. Only the lowermost flight of steps of the staircase remains, and it is in a rather poor state of preservation. The limestone blocks forming the steps have deteriorated – especially due to the impact of weather after the removal of the ceiling (see *fig. 4.1.14*). Only some parts of the edges belonging to a few steps are still traceable. The blocks forming the steps also created the footings of the side walls. Because of this, it is possible to reconstruct the width of the staircase. The casing of the side walls has now been completely removed and only the core masonry of the staircase is visible. It is formed by ashlars of yellow limestone, quite

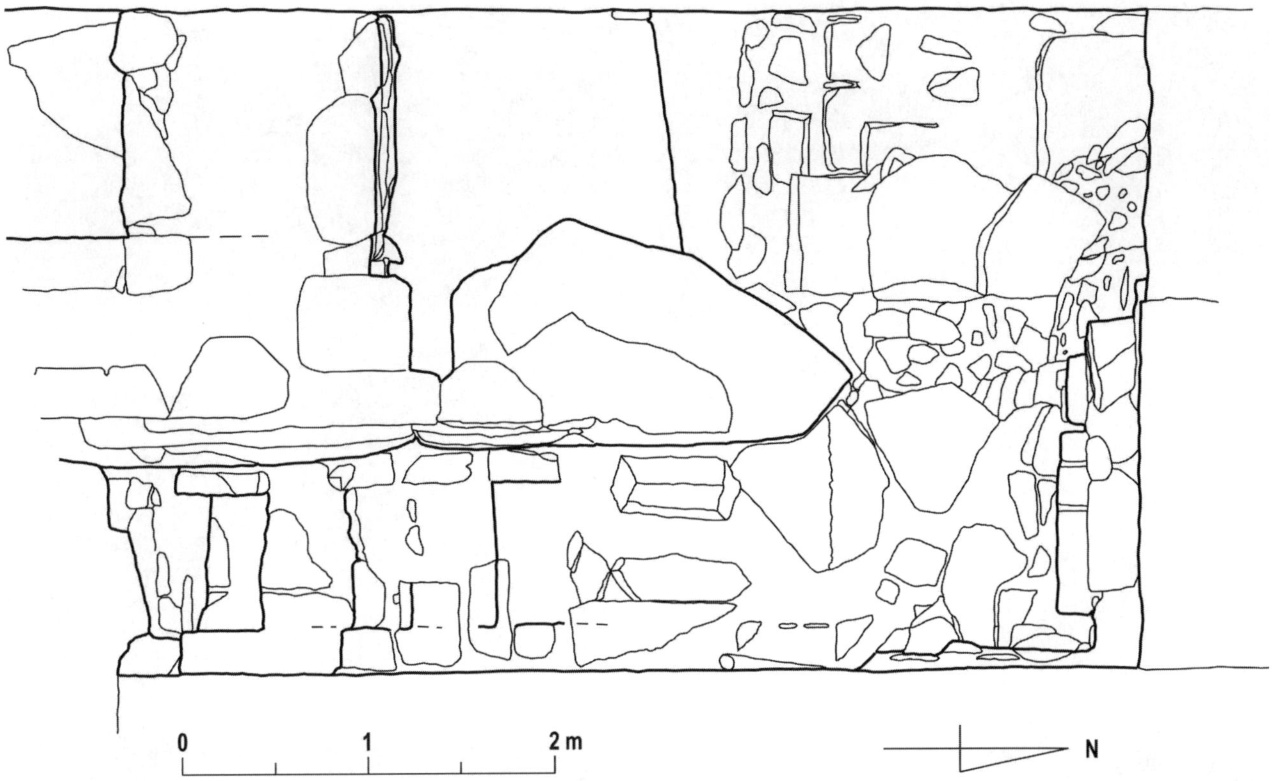

Fig. 4.1.14 Plan of the staircase – Room no. 24

carefully joined together. The western part of the staircase is more poorly preserved than the eastern one. Only the masonry creating the base for the under floor blocks of the staircase remained *in situ* (see *fig. 4.1.15*). This masonry consisted of two types: the main constructional parts were built of large blocks of the same character as the blocks in the western core masonry which has already been described in *chapter 4.1.4*. Smaller stone fragments and low-grade masonry filled the free space of chamber-like constructions, thus creating the base of the staircase. As it happens, both types of masonry were comprised of local limestone.

As one can see from *figs. 4.1.15* and *4.1.16*, this masonry was connected with the partition wall which defined the shape of the staircase. This partition wall, which adjoined the southern wall of Room no. 23, was constructed by using the method standard in the times of the mastaba's construction. These local limestone ashlars were built in alternate layers of headers and stretchers.

Due to the edges of the steps (partially still visible – see *fig. 4.1.14*), we can reconstruct the width of the staircase, which was 0.72 m. It seems that the staircase itself was formed by low steps, only up to 5 cm high. Their upper faces were sloped and they matched the overall angle of the staircase. Following on from the masons' lines documented by M. Verner on the face of the eastern wall of the staircase, this angle was, 23° 30′ – 24°.[200]

As the stone robbers removed the ceiling, then the casing of the side-walls and the majority of blocks with the steps themselves, the upper parts of the staircase began to deteriorate rapidly. As a result, the reconstruction of the original number of steps and flights of stairs is complicated. Having in mind the estimated height (5.20 m) of the Initial Mastaba in the area of the staircase and the documented angle of the staircase, it is possible to suppose that the staircase originally had three flights of stairs.

The first, lowermost wing of the staircase was oriented in a north-south direction. It was connected with the upper parts of the staircase by means of a small landing. The upper part of this flight of stairs, as is the case with the upper flights of the staircase, has been destroyed to a high degree. Only several blocks in its eastern

[200] Verner, *Baugraffiti*, D – Plan Nr. 8, room 24, east wall.

Fig. 4.1.15 Staircase (Room no. 24) from the south

Fig. 4.1.16 Staircase (Room no. 24) from the north

part still remain. Therefore, it is not clear whether the landing was constructed horizontally – as we can see in the similar example of a stairway leading to the roofing terrace of Sahure's mortuary temple.[201] On the other hand, this apparent landing might have actually been another gradual flight of stairs, or even a ramp (with notches). Such a hypothesis concerning the reconstruction of the original form of connection between two long flights of steps was Ludwig Borchardt's choice with regard to the ascending corridor leading to the obelisk in the sun temple of Niuserre.[202]

The second flight of steps in Room no. 24 ascended from the north to the south and the uppermost, shorter flight, might have ascended from east to west. Due to the poor state of preservation it is, however, not possible to ascertain the length of this staircase. As the upper end of the lower flight of the staircase is not preserved, its height had to be calculated. It seems that this flight probably ended at a height of 1.75 m. If the middle flight of the staircase was constructed at the same angle as the lower one, then its upper end must have been at a height of 3.6 m; this second flight would then have been possibly 4.3 m long, thus being 0.5 m longer than the lowermost flight of the staircase (which was 3.8 m long). This fact means that this second flight could not have reached the rooftop terrace of the mastaba and, therefore, it would have been necessary to construct a third, shorter (its length is not possible to ascertain) flight of steps which led in an east-west direction to the mastaba's roof terrace.

[201] Borchardt, *Sahure* I, 25–26, Abb. 21, Bl. 16. As a matter of course, the technology used for the construction of the staircase is different (and more sophisticated than that of staircases in the storerooms in the royal mortuary temples of the time, *e.g.* that of Sahure and Niuserre). We encounter this different technique also in a staircase located in Room no. 6, built during the second building stage (see page 97–98).
[202] Borchardt, *Re-Heiligtum* I, 32, Abb. 20.

There is no information as to how the upper end of the staircase itself was designed – *i.e.* whether a kind of a shelter was built around the upper opening of the staircase, or not (as has been reconstructed, for example, in the case of the exit of the staircase leading to the roofing terrace of the valley temple in Niuserre's mortuary temple).[203] On the other hand, following a common sense approach, one could suppose that the opening of the staircase would have to have had some form of closure – not necessarily a door. It might have been covered by means of a wooden cover, for example.[204] This might have protected the staircase from the heavy winter showers that sometimes fall in the region of the Memphite Necropolis. In the area where we can reconstruct the exit from the stairway onto the terrace there is some ruined masonry (see also *fig. 4.1.16*), although it is not possible to connect these remains with any hypothetical shelter. Apparently, this masonry is of a secondary character and it differs from the core masonry in this part of the mastaba. We can therefore infer that the uppermost flight of the staircase represented the actual access to the roof of the mastaba and the stairway was not topped by any shelter, but by a wooden cover.

Unfortunately there is no direct proof of the level at which the ceiling of the staircase was constructed. It can be only estimated that it was built on the same level as the stair vestibule, *i.e.* 2.15 m above the steps of the staircase. One can suppose that the ceiling had the same angle as the angle of the staircase. Very probably, the roof of the staircase was constructed in a similar way to that of the vestibule below it, *i.e.*, that it was formed by flat blocks of limestone placed on the top of the casing of the side walls. There is however no available information concerning the shape of the ceiling blocks, that is, whether they represented a few long beams laid down along the main axis of the staircase, or, whether the ceiling consisted of smaller blocks placed in the masonry transverse to the main axis of the stair flights.[205] The latter eventuality is more possible.

The existence of such a large staircase is quite extraordinary within the corpus of non-royal tomb architecture. Beside examples already mentioned which we can document in Sahure's and Niuserre's pyramid complexes and in the sun temple of the latter king, large stairway constructions are also attested in Khafre's valley temple,[206] in Userkaf's,[207]_Neferirkare's,[208] and Pepy's II pyramid complexes,[209] as well as in the pyramid and tomb complexes of queens (*e.g.* of Nebet).[210] The examples coming from other non-royal tombs (Ptahhotep I, Akhtihotep Hemi, Neferseshemre, Kagemni Ankhmahor, Nikauisesi, *etc.*) do not match the dimensions and the complexity of layout that we see in the staircase in Ptahshepses' Initial Mastaba. The intricate construction of the staircase is typical of the architecture of Abusir and it is one more attestation to the unique character of this tomb. Moreover, this especial element of the architecture presents additional proof of the esteem and wealth that Ptahshepses must have held at that time.

The construction of the stairway implies that it was an important component of the mastaba and this raises the question about the function it served. Was it to facilitate the guarding of the tomb, or did it serve a more sophisticated function? This is not easy to answer. However, the care devoted to the construction shows clearly that the staircase possessed an important religious function. As was quite recently shown by Nicole Alexanian, the main function of the staircase in large tombs of the Fifth and the Sixth Dynasty probably was to enable access for the tomb

---

203 Borchardt, *Neuserre*, Bl. 3.

204 Such a reconstruction was proposed for the staircase of Nebet's mastaba in Saqqara – see Munro, *Unas-Friedhof*, Taf. 6.

205 *Cf.* Borchardt, *Re-Heiligtum* I, 33, Abb. 20. As a matter of course, the dimensions of hypothetical ceiling blocks were in relevant proportion to the dimensions of the stairway.

206 Hölscher, *Chephren*, 46, Bl. XVII.

207 Labrousse, Lauer, *Ouserkaf*, 43, fig. 43, 45, pl. 17a; *MRA* VII, Tav.1.

208 Borchardt, *Neferirkare*, 33-34, Abb. 37–38; *MRA* VII, 134, Tav. 12.

209 Jéquier, *Pepi II*, vol. III, 3, pl. 2.

210 Munro, *Unas-Friedhof*, 43–44, Taf. 6.

owner's mummy and statue to the roof of the tomb, in order that the ascension of the dead would be secured. This belief concerning the tomb owner's ascension was connected with the sun cult. In doing this, the mummy and the statue would be exhibited to the effect of the rays of the sun. Contrary to the situation in many other mastabas, the entrance to the burial apartment of Ptahshepses was not from the roofing terrace, but from the inside of the mastaba. For that reason, during the burial of the tomb owner, one had to transfer his mummy downstairs to the mastaba and through the descending corridor to the burial chamber. Perhaps, too, the statues of the tomb owner may have been brought to the roof of the mastaba in order to become there the object of the ceremonies connected with the sun in a regular way.

4.1.9 Room no. 25 – Major offering chapel

This room was entered from Room no. 22 *via* an entrance. As it follows from the imprints on its side walls, the doorway itself was 0.80 m wide. Unfortunately, the pivot-holder of this doorway is not preserved, nevertheless, a niche apparently adjoined it from the north, *i.e.*, from the inside of Room no. 25. Therefore, we can only suppose that the wooden door-leaf opened *into* the room. The other doorway was located in the eastern part of the northern wall of the chapel, which makes an entrance to Room no. 26. This door opened to the outside from Room no. 25 (see further).

Room no. 25 was a large, oblong, east-west oriented space. It was located almost precisely on the line of the east-west axis of the burial apartment of Ptahshepses. This alignment underlines the connection between the room and the person buried in the burial chamber (or more precisely in the larger sarcophagus located there). This position (and also its oblong, east-west oriented ground plan) shows that the mortuary cult for Ptahshepses was conducted here, *i.e.*, that this room represents an offering chapel. As a matter of course, we can suppose that a false door was placed in the western wall of the chapel.

It is also true that this room is the most demolished above-ground space in the Initial Mastaba (see *fig. 4.1.17*): only the core masonry of the northern, eastern and southern wall still remain, the tomb owner's false door and other parts of chapel's inner facilities, the relief decoration as well as the ceiling of the room were removed or destroyed. Moreover, the core masonry of the western wall was completely removed. The almost total destruction of the chapel was certainly due to the existence of the burial chamber behind the chapel's western wall: the burial chamber was one

Fig. 4.1.17 Major offering chapel (Room no. 25) from the east

Fig. 4.1.18a Room no. 25, close-up of the western end of the southern wall

Fig. 4.1.18b Room no. 25, the southern wall from the north

of the main targets for the stone robbers and it seems that in order to get into it, this part of the chapel was demolished.

Judging by its dimensions, it is clear that the main offering chapel was the largest room in the Initial Mastaba. Due to the destruction of the western wall, the length of the room can be only suggested by an estimation based on the measurement of the surviving masonry and of the masons' marks: without the casing, the preserved length of the chapel is 8.34 m; with casing, it probably measured 7.3 m (14 cubits). On the other hand, we know the width of the room more precisely because this was better preserved: it now measures 3.75 m. If we should add the supposed width of the casing of the chapel (1 cubit), we can suppose that the chapel would have been about 2.75 m wide. Such a span could easily have been roofed by ceiling slabs which might have been similar to those beams found in Room no. 23. The height of the room, however, is not known. The highest preserved point in the masonry of the chapel's side walls is 4.09 m above the room's pavement. From the way in which the doorway to Room no. 26 (see *fig. 4.1.20*) was constructed, it can be assumed that the height of the major chapel was ca. 3.27 m but it could have been even higher.

Indirectly, the existence of the false door seems to be supported by evidence provided by a roughly-worked limestone block. This block, which is partially built into the southern nucleus wall of the room, could be either a part of a base, or some of the backing masonry for the stela of the false door, or, alternatively, an altar (see *figs. 4.1.18, 4.1.19*). It is important to note that, structurally, this block does not correspond with the aforementioned podium built in front of the western wall of Room no. 22.

The pavement of the room was destroyed to such a high degree during the activities of the stone robbers that it does not allow us to reconstruct the precise position of an offering bench which once probably stood below the northern wall of the chapel in its western part.[211] As it happens, there is no further clue as to the precise size or shape of the bench, though it was probably an oblong block in shape.

[211] We can see such arrangement also in other east-west oriented offering chapels of the second half of the Fifth Dynasty and the beginning of the Sixth Dynasty: Ptahshepses Junior (Bárta, *Ä&L* 10 [2000], 54, pl. 8, fig. 2); Senedjemib Inti in Giza (Brovarski, *Senedjemib*, 19, pl. 46a), Kagemni (Bissing, *Gem-ni-kai* I, 4–5, Taf. 1–2), Khentika (James, Apted, *Khentika*, 26, pls. III, XVIII); Ankhmahor (Badawy, *'Ankhm'ahor*, 34, fig. 16, pl. 60), Nihetepptah (Badawy, *'Ankhm'ahor*, 1, fig. 1, partially on pls. 3 and 6), Wesernetjer (Murray, *Saq. Mast.* 23, pl. XXXII), Nebkauhor (Hassan, Iskander, *Neb-Kaw-Her*, 52, pl. XLIA), Ptahhotep I (Hassan, Iskander, *Ny-'ankh-Pepy*, 45, pls. XXXIVB, D, XXXV).

Fig. 4.1.19 Core masonry in the central part of the Initial Mastaba – in the right foreground is part of the destroyed Room no. 25 (major offering room), in the centre, the block of masonry of Room no. 27 – the serdab

However, having in mind the refinement of a podium in Room no. 28 (the minor offering hall), we can suppose that this bench might also have been decorated with torus moulding and a cavetto cornice).

Another important feature which also might have once existed in the offering chapel was a basin. In the non-royal tombs, the installation of a basin was not very frequent. On the other hand, we can find such an example in the east-west oriented offering chapel of Senedjemib Inti's tomb,[212] in the rock-cut chapels of Niankhre[213] and Ankhmare.[214] We also encounter a basin in the offering place of G 1205[215] and G 4430.[216] At least in one case, a basin became part of the offering chapel built as an extension to the cultic niche of G 4350.[217] In Abusir, we encounter libation basins in the offering rooms of the royal mortuary temples of Sahure,[218] Neferirkare[219] and Niuserre.[220]

We can suppose that the basin in Ptahshepses' mastaba was located in a kind of niche (also only reconstructed) in the south-east corner of the chapel. This supposition is, however, based only on the existence of an outline of a drainage canal which was exposed during the archaeological excavations below the core masonry of the eastern outer wall of the Initial Mastaba (see *fig. 4.3.27, 4.3.28*). This place is about 1.5 m away from the place where the supposed basin would have been located; a more precise location of the basin cannot be confirmed as the core masonry at the south-east corner of the chapel was extensively damaged by the stone robbers – probably while removing the basin. After its excavation, this spot

---

[212] Brovarski, *Senedjemib*, 19, fig. 3, pl. 50a–b.
[213] Hassan, *Gîza* IV, fig. 107; Jánosi, *Giza*, 384, Abb. 104.
[214] Hassan, *Gîza* VI/3, 38, fig. 28; Jánosi, *Giza*, 407, Abb. 114.
[215] Reisner, *Giza Necropolis*, 393, Jánosi, *Giza*, 159, Abb. 16.
[216] Reisner, *Giza Necropolis*, 487; Jánosi, *Giza*, 173, Abb. 29.
[217] Junker, *Gîza* I, 194, Abb. 39; Jánosi, *Giza* 172, Abb. 27.
[218] Borchardt, *Sahure* I, Bl. 16; *MRA* VII, 64, Tav. 6 – here it was located in the south wall, by its east end.
[219] In the case of Neferirkare's offering chapel, the cavity for the basin was inserted in the axis of the east wall and, it seems, due to the fact that the surface of the niche was only roughly worked, that in this case a copper basin was inserted into the niche. The niche was not connected with any kind of canal or pipe as had been well documented by the example from Sahure's temple – Borchardt, *Neferirkare*, 31–32, Abb. 34, Bl. 10; *MRA* VII, Tav. 10.
[220] In the case of Niuserre's offering room, the existence of the basin can be assumed from the existence of a canal – as it is shown on the plan of the temple in *MRA* VIII, 30, Tav. 4.

Fig. 4.1.20 Doorway between the Room nos. 25 and 26 from the south

was partially reconstructed and modern masonry has been built here, and it is therefore, not possible to attest the existence of the basin today. On the other hand, the basin might also have been placed not in the especially constructed niche, but along the eastern part of the southern wall of the chapel, or along the eastern wall of the offering room – both possibilities are likely.

If the supposed reconstruction is right, then the offering room represented an east-west oriented chapel with a false door in its western wall and an altar (accessible by a small staircase?) located below it. It would thus be an example of Reisner's chapel Type VII.[221] In the opinion of Peter Jánosi, the major offering room in the Ptahshepses mastaba (together with that of Djadjaemankh) is among the first examples of a non-royal offering room oriented along an east-west axis.[222]

This orientation of the offering room was quite a new innovation in the framework of burial architecture. It was only introduced into the royal mortuary temples during the reign of Sahure.[223] In George Reisner's opinion, the east-west oriented offering chapels were introduced to the architecture of the non-royal tomb in the middle of the Fifth Dynasty. This fact was shown by the appearance of these chapels in many of the mastaba complexes built in Giza and Saqqara in the later part of the Fifth Dynasty.[224]

4.1.10 Room no. 26

The entrance to Room no. 26 survived in a better condition than most of other doorways in the Initial Mastaba. Some parts of the white limestone casing of its side walls still remain *in situ* (see *figs. 4.1.21, 4.1.22, pl. 9*). Therefore, it can be said that its width was 1.17 m.

Room no. 26 is an oblong north-south oriented room with dimensions 2.12 × 3.88 m. Another doorway opens in its northern end and this entrance lead to Room no. 28. It happens to be the best preserved above-ground room of the Initial Mastaba – its casing is preserved on all its walls up to a height of 1.26 m (see *fig. 4.1.20*).

Fig. 4.1.21 Room no. 26, western wall; in the background Room no. 27

Fig. 4.1.22 Room no. 26, western wall

221 Reisner, *Giza Necropolis*, 260–272.
222 Jánosi, in: *Abusir and Saqqara in 2000*, 454, note 40. As quoted by Jánosi ('Les tombes privées »des maisons d'éternité«', in: *L'art égyptienne*, 62), the first example of this type of offering room is representative of the chapel in Persen's tomb in Saqqara – Petrie, Murray, *Seven Memphite Tomb Chapels*, 9, pl. XIX-4; for the dating of Persen's tomb see – Harpur, *Decoration*, 107.
223 Jánosi, 'Die Entwicklung und Deutung des Totenopferraumes in den Pyramidentempeln des Alten Reiches', in: *Ägyptische Tempel*, 156f.
224 Reisner, *Giza Necropolis*, 260–261. The same conclusion can be found in Strudwick, *Administration*, 30.

Behind the western wall of Room no. 26 another room is located: this is Room no. 27, interpreted as a "serdab" (see below). This function was probably the main reason why a large breach was made in the middle of the western wall of Room no. 26. Such a break could be used for removing the statues usually placed in this serdab-room. Room no. 27 was very probably connected to Room no. 26 by means of a slotted aperture in the wall. Unfortunately, this supposition cannot be verified, mainly due to the existence of the breach mentioned above. In regard to the height of this room, we can only assume, that the ceiling of Room no. 26 was constructed at approximately the same level as the ceilings of Rooms nos. 23 or 22.

Room no. 26 also has the best preserved decoration among all the rooms of the Initial Mastaba. The whole length (and also height?) of the western wall of the space was covered by the decoration of palace façade. This peculiar type of decoration was certainly connected with the entrance to the burial apartment and the existence of the serdab behind this wall as well. As follows from the description, only the lower part of the decoration is preserved now. The "façade" was depicted in polychrome relief, its separate "columns" being executed as shallow incisions, and details were executed in bold colours which imitated reed mats as well as the wooden parts of the façade (see *pls. 10–12*). Patterns used in this decoration follow designs documented in other tombs of the Fifth and the Sixth Dynasty. We encounter this kind of decoration in the chapel of the neighbouring Mastaba of Djadjaemankh. Its western wall was also decorated with the palace façade motif, which was located above the entrance to the descending corridor leading to the owner's burial chamber (*pls. 13–15*). Also in this case, the entrance to the burial chamber was in a room located to the north of the main offering chamber.[225]

On the opposite, eastern wall of the room, a small part of the relief decoration depicting the lower half of a standing male figure was still preserved up until the 1970s.[226] This small piece of decoration is no longer *in situ* and is unfortunately lost. The core masonry of the room's eastern wall, built of regular ashlars of local limestone is well preserved and it reaches a height of about 4 m.

An originally sealed opening of a vertical shallow shaft is in the pavement, in the north-west corner of the room. This shaft, located below the western wall of the room with the palace façade decoration (see *fig. 4.1.23*), provides access to the

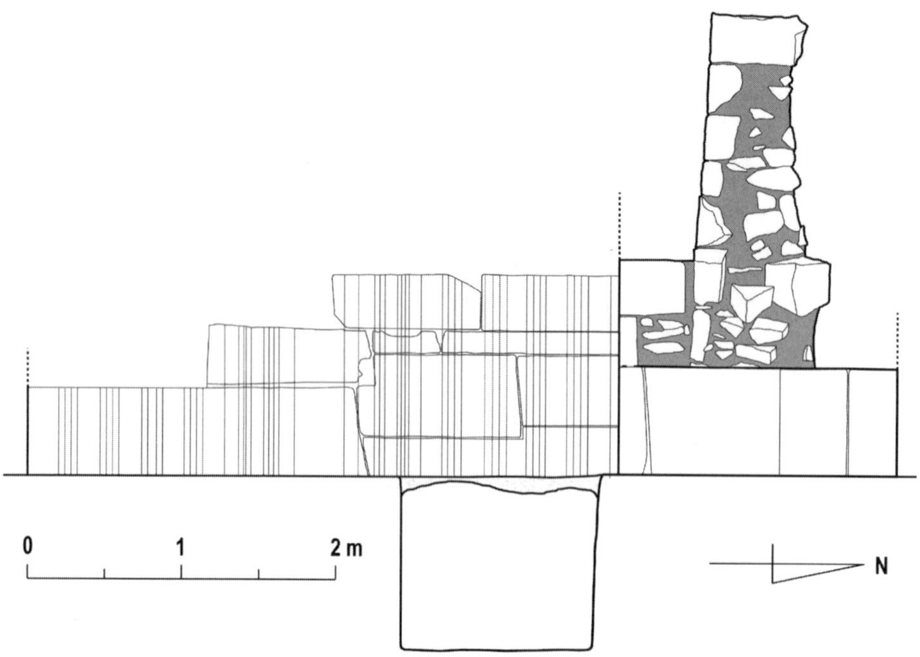

Fig. 4.1.23 Room no. 26, view of the western wall and of the mouth of the descending corridor and the side view of the northern wall of the room

[225] Borchardt, *Neuserre*, 119, 124–126. Bl. 22, 23, 24, Abb. 106.
[226] Verner, in: *Preliminary Report*, 71. Is it possible to suppose that this figure represented an offering bearer?

corridor descending to the burial apartment. The side walls of the shaft have the dimensions of 1.20 × 1.24 m. Its depth rises from the east to the west (0.98 m in the east, 1.13 m in the west). This fact is certainly connected with the way in which the descending corridor was constructed and also with the building history of this part of the mastaba. The same can also be said about the orientation of the side walls of the shaft – its northern and southern side walls do not follow the orientation of the walls of Room no. 26, but that of the descending corridor (the axis of which was shifted to the south from its east-west orientation). The fact that the entrance to the descending corridor was not located outside, but inside of the Initial Mastaba is of great chronological importance (it will be discussed in the concluding chapter).

Room no. 26 had a dual function: on the one hand, it served as a kind of corridor as it allowed access to Room no. 28, located to the north of it and, on the other hand, it enabled access to the descending corridor leading to the underground chambers of the tomb. This function was also very important, and it is underlined by the decoration of the room's western wall which marks the entrance to the burial apartment, the house for the deceased.[227]

The location of the entrance to the descending corridor to the burial chamber presents a significant fact which was very important for the development of the non-royal tombs. Before the construction of the tombs in the Abusir Cemetery of Nobles, the entrance to the burial apartments of the mastabas was located in the roofing terrace. From the time of the construction of these Abusir tombs onwards, mastabas with the entrances to their burial chambers located at the level of their ground floors were built (for further discussions on this alteration, see *chapters 5* and *6*).

4.1.11 Room no. 27 – serdab (*figs. 4.1.24, 4.1.25*)

Another room of the Initial Mastaba is located to the west of the corridor Room no. 26 and it lies immediately behind the western wall of this room. The most interesting fact concerning this room is that the level of the room's floor is 1.27 m *above* the floor of Room no. 26.[228] The dimensions of the room are 5.31 × 2.17 m – it seems that there was no casing along the preserved side walls of the room. The walls of the room were built with limestone of inferior quality with reddish and orange

Fig. 4.1.24 Room no. 27 (serdab), plan

[227] This has been clearly shown by H. Altenmüller in his article 'Der Grabherr des Alten Reiches in seinem Palast des Jenseits', in: *Homm. Lauer*, 11–19.

[228] *Cf.* with the situation in the serdabs of Seshemnefer II and III in Giza: Junker, *Gîza* III, 188, 199, Abb. 33, 37.

colouring.[229] It is hard to say whether the use of stone of such colour was intentional or whether it has any connection with the ritual function of this room. There is a possibility that it was connected with the casing made of red granite which was used in the niches for statues in Sahure's mortuary temple.[230] It seems probable that the usage of reddish limestone presented a ritual substitute for red granite.

Fig. 4.1.25 Room no. 27 from the north

As is the case with other rooms of the Initial Mastaba, the height of the room, due to the bad state of preservation of the masonry, can only be estimated. If we assume that the major offering room was 3.27 m high, then the serdab might have been constructed some 2.00 m high (*i.e.* ca 4 cubits).

The assumption that this room served as a serdab is based on the room's position, secluded nature and the fact that there is no other room which could be considered as a serdab. Unfortunately, this supposition regarding Ptahshepses' serdab cannot be confirmed by the finds of the fragments of statues in this room. As Barbora Patočková states: we are unable, due to the poor preservation of the mastaba, to ascertain from any statue fragment that it was found in its original location.[231]

229 This colouring was not caused by the proximity of flame, as it might at first be thought. This assumption was rejected by petrogeologist Jaromír Leichmann, the Masaryk University, Brno, in a personal communication to the author.

230 Borchardt, *Sahure* I, 57. S. Aufrère (*Univers minéral*, 703) mentions, on the base of the later written sources, that the usage of the granite might have had symbolical meaning. It might have presented a reference to the region of the first Nile cataract, in which are large areas of outcrops of granite. Moreover, the ancient Egyptian located there springs of the Nile river. In Aufrère's opinion the usage of the red granite might have also been a reference for the primordial waters of chaos.

231 Patočková, *Fragmenty soch*, 134; Patočková, 'Fragments de statues découverts dans le mastaba de Ptahchepses à Abousir', in: *Les critère de datation*, 229.

Patočková thinks, however that it was possible for several statues to have been put in this room.

Serdabs, or better to say the burials for the *ka*-statues of the kings, had already been introduced into the framework of royal mortuary architecture in the Archaic Period, as we can see in the Den tomb in Umm el-Qab.[232] In non-royal architecture, serdabs became inseparable components from the time of Third Dynasty,[233] although the first attestation can be also dated to the Archaic Period, to the First Dynasty.[234]

In regard to the level of the floor of the serdabs, Peter Jánosi mentions,[235] that until the end of the Fourth Dynasty / beginning of the Fifth Dynasty, serdabs constructed in the Giza tombs, were located at a higher level than the level of the chapels with which they were connected. This discovery for Giza is not reflected at Abusir, where the date of the Mastaba of Ptahshepses shows that Abusir retained the old tradition a little longer. The Initial Mastaba was constructed before the end of the first middle of the Fifth Dynasty (for the discussion on this topic see the concluding chapter). What we see here is probably a piece of evidence for the imitation of some architectural elements from Giza in the tombs in Abusir-Saqqara area in a somewhat later period. Nevertheless, it is more probable that the higher level of Room no. 27 was apparently connected with constricting constructional reasons, related to the existence of the descending corridor below this room. The height of its ceiling apparently caused an increase in the level of the serdab's floor.

4.1.12 Room no. 28 – Minor offering chapel

The doorway to the last, as yet unmentioned, aboveground room of the Initial Mastaba leads from corridor Room no. 26. The doorway was 1.03 m wide and 1.05 m long. It is followed by a small recess (0.67 × 1.35 m), which shows that the door opened *into* Room no. 28. Following its east-west orientation and its ground plan (the room was 6.95 m long and 2.64 m wide) it is apparent that it served as an offering chapel. The chapel comes under the same category as the chapels of Reisner's Type VII[236] and a close relative, aside from the aforementioned chapel in Djadjaemankh's tomb, is the offering room in the tomb of Ptahshepses Junior II.[237] Very probably, the chapel served for the mortuary cult of Ptahshepses' spouse and it was a smaller variant of her husband's offering chamber.

The side walls of the chapel have been almost completely destroyed. Despite this fact, the casing here is better preserved than in the major offering chamber Room no. 25 (see *fig. 4.1.26*). There are no direct clues for ascertaining an approximate height of the room. We can hypothetically assume that the original ceiling in this room was at the same height as that in Room no. 25 – *i.e.* 3.27 m. The ceiling of Room no. 28 was apparently constructed in the same way as the major offering room – beams were laid transversely to the main, east-west, axis of the chapel.

Even as we found in the major offering chapel, we also note that in the minor offering chapel (no. 28) almost the entire western wall was completely destroyed and only the lowermost part of its casing remains *in situ*. In its original state, this wall probably featured a false door. Z. Žába mentioned in his report on the work made in the year 1968 that in Room no. 28 fragments of "a granite false door, shattered

---

[232] *Cf.* Bard, 'The Emergence of the Egyptian State (c. 3200–2868 BC)', in: *OHAE*, 72. K. Lehmann describes the annex to the Den tomb as a *ka*-burial (Lehmann, *Serdab*, 277–284). However, it is apparent for her that the royal *ka*-burials were functional models for the non-royal serdabs (*op. cit.*, 284).

[233] Brescianni, 'Serdab', *LÄ* V, 875; Lehmann, *Serdab*, 19–20.

[234] This example comes from one of the tombs excavated by the Cairo University in Abu Gurab by Abusir (Radwan, 'Recent Excavations of the Cairo University at Abusir. "A Cemetery of the 1st Dynasty"', in: *MÄU* 4 (1995), 313). K. Lehmann underlines that this tomb is the oldest known non-royal tomb with a serdab (Lehmann, *Serdab*, 18–19; *cf.* Bárta, 'Serdab and Statue Placement in the Private Tombs down to the Fourth Dynasty', *MDAIK* 54 [1998], 65).

[235] Jánosi, in: *Abusir and Saqqara 2000*, 454, n. 36.

[236] Reisner, *Giza Necropolis*, 260–261.

[237] See Bárta, *Ä&L* 10 (2000), 53–54, fig. 2, pl. 8.

Fig. 4.1.26 Room no. 28 (minor offering room) from the west

to pieces" were found there.[238] The door was apparently removed by stone robbers. As opposed to the situation regarding the false door in the other room we looked at earlier, a part of an offering altar is still preserved in front of the western wall: today, its southern, larger, part is still *in situ* (the dimensions of the preserved part: 1.03 × 0.61 m). Originally, the altar had the form of an oblong podium with the dimensions of 1.52 m (L) × 0.61 m (W) × 0.74 m (H). The podium's side walls are topped with a simple cavetto cornice. Bellow it, there is a simple torus moulding (see *figs. 4.1.27, 4.1.28*). The podium was accessible by means of a series of at least four steps with a total length of 1.25 m and height 0.74 m. Unfortunately, the upper surface of the altar has not been well preserved, but has been weathered to a high degree; it is therefore impossible to reconstruct its original appearance. As the analogies from other non-royal tombs show, the upper surface might have been left undecorated, or it could have been adorned with a *ḥtp* sign in low relief.[239]

Fig. 4.1.27 Room no. 28, remains of the altar from the west

[238] Žába, in: *Preliminary Report*, 26. It should be underlined here that, as was true for Room no. 25, there is no direct proof (find of fragments of the false door, *etc.*), that in this room the false door had ever really existed.

[239] Such decoration on the offering tables we can see, *e.g.*, in other tombs of the period: Ptahshepses Junior II (Bárta, *Ä&L* 10 [2000], 53–54, fig. 2), in the chapel of the tomb of Ti »

Fig. 4.1.28 Room no. 28, front view of the altar

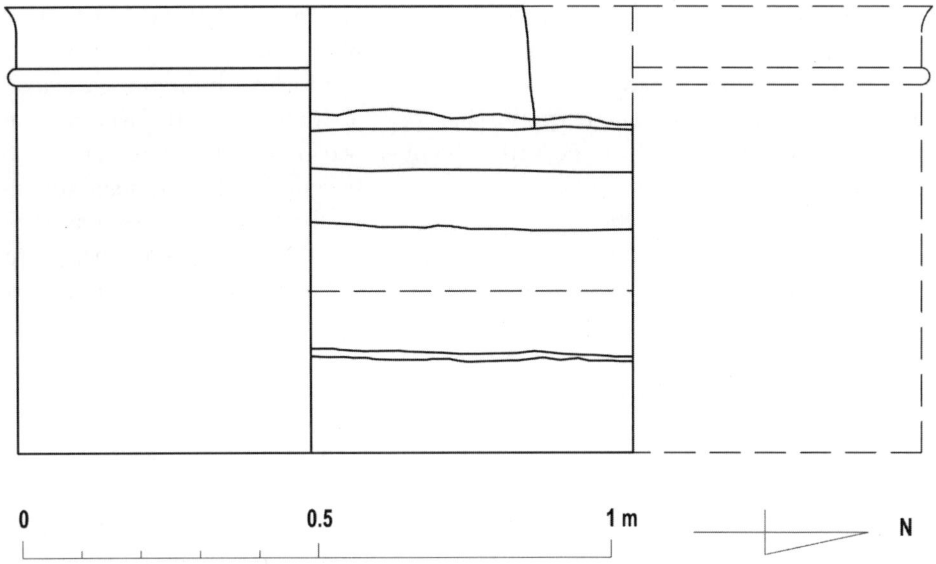

Unlike the major offering room, this room was not, as far as the documentation made during the archaeological excavation informed us, equipped with a libation basin; no trace of it or of a waste canal was found. If this impression should be true, then we could assume that, firstly, a kind of removable basin was used in this chapel, or, secondly, some of the rituals for Ptahshepses' spouse connected with the basin were hypothetically made in her husband's offering chapel (the latter room was only a few metres away from that of Khamerernebty). It should be underlined here that there is no direct attestation for either of these propositions.

4.1.13 Room nos. 29–31 – funerary apartments

The funerary apartments which were part of the project of the Initial Mastaba and consisted of three parts: the descending corridor (no. 29), the burial chamber (Room no. 30), and the Niche for Canopic Jars (no. 31). A thorough study of the mastaba's substructure is important for our knowledge of the constructional and architectural development of the Initial Mastaba (see hereafter).

Fig. 4.1.29 Construction pit for the burial chamber, western wall, view from the north-east

Our initial approach to this study lies in the way in which the burial apartment of the mastaba is discernible in the masonry of the tomb. It was built in a large construction pit, a method that was apparently adopted because of the low quality of subsoil in Abusir, and this sort of construction is noticeable in the case of other tombs in the Cemetery of Nobles. This method is especially evident in the Mastaba of Djadjaemankh, Mastaba of the Princesses[240] as well as in the Mastaba of Ptahshepses Junior II[241] and in other instances on the Memphite Necropolis. If we follow the contours of this pit, still visible in the masonry of the mastaba (*fig. 4.1.29, pl. 16*), then we might suppose that the pit would have been "opened" to the north. The orientation would then be the same as the orientation of the constructional pits cut in the subsoil for the burial chambers of the pyramids, mainly those built in Abusir. Whether it might have been a result of coincidence, or of the intentional choice of the constructional method of the tomb owner who was well acquainted with the methods used in the royal monumental constructions, is not possible to discern. This method of construction, however, was used only during a limited period of time. It was used to facilitate the cutting of the subsoil and its transportation outside the pit while (moving in the opposite direction)

» (Épron, *Ti*, pl. 1.), in front of the false door of located in the offering chapel of Niankhnum and Khnumhotep (for the location the basin see: Moussa, Altenmüller, *Nianchchnum und Chnumhotep*, Abb. 1), or, to mention a later example, in the pillared chapel of Mereruka (Duell, *Mereruka* I, plan facing pl. 2).

[240] Borchardt, *Neuserre*, Bl. 22, 23, 25, 26.

[241] Bárta, *Ä&L* 10 (2000), fig. 2.

limestone and other construction materials were taken into the pit. At a time when the construction of the side walls of the burial chamber was started, this approach path was lined with limestone blocks and a new corridor was built along the axis of the future descending passageway. This corridor was apparently used for the placing of the sarcophagi into the burial chamber (see later in this chapter).

As a matter of course, the orientation of Ptahshepses' subterranean rooms was different from that of the royal pyramids. While the latter had their entrance corridors oriented along their north-south axes and their burial chamber were oriented in an east-west direction, the orientation of Ptahshepses' funerary apartment was different. The descending corridor was constructed along a southwest-northeast axis and the burial chamber, as was standard with non-royal tombs, was oriented in a north-south direction.

4.1.13.1 Room no. 29 – descending corridor (*figs. 4.1.30–4.1.33*)

The entrance to the descending corridor of the Ptahshepses mastaba is in the western wall of the above mentioned, shallow vertical shaft located in the pavement of Room no. 26. As it has been already discussed, it was not by accident that this entrance was situated below the wall with the palace façade decoration. During excavation, the descending corridor was found filled with large blocks of white limestone which blocked-up the whole track of the corridor (see *figs. 4.1.31* and *4.1.33*). These blocks were intended to prevent looting within the burial chamber. Nonetheless, despite all this effort, the burial chamber was plundered, as was discovered by Z. Žába during the archaeological excavations of the Czechoslovak mission. The tomb and stone robbers then entered the chamber from the direction of the roof of the Mastaba. As a consequence of their destructive opening of the tomb, the area of the burial apartment was later used as a secondary cemetery.

In contrast to other rooms in the Mastaba of Ptahshepses, the descending corridor is in a good condition, its side walls and the ceiling of the corridor being preserved particularly well and in this respect it is the most intact space in the mastaba. The

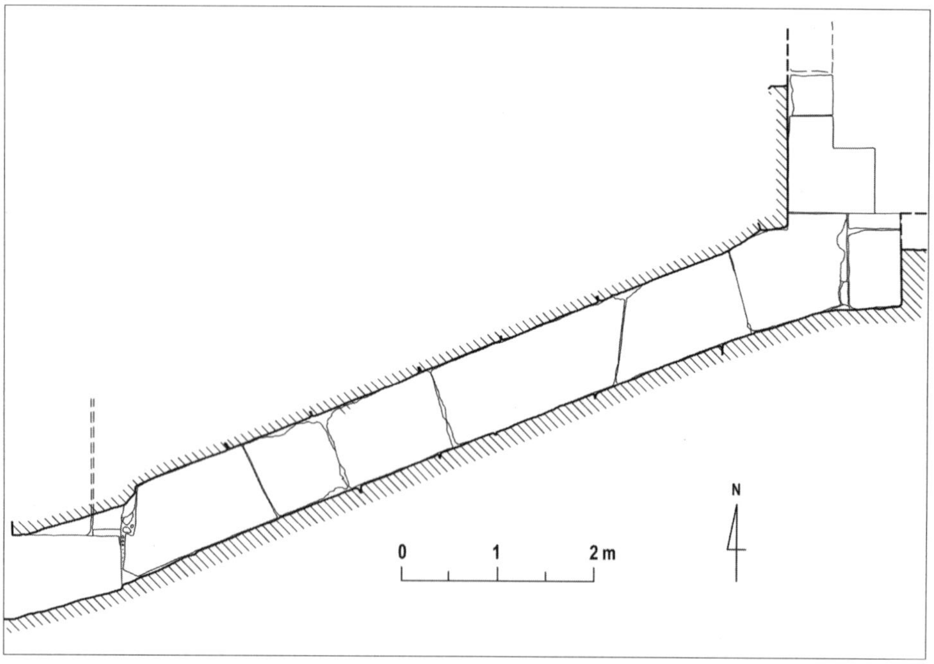

Fig. 4.1.30 Descending corridor to the burial apartment, northern wall

main reason for this state of preservation was due to the plugging of the corridor by the limestone blockage. Therefore, it is astonishing that, in the middle part of the corridor, there is an aperture that apparently was made secondarily. Its dimensions are ca. 0.75 × 0.35 m. Because of the fact that the corridor was sealed by the blockage mentioned above, the only solution for this unusual fact would be to suppose that

Fig. 4.1.31 Vertical shaft in the pavement of Room no. 26 giving access to the corridor descending to the burial apartment. Picture taken during the archaeological excavation. In the descending corridor the stone blockage is still to be seen *in situ*

this hole had been made by tomb robbers. Surprising as it may seem, such an action was possible only during the period before the blocking of the burial chamber, *i.e.* at a time around the burial ceremonies.[242] This aperture represents an important element in our knowledge of the mastaba's building history (see below).

The length of the descending corridor – whose walls are cased by smoothed blocks of white limestone – is 7.80 m and its sides measure 1.16 × 1.16 m. The angle of the slope differs a little in three parts of the corridor: at the mouth, the angle of the bottom of the entrance shaft is ca. 16°30′; after this point, a passage

Fig. 4.1.32 Descending corridor to the burial apartment, view from the upper end of the corridor

[242] Due to the fact that in the burial chamber at least two sarcophagi have been inserted, one cannot to exclude the idea that, after the funeral concerning one of the persons buried there, some unknown space of time elapsed between the funeral ceremonies connected with these persons buried in the chamber. During this time the corridor might have been left unplugged by stone blocks and therefore accessible for any attack executed by tomb robbers. There is evidence from the Abusir-Saqqara area that the burial chambers and shafts of tombs were attacked by the tomb robbers even before they were sealed (see Bárta *et al.*, *Qar*).

begins whose first section is 6.54 m long and has a slope of 20°40′. The lowermost part of the corridor, shortly before the corridor opens into the burial chamber, is 1.24 m long and has an angle of 15°50′. This type of descending corridor can be classed as Reisner's type 9 – *sloping passage* – in his list of tomb shaft types.[243] Most of the passageways of this type lead into the burial chamber, which contains the stone sarcophagus. Their lower openings were located at the level of the burial chambers' floors. This is also the case with the descending corridor in the Mastaba of Ptahshepses.

Fig. 4.1.33 Limestone blocks used in the blocking of the corridor descending into the burial apartment; now located to the north-east from the mastaba

As a matter of course, one can study more easily the way how the corridor's floor, side walls and ceiling was constructed, which is not so apparent in the case of the construction trench for the corridor (see below). At first, we can state that the method of construction of the corridor floor differs a little in the course of its track (see *fig. 4.1.30*). The corridor ceiling was constructed by means of the same technique as other rooms throughout its entire length. The ceiling blocks, about 0.36–0.40 m high, were laid across the tops of the corridor side walls. The previously mentioned secondary aperture which opens about 3.1 m from the upper mouth of the corridor allows us to study the way in which the masonry around the corridor was constructed. The filling of the space above the ceiling of the corridor consists of larger blocks of local limestone (larger than the blocks used for the faces of the descending trench), joined quite carelessly without mortar and, on the other hand, of fragments of mud bricks, sand and small limestone splinters.[244] This filling masonry is at least 1.50 m high (above the top of the ceiling block of the corridor where the aperture is located). Thus, it reaches a level 0.10 m above the pavement of Room no. 26.

As the masonry exposed by the aperture in the descending corridor securely shows, the corridor was built within the descending trench that had been used during the construction of the burial chamber for transporting both the building material and the sarcophagi later placed in the burial chamber. The trench apparently followed the same route as the descending corridor, *i.e.* from the north-east to the south-west. It was possible to document it from following facts:

1) The existence of both facings of the trench built in the core masonry and the trench can be detected along the track of the descending corridor on both sides.

---

[243] Reisner, *Giza Necropolis*, 150–155.

[244] The quality of this masonry was as inferior as the filling masonry in the pyramids' construction used in the time of the building of Ptahshepses' mastaba, in Abusir, *e.g.*, in the pyramid Lepsius no. 24, *cf.* Verner, in: *Stationen*, 145–150.

These facings are visible at the lower end of the corridor (in the area of the burial chamber) and in the above mentioned aperture made by the stone robbers. The southern face of the construction trench runs much nearer to the side wall of the corridor – at a distance of 0.40–0.42 m from the corridor's southern wall.

2) The trench is also documented in the area of the shallow shaft in the entrance to the descending corridor. Here the northern face of the trench runs 0.94 m behind the wall of the actual corridor. This means that the construction trench began in the area that was later built over by the eastern outer wall of the Initial Mastaba. This eastern wall thus blocked the opening of the descending corridor and it became necessary to provide another entrance to the descending corridor by means of a vertical shaft.

To sum up: it seems to be the case that the descending corridor was placed within the trench, but out of alignment with its axis, and that the corridor was shifted towards the southern face of the trench.

The detected parts of the trench's facings also demonstrate that they were built with the same type of masonry and similar building methods as was the case in the Unfinished Pyramid of Raneferef – by means of oblong, rough cut blocks. As a matter of fact, the format of these blocks in the Ptahshepses mastaba is smaller in comparison than the format of the blocks used in the king's tomb. The blocks made of local limestone in the trench side walls are joined by mud mortar.

As a consequence of these facts it is possible to assume that this trench had a width of ca 2.52 m (= 4.84 cubits, *i.e.*, the width of the descending corridor 1.16 m + the distance of the faces of the trench from the side walls of the descending corridor). Thus, even though the finished corridor would not permit the passage of the sarcophagi at a later stage of the construction of the tomb, the construction trench was certainly wide enough to be used as a transport track for the building blocks and for the sarcophagi positioned consecutively in the burial chamber. Unfortunately, it is not possible to ascertain the length of this trench. As has already been mentioned, the upper end of the corridor probably lies below the eastern wall of Room no. 26. Moreover, the lower end of this trench should certainly be located under the pavement of the burial chamber, and this was not removed by the excavators.

An interesting feature appearing in this descending corridor is a zigzagging masons' line[245] which has survived on the lower face of the ceiling slabs of the corridor. The directions along which these separate zigzags are designed, are pointing to the main cardinal points. The interpretation of the meaning of this line seems to be impossible today. Its appearance in the corridor is extraordinary in the corpus of ancient Egyptian architecture and therefore there is no analogical material for comparison. Miroslav Verner suggested it might have originally represented a line aiding the transfer of precise directions – such as indicating the cardinal points – into the area of the burial chamber. It is possible, that during the finishing works – mainly during the polishing of the chamber's casing – such a contribution was important. This hypothetical method of transferring the directions to the cardinal points from this zigzagging line, might have caused some mistake in the orientation of the eastern wall of the burial chamber (see below).

4.1.13.2 Room no. 30 – burial chamber

The burial chamber is one of the most extraordinary architectural elements of the Mastaba of Ptahshepses in relation to its dimensions, unusual design and to the techniques used during its construction. In comparison with the rooms in the superstructure of the Initial Mastaba, its preservation, with the exclusion of its ceiling, is relatively good. The casing of the side walls, made of the smoothed blocks of white limestone is preserved mostly up to the level of the chamber's ceiling. In

[245] See: Verner, *Baugraffiti*, 175, loose plan E – no. 8, Room 29.

contrast to that, the ceiling itself is almost destroyed (see the discussion below). To the south, there was an entrance to Room no. 31 (Niche for the Canopic Jars) which shall be discussed later.

Dimensions and layout of the burial chamber

The chamber has been oriented in a north-south direction (however, the eastern wall of the burial chamber is not oriented directly in a north-south direction, but deviates 0.5° to the west from this orientation). The chamber consists of a narrow northern and southern part and a substantial middle section with a recess for Ptahshepses' sarcophagus (see *fig. 4.1.34, 4.1.35*). The dimensions of the chamber are: maximum length 6.22 m (11.96 cubits, *i.e.* 12 cubits), width of its northern and southern narrow parts 2.09–2.15 m (4–4.13 cubits), the length of the niche – located in the middle part of the burial chamber – is 3.20 m (6.15 cubits) and its width was 2.30 m (4.42 cubits). The width of the middle and broader part of the burial chamber was thus 4.45 m. The area which covers the burial chamber, excluding Room no. 31, is 20.36–20.73 m^2. The pavement of the burial chamber consists of large, flat and well worked limestone blocks: they were partially removed by the stone robbers.

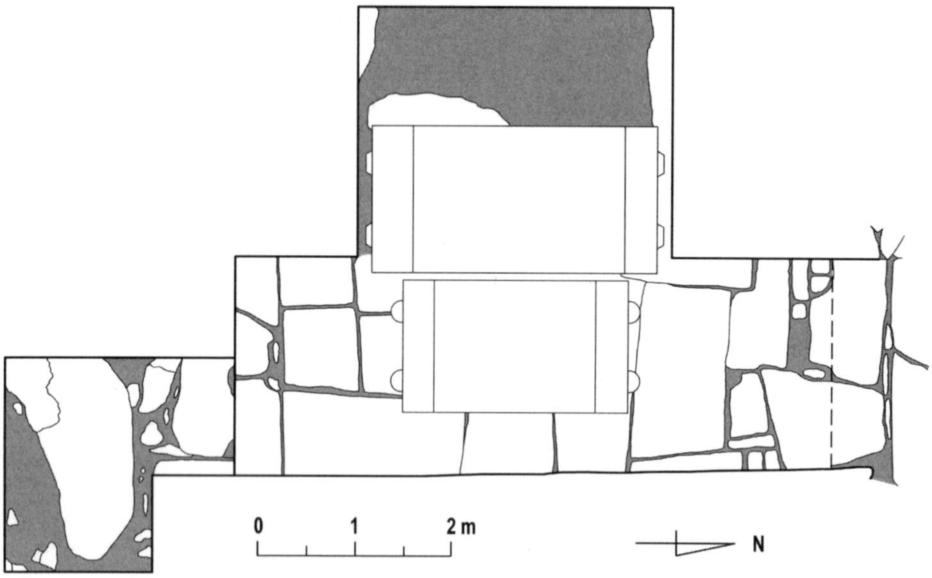

Fig. 4.1.34 Burial apartment, ground plan

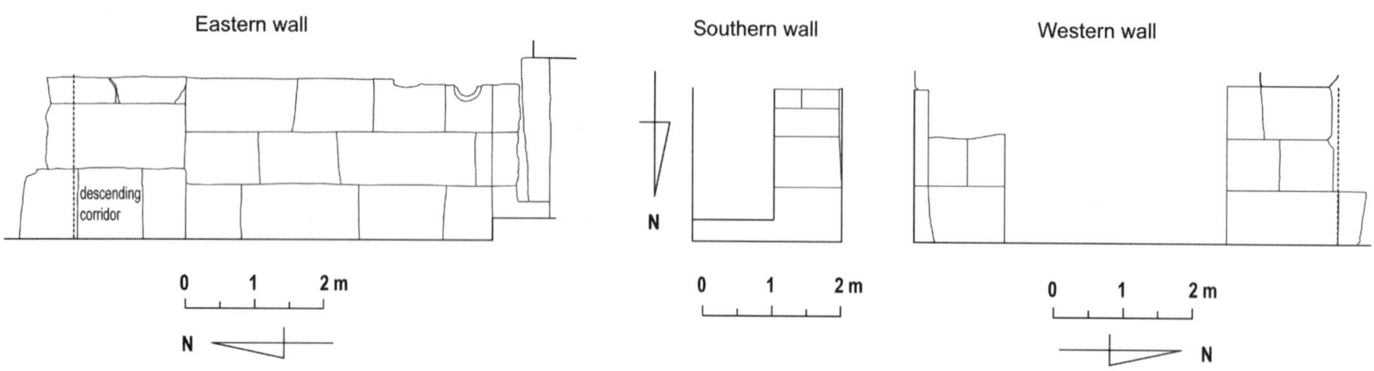

Fig. 4.1.35 Burial chamber, front views of the walls

The ceiling of the burial chamber

The ceiling was badly damaged, however, from a survey of the preserved tops of the chamber's side walls it follows that the ceiling of the chamber was constructed by means of two techniques. In the northern and southern – narrower – parts of the burial chamber, the ceiling consisted of limestone beams placed over the tops of the side walls in an east-west direction. Therefore, this part of the ceiling was flat.

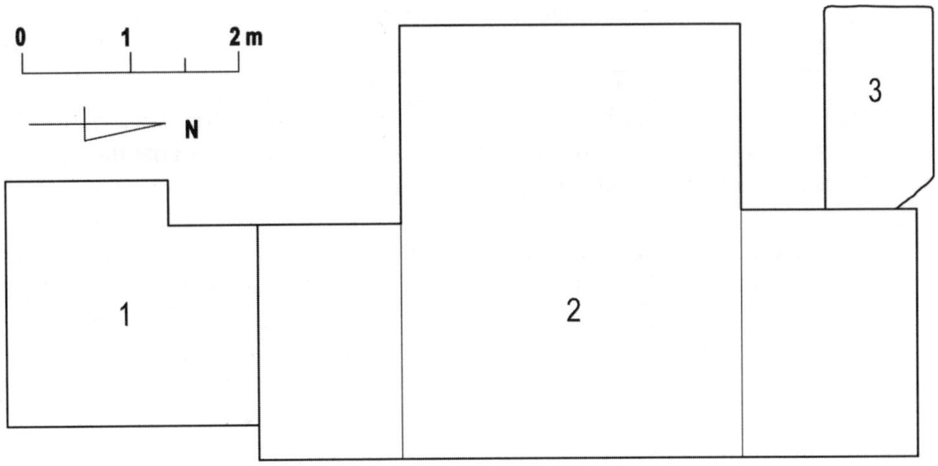

Fig. 4.1.36 Burial apartment, north-south section with the reconstruction of the roofing levels (*1* Niche for the Canopic Jars; *2* burial chamber; *3* trapezoidal roofing slab – see also *fig. 4.1.37*)

The ceiling in these two parts of the burial chamber was not constructed at the same height, however. In the northern part, the ceiling height reached 2.25 m, and in the south, the height was 2.14 m (see *fig. 4.1.36*). The only slab preserved *in situ* is located in the northern end of the chamber. It is a huge block of quality limestone. The dimensions of this block are: 1.87 × 1.01 m in width, while its length varies between 3.02 and 3.77 m (see *fig. 4.1.37*). The dimensions of this block are almost comparable to the dimensions of the blocks documented in the burial chambers of the royal pyramids, *e.g.*, in Niuserre's burial chamber.[246] This pattern follows the typical trapezoidal shape of the blocks used in the saddle ceilings of the royal burial chambers in pyramids. But why were such ceiling slabs used in the burial

Fig. 4.1.37 Trapezoidal roofing slab originally intended for a royal pyramid

[246] The ceiling beams in this pyramid were larger: 4.40–5.77 × 1.82 m. The width of the blocks is not discernible on the plan of the burial chamber, but it follows from the plans that they varied from 1.13 to 1.82 m (see Borchardt, *Neuserre*, Blatt 7, north-south section through the pyramid); *cf.* also the stone ceiling of the burial chamber in Neferirkare's pyramid: Borchardt, *Neferirkare*, Blatt 2, north-south section through the pyramid.

chamber of Ptahshepses? The following hypothetical explanations are offered for consideration:

1) The above-mentioned block was left-over material from the construction of Niuserre's pyramid. In opposition to this idea, due to the different dimensions already mentioned, this might not be a suitable explanation.

2) The block was made for Ptahshepses' mastaba, for the construction of the saddle ceiling above the middle, broader part of the burial chamber. The block which is under discussion was not finally used there (the reasons for this omission are not clear) and therefore it was utilised in a different construction from the one originally supposed.

In the discussion on this block one has to mention an interesting feature: the masons' lines and marks which have been documented on the northern face of the discussed trapezoidal ceiling block.[247] It should be underlined here that the face was then obscured by the masonry constructed to the north of the burial chamber. The masons' lines apparently present experimentation (they represent two sets of lines made in red paint) with a form of a saddle roof. However, having in mind the height of the saddle roof above the middle section of the burial chamber, these lines do not seem to have corresponded with it. Therefore, one cannot exclude that this block was originally intended to be used in another context. In this way, the first offered explanation for the use of the ceiling block seems to be the more appropriate.

Fig. 4.1.38a–b Burial chamber, remains of slabs used in the saddle roof; *a* view from the east, *b* view from the south-east

Certainly, the most notable feature of the burial chamber was the construction of the ceiling above the middle part of the chamber. A fragment of a ceiling slab in the north-western part of the niche for the sarcophagus (see *figs. 4.1.38a–b*) shows that in the middle section of the burial chamber the ceiling was not covered by means of a flat ceiling, but by means of a saddle ceiling. This fragment of the ceiling slab represents the bottommost part of a limestone block with a well worked under side. Unfortunately, the other ceiling beams that have been preserved are

[247] Verner, *Baugraffiti*, 107, Abb.3, Taf. XXV/183.

in an even worse state of repair and no part of any other block with an inclined lower side of the saddle ceiling has been preserved. The remainder of the ceiling slabs were cut and destroyed during stone mining in the area of the chamber and especially at the time when the spot was used as a secondary cemetery.[248] The shape of the block can be reconstructed and it seems that it also had the same form as the already mentioned trapezoidal block from the northern part of the burial chamber. Unfortunately, the documentation of the archaeological situation is not sufficient and it is not possible to say whether any other, loose fragments of trapezoidal ceiling blocks were found there. Such a find would have helped us especially with assessment of the number of the ceiling blocks used in this saddle ceiling (see below).

The angle of the saddle ceiling

As the slope of the remaining part of the ceiling slab shows, the inner angle of the saddle ceiling was 35°. If this angle was really the angle used in the case of the whole ceiling, the top of the ceiling must have been at a height of 3.90 m above the pavement of the chamber (see *fig. 4.1.39*).

Fig. 4.1.39 Burial chamber, east-west section with the reconstructed level of the mastaba roof

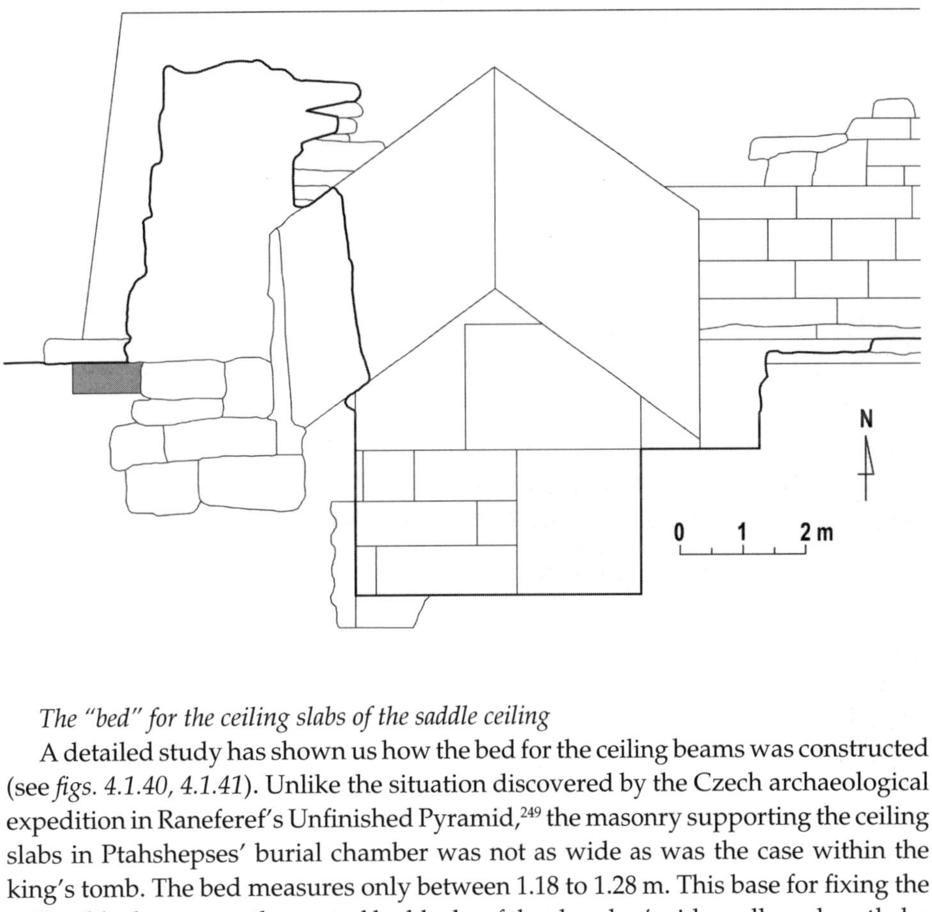

The "bed" for the ceiling slabs of the saddle ceiling

A detailed study has shown us how the bed for the ceiling beams was constructed (see *figs. 4.1.40, 4.1.41*). Unlike the situation discovered by the Czech archaeological expedition in Raneferef's Unfinished Pyramid,[249] the masonry supporting the ceiling slabs in Ptahshepses' burial chamber was not as wide as was the case within the king's tomb. The bed measures only between 1.18 to 1.28 m. This base for fixing the ceiling blocks was partly created by blocks of the chamber's side walls and partly by the core masonry of the western outer wall of the Initial Mastaba. The ceiling beams leaned against the latter masonry. The specially formed "bed-blocks" of the burial chamber's casing have their upper faces inclined at the same angle as the ceiling. The gap in the join between the side walls of the burial chamber and the ceiling beams was 0.10 m broad, therefore, the uppermost parts of the side chamber's side walls were modelled in plaster.[250] In this connection it should be underlined that this

[248] Strouhal, Bareš, *Secondary Cemetery*, 16–21, Plan 1–2.
[249] Verner, in: Verner *et al.*, *Raneferef*, figs. 1.1.7, 1.1.20, 1.1.22.
[250] Such a method is also attested in the case of the ceilings in the royal pyramids – *cf.* in the case of Unas' pyramid – see: Labrousse, *L'architecture à textes*, figs. 16 and 22.

crown of the chamber's side walls made of plaster had only an aesthetical function to fill the gap between the large limestone blocks of the walls and the ceiling, it did not have to support the the ceiling block.

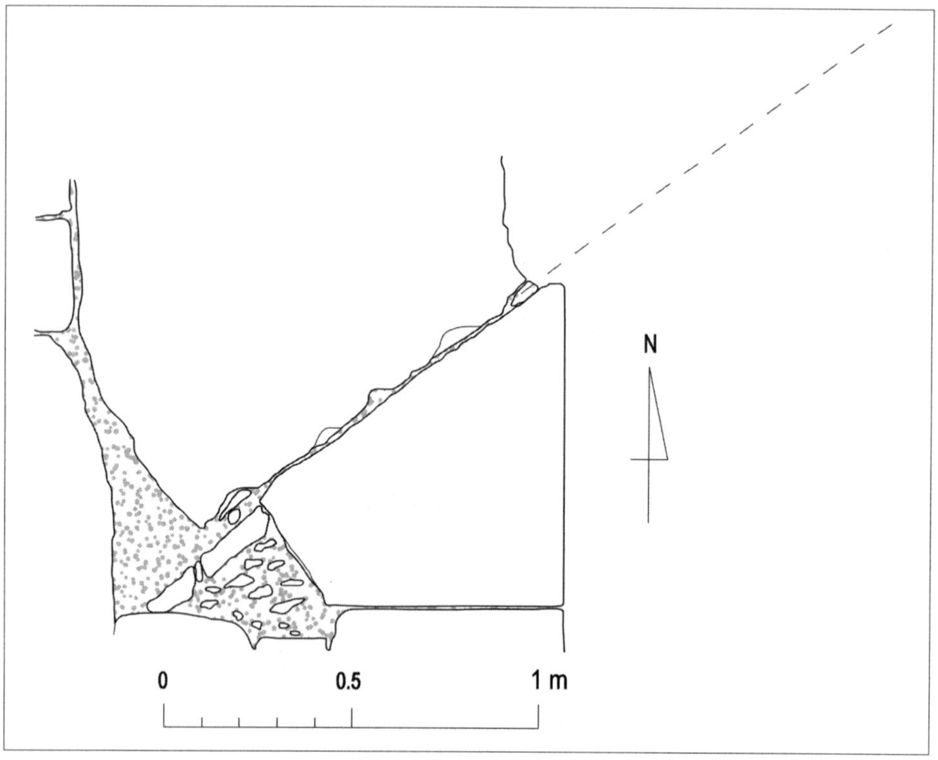

Fig. 4.1.40 Burial chamber, lower part of the southernmost preserved roofing beam and the bed for the roofing beams

Fig. 4.1.41 Burial chamber, the bed for the roofing beams

Groundplan of the burial chamber

Why the middle part of the burial chamber was roofed by means of a saddle ceiling and not a flat ceiling – as was the standard way in non-royal tombs – is a matter of some debate. It seems that the main reason was due to the width of this part of the burial chamber, *i.e.* 4.45 m. Evidently, a pillar (or pillars) apparently could not be constructed, perhaps because of the existence of the second sarcophagus in front of the large sarcophagus placed in the niche. Without the use of a pillar (or pillars) the width of the chamber then outgrew the technical capabilities of horizontal roofing, or, more precisely, the standard techniques used in the burial chambers of the non-royal tombs. Therefore, the technique used in the burial chambers of royal pyramids of the period was applied to the Mastaba of Ptahshepses. As is well known, this technique involved using a saddle ceiling. In this connection it should be mentioned here, that the width of the royal burial chambers of the Fifth and the Sixth Dynasty did not exceed 3.15 m.[251] In this instance, however, the width of Ptahshepses' burial chamber in its middle section was larger in comparison to those of the royal examples.

It can be assumed that the major problem presented to the architects of the Ptahshepses burial chamber must have been the weight of masonry above the burial chamber and also the low quality and instability of the subsoil on which the mastaba was built. On the other hand, it is well documented that in the case of some of the other aboveground buildings from the same period, a width equal to the broader part of the burial chamber (4.45 m), or even larger, was possible to surmount without using any support. This can be documented, for example, by the 5 m wide offering chapel in Neferirkare's mortuary temple.[252] In this case, large limestone beams were also used. They were worked into the shape of a false vault from below.[253]

In general, the ground plan of Ptahshepses' burial chamber shows a strong resemblance to the burial chambers of some of the other Abusir tombs – they also contain deep niches. In contrast to the tomb of Ptahshepses, though, the ceilings in these burial chambers were supported by pillars. Among these examples belong the following tombs: Userkafankh's,[254] Nebtiemneferes'[255] and Ptahshepses' Junior II's tomb.[256] Pillars are also attested in the burial chambers located in the Mastaba of Princesses – *i.e.* in the burial chamber of Kahotep and in the burial chamber of an unknown person located to the north of his funerary apartment.[257] It is highly possible that, in the case of the burial chamber of Meretites in the Mastaba of the Princesses, the ceiling was also supported by a pillar.[258] As was noted by Miroslav Bárta: the main reason for the use of pillars in the burial chambers of the Abusir tombs can be primarily to be due to the poor quality of the gravel terrace on which the mastabas and the whole of Abusir cemetery site were built.[259]

Another question concerning the saddle ceiling in the burial chamber is whether it was constructed by means of pairs of slabs or by means of slabs whose joins did not match with the joins of blocks built into the opposite side of the saddle ceiling.[260] Due to the aforementioned poor state of preservation of the ceiling slabs *in situ*, answering this question is problematic. If the ceiling consisted of pairs of slabs, then the most probable number of pairs is five, *i.e.* altogether ten blocks would have been be used in this way. Contrary to this reading, Vladimír Fiala supposed that there were four pairs of ceiling beams used for roofing the burial chamber.[261] The first

---

[251] *Cf.* Naggar, *Voûtes*, 95–111.

[252] See *MRA* VII, Tav. 10.

[253] Further examples which are closer in nature to the burial chamber of Ptahshepses are the burial chambers in the substructures of the royal tombs dated to the end of the Fourth Dynasty – those of Menkaure (2.40 m, *MRA* VI, 44–45, fig. 7–8), and Shepseskaf (3.90 m; *MRA* VI, 142, 156, fig. 8).

[254] Borchardt, *Neuserre*, Bl. 20.

[255] Verner, *Forgotten Pharaohs*, plan on the p. 84.

[256] Bárta, *Ä&L* 10 (2001), fig. 2, pl. 9.

[257] Borchardt, *Neuserre*, Bl. 25, 26, 27.

[258] *Cf.* Jánosi, in: *Abusir and Saqqara*, Abb. 4.

[259] Bárta, *Ä&L* 2001, 57.

[260] See, *e.g.*, Borchardt, *Neuserre*, Blatt 7.

[261] Fiala, in: *Preliminary Report*, 53; this reading was adapted by Naggar (Naggar, *Voûtes*, 132).

reading is, however, more probable than Fiala's hypothesis. Evidently, the block which survived in the north-western corner of the niche was not broad enough to reach the northern wall of the burial chamber, which supported the ceiling in this part of the burial chamber. Therefore, another beam needed to be placed beside it. To the south of the remaining beams there were apparently three more ceiling beams.[262] Therefore, we can suppose that five beams on each side of the burial chamber were used, thus making ten beams in all for the construction of the burial chamber's ceiling.

On the other hand, with the unmatched blocks on both sides of the ceiling, the number of blocks used is uncertain. We therefore must accept from the width of the ceiling beams that partially survive that the total number of beams present may have been anything between eight and eleven.

As was adumbrated earlier, beside its technological aspect, the use of the saddle ceiling testifies to the high rank of Ptahshepses held in his society. This type of ceiling construction was reserved almost only for royal tombs during the Old Kingdom.[263] Other examples of saddle ceilings in non-royal tombs are rare. One of them is provided by Iinefer's mastaba (dated to the Fourth Dynasty) located in the Central Dahshur Cemetery (*Dahschur-Mitte*). Unlike the situation in the Mastaba of Ptahshepses, Iinefer's burial chamber was built at the bottom of a deep construction shaft and it seems that the saddle form of the ceiling had a technical purpose.[264]

The other example of a saddle construction is found in slightly earlier Far Western Tombs at Meidum, dated to the time of the construction of the local pyramid.[265] In several of these tombs, their burial chambers were also cut into the rock as was the case for Iinefer. Their ceilings had saddle shapes (they were named as "pent-roofed tombs" by the excavators) and were cut into the soft rock without the use of additional masonry. In this case, an explanation based on purely technological grounds is not possible. We can only hypothesise that it was done for reasons of instability in the subsoil and the supposition that the saddle form of the ceiling could improved this situation. E. Mackay underlines the poor quality of the bed-rock, which was cracked and falling from the ceiling during the excavations of the burial chambers. In Meidum, another tomb had a burial chamber that had been roofed in this royal manner. The method of construction for this ceiling could be compared with the construction of Ptahshepses' burial chamber.[266] The main difference between the burial chambers of the minor Meidum Far Western Tombs with the saddle ceiling and that of Ptahshepses are the dimensions. The Meidum burial chambers were much smaller than that in Ptahshepses' monument.

We need to ask one further question regarding Ptahshepses' burial chamber: Why was the middle part of the burial chamber built so wide if it was not possible to cover it by using the standard methods? Apparently, the main reason was that the placement of a large sarcophagus for Ptahshepses and a smaller one, presumably belonging to his wife, Princess Khamerernebty (see *figs. 4.1.42, 4.1.43*), had already been made before the problem of the ceiling was confronted.[267] Aside from other

---

[262] See Fiala, in: *Preliminary Report*, fig. 17.

[263] Arnold, *Building*, 191. There is one exception: the burial chamber of Queen Neferhetepes in her pyramid complex in Saqqara. As we can see in the pyramids of kings, the burial chamber was ceiled by means of a saddle roof (Labrousse, Lauer, *Ouserkaf*, 144–145, fig. 345–346, 348, pl. 30). One can only hypothesize that this non-standard use might have been somehow connected with an exceptional role which is suggested for this person at the turning point of the Fourth and the Fifth Dynasty.

[264] It follows from the figures in Barsanti's report on the excavation of the tomb (Barsanti, 'Rapport sur la fouille de Dahchour', *ASAE* 3 [1902], 200–201, figs. 5–6) that the roof-beams would hold filling masonry above Iinefer's burial chamber. See also: Alexanian, *Netjer-aperef*, 18; Naggar, *Voûtes*, 131, fig. 157.

[265] Mackay in: Petrie, Mackay, Wainwright, *Meydum and Memphis*, 26–27, pl. XVIII.

[266] Reisner, *Tomb Development*, 209, fig. 104.

[267] For the technical data, description and historical consequences see M. Verner, 'Newly discovered royal sarcophagi from Abusir', in: *Abusir and Saqqara 2000*, 568–569, fig. 6.

Fig. 4.1.42 Burial chamber, view from the south at the time of its unearthing

features, it is worth underlining that both sarcophagi were made of granite. It is well known that granite was under the full control of the ruler. As in many cases in this tomb, the dimensions and workmanship with which especially the larger – the owner's – sarcophagus was made offer further evidence of the extraordinary position of this tomb among other non-royal tombs from the period of the Old Kingdom. This material was not used only for the sarcophagi of the members of the royal family,[268] but also for the manufacture of sarcophagi belonging to persons of non-royal origins, but only those of an elite status (see also *pl. 17*).

The supposition that the larger sarcophagus belonged to Ptahshepses and the smaller to Khamerernebty cannot be fully confirmed, due to the lack of anthropological material which could be confidently attributed to both persons. It seems that, during the archaeological excavations of the burial chamber, remains of *two male* skeletons were found. Following the opinion of the palaeopathologist Eugen Strouhal, these two skeletons were datable to the period of the construction of the Initial Mastaba.[269] It is a puzzle why we had the remains of two males and not, as it would be expected, the bones of *a female and a male*. Several items of the burial equipment (copper models of bowls)[270] were found during the excavation of the burial chamber. This fact, however, cannot be used as confirmation for our supposition that the smaller sarcophagus was intended for the tomb owner's wife.

Fig. 4.1.43 Burial chamber with its two granite sarcophagi, view from the east

A complex problem is connected with the find of fragments of a third sarcophagus. Following personal communications from the then members of the archaeological

[268] *Cf.* Jánosi, *Giza*, Tab. 10 on the p. 215.

[269] Personal communication from Eugen Strouhal, spring 2001. Professor Strouhal was unable to obtain consent from the authorities for an investigation into the anthropological material found. The anthropological material has since become lost, therefore verification was not possible.

[270] Žába, *Excavation Notebooks* 2/1968, 3/1968; *cf.* Verner, in: *Abusir and Saqqara in 2000*, 568, n. 32.

expedition in the year 1968 (M. Verner and E. Strouhal),[271] during the excavations in the area of the burial chamber certain fragments of a third (!) sarcophagus were found. As already M. Verner mentions, however, these fragments might be an intrusion. Moreover, there is no documentation made by Zbyněk Žába proper to this find, so this piece of information cannot be checked. If it were true that in the burial chamber a third sarcophagus was placed, there would have been serious problems connected with the limited space available in the burial chamber for this third, hypothetical sarcophagus.

It is a complex problem to ascertain whether the saddle ceiling was planned from the beginning, or whether it represents a later change in the architectural plan of this part of the mastaba and the reconstruction of the masonry above the burial chamber. From a thorough study of the masonry, it follows that the present layout of the burial chamber was part of the plan of the mastaba from the very beginning (see further). The layout of the burial chamber was not apparently changed in order to include the second granite sarcophagus. There is no feature which would enable us to suspect such a change in the chamber's ground plan. On the other hand, the second, smaller sarcophagus was apparently put inside the chamber not only after the layout of the chamber's ground-plan had been executed, but it is even possible that this deposit was made after the building of the side walls had commenced. Despite this likelihood, how *could* the second sarcophagus be installed in the burial chamber after the building of the walls already begun? The finished descending passage into the chamber was too small to allow the transfer of the sarcophagus into the tomb by this route. After careful analysis, it now appears that the answer is available in the masonry of the mastaba.

Methods used during the construction of the burial chamber

As has already been mentioned, the technological process which was used during the construction of the burial chamber is similar to that used in the construction of the pyramids of the kings and queens at Abusir.[272] At first an open construction pit was built with an access probably leading from the north (see p. 61). In this excavation, the construction of the burial chamber was started. To the south-west, west, north and the north-east of the pit, the core masonry of the above ground parts of the Initial Mastaba was already under construction (see p. 43). Then, the funerary apartment was constructed within the pit, together with its descending trench intended for the construction of the descending corridor. This trench for the descending corridor was broad enough to be used for the transportation of both sarcophagi. It is very probable that this manoeuvre was carried out *after* the layer of the under-pavement blocks and the blocks of the pavement itself in the burial chamber had been put down.

The methods used during the building of the Initial Mastaba seem to be documented by the existence of a construction join which is clearly noticeable in the masonry of the Initial Mastaba (see *figs. 4.1.46, 4.1.11*). It runs through the south-eastern part of the mass of the mastaba. From its existence, it follows that the core masonry of the Initial Mastaba was built in two sub-phases (at first, in its western, then secondly in the eastern and south-eastern parts). Recently, an assumption has been made that this break in the masonry is related to the reconstruction of the whole Initial Mastaba in connection with the insertion of the smaller sarcophagus into the burial chamber.[273] In contrast to this theory, however, it is more plausible that the main reason for existence of this join in the core masonry should be found

---

[271] *Cf.* Verner, in: *Abusir and Saqqara in 2000*, 568, n. 31.

[272] Ptahshepses was certainly familiar with the methods used in the construction of the royal pyramids, mainly due to his role as Overseer of all the Kings' Works. (see Krejčí, 'Some Remarks on the "Overseers of Works" During the Old Kingdom', *Ä&L* 10 [2000], 67–75; *idem*, *Stavebně-historický vývoj*, 86–93). He was, therefore, able to make use of these methods during the construction of his own tomb.

[273] Verner, in: *Abusir and Saqqara in 2000*, 574.

in the construction history of the mastaba. Because of the need to transport and insert huge blocks of the ceiling of the burial chamber and megalithic blocks that made up the side walls and ceiling of Room no. 31, the construction to the east and the south-east of the burial chamber was halted at one point in time. These blocks (separate blocks make up almost the whole surface of a niche side wall or of its ceiling) weigh up to 10 tons each. In order to manipulate them, and in order to insert them in their place in the masonry of the burial chamber, a space to the east and south-east of this recently constructed masonry had to be left free. After the burial chamber was finished, Room no. 31 and the descending corridor, the rest of the core masonry, the filling and the core masonry of the Initial Mastaba were built (for further discussion see *chapter 4.1.14*).

4.1.13.3 Room no. 31 – Niche for the Canopic Jars

In the south-east corner of the burial chamber a short passageway connects the burial chamber itself with a small chamber, traditionally described as the "Niche for the Canopic Jars". The passageway is certainly not preserved in its original form. The passage is 0.84 m long, 1.82 m high and 1.22 m wide now. On its eastern wall, there are clear marks which refer to the fact that in this place a partition, possibly made of one block of stone, was originally located. This limestone block narrowed the passageway and so created a doorway in it. This stone was very probably removed by tomb-robbers, who also shifted the smaller sarcophagus from the burial chamber into this passageway (see *fig. 4.1.44*). In this position the sarcophagus was found by Z. Žába in 1968. The present width of the passageway perfectly fits the width of this sarcophagus. This operation made enough room for access to and the opening of the sarcophagus of Ptahshepses. Because of the removal of the block from the passageway and because of the rather poor preservation of the passageway pavement, it is not possible to reconstruct the original width of the entrance to the niche; how wide it was originally and what form it had (the width of the entrance could have been 0.80 m as, theoretically, the discussed block could have been 0.52 m wide). The floor of the doorway was constructed some 0.32 m higher than the pavement of the burial chamber.

Fig. 4.1.44 Passageway to Room no. 31 (Niche for the Canopic Jars) from the north

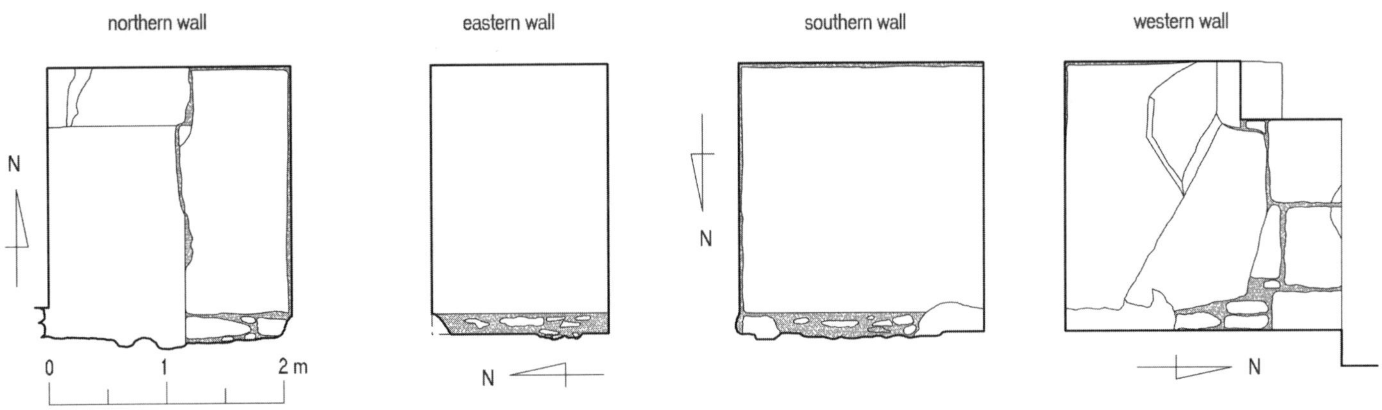

Fig. 4.1.45a–d Room no. 31, front views of the walls

The Niche for the Canopic Jars in fact is very well preserved room: the tomb robbers did not remove its ceiling and they also did almost no harm to its side walls. Only the pavement of the floor was damaged to any great extent. The room is 1.40 m wide, 2.13 m long and 1.82 m high (so that its height was the same as the entrance passageway to it).

Together with Room no. 31, the entire burial apartment of the mastaba covered an area of about 24 m^2. The eastern and northern walls of the room were constructed of one large block each of white limestone (see *figs. 4.1.45a–d.*). The north wall consists of two blocks and the western wall of blocks that are smaller. Because of the removal of the pavement of the room, the lowermost parts of the walls were left uncovered. This fact allows us to see that the large blocks of the walls were laid on a layer of small fragments of limestone and plaster, a layer which is 0.18–0.20 m high.

Only in the case of the western part of the northern wall do the larger limestone blocks reach the level of the under-pavement blocks. The flat ceiling is made of one huge monolithic block of white limestone which weighs at least 9.125 tons. This block lies upon the side core walls and their casing. The walls are carefully smoothed and processed.

On the basis of the thorough study of the masonry around Room no. 31, it is possible to distinguish the successive technological steps by which the room was made. Construction of the niche and of the burial chamber required free space for the lowering and positioning of the large monolithic blocks used in the niche's side walls and its ceiling. This presented the main reason for leaving the masonry in the space around and above of these two underground chambers open to the south-east. The technical process for the building of the room was as follows:

1) Digging of the constructional pit for the room (together with digging of the space for the burial chamber).
2) Laying of the under-pavement blocks.
3) Laying down of the blocks creating the side walls of the passageway at the same time as the blocks of the side walls of the burial chamber.
4) Laying down the "bed-layer" on which the later side walls of Room no. 31 were laid.
5) Putting down the monolithic blocks of the north and south walls.
6) Putting down the monolithic block in the eastern wall.
7) Construction of the west wall of the room.
8) Laying of the east side block of the doorway.
9) Setting the upper pavement blocks of the room.
10) Lowering of the huge ceiling slab onto the tops of the side. During this operation, the room – as was also the case with the burial chamber – was certainly filled with sand in order to ease the ceiling block into position and in order to prevent potential cracks opening up, not only in the ceiling block, but also in the blocks of the walls.

It is possible to assume that the side walls of Room no. 31 were built in the same period of time as the construction of the walls of the burial chamber, or only little later. Whether the ceiling slab of the Niche for the Canopic Jars was put down before construction of the saddle ceiling of the burial chamber itself is not possible to say.

As the burial apartment had been thoroughly plundered, there is no direct attestation for the function of Room no. 31. On the other hand, its position, layout and dimensions from other tombs of the period seem to show, that it served for the deposit of the canopic jars (or chests) of the buried persons. This hypothetical function was the origin of the modern designation for the room. Because two persons were buried in the burial chamber, we have to suppose the existence of two sets of canopic jars which might have been originally kept in Room no. 31. There is a question of whether only the canopic jars were put inside the room, or whether it originally also held other parts of the burial equipment. The room seems to be too large (5.43 m^3) if intended only for the canopic jars or canopic chests. It is thus likely that we can also presume that other burial equipment could have been deposited here.

It should be mentioned here, that a niche was also attached to Khamerernebty's burial chamber in the Mastaba of Princesses.[274] As is also the case with the burial apartment in the Mastaba of Ptahshepses, the niche in original Khamerernebty's tomb, which has the form of a very small, separate room, was located to the south of the burial chamber. The entrance to the room was from the north in the form of a doorway without a door leaf. There is also a very close analogy to the design of Room no. 31 in the neighbouring tomb of Ptahshepses Junior II. Here we also

[274] Borchardt, *Neuserre*, Bl. 25.

encounter a niche, which is connected with the main burial chamber by means of a narrow doorway located in the chamber's south wall.[275] From other cemeteries of the Fifth Dynasty, we do not have a lot of other analogous examples. There is one further example that might be mentioned: in tomb GIS VIII S (Sekhemka),[276] we encounter a recess in a burial chamber dated to the late Fifth Dynasty (in the south wall of the burial chamber, by its south-west corner and quite high up in the wall).

4.1.14 Core masonry in the south-eastern part of the Initial Mastaba

In the context of problems connected with Room no. 31 and the burial chamber, the way in which the core masonry of the eastern parts of the Initial Mastaba was constructed should be described. After the insertion of both sarcophagi, construction of the side walls of both the burial chamber and Room no. 31 and the finishing of their ceilings began. At the same time, other parts of the superstructure of the Initial Mastaba located in its eastern and south-eastern sector were also built.

Fig. 4.1.46 Southern outer wall of the Initial Mastaba, the join between the construction sub-phases of the Initial Mastaba as it appeared in its greatly destroyed state

Unlike the core masonry in its western part, the masonry lying to the east (and south-east respectively) around the aforementioned join was built in a clearly distinct way. In contrast to the core masonry in the western part of the Initial Mastaba (see *chapter 4.1.4*), the core masonry of this second sub-phase of the Initial Mastaba was constructed by smaller sized (0.50–1.20 × 0.37–0.47 × 0.45–0.54 m) and regular ashlars made of local limestone. These blocks, in contrast to other like ashlars used in the western and north-western part of the mastaba, were rather well worked (see *figs. 4.1.8.–4.1.11* and *4.1.46*). They were then carefully joined together by means of quality mortar. Afterwards, this core masonry was covered by the casing of the side walls and roofed by, seemingly flat, blocks of limestone. After adding the filling masonry above the ceilings of the separate rooms, the rooftop terrace of the mastaba (or terraces in different levels) was constructed and the casing of the outer walls of the mastaba was finished. As was already mentioned earlier, there is no evidence to determine whether or not the Mastaba of Ptahshepses already at this building stage, possessed any kind of exterior structure along its eastern façade. Such a construction could have been built of light materials such as mud bricks and wood, *etc.* and therefore consist of impermanent materials. Its existence, therefore, cannot be totally discounted as there are many instances of these installations in the non-royal cemeteries in Abusir (*e.g.* Djadjaemankh's tomb), Giza and Saqqara.

[275] Bárta, *Ä&L* 10 (2000), fig. 2.
[276] *PM* III, 221; Junker, *Gîza* IX, Abb. 1.

4.1.15 Summary of chapter 4.1

The first building stage of the Ptahshepses mastaba consisted of over ten rooms and spaces of varying sizes. Of these, the most important were the rooms of the monumental burial apartment, where (at least) two large granite sarcophagi were positioned. This fact, together with the existence of two offering chapels (with the remaining part of the offering table in the minor offering chamber – Room no. 28) attests that the Initial Mastaba was used as the burial place for two persons. Unfortunately, the burial of a third person which has been discussed by the palaeopathologist cannot be documented. Moreover, the way in which the burial chamber was given its ceiling – by means of the saddle roof – is an extraordinary episode in the corpus of non-royal Old Kingdom tomb architecture. The staircase leading to the mastaba's roofing terrace, which is one of the oldest examples of its kind in a private Old Kingdom tomb, also seems to show a high social rank of the tomb owner. Besides these features, it also implies the complexity of the burial of the tomb owner (and his wife) and hints at the possibility of complex tomb rituals that might have taken place as well. There is no doubt that the Initial Mastaba was fully completed, as is documented by its casing hidden behind the later additions. Already in this early form of the Initial Mastaba, the tomb of Ptahshepses was the largest tomb built for a non-royal person in the Abusir Cemetery of Nobles. These facts all seem to support the supposition that Ptahshepses was already a quite powerful person when he started the construction of his tomb.

4.2 The second building stage

In what was likely to have been only a short time after the completion of the first building stage of his existing tomb, Ptahshepses decided to enlarge it by building an annex along the northern part of the eastern façade of the Initial Mastaba (see *fig. 4.2.1*). As previously discussed in *chapter 3*, it is not possible to refute the existence of earlier buildings in the space where the Initial Mastaba was built. Theoretically, any such earlier constructions would have prevented the construction of an annex covering the whole eastern face of the Initial Mastaba (see further discussion in this chapter). If no older constructions were built in the area to the south to the new annex, then one can suppose that a large open courtyard, encircled by an enclosure wall, was constructed or planned (see below) to the south of this new annex. In this way, the annex would make a logical part of the mastaba, the courtyard would then fill in the rectangular ground plan of the entire tomb.

The larger part of the masonry of the second building stage has been hidden behind the masonry of the third building stage. This means that the study of the core masonry of this annex was not an easy task. On the other hand the study of the casing of the inner rooms of this building stage was not as difficult. These rooms are in fact the best preserved rooms of the whole mastaba – especially the Chapel with Three Niches (Room no. 4) and the so-called "Old Portico" (Room no. 3). These are the rooms which were excavated by Jacques de Morgan in 1893.

4.2.1 Casing of the second building stage

The state of preservation of the second building stage's casing is better than that of the Initial Mastaba. This is true particularly with the northern and southern outer walls. We can study the polished casing blocks belonging to the masonry of the annex preserved *in situ* in the north-east sector of the mastaba. The casing was, at least in this area, finished. This fact is important for the building history of the mastaba. The angle of the casing was measured at 82°20´ here. Contrary to the situation in the northern sector, the stone robbers removed not only the upper parts of the masonry, but also the lower part of the eastern façade of the annex with its casing. The north-east corner of the annex itself, therefore, did not survive. We can, however, extrapolate the dimensions of the annex (see further in this chapter; see also *figs. 4.2.2a–c*). Fortunately a block of the casing has survived in the

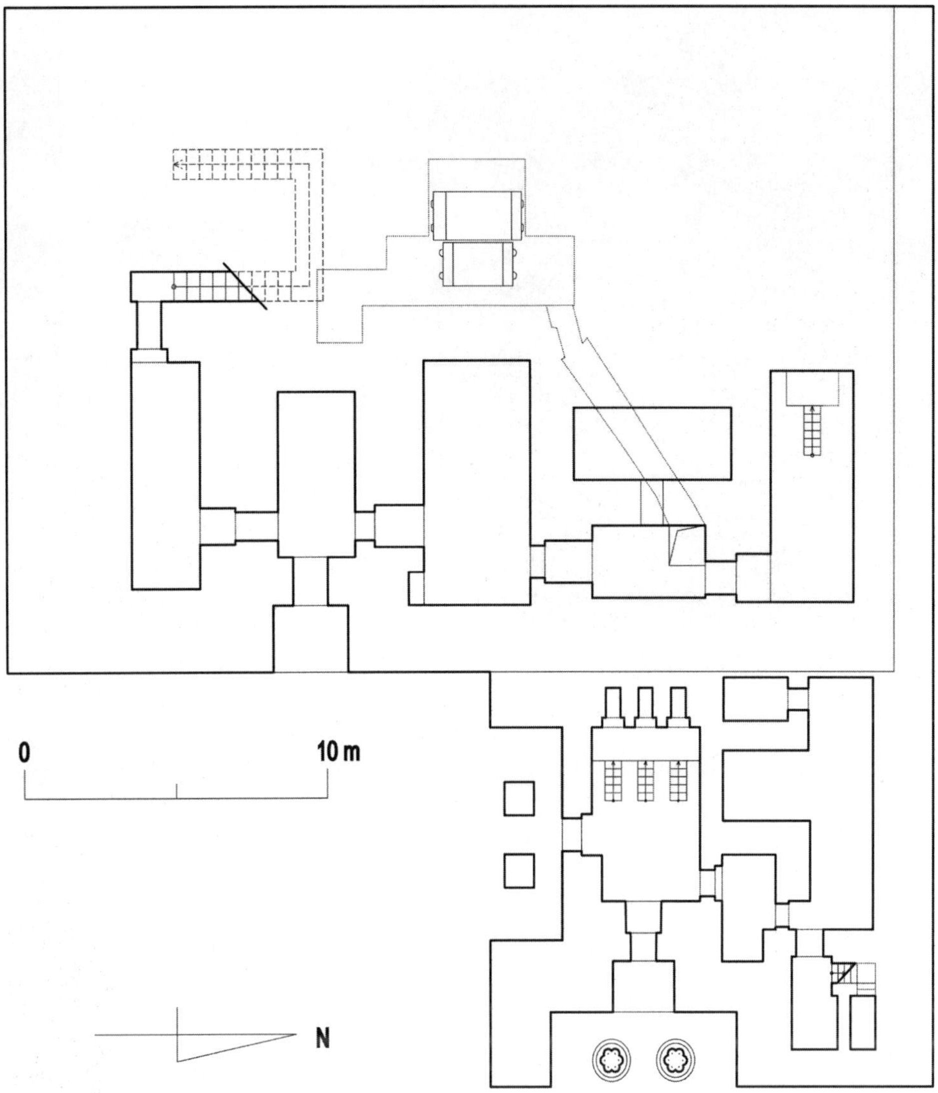

Fig. 4.2.1 Overall plan of the mastaba during the second building stage

masonry which certainly belonged to the casing of the second building stage (see *figs. 4.2.2a* and *4.2.2c*). This block helps us to locate the eastern face of the annex, at least in regard to its northern part: the southern part was covered during the subsequent building stage. In addition to that, the original situation in this area was obscured during the restoration work done after the excavation. It is highly probable that the eastern façade of the new annex was in line with the eastern face of the aforementioned block.

More problematic than the north and east faces of the annex seems to be its southern façade. The situation in the area of Room no. 10 (the Southern Portico) is not clear. The area to the south of it and the room itself has been altered at a later date, during the third building stage. Originally, the southern outer wall of the annex created a north wall for the above mentioned hypothetical open court located to the south of the annex. This wall was sloped (it was built at the same slope as attested in the case of the north wall of the Room no. 11 – 82°20´). During the third building stage, the Southern Portico was enlarged and, along the eastern part of this wall, new Room no. 12 was constructed (see *chapter 4.3.6*). During these changes, the slope of the wall was cut back (for 15 cm at the base of the wall), in order to create a vertical wall for the new Room no. 12 and the eastern part of the enlarged Southern Portico. In this way, the actual eastern and western walls of the Southern Portico do not have identical dimensions and the original measurements were slightly changed.

Fig. 4.2.2a–c The north-eastern corner of the second building stage (*a* view from the east and *b* view from the north-east; *c* close up of the surviving casing block and of the core masonry)

4.2.2 Dimensions of the second building stage annex

The annex built during the second building stage formed an east-west oriented rectangle which was 12.85 m (= 24.71 c) broad and 14.20–14.30 m (= 27.30–27.50 c) long.[277] It follows that it covered a space of 182.47–183.76 m^2 and the mastaba's superstructure as a whole then covered 765.07–784.22 m^2. These calculations relate to the tomb's area without the above mentioned hypothetical court located between the newly built annex and the eastern façade of the Initial Mastaba. Such a space, whose dimensions might have been at least 15.2 × 12.85 m, should then have covered 195.32 m^2. At this stage, the entire complex of Ptahshepses' mastaba with this alleged court would have encompassed 958.59–977.74 m^2.

In the second building stage, it is very probable that the roof terrace of the annex was constructed in two levels. Its lower part was located above the Chapel with the Three Niches and the Northern Storerooms. The roof above the Old Portico was constructed on a higher level than above the rest of the annex. The same might have also been true for the Southern Portico (no. 10). The lower roof terrace could have been on the same, or on an almost equal level – as was the case with the roof terrace

[277] This equivocal reading is caused by uncertainty over where the south face of the annex originally ran, see above.

of the Initial Mastaba, *i.e.*, at least 5.06 m (see *chapter 4.1.2*). The level, at which the ceilings above the both porticos were built, is difficult to ascertain. The height of the columns in the Old Portico is not known, even though it can be estimated as being from 4.5 to 5 m (see *chapter 4.2.4* for further information concerning the columns). If we add the height of the architrave above them, *i.e.* ca 0.60 m (equal to the width of the capital of the columns) and at least 0.50 m for the roofing masonry we would get readings of between 5.6 m to 6.1 m: this was very probably the height of the Old Portico.

4.2.3 Ground plan of the annex built during the second building stage

4.2.3.1 Annex with cultic and storage rooms (see also *pls. 18–20*)

As it follows from its dimensions, the new annex formed a rectangular building whose main communication axis was oriented in an east-west direction. On the other hand, its longer axis was oriented in a north-south direction (see *fig. 4.2.1*). The main entrance was located in the centre of the annexe's eastern façade. This present-day Room no. 3 – the Old Portico – was changed into an internal room during the third building stage. A doorway opens in the western wall of this room and leads into the most important room of this annex, the Chapel with Three Niches (no. 4). In the north-eastern corner of Room no. 4, there is an entrance to a group of storerooms (Northern Storerooms). In the southern façade of the annex, there was another entrance, allowing access to the Chapel with Three Niches; this has been called the Southern Portico by the author of this monograph. The annex built during the second building stage represents a turning point in the building development of the entire mastaba. In addition to that, it is possibly one of the most significant points in the development of non-royal tomb architecture of the Fifth and Sixth Dynasties. Ptahshepses was by this time already in a very high position (we think that by now he was already married to the royal princess – see *chapter 3*). He was able to start to turn his tomb into a kind of private temple-tomb. This change – apart from his wish to show his high social status – is marked by the erection of statues of himself and, possibly, of other members of his family. During this building stage, the architectural transformation was manifested also in the use of selected elements of architecture – especially those of the niches in Room no. 4 and by the use of floral columns in the New Portico. As has already been shown in the instance of the first building stage, Ptahshepses' aim was to match in its scale, exquisite construction, sculptural and relief decoration and also in the used elements of architecture the model of a royal mortuary temple.[278]

4.2.3.2 Hypothetical open court

What is quite interesting is the way in which Ptahshepses began all these constructional changes in his own tomb. As a comparison, the neighbouring tombs of other magnates in Abusir might be used in this respect. These tombs were also enlarged. In their case, however, these later additions were built along the *entirety* of the eastern façades of these tombs, as we can see in the monuments of Userkafankh[279] and Djadjaemankh.[280] In a manner different to these others, Ptahshepses added an annex to his tomb which did not cover the whole eastern façade of the Initial Mastaba. On the other hand, we can find annexes which do not hide the whole eastern façade of the tombs in other sites as, *e.g.*, in Giza.[281] As the reasons for these sorts of additional ground plans remain obscure, two hypotheses can be rendered for explaining Ptahshepses' alterations. The first, which is connected with the practical side of the problem, could be based on the hypothetical precondition that

---

[278] See also Jánosi, in: *L'art égyptienne*, 62.
[279] Borchardt, *Neuserre*, Bl. 20.
[280] *Op. cit.*, Bl. 22.
[281] *Cf.* for example Jánosi, *Giza*, Pl. 1–4; these tombs are, however, dated in their majority to the previous periods of time to the Fourth Dynasty.

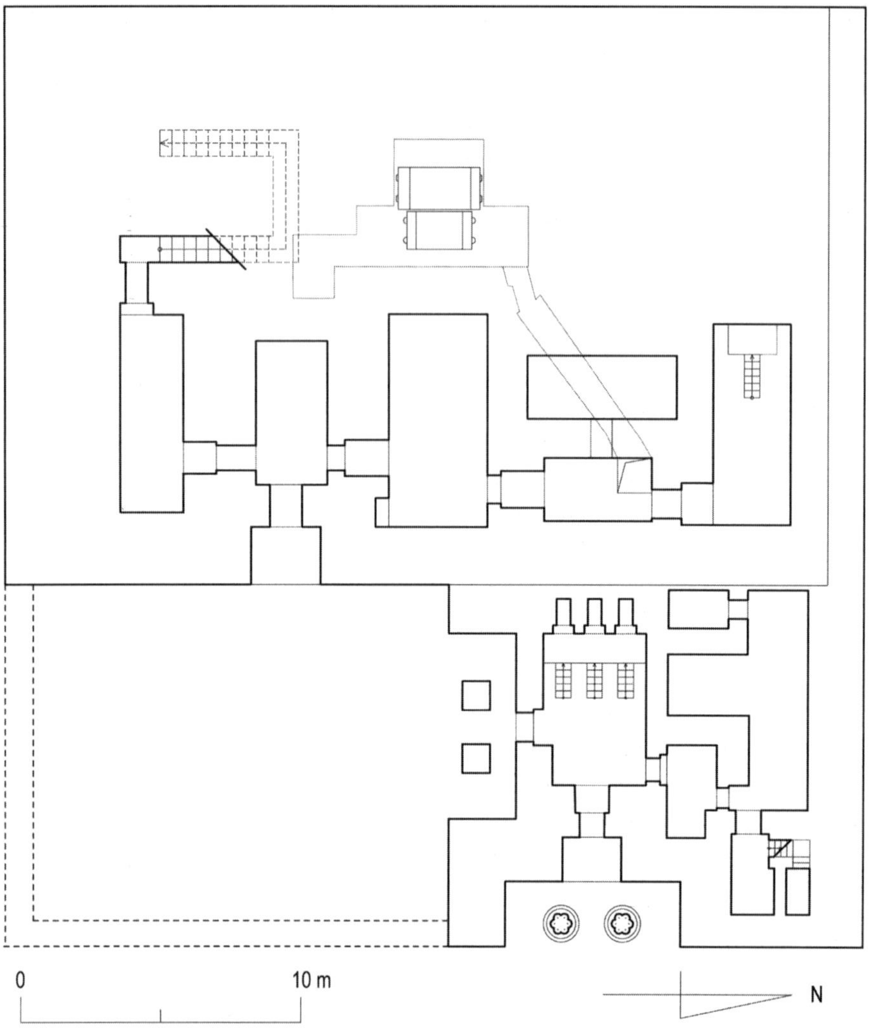

Fig. 4.2.3 Overall plan of the mastaba during the second building stage with the hypothetical enclosure wall

the area to the east of the Initial Mastaba could have been filled with the clutter of constructional ramps and piles of building material. To the same category might have been included the hypothetical (older) cultic or tomb constructions in this area (see also discussion in *chapter* 3). These hypothetical constructions or/and rubbish might have prevented the construction of masonry – cultic rooms, magazines, *etc.* – along the whole eastern façade of the Initial Mastaba. Another and a more plausible explanation lies in the design of the space between the eastern face of the Initial Mastaba and the new annex and its function. The southern entrance to Room no. 4 certainly connected this chapel with the inner rooms of the Initial Mastaba. Unfortunately, the precise character of this connection is no longer clear. It is plausible that the rituals, or "processions" were conducted between Room no. 4 and rooms in the Initial Mastaba.

An open space, which came into existence by the construction of the new annex, might have served these purposes. This area was possibly enclosed by a surrounding wall (see *fig. 4.2.3*). Such a wall could protect an enclosed courtyard against any unauthorised entry to the Initial Mastaba, or it might stop passers-by from viewing the progress of the ceremonies. These ceremonies might have been held in this courtyard. The construction of enclosure walls around the areas where religious rituals were taking place was one of the fundamental characteristics of ancient Egyptian architecture.[282] These principles, used in the tombs dated to the

[282] One also notes from this same Old Kingdom period, the enclosure walls around the pyramid complexes and pyramids themselves, as well as the presence of walls around the more prestigious non-royal tombs. In addition, there are the enclosure walls around the opencourtyards in both the known sun temples in Abusir and Abu Ghurab, as well as the walls built in order to protect the open spaces of the divine temples located in the provincial centres (*e.g.* in Medamud).

same period, we can encounter in the case of mastaba G 6010 (Neferbauptah) and especially G 6040 (Shepseskafankh).[283] In this case, we can see a clear endeavour being made to separate the open courtyard (here with a pillared portico) from the outer world by means of an enclosure wall.

On the other hand, also from the period of the Old Kingdom, there are several cases which seem to document that the endeavour to close off these cultic rooms was not so strong. In these cases the free space between the separate parts of tombs and their cultic spaces was not closed. In the tomb of Minkhaef (G 7430) located in the Giza East Field, a hall with (in this case four) niches had been constructed. To the east of this chapel, an annex was added which was enlarged twice (the first enlargement was built of limestone blocks, the second was built of mud brick). There is another entrance to the cultic rooms in this annex. Therefore, the cultic installations of Minkhaef's mastaba had two entrances.[284] Contrary to the situation in the Mastaba of Ptahshepses, its chapel with niches is connected, *via* a small rectangular room, with the cult chapel, but this provision of a room could have been influenced by the lack of space in the narrow street between the mastabas. The main reason for the absence of a surrounding wall can be seen in the fact that the annex with the cult rooms was built in the street between the tombs of this cemetery and therefore there was not enough space to enclose it all. In a simpler form, we find cultic installations with two entrances in the case of anonymous mastabas G 7240[285] and G 7340.[286]

4.2.4 Room no. 3 – the Old Portico

4.2.4.1 Casing and dimensions

This room, now partly creating an internal room of the mastaba, originally represented a monumental entrance to the newly built annex of the Mastaba of Ptahshepses. As was already indicated, some parts of the original masonry of the Old Portico are now hidden, not only behind later additions, but also behind modern reconstructions (see p. 78). Because of this reason, the precise dimensions of this new entrance need to be extrapolated. After the construction of the New Portico during the third building stage, this original entrance became a closed room, nowadays called the Old Portico, and the new masonry covered the original eastern façade and its casing. Despite these coverings, the line of the portico's outer wall can still be estimated by using the face of the single annex casing block preserved *in situ* to the north of the room (see above). The room now has an oblong layout with its longer axis oriented in a north-south direction; it is 6.32 m long and 4.40 m wide. Originally, the width of the portico was 2.63 m. The niche for the doorway leading to the chapel no. 4 was 2.04 m wide and its side walls were 1.49 and 1.52 m long. As follows from this description, the portico had a form similar to the form of the porticos used in the royal pyramid complexes of this time – *e.g.* of Sahure.[287] The inner western wall of the portico was battered at an angle of 86° 30′ (see *fig. 4.2.4*).

Fig. 4.2.4 Old Portico, northern part of the western wall from the south-east

4.2.4.2 Columns

The most remarkable feature in this room is represented by a pair of six-stemmed lotus columns (see *fig. 4.2.5*).[288] These very fine columns did not survive the attacks

---

[283] Weeks, *Cemetery G 6000*, pls. 3–5.

[284] *PM* III, 195, Reisner, *Giza Necropolis*, 206–207, fig. 7; Jánosi, *Giza*, 253–254, Abb. 46. Jánosi also underlines the strangeness of this layout.

[285] Jánosi, *Giza*, 193–194, Abb. 46.

[286] Nevertheless, in this case, the second entrance represents an approach to a storeroom; *ibid.*, 253, Abb. 46.

[287] *Cf.* the secondary entrance to the mortuary temple of Sahure, see: Borchardt, *Sahure*, Bl. 16, or the western part of the inner chapel in that ruler's valley temple – Bl. 13.

[288] De Morgan, *RevArch* 24 (1894), 28–29, figs. 2, 5–9; Borchardt, *Pflanzensäule*, 6, Abb. 9; Borchardt, *Denkmäler* II, p. 173, Bl. 99; Jéquier, *Architecture*, 204, note 2, fig. 130; Verner, 'Ein »

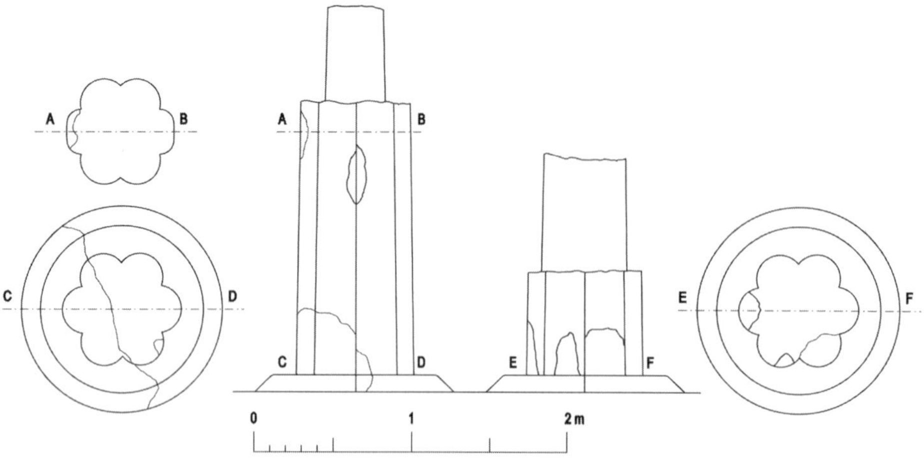

Fig. 4.2.5 Old Portico, lower parts of the columns remaining *in situ*

Fig. 4.2.6 Old Portico from the east

of stone robbers and their preservation is, in comparison with the columns of the New Portico (see *chapter 4.3.3*) much worse. Only the column bases and lowermost parts of the column-shafts have survived *in situ*. Both bases have the same form; their upper diameter is 1.04 m (*i.e.* 2 cubits), the lower diameter 1.26 m and the height 0.10 m. The base of the south column was made from one block, the northern one was made of one large block with an added limestone appendage.[289] The shaft of the southern column has survived to a height of 1.78 m above the room floor, the northern shaft to a height of 0.74 m. The surviving parts of both the columns were also, at an unknown time, but very probably not long after de Morgan's excavations, partly moulded by the use of concrete (see p. 9). Possibly in connection with the construction of the wooden ceiling above Rooms no. 3 and 4, simple, featureless shafts (*fig. 4.2.6*) have been moulded onto the surviving parts of the columns. There is no piece of evidence concerning the time when these featureless shafts might have been moulded. It might have been done directly after the 1893 excavation, but also in concern with the reconstruction of the roof in the year 1924 (compare with p. 11). These restored columns reach all the way to the ceiling.

»entfallener und ein neuer Beleg zur Geschichte der achtstengligen Lotossäule' *BSE* 9–10 (1984–1985), 324; *idem*, 'The Columns of Abusir', in: *OKAA*, 346.

[289] Unfortunately, it is not possible to answer the question of whether the base was originally made of more than one block or whether this appendage has been made by J. de Morgan or A. Barsanti. The situation is, as with many places in the Mastaba, obscured by modern restoration.

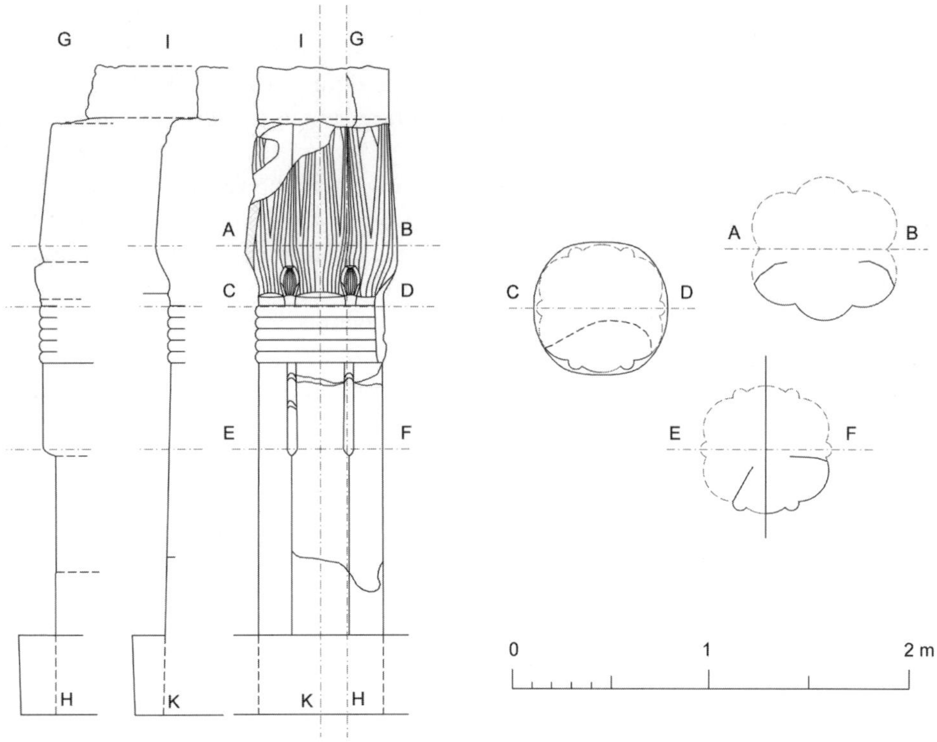

Fig. 4.2.7 Preserved part of the six-stemmed lotus column originally erected in the Old Portico, Cairo Museum

Fig. 4.2.8 Preserved part of the six-stemmed lotus column originally erected in the Old Portico, front view and sections

The fragments of a capital, with part of a shaft belonging to one of the columns, was excavated by J. de Morgan. These fragments were pieced together by A. Barssanti[290] not long after this time and also in addition, largely remoulded. This part of the column is now kept in the Egyptian Museum in Cairo (CG 1748; see *figs. 4.2.7, 4.2.8*). It clearly shows that the columns were formed as a bundle of six lotus stalks with closed buds, bound by five ropes. Between the stalks, smaller lotus buds with 0.45 m long stalks with rounded ends have been thrust into the bundle in six different places. Despite the fact that the separate stems were, in the lower parts of the pillars, positioned in a circle (or regular hexahedron), the half-open buds were grouped into an ellipse, so that the capital is not circular in cross-section, but slightly distorted. After assembly of the fragments found during de Morgan's excavations, it was possible to reconstruct the upper part of one of the columns. Also a square abacus survived; it is 0.254 cm high and 0.64 m wide. No parts of original colouring have remained on this reassembled part of the column. Altogether this restored part of the column measures 2.54 m (together with its moulding 2.78 m).

Unfortunately, due to their poor state of preservation, the complete height of the columns is not easy to ascertain. There is no direct preserved analogy to the columns from the Old Portico (*i.e.* stone six-stemmed lotus columns). Therefore, the columns erected in the New Portico were used as a reference for the width/height index of the columns erected in the Old Portico. These New Portico columns, however, represent eight-stemmed lotus columns, so some proportional changes may be inaccurate. Therefore, the following numbers should be taken only as a guide.

If we take as the basis for our reconstruction the ratio of the columns' height to their width at their butt ends (1:5.90), then the overall height of the column together with the abacus could be 4.48 m (8.61 cubits). On the other hand, by taking into account the ratio of the height of the capital (without the abacus) to the entirety of its length (1:5.33), then the height might have been 4.83 m (9.28 cubits). Both readings do not include the height of the column bases.[291] Having in mind

[290] Žába, *Find of Columns in the Mastaba of Ptahshepses in Abusir*, 20.

[291] M. Balík came to the result of 4.16 m (Balík, *Mastaba*, fig on. p. 63), but he did not mention the description of the method used for obtaining this figure.

that Room no. 4, which adjoined the Southern Portico and was connected by a doorway, had its ceiling at a height of 3.54 m, it seems to be more probable that the height of the columns in the portico was the lower figure – ca 4.48 m. This reading would be almost precisely two cubits (1.04 m) larger than the level of the ceiling in Room no. 4.

It is possible that one of the fragments coming from the capital of one of the columns located in the Old Portico was found by Ludwig Borchardt during the excavations in a non-specified area during his work in Niuserre's pyramid complex and its vicinity,[292] and that this fragment is kept in the Egyptian Museum of the University of Heidelberg (see *fig. 4.2.9*).[293] The fragment is 57.5 cm long and 22.5 cm wide. As Borchardt has mentioned that the fragment bears remains of its original green colour, it is highly possible that this column-fragment came from one of the two columns in the Old Portico as well.

Fig. 4.2.9 Fragment of the six-stemmed lotus column originally erected in the Old Portico, now kept in the Heidelberg University Museum

An important fact is that there are small residues of the original colouring on the parts of the *in situ* surviving shafts of the columns. Unfortunately, the situation is to the some degree obscured by the fact that there is no appropriate documentation made by J. de Morgan. Therefore, it is not possible to compare the original situation on the discovery of these column-shafts with the present state. Such a possibility would be very important for our understanding of the building history of this area and of the whole mastaba (see discussion later).

Seeing that the plant buds are represented in the column-fragment from the Egyptian Museum in Cairo, the flowers can be identified as being *Nymphea caerulea Sav.*,[294] a plant which is almost impossible to find in Egypt in the present day.[295] The use of the vegetal column is closely connected with Abusir – and this tradition began right here.[296] In the repertoire of non-royal mortuary architecture from the Old Kingdom, the use of these vegetal columns is rather exceptional. At the same time, this pair of columns represents the first piece of evidence for the use of stone columns in a private tomb.[297] As in many cases in this tomb, the high rank of Ptahshepses should be taken into the consideration, when one wishes to explain the use of this component of architecture: it must be linked with some attempt by the tomb owner to emulate the architecture of the mortuary temples of his lord(s), as well as with the expression of religious ideas, traditionally connected with the lotus flower. For further discussion, see *chapter 5*.

One very important factor in our knowledge about the history of the tomb may be the remnants of colouring which survived on the both of the column parts still preserved *in situ*. It seems that the first stage of the decoration of the columns had the form of a very simple geometrical pattern painted in white/grey and beige colours (see *pl. 21*). The decoration consisted of different horizontal bands of unequal width (see *fig. 4.2.10, 4.2.11*) and these were not made with great care. We can see individual lines made with a paintbrush.

This gives rise to the question of whether or not this decoration was hypothetically (as a matter of course, for unknown reasons) made by modern masons during one of the restorations carried out since the time of the unearthing of this part of the mastaba. In this case, we should ask why somebody would have executed such a primitive decoration and why such a person would not have used brighter colours. Therefore, this alleged "modernity" seems not to be the case and this simple decoration should be dated to the period of the mastaba's construction.

---

292 Borchardt, *Neuserre*, 136, Abb. 115, 116.
293 Inv. No. 1728; see Feucht, *Vom Nil zum Neckar*, 42.
294 Germer, *Flora*, 37–39; Boulos, *Flora* I, 152, Pl. 29.
295 Meader, Demeter, 'On closer Inspection. The Egyptian Blue Water Lily', *Kmt* 15:2 (Summer 2004), 59–63.
296 Verner, in: *OKAA*, 343–355.
297 On the other hand, the plain (wooden) columns were used for the construction of a colonnade in the courtyard of the tomb neighbouring that of Ptahshepses, the Mastaba of Djadjaemankh (Borchardt, *Neuserre*, Bl. 22). As a matter of fact, one can encounter columns also in other tombs in the cemeteries dated to the Old Kingdom.

Fig. 4.2.10 Old Portico, remains of the southern column *in situ*

Fig. 4.2.11 Old Portico, remains of the northern column *in situ*

Tiny remnants of the blue and green-blue original colouring have remained on the surviving part of the south column, whose cover quite clearly displays the same simple white-grey and beige decoration (see *pl. 22a-b*). From this fact it seems to follow that the decoration of the column could have progressed in two phases – the first "provisional" and the second "final". The provisional phase of the decoration is, hypothetically, connected with the time of the completion of the second building stage and the final phase with the third construction phase. We have, therefore, to inquire whether or not the entire decoration of Room no. 3 and Room no. 4 was not carried out during the third building stage. Beside these considerations, there are other grounds for this supposition which are more obvious: in the decoration of the Old Portico, as is also the case in Rooms no. 4 and 10, there is no distinct line which would mark the extent of decoration which might have been finished during the second stage and that which might have been completed during the third building stage. We can, therefore, suppose, that either the decoration of the Rooms no. 3, 4 and 10 was under preparation and partially completed before Ptahshepses' decision to enlarge his mastaba during the third building stage and the decoration was then remodelled in its entirety, or that the decoration was not yet begun at this time but was created in its entirety during the third building stage. On the other hand, the above mentioned "first phase of decoration" of the column was not documented in the case of the reassembled fragment of the column from the Cairo Museum (earlier mentioned on p. 85).

4.2.5 Room no. 4 – Chapel with Three Niches

This room is the most prominent and important room in the annex of the second building stage. The room has an oblong, east-west oriented shape. The chapel is 3.08 m wide in its eastern part and 3.50 m wide in its western part. It is 5.24 m long and, if we add the depth of the niches in the western wall of the chapel, then the room's overall length becomes 6.14 m. As it follows from the height of the decoration which has survived *in situ* in the north wall of the chapel, the original height of the chapel can be estimated at 3.46 m.[298]

There are three doorways which open into the chapel. The main entrance leads from the Old Portico, *i.e.* from the east. It was closed by a door with a single leaf. The entrance comprises a doorway 0.95 cm wide, and a kind of a niche (1.25 × 0.95 m)

[298] Balík, *Mastaba*, 45.

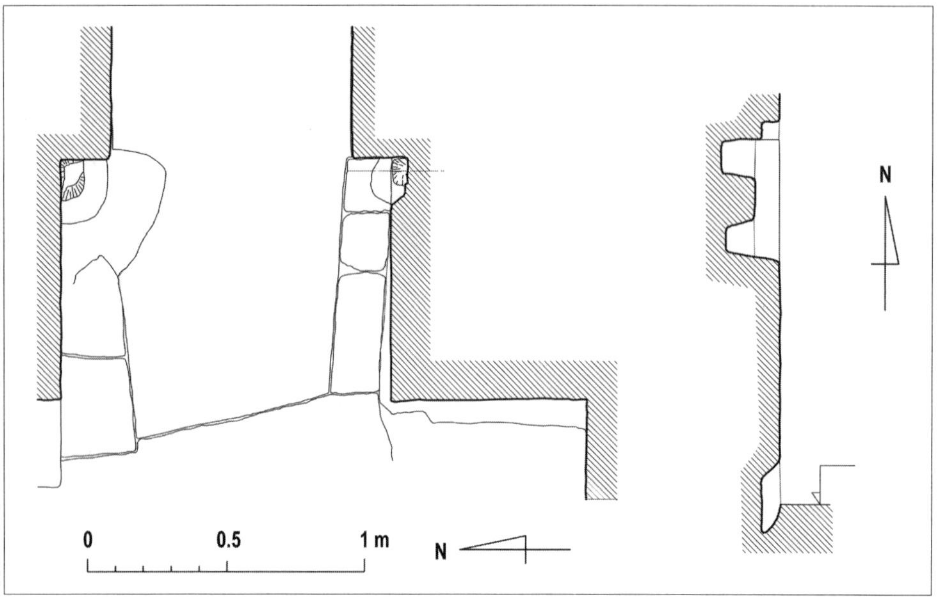

Fig. 4.2.12 Doorway between Room nos. 3 and 4, situation plan and section through the bolt hole of the door latch

in which the wooden door leaf was operating. The door opened into the chapel and therefore would have been sealed off to outsiders by those inside who performed the mortuary rituals. On the south wall of the doorway niche a hollow for the door latch remained in situ (see *fig. 4.2.12*). The other doorway, leading to the Northern Storerooms (Nos. 5–9) is located in the north wall of the chapel; it was 1.98 m high and 0.78 m broad. The niche (1.03 m wide and 0.32 m long) of the doorway clearly shows that a wooden door of one leaf opened into Room no. 5,[299] a room adjacent to the chapel from the north.

The doorway to the Southern Portico is located in the south wall of the chapel, 1.10 m from the south-eastern corner of the chapel. It is 0.95 m wide and had a small niche 1.25 m wide and 0.32 m long. In the niche, there was a one leafed wooden doorway which once opened into the chapel. Due to the fact that its side walls have been destroyed in its upper part, the height of the doorway has had to be reconstructed. If one follows the length/width index coefficient of the doorway between Rooms no. 4 and no. 5, then one can assume that the doorway was about 2.40 m high.

The most remarkable feature of Room no. 4 is located in its western wall, where there are three niches constructed above a podium built along the western wall of the chapel (see *pl. 23*). The podium has the same width as the chapel (3.50 m) and a height of 0.54 m. The majority of the podium was constructed by means of a monolithic, well worked block of white limestone. As the plan of this part of the chapel (*fig. 4.2.13*) and the view of the niches (*pl. 24, fig. 4.2.14*) show, the construction of the niches and podium was interconnected to each other. At first, the niches were constructed, then the large, smoothed block of quality white limestone already mentioned was laid in its position. Finally, after adding the small staircases leading to the separate niches, paving blocks in front of every niche were added. The separate joins between the limestone blocks were filled with quality calcareous mortar.

Each individual staircase is made of one block of fine limestone and it consists of five low steps. As was the case with the large limestone block of the podium, the faces of the staircases were carefully worked and smoothed. The last step of each staircase is formed by the edge of the large limestone block of the podium. The main axes of the staircases were laid along the axes of the individual niches. The dimensions of the individual staircase blocks are the same: 1.15 (L) × 0.52 (W) × 0.43 (H) m and also the height of the individual steps oscillates around 11 cm.

---

[299] The doorway was blocked up by de Morgan after his excavation ceased (Fiala, in: *Preliminary Report*, 49).

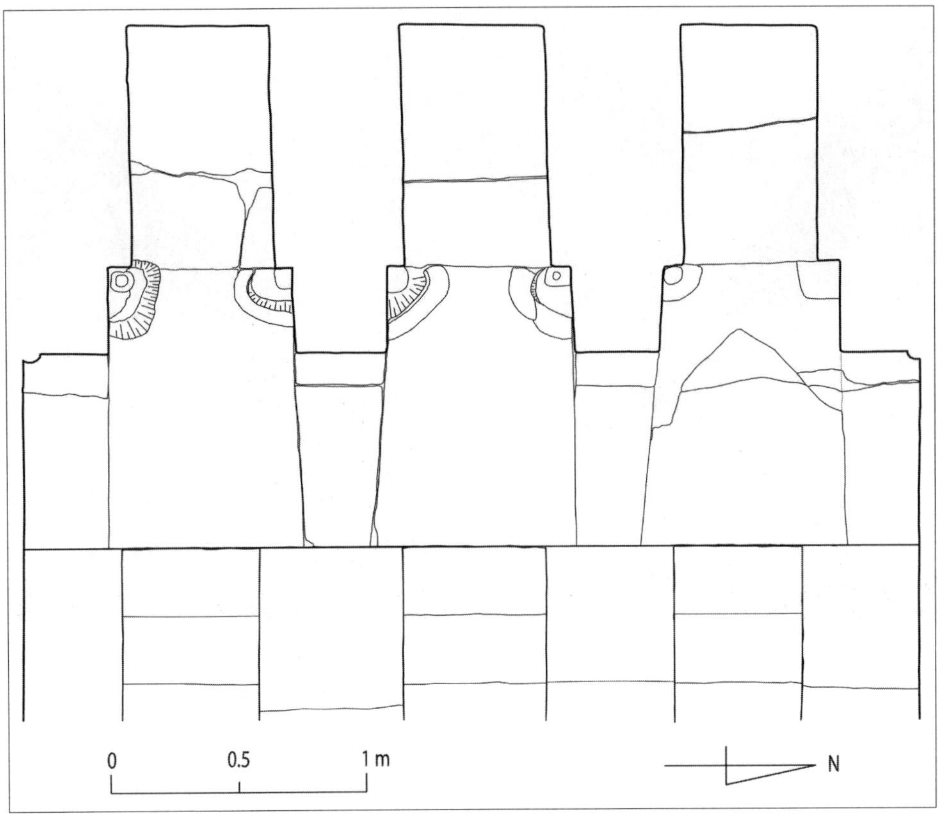

Fig. 4.2.13 Room no. 4, plan of niches in the western wall

The niches in the western wall of Room no. 4 incorporate two parts: a "mouth" which was between 0.71 to 0.73 m wide and from 0.33 to 0.35 m deep and the niche itself; the south niche is 0.55 m wide and 0.925 m long, the middle one is 0.57 m wide and 0.92 m long and the northern niche is 0.54 m wide and 0.90–0.91 m long. The height of the niches is not possible to discern exactly, mainly due to the fact that the upper section of the west wall is missing, because of stone robbery and weathering (for the discussion on the layout of the whole western wall of the chapel see below)

The masonry of partitions (or "narrow walls" as they have been named by M. Verner) between the niches and their back walls consist of smoothed ashlars of white limestone. The blocks are joined, as is the case with the blocks of the podium and of the staircases, by means of quality calcareous mortar. The faces of these "narrow walls" were decorated in polychrome relief decoration; this decoration consists solely of figures of Ptahshepses, his names and titles.[300] The rims of the mouths of the niches were decorated with the polychrome block border that was a characteristic of the Fifth Dynasty. The border strips are framed on each side by thin lines of dark-green colour. Within those lines there is a block border of squarish blocks of the following colours: dark-green, light blue, red and narrow strips of black interchanging with each other.[301] The side walls of the partitions between the niches are decorated by a simple pattern of interchanging strips of green (0.055 m wide and 0.30 m long) and yellow-beige (0.02 m wide, see *pl. 25, fig. 4.2.14*) The black painted dado of the "narrow walls" is 0.40 m high.

One interesting fact that came to light in the measuring of this room, is that the axes of the niches are shifted by 1° to the southwest (see *fig. 4.2.13*). This fact can be clarified by two explanations: either it was caused by a mistake which was made during the surveying and planning of this construction, or else, the shift of niche-axes was caused by the method of the construction – large, white limestone blocks

[300] Verner, *Reliefs*, 89–91, pl. 45–48, photos 76–80.

[301] M. Verner (*Reliefs*, 91) directs the reader's attention to the frequent use of blue colour in the background, especially for the hieroglyphic signs in the chapel. He connects this fact with the Pyramid Texts whose hieroglyphic signs were filled with blue colour.

Fig. 4.2.14 Room no. 4, mouth of the central niche from the west

were used for the construction of the partitions between the niches, they might have not been worked accurately. In this way, these blocks could have caused this distortion.

The individual niches were closed by two narrow wooden leaves which were fixed into pivot holders. These were placed in the corners of the mouths of the individual niches. In the case of the south and middle niches, the pivot holders are still *in situ*. The holders have the standard form of a limestone frame in which the door-leaf pivot was fixed. Below the pivot holders, there were basalt washers measuring 5–7.5 × 6–10 cm (see *fig. 4.2.14* and *pl. 26*) as is documented in the preserved examples. The washers were cemented in their places by quality, light-pink mortar. These basalt washers would have improved the stability of the pivots and also prevented the deterioration of the bottom of the pivot-holders. From the dimensions of the mouths of the niches, it clearly follows that the door-leaves were quite narrow, *i.e.* ca 27.5 cm wide. The doors opened outwards, towards the chapel room. The form of the wooden-leaves possibly resembled those examples shown in the decorations of tombs of the period when the mastaba was constructed.[302] In the shrine's original state, the interior of the separate niches bore no decoration. There are only a few simple signs and lines painted in ink on several places of the internal walls of the niches. They are, however, of later date and therefore will not be discussed here.

The upper rims of the niches were probably also decorated by the same polychrome bands as is the case with the side rims of the niches. Unfortunately, there is no direct proof which would help us with the reconstruction of the space above the niches. In this connection it is important to mention that there are no torus mouldings beside the rims of the individual niches. Therefore, it is rather improbable that every single niche might have been topped by a concave cornice.[303]

However, at the northern and southern end of the western wall of the chapel, there is a torus of about 7.7 cm wide with typical zigzagging.[304] Most likely, the

---

[302] See, *e.g.*, the illusive doors which decorated one of the walls in the serdab building belonging to Seshemnefer II – Junker, *Gîza* III, 188, Abb. 33–34; Brunner-Traut, *Seschemnofer*, Taf. 32.

[303] We cannot fully rule out that concave cornices were originally located above the individual niches, although there is no proof of this. The nearest comparable example, the niches in the Saqqara tomb of Djedkare's vizier Rashepses (*Cf. LD* I, Bl. 39) were not topped by such cornices. Also, in the case of the niche with the statue located in the pillared chapel in Mereruka. In his account on the results of his excavations of Sahure's pyramid complex (*Sahure* I, Abb. 31), L. Borchardt published the typical form of a torus topped by a concave cornice.

[304] Verner, *Reliefs*, Pl. 46, 48.

continuation of the torus was located above the niches. The existence of this torus seems to support our supposition, that the whole western wall of Room no. 4 represented one functional unit – a kind of false door (see discussion on this topic below in this chapter).

From the design of the niches, we can suspect that they once incorporated statues of Ptahshepses.[305] Nevertheless, it is not clear which types the statues were. As was already mentioned, in the decoration of the "narrow walls" we can see the figures of Ptahshepses. The figures always face towards the middle niche (*i.e.* to the right or to the left). Ptahshepses is depicted as a lector priest and as an official. Having in mind this fact we can hypothesize that the statues Ptahshepses erected in the niches presented him as an official and/or a priest. To answer this question, we should await the full publication of the statuary found in Ptahshepses' mastaba.[306] In the opinion of Barbora Patočková, the statues were life-sized and that the statues were standing.[307] However, having in mind the width of the niches (ca. 0.54–0.57 m), it is more than probable that the statues were slightly under-life sized. Standing statues in the niches of Room no. 4 are also hypothesized by M. Verner.[308] Contrary to these two suggestions, M. Rochholz supposes, that in the niches of Room no. 4, not only standing, but also seated statues of the tomb owner might have been erected.[309] His opinion is based on the relief decoration of this chapel and he links statues depicted on the eastern wall of Room no. 4[310] with those which were – in the opinion of Rochholz – likely to have been erected in the niches of the same room. Nevertheless, there is no possibility to make such connection as there is no direct proof for this hypothesis. More probable, in my opinion, remains the supposition of Patočková and Verner.

Beside the question of whether the statues had a standing, striding or seating form, there is also a question over whether or not the statues in the niches might have been erected on bases. We can encounter such a base in a similar situation in the instance of the engaged statue in the pillared room of Mereruka's mastaba in Saqqara.[311] Nevertheless, on the pavement and on the side walls of Ptahshepses' niches, there are no signs of mortar which would document the use of such a base, so it is not possible to ascertain whether the statues of Ptahshepses had bases or were without them. The same should also be said in connection with the material of which the statues were made: there is no piece of information available as yet which could help us to ascertain what materials would have been used and we need to wait for the publishing of the statuary from the mastaba.

On the basis that the statues of Ptahshepses were erected in the niches, one may suppose that the whole of the western wall of the chapel was composed as one large false door.[312] The alleged standing statues might have been depicted here as

---

[305] For this suggestion see, Smith, *HESPOK*, 55; Verner, *Reliefs*, 91, Patočková, *Fragmenty soch*, 139–140.

[306] This publication is in preparation by B. Patočková. In her M.A. thesis, she states that Ptahshepses might have been portrayed in his various roles and offices in these niches (Patočková, *Fragmenty soch*, 139). To answer this question, one can suppose that the easiest way would be presented by the comparison of the niche-statues in Ptahshepses' mastaba with those in the royal mortuary temple. Nevertheless, despite several suggestions, there is no clear indication of the form of statues erected in the chapels with five niches of the royal pyramid complexes (see: M. Rochholz, 'Sedfest, Sonnenheiligtum und Pyramidenbezirk. Zur Deutung der Grabanlagen der 5. und 6. Dynastie', in: *Ägyptische Tempel*, 265–266, notes 71 and 73) and all one can say is that different aspects of the kings were venerated in them. Such testimony seems to be hinted at in Neferirkare's papyrus archive (Posener-Kriéger, de Cenival, *Abu Sir Papyri*, Pls. IV and V; Posener-Kriéger, *Les papyrus d´Abousir*, 502).

[307] Patočková, *Fragmenty soch*, 138.

[308] Verner, *Reliefs*, 91.

[309] Rochholz, 'Statuen und Statuendarstellungen im Grab des *Ptḥ-špss*', *SÄK* 21 (1994) 262.

[310] Verner, *Reliefs*, 47–49, pl. 26, photos no. 41–42. Rochholz, *SÄK* 21 (1994) 262.

[311] This base bears the name and title of Mereruka on its front side (Duel, *Mereruka*, pl. 147–148).

[312] Verner, *Reliefs*, 91; Patočková, *Fragmenty soch*, 140.

"coming out" of the false door[313] in the same fashion as seen in Mereruka's tomb. From the existence of the torus (see discussion above), there is an implication that the existence of a concave cornice ran above all three niches. The concave cornice was a standard part of the false door in the period of the mastaba's construction.[314] Unfortunately, there is no direct proof for our hypothesis concerning the concave cornice running above Ptahshepses' statue niches. If the torus did continue above the niches, then we cannot rule out the idea that the frieze of *khekers* (and *djeds*) was placed above this torus. This supposition seems to be documented by fragments of such friezes which were found during the excavation of the mastaba. Moreover, it is very probable that this type of frieze crowned the side walls of Room no. 4.[315]

As the third eventuality of our tentative reconstructions of the original appearance of the upper part of the wall with niches, we can propound the idea that above the niches an architrave with one or more lines of hieroglyphic text was positioned (such an architrave might have been also the part of the hypothetical wall's design using the concave cornice and *kheker*-frieze). The existence of such an architrave cannot be excluded. Along the sides of the niches, there were the columns of hieroglyphic texts with the names and title of Ptahshepses. Such vertical lines of texts were usually complemented by horizontal texts in the case of false doors, niches with engaged statues, *etc.* Therefore, such horizontally arranged text(s) should also be presumed for the upper part of the wall.

The maximum height of the niches in Room no. 4 might have been 2.80 m (the proposed height of the room is 3.46 m, minus the height of the podium in front of the niches, and the distance of the torus from the ceiling of the room). The width of the niches is only 0.54–0.57 m. Therefore, if we take 2.80 m as the height of the niches, then such hypothetical "narrow" niches would have been too high for the life-sized (or even slightly under-life-sized) statues which were kept in them. Therefore, the niches were certainly lower (1.60–1.80 m?) than the above-mentioned maximum height. The free space between the ceiling of Room no. 4 and the upper level of the niches was undoubtedly filled by decoration in some way. As has been suggested, it seems that the vertical lines on the "narrow walls" of the niches were very probably supplemented by horizontal hieroglyphic text(s) above the niches. Such line(s) of hieroglyphic inscription might have filled the space between the upper rims of the niches and the torus. Whether the whole wall was crowned by the concave cornice or the *heker*–frieze, it is not possible to document, therefore, the answer for this question still remains open (for a schematic reconstruction of the chapel's western wall, see *pl. 27*).

Ludwig Borchardt had already mentioned the resemblance between the layout of Room no. 4 with that of the chapel with five niches in the royal mortuary temples of the same period of time.[316] These chapels with niches can be found in the royal mortuary temples from Userkaf's reign onwards.[317] In many cases, we can see that in front of the individual niches, small staircases were placed – a feature which is also attested in Room no. 4 in of the Mastaba of Ptahshepses. As is the case with Room no. 4, the niches were closed by wooden doors. On the other hand, a wider

---

313 Patočková, *Fragmenty soch*, 140.

314 Both false doors in Ti's offering chapel, which are chronologically close to the construction date of the Mastaba of Ptahshepses, can be mentioned here – Steindorf, *Grab des Ti*, Taf. 135, 139 and Wild, *Le tombeau de Ti* III, Cl. CLXXXII and CLXXXIV.

315 See Verner, *Reliefs*, 66; Vachala, *Relieffragmente*, Bl. 16, 37. Also E. Brovarski considers that the uppermost parts of the walls in Senedjemib Inti's tomb may have been topped by the *kheker*-frieze: Brovarski, *Senedjemib Inti*, 22.

316 Borchardt, *Sahure* I, 20–21. Abb. 16; Brinks, *LÄ* III, 1225.

317 See Labrousse, *Userkaf*, Borchardt, *Sahure* I, 9–10, 20–21, Abb. 16, Bl. 16; *MRA* VII, Tav. 6, 7; Borchardt, *Neferirkare*, 7–8, 27–28, Bl. 20; *MRA* VII, Tav. 10, 12, 14. In the case of the mortuary temples of Niuserre: Borchardt, *Neuserre*, *MRA* VIII, 24–26, Tav. 4–5; Djedkare: *MRA* VIII, 78, Tav. 15; Unas: Labrousse, Lauer, Leclant, *Le Temple haut du Ounas*, 46, Fig. 32; Teti: Labrousse, Lauer, *Teti*, 27–28, pl. XXXV; Pepi I: Leclant, *Pépi* I, 20–21, Fig. 3; Pepi II: Jéquier, *Pepi II*, 24–26, pl. 1, 34), the halls with niches are destroyed to a large extant.

range of materials was used for the construction of the royal halls with niches than were used in Room no. 4. Travertine, basalt, black and red granite, white limestone and wood were used for the construction of niches in the royal temples. Ptahshepses only used limestone and, in a very restricted extent, some basalt. Unlike the royal temples, we cannot suppose that the ceiling of the niches for Ptahshepses was decorated with stars – no fragment of such a decoration was found. One can see such decoration in the case, *e.g.*, of Sahure's hall with niches.[318] Thus we can see that Ptahshepses – despite the fact that he was a powerful magnate and the highest official in the country – was limited in his endeavour to make use of the "royal" elements of architecture. This limitation was presumably imposed because he was of non-royal stock.

We should also add here that in the queens' mortuary temples we can encounter chapels with niches. The number of niches is, in the majority of cases, the same as in Ptahshepses' Room no. 4: three niches.[319] The halls with three niches represent a kind of standard for the pyramid complexes of queens.[320] In these niches, located in the western walls of the chapels, the statues of queens were housed. As is the case in the chapel of Ptahshepses, we do not know in which form the queens were portrayed in the individual niches. However, the arrangement of the queens' chapels with niches was different to that in the Mastaba of Ptahshepses. The main communication running through these offering chapels was oriented in a north-south direction, on contrary to that the main communication in Ptahshepses' chapel lies along an east-west direction. On the other hand, despite the fact that they were not equipped with staircases, the queens' niches are – in a majority of cases – elevated above the floors of the chapels.

Room no. 4 in the Mastaba of Ptahshepses is rather extraordinary in its design as regard to the usual layout for non-royal architecture. Leaving aside the examples from the royal mortuary temples, the closest analogies coming from the Fifth and the Sixth Dynasties can be found in two Saqqara tombs – those of Rashepses and Ankhmare. They have been chosen here especially because of the number of the niches in their chapels. The tomb of Rashepses was built to the north west of Netjerikhet's pyramid complex in Saqqara during the reign of King Djedkare.[321] In this mastaba, we encounter a complex ground plan consisting of an open courtyard, an offering room, serdab, corridors and halls and also a pillared hall with three niches in its western wall. In contrast to those in Ptahshepses' mastaba, the niches in this tomb had a different design. The most important difference is the absence of a podium in front of the niches and of small staircases leading to the separate niches. Unfortunately, Lepsius' documentation does not tell us whether the niches were equipped by wooden doors, nevertheless, it is more probable that if there had been, there would have been some indication of pivot holders, and Lepsius would have recorded them. Thus it seems that the niches were not equipped with door-leaves.[322] The niches in Rashepses' tomb were wider (and had a larger length/width ratio) to those in the Mastaba of Ptahshepses.[323] Another close analogy to the niches in Ptahshepses chapel is found in the tomb of Ankhmare.[324] In this case we can

---

[318] See Borchardt, *Sahure* I, 56.

[319] In the case of the double tomb of Queen Nebet and Khenu (Munro, *Unas-Friedhof*, Taf. 1) there are four niches and in Wedjebten's mortuary temple only two niches (Jéquier, *Oudjebten*, 12, pl. 1).

[320] Jánosi, *Pyramidenanlagen*, 145–149.

[321] *PM* III, 494–496, plan XLIX; L*D* I, Bl. 36, L*D* Text I, 165–167.

[322] L*D* I, Bl. 39, *PM* III, Pl. XLIX.

[323] Rashepses, like Ptahshepses, not only obtained the title of *ỉmj-rꜥ k3(w)t nbt nt nśwt* but during the course of his lifetime also rose to be *ṯ3tj tꜥjtj n s3b* (Baer, *Rank and Title*, 101, 292; Strudwick in his *Administration*, 116–117, dates him to the middle of Djedkare's reign.) We can, therefore, ask whether his high position can make a kind of connection between these two tombs and their owners. Both of men might have been able to incorporate niches, the element of "royal" architecture also in their tombs, because of their high rank.

[324] *PM* III, Mariette, *Mastabas*, D 40, 280–284, plan on p. 280.

see a wide hall with three niches. It is not possible to discern from Mariette's plan whether they were equipped with wooden doors or not. In the plan of the cultic rooms of the mastaba it clearly shows that the chapel with three niches was directly connected with the main (also east-west oriented) offering hall of the tomb. This layout was quite similar to that of the mortuary temples of queens.[325]

In the Memphite area, the use of niches in non-royal tombs was not infrequent – as is shown by several examples in Giza. These tombs belonged to both the highest echelons of Egyptian society, as well as the middle strata of the Egyptian bureaucracy. The older examples, dated to the Fourth Dynasty, are those of Kawab (G 7120)[326] and Minkhaef (G 7430, G 7440).[327] Contrary to the previous examples, the owner of another tomb, Rawer, did not possess these high-ranking titles,[328] but he was able to build a complicated tomb, adorned with an extensive number of statues. Altogether, the tomb comprised twenty niches,[329] some of them with similar niches to those attested in the Mastaba of Ptahshepses.

We also have examples of the use of niches in rock-cut tombs – not only in the Memphite necropolis,[330] but also from the provinces.[331]

We can see from the previous list of the analogies that rooms with niches were not exceptional in private tombs of the Old Kingdom. The Chapel with Three Niches in the Mastaba of Ptahshepses, on other hand, is outstanding in the way the niches were architecturally designed. In this connection, Room no. 4 represents another attestation of Ptahshepses' efforts to follow the forms of royal mortuary architecture. The form of the western wall with niches was apparently influenced by its models in the royal mortuary temples – as in those of the kings (in its architectural forms) – or as in those of queens (in the number of niches).

One further problem we need to look at is the question of the rituals that were connected with Ptahshepses' Chapel with Three Niches. The chapel is located in the central position of the annex, which was constructed during the second building stage; it lies at the intersection of the supposed main route from the Old Portico (no. 3.) to the Chapel with Three Niches (no. 4) and the route between the Southern

---

325 The dating of this tomb owner is found in Baer, *Rank and Title*, 64: Baer estimates that Ankhmare belongs to the time of Menkauhor or later. It follows, from the titles documented on his false-doors, that Ankhmare was of lower rank than Ptahshepses and Rashepses.

326 The chapel with niches is located in the chapel's western wall. Two of Kawab's niches were constructed on the same level and two or three statues of the tomb's owner were placed in them. See *PM* III, 187; Reisner, *Giza Necropolis*, fig. 6; Simpson, *Kawab*, 2, Fig. 5; Jánosi, *Giza* I, 193–194, Abb. 46.

327 The chapel was equipped with four niches located in the west wall – Reisner, *Giza Necropolis* , fig. 7. Both Minkhaef and Kawab were of royal descent and they possessed titles which closely connected them with the king (*s3 nśwt n ẖt.f, rpꜥt ḥ3tj-ꜥ, ṯ3tj tꜥjtj n ś3b, pr ḏḥwtj, imj-rꜥ k3t nbt nt nśwt, s3w nḫn, r P nb, śmr-wꜥtj, ẖrj-ḥb, ḥrj-tp* – see: Smith, *JEA* 19 (1933), 150.

328 See Hassan, *Gîza* I, 2–3.

329 *PM* III, 265–269, plan XXXIII, Hassan, *Gîza* I, 4–38, plan on the frontispiece, see especially the site plan, and the room showing a hall with five niches in its western wall on pl. 5.

330 Nebemakhet's tomb in Giza dated to the Fourth Dynasty (*PM* III, 230–232; Hassan, *Gîza* IV, fig. 72; Jánosi, *Giza* I, Abb. 90). It is apparent that the introduction of niches was not part of the original plan of the room and that they were cut into the rooms at a later date – see Jánosi, *Giza*, 362–363.

331 Tjauty's tomb in Qasr es-Saijad (Brunner, *Felsgräber*, 46–47, Abb. 24). In this tomb, we encounter a chapel with niches in its western wall. On the other hand, there are several contextual problems. Firstly, the tomb is dated to the Sixth Dynasty; secondly the number of niches is four, not three as in the example of the Chapel with Three Niches in the Mastaba of Ptahshepses; thirdly the dimensions of the niches are quite small. As was mentioned by H. Brunner (*Felgräber*, 46–47), the layout of the tomb and also that of the respective chapel has been influenced by the mastaba-tombs of the Residential area. The explanation for this we can see in Tjauty's engagement in high offices within the Residence. In another provincial tomb – that of Inti, located in the cemetery of Deshasha (Petrie, *Deshasheh*, 5, pl. III), we can also see three niches in the western wall of the rock-cut tomb. However, the niches did not have the same layout nor the same function as those in the Mastaba of Ptahshepses. The middle niche was broader; moreover, its rear panel hid the entrance to the corridor leading to the burial chamber. The side niches functioned as serdabs.

Portico (no. 10) and the Northern Storerooms. Moreover, the decoration of both the north and the south walls of Room no. 4[332] depicts offering bearers and the offerings which were meant to be brought to Ptahshepses. As well as these stylistic offering bearers, Ptahshepses' sons bringing the offerings are also depicted on these two walls.

Having in mind the supposition that the entire western wall was designed as a large false door, the section with its three niches might have functioned as a place where some types of offering rituals for the deceased tomb owner, symbolised by his three statues placed in the niches, were likely to be made. As distinct from the standard examples of other offering rooms (see *chapter 4.1.9*), there was no side altar attested in this chapel. There would have been no purpose to the flights of steps before each niche if they did not serve as a pathway to the podium located below the niches at the top where, no doubt, the offerings were placed. This use of the steps may serve to explain why no side altar was found in this room. Be that as it may, there is no direct proof for any hypothesis concerning the ritual which might have been once executed in connection with the statues erected in the niches nonetheless, the architectural forms used in Room no. 4 of the Mastaba of Ptahshepses are rather close to their royal models. This fact seems to indicate that similar rituals were also connected with the niches in Ptahshepses' Room no. 4, although we have no evidence for this. [333]

4.2.6 Rooms nos. 5–9 – Northern Storerooms

To the north of Room no. 4, there is a group of five rooms (nos. 5–9). The walls of these spaces, dressed by well worked and smoothed blocks of white limestone, are quite well preserved. The floor of these rooms was also made of well worked flat limestone blocks. No part of a ceiling in any room in this sector of the mastaba remained *in situ* but the originally masonry is preserved up to ca. 3.30 m above the pavement of these rooms. Because the width of the rooms does not exceed 2.11 m, it is very probable, that the rooms were roofed by large limestone beams. They were probably positioned above the respective spaces transverse to their longer axes. No trace of a support was found in this area. It is not possible to ascertain the precise height of the rooms in this sector of the mastaba. The ceilings in this part of the mastaba – at least in the spaces which directly adjoin Room no. 4 (*i.e.* nos. 5, 7 and 8) – were probably constructed at the same height as that of the chapel (3.46 m, see p. 92). Constructional reasons are responsible for this supposition.

Room no. 5 has an irregular ground-plan and was 2.5 m wide in its west part, 2.08 m wide in the east side and 3.78 m long. Its southern wall once had a door leading to the Chapel with Three Niches. Very probably, this door had been blocked up by J. de Morgan after his excavations of the mastaba. In the north wall of Room no. 5, there is a doorway to Room no. 9 (see *figs. 4.2.15, 4.2.16*). This doorway is 0.74 m wide and 0.58 m long. Originally in the doorway, there had been a wooden door leaf. The limestone holder for the door pivot survived. Its form, together with the scratches made by the door leaf on the floor pavement, confirm that the door opened into Room no. 9. There is no relief decoration detected in this room, so it is hard to ascertain its function. The eastern half of the room forms a kind of "niche", therefore, it is not impossible to assume that this part might have been used for depositing of some goods and instruments.

Room no. 9, connecting the individual rooms in this part of the annex, is quite a large space, oriented in an east-west direction. Its width is 2.11 m and the length

---

[332] Verner, *Reliefs*, 64–91, pls. 31–44, photos 48–75.

[333] Having in mind all the differences in the status of a king and an official, it can be mentioned here, that Neferirkare's papyrus archive informs us that all the statues of the king kept in the hall with five niches of his mortuary temple experienced a daily cleansing, they were enrobed and also censed in the regular way (Posener-Kriéger, *Les papyrus d´Abousir*, 52–57, 501–504, 537, 544) and one would expect that their ritual meals were then presented to them at the proper hours.

Fig. 4.2.15 Doorway between Room nos. 5 and 9

Fig. 4.2.16 Doorway between Room nos. 5 and 9, door-jamb with pits for the door latches

Fig. 4.2.17 Room no. 9, one of the re-used blocks with erased relief decoration

6.68 m. As was already mentioned, its western wall was formed by the original eastern façade of the Initial Mastaba. It goes without saying that the wall is sloped at the same angle as the casing of the Initial Mastaba (82°). Following the alleged method of construction regarding the ceilings in this part of the annex, we can reconstruct the original height of the ceiling at a level of 3.46 m. Most probably, the ceiling blocks were laid in a north-south direction. The room was apparently used as a corridor, linking Room nos. 5, 6, 7 and 8.

Fig. 4.2.18 Room nos. 7 and 9 – present situation

As was the case with Room no. 5 and all of other rooms in the northern sector of the annex, there is no relief decoration on the wall casing of Room no. 9. Nevertheless, some blocks built into the wall casing are re-used blocks, originally decorated with relief decoration. One can quite easily recognize the original relief decoration. On the photograph (*fig. 4.2.17*), the traces of the original scene – offering bearers – can be identified. There is no idea from which building it might have come, but one can suppose that it might have represented some non-royal tomb whose construction was dismantled.[334] Moreover, one can only assume that this tomb might have been originally built somewhere in the area of the Abusir pyramid plateau.[335]

In the southern wall of Room no. 9, between the entrances to Rooms no. 5 and 8, there is a deep niche – Room no. 7. It is 2.77 m long and 2.08 m wide. If the supposition concerning the construction of the ceilings in this part of the annex is right, then its ceiling was at a height of 3.46 m. The function of this room, which is also dressed by well worked limestone blocks, is not fully clear. Most probably it served as a storeroom. This niche is distinguished by its "openness", therefore the less precious implements might have been kept there (see *fig. 4.2.18*).[336]

Another doorway was located in the southern end of the east wall of Room no. 9. It gave access to Room no. 6. The room is 2.70 m long and 2.58 m wide. Originally, the room was paved with large, flat limestone blocks: nevertheless, the paving survived only in the doorway to the room. Apart from the small staircases in the Chapel with Three Niches, Room 6 was the only room in the annex which was equipped with a staircase. The staircase is 0.76 m wide and only five steps of the lowermost wing of the staircase have survived until the present day (see *figs. 4.2.19, 4.2.20*). Each step of the staircase is 0.19 m high. The larger part of the first four steps was cut out of one large piece of white limestone,[337] however, the other (circa one fifth of the width of the staircase) was created by another block, forming also a part of the side wall. This latter part has been made of apparently inferior limestone, therefore, this part of the staircase is less preserved than the other one. Nevertheless the fact that its surface was well worked and smoothed it survived with well visible marks of use on its faces. The last (uppermost) surviving step in Room no. 6 represents a small landing (0.64 × 0.76 m) created by another large block of white limestone. This landing was cut into the casing of the north wall of

---

[334] This habit of re-using of building material is not exceptional. It has been, for example, documented in the masonry of partition walls secondarily built in the court of Qar's tomb in Abusir-South. But also the re-using of the building material in the royal monuments was rather widespread.

[335] As was already mentioned in *chapter 3*, due to the large number of constructions and late activities (stone-mining, secondary burying), the area of the Abusir Pyramid Necropolis does not offer until now no direct attestations of the older tombs than those located in the Cemetery of Nobles. Despite it, their existence might have been presupposed.

[336] The ground plan of the niche might lead us to the supposition that the niche was the place where the statue of the deceased was erected and its cult was running. Such hypothetical supposition which can arise is not possible to support with evidence. Due to the non-existence of decoration in this room the other functions might be considered preferable.

[337] The same technique, using one piece of the stone, but as a matter of course on a larger scale, can be encountered in the storerooms of Sahure's mortuary temple – see Borchardt, *Sahure* I, 60–62, Abb. 76–78.

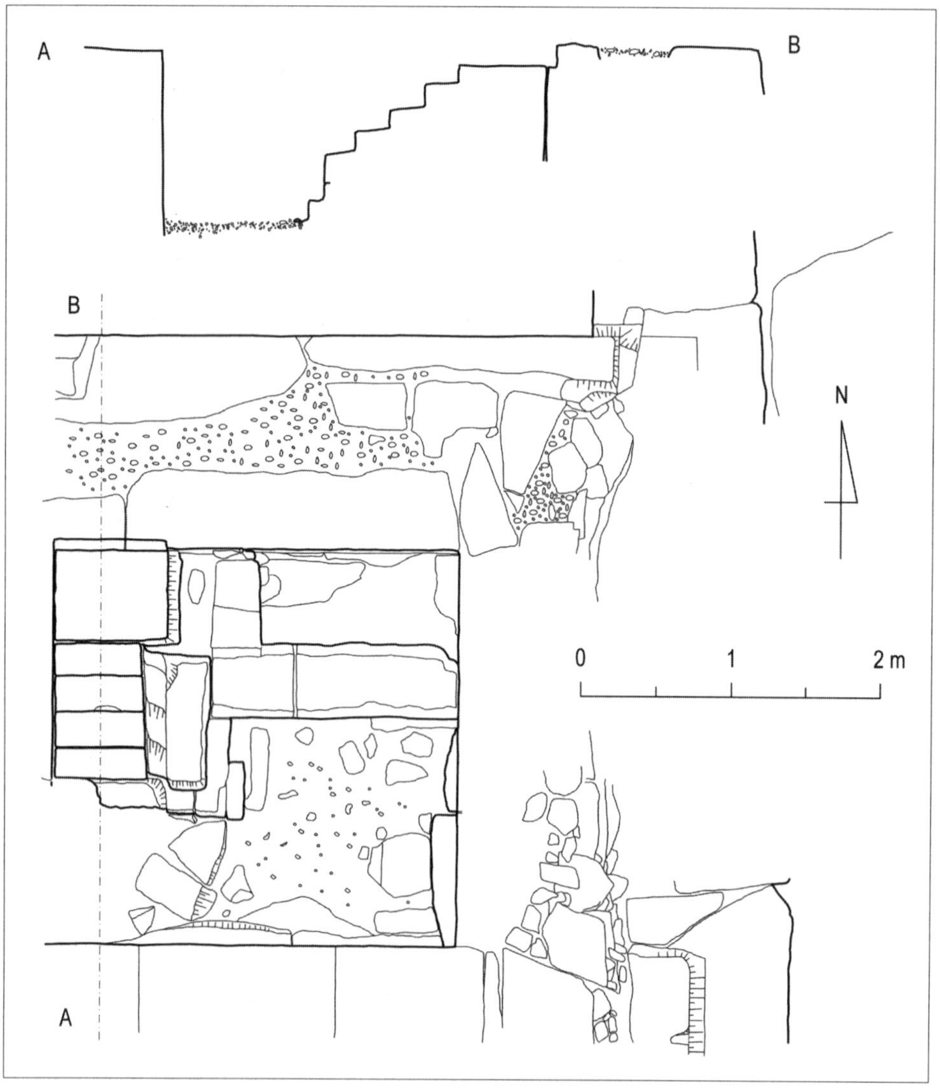

Fig. 4.2.19 Room no. 6, plan and section through the stairway along its western wall

the room to a depth of 0.07 m (see *figs. 4.2.19* and *4.2.21*). As was the case of the lower fly of the staircase, also the surface of the landing was carefully worked and smoothed.

To the east of the staircase itself, there are several blocks of a wall which had a north-south direction; unfortunately, this wall is now almost lost. The wall was originally 0.50 m broad (it probably supported the ceiling of the room). Only several remaining blocks show that an auxiliary wall running at a distance of 0.70 m in parallel to the north wall of Room no. 6 was once constructed of flat fragments of limestone.[338] The masonry, which once had filled the space between the auxiliary wall and the northern wall of the room, was also built quite carefully with flat fragments of limestone. They can be still partially seen *in situ* (see *fig. 4.2.19*), too. Both the above mentioned walls – the wall built in the north-south direction as well as the wall running in parallel to the north wall of the room – were connected with another wall built in parallel to the north wall of the room.

Apparently, the auxiliary wall running in parallel to the north wall of the room and the filling masonry created a kind of a base for the second wing of the staircase. In this way, it is possible to say, that this wing was built in an east-western direction. The existence of this second wing seems to be proved by the landing which crowns the preserved part of the staircase. A very small part of the first step of the second wing of the staircase which was cut partially into the casing of the room is preserved. This small detail, together with the presence of the above mentioned auxiliary wall,

[338] See also Fiala, in: *Preliminary Report*, 49–50.

Fig. 4.2.20 Room no. 6 from the south

Fig. 4.2.21 Room no. 6, notch of a step made into the northern wall of the chamber

documents the fact that the direction of the staircase changed from north-south to east-west on this landing.

The faces of the room's casing in the space closed by this auxiliary wall below the second wing of the staircase are smoothed. The smoothing of the blocks seems to confirm that the layout of Room no. 6 was changed after the completion of the room's casing, or more precisely, of its lower part (the masonry of the room is preserved only up to 1 m above its pavement). When this decision for change was made, a supporting wall was added and the northern part of the room was filled in with masonry. After this, the construction of the staircase was started.

Any conclusion in respect of the height and number of wings of the staircase can be verified. If we would assume that there was another wing of steps then we should also suppose the existence of the upper floor (or "semi-floor") in Room no. 6. From actual observation at the site, and the way in which the staircase might have been constructed, we can suppose that the ceiling of the lower floor might have been at a height of 1.90 m above its pavement. The hypothetical upper floor then could have been constructed to a height of 2.40 m. As the tentative reconstruction shows, this upper floor could not have been built above the entire lower floor. The ceiling of this upper floor might have been constructed at a height of ca 3.90 m above the pavement of the lower floor of Room no. 6.

On the other hand, it cannot be fully ruled out that there was another, third, staircase wing, running, most probably, along the eastern wall of the room. In this case, the second floor would be, as a matter of course, constructed at a higher level – in ca 2.90 m. The rougher nature of the southern half of the eastern wall of Room no. 6 may suggest that another supporting wall for the staircase might also have been constructed along this wall. It represents the only evidence for this hypothetical proposition which cannot be documented in any other way.

The function of Room no. 6 seems to be obvious: it served as a storeroom. In his account on the mastaba's architecture, V. Fiala supposed that this room, because of the width of its walls and because of the existence of the doorway (opening inside the room), contained more valuable goods.[339] This supposition cannot be confirmed, *e.g.*, by finds of such goods during the archaeological excavation.

From the previous discussion it follows that the staircase in Room no. 6 was designed in the same way as the staircase in the "treasury" of Neferirkare's mortuary temple – along the side walls of the room.[340] In this case, however, we find a combination of mud bricks and of limestone masonry which was the consequence of the non-standard development of the mortuary temple. In the standard method, the storerooms of the royal mortuary temples were of greater length/width index (Room no. 6 is almost squarish) and the staircases in these storerooms are designed in a different way, *i.e.* along one of the longer walls of the storerooms. The staircase of royal mortuary temples consisted in many cases of one, or at most of two wings of steps.[341]

V. Fiala supposed that the upper floor of Room no. 6 extended over the area marked by Z. Žába as "Room no. 2". As Fiala himself adds, this supposition cannot be confirmed by the remaining masonry.[342] Moreover, we know that the casing of the eastern façade of the annex constructed during the second building stage was laid down and (at least partially) finished. If the upper floor of Room no. 6 had really been extended above "Room no. 2", then it would have been confronted by considerable difficulties. The builders would have had to cut through not only the core masonry, but also through the casing of the annex which had already been finished.

Room no. 8 is the smallest room in the annex of the second building stage: it also represents "the most confined" room in this complex of storerooms (see *fig. 4.2.22*). Its entrance is located in the south-western corner of Room no. 8 by a doorway which is 1.59 m high (the lintel of the doorway is designed on two levels, the recess thus formed in the lintel enabled the insertion of the wooden door frame 1.65 m high and 0.79 m wide (*fig. 4.2.23*). The pivot holder in the floor of the room did not survive and the block which housed it was removed (very probably by stone robbers). However, the pivot block has survived in the lintel of the doorway. The lintel above the doorway consists of one large limestone block whose dimensions are 1.14 (1.08) × 0.79 × 1.65 m. The pivot holder is represented by a circular hollow with a diameter 7.5 cm and a depth of 1.8 cm. There is an oblong, shallow recess around it. It served for the insertion of a wooden beam, which might have reinforced the whole construction of the door. As we find quite frequently in this mastaba, the

---

339 Fiala, in: *Preliminary Report*, 49.

340 Borchardt, *Neferirkare*, Bl. 10. In this case, however, we find a combination of mud bricks and of limestone masonry.

341 *Cf.* Borchardt, *Sahure* I, 22–24, Abb. 17, 19.

342 Fiala, in: *Preliminary Report*, 50.

Fig. 4.2.22 (right) Room no. 8 during the archaeological excavation

Fig. 4.2.23 (left) Room no. 8, entrance from the north-east

doorway also contained a hollow for the latch. This hollow is located in the west wall of the doorway and it had an oblong shape (width 9 cm, length 10 cm, depth 8 cm). It is not possible to discern whether some part of the door construction was made of metal as we can see, *e.g.*, in several examples in Sahure's mortuary temple.[343]

Room no. 8 is 2.00 m long and 1.25 m wide. Its western wall formed the eastern façade of the Initial Mastaba. Therefore, it is inclined at the same angle (82°), as is also the case with Room no. 6, V. Fiala suggested that the more precious items of the tomb's utensils might have been kept here.[344] This supposition has been made mainly because of the existence of the lockable doorway and the quite small dimensions of the room. As was also the case for Room no. 6, this hypothesis cannot be verified (*e.g.* by the discovery of any such instruments).

4.2.7 Room no. 10 – the Southern Portico

This space is represented by a broad recess constructed to the south of the Chapel with Three Niches; it is situated in the southern outer wall of the annex of the second building stage. The dimensions of this space are 2.30–2.45 × 6.40 m. From these figures, it follows that the side walls of the portico are not equally long.[345] The original length of both the side walls would certainly have been 2.45 m (see *fig. 4.2.24*).

Fig. 4.2.24 Room no. 10 (Southern Portico) during the archaeological works of Z. Žába, view from the south

[343] Borchardt, *Neuserre*, 38, Abb. 34–35.

[344] See Fiala, in: *Preliminary Report*, 49.

[345] For further discussion concerning explanation of this fact see *chapters 4.2.1* and *4.3.5*.

The ground plan of the portico shows that this space served as an entrance leading to Room no. 4 (or *vice versa* from Room no. 4 to the above discussed hypothetical courtyard). Its walls were decorated with polychrome reliefs which certainly needed to be protected by a ceiling. Room no. 10 is quite long, therefore, it is surprising that no support for such a ceiling survived or was documented. It was certainly not possible to span such a length without the use of supports. Very early on, J. de Morgan was intrigued by this area. Despite the fact that he did not find any traces of them, he supposed that two "columns" had supported the ceiling in this recess.[346] As it is possible to see on the plan of the part of the mastaba excavated by de Morgan,[347] he was not sure about the existence of these supports. He traced these supports as pillars by dotted lines in the plan (see *fig. 1.4* and *pl. 28*). Although Z. Žába wanted to prove the existence of these ephemeral pillars by new excavations in 1961, he was unable to confirm their existence. Despite this fact, the existence of supports in the entrance-recess should be taken into the consideration.[348]

The ceiling of the recess once covered quite a large area (15.7 m^2) and even though no evidence for them was found, it should be assumed that a pair of supports might have existed here. These supports were likely to be two columns, rather than two pillars.[349] If two columns were erected in the Old Portico, it is logical to suppose that a pair of columns was also erected in the Southern Portico. If this was the case then the issue of which column type might have been used in the portico still remains. It could have been a plain shaft column type. We can encounter such columns in entrances to the Giza tomb of Neferseshem IV,[350] Rawer[351] or that of Senedjemib Inti.[352] The cylindrical columns were also erected in the side entrances to Sahure's valley and mortuary temples in Abusir.[353] On the other hand, the use of floral column types should be taken into consideration. Should this supposition be correct, then it should be pointed out here that only lotus columns were used in the Old and the New Porticos. Following on from this, it is possible to suppose that the ceiling of the Southern Portico might have been supported by two, bundle lotus columns (for the three-dimensional visualisation of this hypothesis, see *pl. 29*).[354] For the use of plain or even papyrus bundle column types there is no evidence (not even of indirect nature; for further discussion, see *chapter 5*).

As already mentioned in the case of Room no. 4, it is not clear whether in this building stage the walls of the portico were already decorated by coloured reliefs, or, whether their completion was part of the third building stage. There is no distinct indication between the parts of the decoration which might have been assigned to the second and which to the third building stage. In the light of this uncertainty, we shall assume that its decoration was a part of work executed in the third building stage. During this building stage, the space of the recess underwent a major enlargement which greatly changed the layout of the Southern Portico (see *chapter 4.3.5* for further details).

---

346 De Morgan, *RevArch* 24 (3e série) (1894), 24.
347 *Op. cit.*, fig. 2.
348 There is a possibility that there might have been a protective roof protrusion running around the edge of the portico. That would protect the reliefs, but yet not need any supporting structures. However, the dimensions of the Old Portico and the Southern Portico are comparable. Therefore, one can expect, that there once were supports in the recess of the Southern Portico.
349 In this connection it is important to mention that the pillars were used in the entrances to the mastabas mainly in Saqqara. We can encounter pillars in the porticos of the tomb of Niankhkhnum and Khnumhotep, Kaemtjenenet, Isesiankh, Ptahhotep I and Ti.
350 Junker, *Gîza* II, 101.
351 Hassan, *Gîza* I, fig. 1.
352 Brovarski, *Senedjemib*, 12–13.
353 Borchardt, *Sahure* I, 35, 62–64, Abb. 28, 79 and 80; Bl. 1.
354 Realistically, there is no possibility of ascertaining the number of stalks in these hypothetical columns.

4.2.8 Expansion of the mastaba to the north

During this building stage, stonework construction which magnified the mastaba along its entire northern façade (together with the newly built annex) was presumably carried out. It extended the mastaba for 2.65 m to the north. The stone enlargement was laid down *after* the casing of the long northern wall of the Initial Mastaba and the new annex had been put into place. On the other hand, as this enlargement was hidden behind the casing added during the third building stage, it is clear that it was constructed *before* this second lot of casing was laid. These facts establish its relative chronological position between the construction of the annex of the second building stage and the casing of the third building stage. The reasons for this enlargement are not fully clear.

The expanded stonework in this area does not include any free spaces or rooms. It seems to us that there was no practical need to enlarge the mastaba at what must have been considerable expense to the magnate. Among the reasons which might have been hypothetically taken into our consideration may have been some aesthetic aspect (mainly having in mind the view from the east, a need for some alteration of the length/height proportion might have arisen).

Fig. 4.2.25 Filling masonry with casing added from the north to the masonry of the Initial Mastaba

The study of the masonry in the northern sector of the mastaba has revealed (see *fig. 4.2.25*) that – as was the case regarding the cladding of the first building stage – the casing of the second building stage was built on a layer constructed of flat blocks of limestone. After the first layer of the casing had been set down, the filling masonry was added. On the level of the upper faces of the lowermost casing blocks the second layer of flat local limestone blocks was constructed. Then another layer of the casing blocks was added. After that came the filling masonry, and then the third layer of flat limestone fragments. Only lower part (up to 1.5 m) of this masonry survived, however, we can hypothesize that it was also constructed in the similar way in its upper parts. The filling masonry not only consisted of fragments of local limestone and detritus, but also of fragments of granite and basalt which were certainly collected from neighbouring construction sites and dumps of the royal pyramid complexes. This building technique resembles the technique used in the case of partition walls built in the royal mortuary complexes. In this case, the filling masonry was covered on both sides by the final casings.[355]

---

[355] See Arnold, *Building*, fig. 4.72.3.

4.2.9 Summary of chapter 4.2

The overall effect of the second building stage was to increase the size of the monument: however, this change of the mastaba's size was only the external and superficial alteration: more important were the alternations in the purpose, function and effect of the entire structure which were realised by the additions of several inner rooms. The newly added annex started a change of what had been, generally said, a standard mastaba form into an edifice that can only be called a temple-tomb. Despite the above mentioned size of the enlarged tomb, the added masonry was not massive as we can still see in the Initial Mastaba, but it incorporated much more free space of cultic and storage rooms. For the first time in Egypt, to our knowledge, a triple shrine derivative of the royal complexes had been included in a non-royal tomb. In this shrine, statues were erected which played an important role in the rituals conducted in the tomb. A new entrance to the tomb was adorned by a pair of lotus bundle columns: this is another feature of architecture which is new to the non-royal tombs of the Old Kingdom and which shows the importance of the tomb builder and his social status. Apparently, Ptahshepses was influenced by the architecture of the neighbouring pyramid complexes, especially that of Sahure. For reasons which are not obvious to us, Ptahshepses decided to enlarge the mastaba to the north after the erection of masonry of the second building stage's annex and one can only suppose that this northern addition which did not possess any internal room came into existence because of the aesthetic impact on the visitors. Nevertheless, it is evident that even all this majesty was not enough for Ptahshepses. Thus, he decided, very probably before the completion of the inner decoration in the newly built annex, to enlarge his mastaba to the enormous dimensions of its third building stage.

4.3 The third building stage

Despite the fact that, from the architectural point of view, the annex built during the second building stage was almost finished, it seems that Ptahshepses decided to enlarge his tomb for a second time. During this third building stage Ptahshepses continued in his efforts to change the above ground part of his tomb into a temple-like monument comprising altogether forty inner rooms and other spaces (see *fig. 4.3.1*). Given that not all the rooms and all the masonry of the tomb

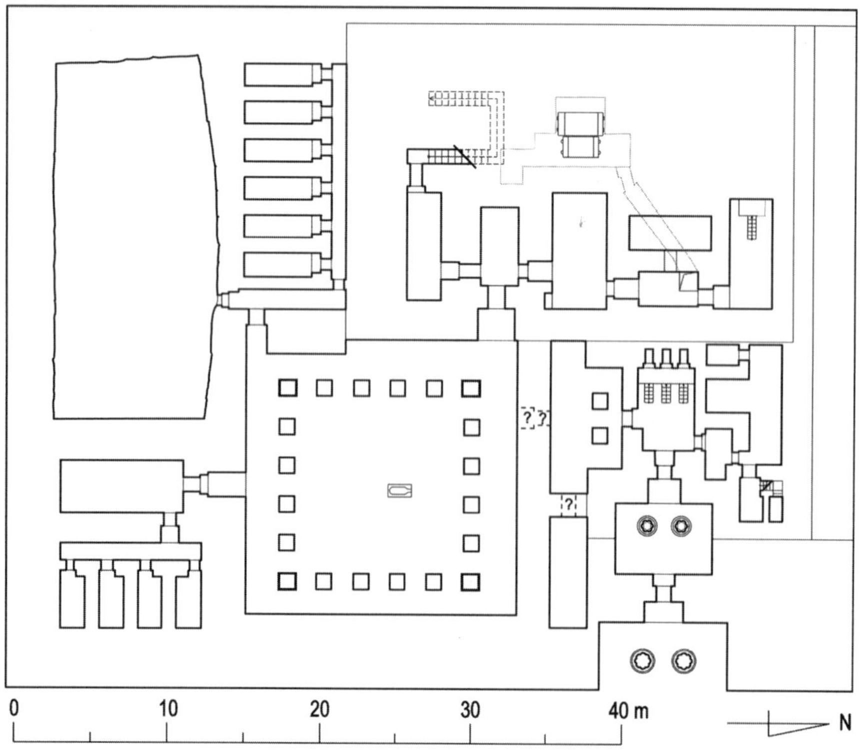

Fig. 4.3.1 Overall plan of the mastaba during the third building stage

were finished by the time of his death (see hereafter), we may be allowed to suppose that he overestimated his potential. It is obvious that his plan was so grandiose, that Ptahshepses had to use lower quality building techniques for the core masonry and also inferior building material (mainly limestone) for the casing and the creation of some of architectural features. Moreover, the core masonry was not built with a great deal of care. The builders depended for strength on the massiveness of the masonry and also on the wall casing. This opinion is borne out by the fact that this masonry ended up being very poorly preserved.

4.3.1 Casing and dimensions of the third building stage

Unlike the stonework built during the two previous building stages (*cf. chapters 4.1.1* and *4.2.1*), the masonry and the mastaba's casing was not hidden by later additions. Therefore, despite the fact that a large part of the tomb's casing had been removed, it is easier to follow the original face of the mastaba. The casing has, in parts, survived along the south outer wall (at its eastern end), the west wall (by its southern end) and the east wall (the casing has survived particularly well only in the area of the New Portico – see *figs. 4.3.2, 4.3.3* and *4.3.6*).

Fig. 4.3.2 Mastaba from the south-east; in the foreground are the remains of the casing of the south-eastern corner built during the third building stage

Fig. 4.3.3 Overall view of the mastaba from the south-west

The original casing of the third building stage of the north wall is the best preserved and it is possible to follow its line in roughly 75 per cent of its length. In fact, this surviving part came into existence before the commencement of the third building stage (see *chapter 4.2.8*). Apparently the ancient builders continued its line and used it during the third stage (see *fig. 4.3.4*). The casing of the western

Fig. 4.3.4 The area to the north-east from Room no. 6 with the masonry joined onto the casing of the eastern and northern outer wall of the second building stage annex during the third building stage

wall, though, represents a more complicated problem. The casing (and also the core masonry) constructed during the third building stage overlaps for 1.06 m the face of the western wall that had been built during the first building stage (see also *chapter 4.1.1*). Unfortunately, in the area of the junction between the Initial Mastaba and the masonry added during the third building stage, the masonry is destroyed. It is therefore not possible to say whether the casing of the western outer wall of the mastaba was lengthened as far as the north-western corner of the tomb, in line with the casing built during the third building stage (see *fig. 4.3.1*), or, whether a corner in the casing was made in the area of this join and no masonry was added to the casing of the Initial Mastaba. Regrettably, Žába's archaeological excavations have not shed any light on the answer to this question.[356] From the architectural point of view, the first option would seem more plausible.

Beside these changes, the mastaba was enlarged to the north. This extension was possibly caused by shifts in the proportional balance of the mastaba which followed the construction of the New Portico. In the north-eastern corner of the mastaba, a new "Room no. 2", came into the existence. The main walls of this space consist of large, up to 2.5 m long blocks made of local limestone. These blocks were quite carefully joined together in order to create this "room" whose dimensions were ca 6.5 × 4.7 m. The archaeological excavations in this area did not reveal any evidence concerning its function. The space was filled by debris when the team of the Charles University excavated it, thus one cannot guess at its original filling (presumably it was filled with sand, see *fig. 4.3.5*).

The basic problem connected with this room is the assessment of its function. Masonry preserved around this room does not bear any indication of the internal construction, nor any part of any kind of doorway, or even of an entryway or construction connected with a staircase. On the other hand, we should mention the poor state of preservation of this part of the mastaba. Hypothetically, any aperture

[356] *Cf.* Jánosi, 'Les tombes privées »des maisons d'éternité«', in: *L'art égyptienne*, fig. 63, and Arnold, *Architecture*, fig. on p. 182.

that could once have been there may have existed in the upper levels of masonry. The masonry still preserved *in situ* could represent the base for upper parts of the room which could have originally incorporated an entrance. Nevertheless, we should also consider the technological aspect of the whole question. "Room no. 2" was constructed in the close vicinity of the New Portico. If we would suppose that

Fig. 4.3.5 Room no. 2 from the west

in the former space a real room was positioned, then the masonry between it and the side walls of the New Portico would not be wide enough to carry the large weight of the architrave and of the roof of the portico.

Having in mind all these facts, it seems more probable that this space, considered by Zbyněk Žába to be another room of the mastaba, was in fact an auxiliary, chamber-like construction. It filled the space which came into existence in connection with the construction of the new monumental entrance to the mastaba (the New Portico). This fact indicates that this space had – more probably – a purely technological function, *i.e.*, that it was not used as a cultic space or as a storeroom. In this connection one can mention here that, already during the previous period, before the construction of the third building stage of the mastaba, the tomb was enlarged to the north. The same hypothetical – aesthetic – reasons might be taken into consideration.

As was already shown in the chapter concerning the second building stage (see p. 100), it seems rather improbable that the area of "Room no. 2" was connected with Room no. 6 belonging to the Northern Storerooms but, as a matter of course, we cannot exclude this possibility fully. If we do accept this hypothetical reasoning, one could suggest that a staircase might have been constructed above "Room no. 2", and in this case, could have lead to the roof terrace of the mastaba. If this supposition were to be right, then the staircase would have been used for the conducting of religious rites connected with the statues erected in Room no. 4.[357] This hypothetical staircase might also explain why no piece of direct evidence for a doorway leading to the area of "Room no. 2" was found.

As was noticed regarding the casing constructed during the first and second building stages, the casing for the outer walls that was constructed during the third

---

[357] The connection between the staircase and the rites in which a major role was also played by statues of tomb owners was recently proposed by N. Alexanian in her article: 'Himmelstreppen und Himmelsaufstieg. Zur Interpretation von Ritualen auf Grabdächern im Alten Reich', in: *Grab und Totenkult*, 27–40. These problems connected with the staircases in the Mastaba of Ptahshepses are discussed in *chapter 5* of this monograph.

building stage was built of blocks of white limestone. They were not only worked well on their faces, but also on their adjacent sides, in order to fit better together.[358] The angle of slope for the casing was 84° 20´.

The height of the mastaba's outer walls reached during the third building stage can be estimated following the assumed height of the columns in the New Portico and those of the pillars in the open courtyard (see also *chapter 4.3.7*). In this way, one can infer that the roof terraces of the newly constructed parts of the Mastaba of Ptahshepses did not rise to one level, but to several levels – as was thought to be the case both with the Initial Mastaba, and with the annex of the first enlargement of the mastaba. In the case of the New Portico, the roof terrace would have been constructed at a level of 8.38 m (= 16.11 cubits; see hereafter *chapter 4.3.3*). The other parts of the mastaba were certainly lower: this follows from the height of the pillars in the courtyard (see hereafter *chapter 4.3.7*). The height of the roofing terrace above the ambulatory of the open courtyard, can be estimated at 6 m and the height of the outer walls of the mastaba at about 6.5 m. As is the case of the Initial Mastaba, so it was for the second enlargement of the tomb: we can thus suppose the existence of a wall encircling the edges of the monument, but also integrating the different roofing terraces of the mastaba in respect of one's view of the building from the outside. The height of this wall probably varied quite a lot in the different areas of the mastaba – no doubt related to the different levels on which the roof terraces were constructed.

In the third stage, the mastaba was enlarged mainly to the south, south-east and to the north and the north-east. Judging by its surviving masonry, or by using an extrapolation following from it, it is possible to estimate that the mastaba finally reached the enormous dimensions of 56.24 × 42.24 m (= 108.16 × 81.23 cubits) during this building stage, thus covering a surface of 2375.58 m^2. Bearing these figures in mind, we should state that the mastaba is not the largest Old-Kingdom non-royal tomb as it is quite often mentioned.[359] The largest so far known non-royal tomb of the Old Kingdom[360] is G 2000, which covers an area of 5586 m^2 (105 × 53.2 m).[361] It is, however, possible to say that the ground plan of the Mastaba of Ptahshepses in its final form is the most complicated among all non-royal tombs of the Old Kingdom. In addition, the Ptahshepses mastaba is the largest of all the large mastabas of nobles dated to the Fifth and the Sixth Dynasties. This vast tomb incorporated 37 spaces in its superstructure alone. Together with the burial apartment for the vizier and his spouse, the Mastaba of Ptahshepses comprised 40 rooms and spaces.[362]

4.3.2 Ground plan of the newly built parts of the mastaba (see *pls. 30–32*)

Viewed from outside, the most remarkable feature of the third building stage was a new portico (Room no. 1) with a pair of columns at the only entrance access to the mastaba. With the construction of this new monumental entrance, the older portico was transformed into an internal room of the mastaba. In the area to the

---

[358] This method is attested already in the masonry of the first building stage of the mastaba and in many instances of Old Kingdom tomb architecture (Arnold, *Building*, 149–153, figs. 4.79 and 4.82.2 and 4.82.3b).

[359] *Cf.* Verner, in: *Unearthing*, 30; Jánosi, in: *L'art égyptienne*, 61, and other instances.

[360] The problem connected with the size of nobles' tombs of the Old Kingdom was studied by N. Kanawati ('The Financial Resources of the Viziers of the Old Kingdom and the Historical Implications', *PASA* 5 [1974], 1–20).

[361] *PM* III, 66; Reisner, *Giza Necropolis*, 414, fig. 4.

[362] If we would compare Ptahshepses' monument with the entire building unit of the room-ensemble of the Mastaba of Mereruka in Saqqara, we would find that the latter consists of 32 rooms and spaces and the tomb covers an area of 1071 m^2 (Duell, *Mereruka*, plan on the opposite page to pl. 2). On the other hand, some of the tombs built by the members of the lower strata of the inhabitants of the Memphite area present us with quite complicated structures. The ground plan of the tomb of Rawer in Giza is a very complicated structure, too (altogether, this tomb comprised of at least 43 rooms and areas – 18 chambers and courtyards with 20 statue-niches and 25 serdabs) – Hassan, *Gîza* I, 1, plan on the front page.

south of the annexe of the second building stage, several spaces were constructed. As well as the confusing area of spaces no. 10, 11 and 12 (see hereafter), a large open pillared courtyard was also built (space no. 13) together with an ambulatory (no. 14). In the axis of the courtyard's south wall, there was a deep recess (no. 15) giving access to the rectangular Room no. 16, which is connected to the storerooms in the south-eastern sector of the mastaba (Room nos. 17–20).

In the south end of the west wall of the courtyard there was another small recess with a doorway leading to corridor no. 32. This doorway connected the courtyard with the Boat-room (no. 40) and with the south-western group of storerooms (nos. 33–39).

In the north-western corner of the courtyard, the entrance (no. 21) of the Initial Mastaba was incorporated into the court's ambulatory. In this way, the courtyard was connected with the cultic rooms of the mastaba. On the other hand, the area of the north-western corner of the courtyard became the most important spot in the expanded mastaba in respect of communication tracks.

4.3.3 Room no. 1 – New Portico

It was mentioned above that by the second tomb's enlargement Ptahshepses intended to emulate a royal mortuary temple. This intention we can see straightaway in the construction of the new monumental entrance to the entire tomb – the New Portico (Room no. 1). In respect of the tomb-owner's endeavour to built a temple-tomb, an important role here was played by the erection of a pair of eight-stemmed columns. By this architectural innovation, Ptahshepses continued the trend of erecting floral columns whose wide use in the canons of royal architecture was effective throughout the entire Fifth Dynasty in Abusir and Saqqara.

4.3.3.1 Casing and dimensions (see *pls. 33–34*)

From the surviving remains of the portico's casing it is evident that it was made from monolithic fine white limestone blocks. In the portico, only a few of fragments of these blocks survived *in situ*. A large fragment of casing in the southern part of

Fig. 4.3.6 New Portico from the east; parts of the surviving casing have been incorporated into the modern restoration of the monumental entryway to the mastaba

the portico shows that the lowermost part of the portico's side walls was painted in black (see *fig. 4.3.6*). This colour was certainly intended to imitate the basalt dados of the royal mortuary monuments built during the same period.[363]

[363] *Cf.* Borchardt, *Sahure* I, 24, 34; Borchardt, *Neuserre*, 56–57.

The upper part of the portico's casing with its relief decoration has been lost. Despite the poor state of preservation of the portico's masonry, however, it is possible to reconstruct the dimensions of the portico – 4.23 × 7.95 m. In connection with this, it should be underlined that the entrance used today for approaching the Old Portico (which came into existence during the reconstruction work), probably does not correspond in its dimensions to the original doorway to the mastaba.[364] Unfortunately the original size and precise location of the doorway cannot be traced. The main reason for this uncertainty, beside the destruction of the masonry itself, is the presence of the recently reconstructed masonry.

4.3.3.2 Columns

As we have seen, the main architectural feature of the portico is the pair of columns. They were excavated by Z. Žába in 1961. The columns fell into a layer of blown sand in ancient times and did not break up into many fragments (see *fig. 4.3.7*). It was therefore possible to reconstruct them later, during the 1980s. Throughout the excavations an important fact also came to light – each column was embedded in its base by means of a peg made of acacia.[365] These pegs survived until modern times (see *fig. 4.3.8, 4.3.9*) and the peg from the northern column has been retained for C^{14} investigation. Unfortunately, the results of these tests were not very helpful in respect with the Old Kingdom chronology (the registered date was 1942 B.C./3892 ± 64 b.p. and the age based on the 5730 years half-life was 2056 B.C.).[366]

Fig. 4.3.8 New Portico, the southern eight-stemmed lotus column, as found during the archaeological excavation

‹ Fig. 4.3.7 New Portico, parts of the columns at the time of their discovery

Fig. 4.3.9a–b New Portico, the northern eight-stemmed lotus column, as found during the archaeological excavations; the original wooden peg is protruding from the column base (see *b* for close-up)

Each column was made of one monolith of porous limestone. This type of limestone is not as stable as the high quality Tura limestone.[367] The columns exhibit

[364] It is apparent, that J. de Morgan did not work as carefully as he might have done during his excavations. We can document this fact with regard to the space of the original doorway, between the New and the Old Portico. In the account of his excavations in the mastaba, he did not mention any piece of information about the nature of his discoveries, nor did he present on the plan the area of by him excavated structures. After the termination of his work, he built a wall in line with the eastern wall of the Old Portico, but he did not make adequate documentation concerning it. He took it for granted that the eastern wall of the Old Portico did not have a doorway. It, again, shows his misunderstanding of the structures he excavated in the area of the Mastaba of Ptahshepses.

[365] *Acacia sp.*, probably *A. nilotica L.* – see: Barker, Burleigh, Meek, 'British Museum Natural Radiocarbon Measurements VII', *Radiocarbon* 13 (1971), 164.

[366] This specimen of the peg material was studied for C^{14}-dating several years after the unearthing of the columns, together with other samples coming from the archaeological sites in Egypt. Unfortunately, due to the overall discrepancies in these tests (*op. cit.*, 159) which were not possible to correct at that time, the results are not usable for a more precise dating of the mastaba.

a high level of damage in those parts which projected from the sand layer in which they had once lain. The columns stood on low rounded limestone bases with a diameter of 1.55 m and which were 16 cm high. The base of the columns have a diameter of 1.04 m (= 2 cubits). The intercolumnium was 2.95 m.

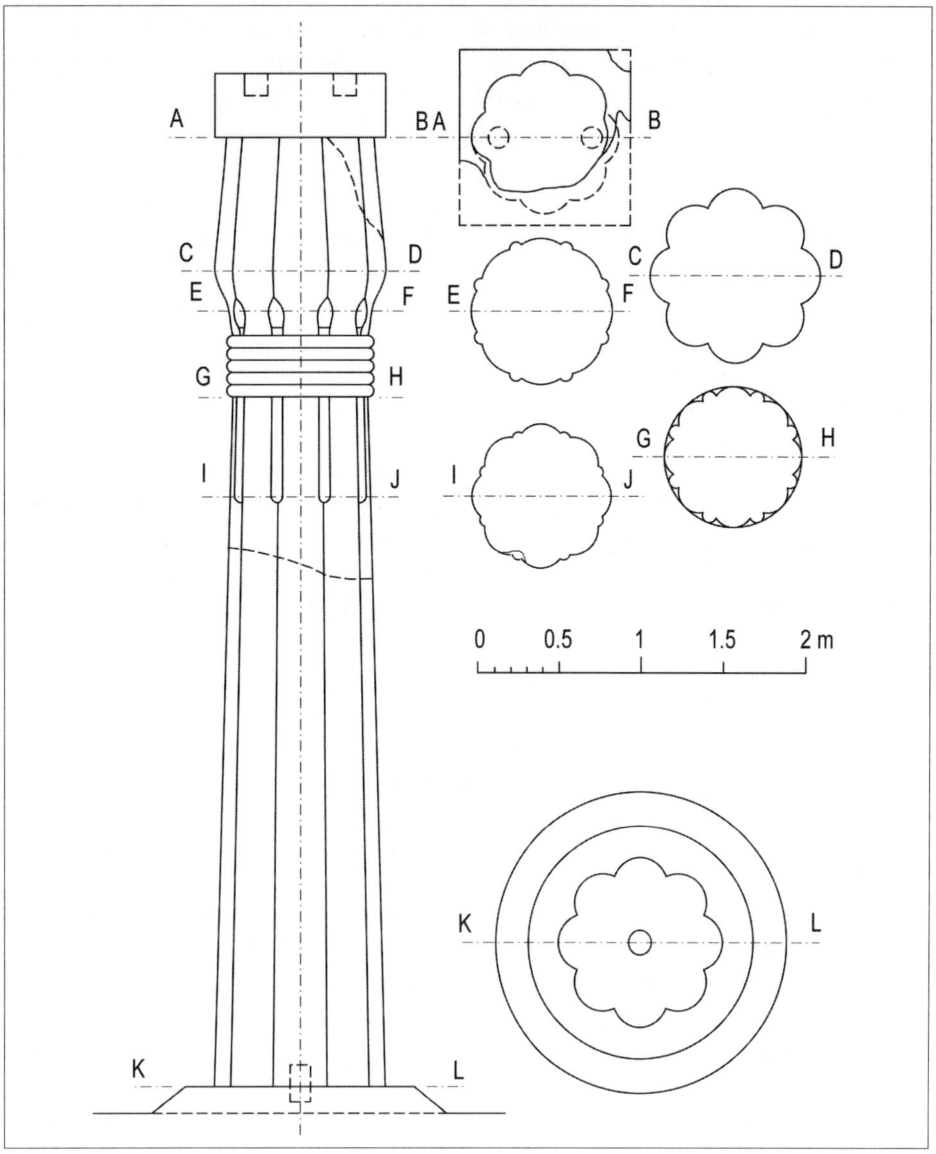

Fig. 4.3.10 Northern column from the New Portico; front view and sections through the shaft and column head

The columns represent an eight-stemmed lotus form used in this instance for the first time in Egyptian architecture.[368] The separate stems were positioned in a circle (or rather, an octagon). As is the case with the columns in the Old Portico, the shafts of the columns are slightly conical, with their radii measuring 52 cm at the base and 48 cm just below the capital (see *fig. 4.3.10*). The capital is created by a bundle of simplified lotus buds. Unfortunately, as no detail of the lotus flowers is modelled in the capital, it is not possible to ascertain precisely which of the two subspecies of *Nymphea caerulea Sav.* – the white or the blue lotus – is depicted in this case. Moreover, no traces of the original colouring of the columns remain on them.[369]

[367] This type of limestone was possibly quarried in the area to the west of "Lion's Hill", to the south of Abusir. These quarries were located by the author and their possible existence in this place was corroborated by Jaromír Leichmann (from the Masaryk University, Brno), November 2004. For its location, see, Krejčí, 'The origins and development of the royal necropolis at Abusir during the Old Kingdom', in: *Abusir and Saqqara 2000*, 473.

[368] Korecký, in: *Preliminary Report*, 117–124; Verner, 'Ein entfallener und ein neuen Beleg zur Geschichte der achtstengligen Lotossäule', *BSEG* 9–10 (1984–1985), 323–336. See also Phillips, *Columns*, 12–14, figs. 22, 25.

[369] For a discussion concerning the species depicted in the columns – see *chapter 4.2.4*.

In between the large lotus heads there are eight smaller lotus buds having 0.43 m long stalks with rounded ends. Unlike the capitals of the columns located in the Old Portico, the separate large flowers and smaller lotus buds were positioned in a circle, making in this way a complex structure of two octagons. Below the capital itself we can see five lines of rope which hold the whole bunch of lotus plants and buds together. Above the capital there is a squared abacus (104.8 × 104.8 × 41 cm). In the upper surface of the abacus there are two insertions which possibly also contained (wooden) pegs, which helped to join the columns to the architrave which they supported.[370]

The extraordinary nature of Ptahshepses' columns is also marked by their height. The columns were 6.14 m high (with their bases 6.30 m). If we compare them with Sahure's *palm* columns from the open courtyard in the king's mortuary temple, then we can see that those of Ptahshepses are almost equal to them. The height of the columns in Sahure's temple was 6.30 m.[371] It is interesting that the *papyrus* columns of the open courtyard in Niuserre's mortuary temple were "only" 5.15 m high.[372] This comparison suggests not only Ptahshepses' high rank and power, but also his right and ability to use large volumes of material for the construction of his tomb.

The columns in the New Portico once supported an architrave (or entablature). No part of such an architrave was found; therefore, we can only estimate that the height of the architrave was two cubits – 1.04 m (*i.e.* that it was same as was the width of the columns' capitals). The same reading might be applicable for the height of the roofing masonry. In this case, the level of the roof terrace would be at a height of 8.38 m.

As already mentioned by Miroslav Verner,[373] the portico was possibly crowned by a cavetto cornice[374] as follows from a relief fragment found by Zbyněk Žába.[375] This fragment presents a part of a scene very probably – as it follows from the accompanying text – depicting procession of the cattle (in front of Ptahshepses?). Only a part of the original scene is preserved – presenting a part of a portico with a lotus bundle column and crowned with a concave cornice. Also tiny remnants of the original colouring were possible to document after its discovery. This hypothesis cannot be confirmed by the archaeological material as no fragment of such a cavetto cornice was found during the archaeological excavations. With uppermost caution, the observer may reconstruct the way in which the uppermost part of the portico entrance was originally designed and compare this with the design of the entrances to the royal complexes built in the Abusir royal necropolis. In the latter instances, some parts of cavetto cornices were found in the royal mortuary temples, and they were used in the visualisations made by Ludwig Borchardt.[376] For the non-royal tombs of the period, there is no direct attestation for the use of a cavetto cornice above a tomb entrance. Hermann Junker reconstructed the original form of the entrance to Seshemnefer's IV tomb in Giza as consisting of only an indistinctly protruding and not very elaborated cavetto cornice built in between two upright flat walls with undecorated faces. In this case, the roof of the entrance portico was strongly supported by simple, cylindrical columns.[377]

---

[370] The same method of attachment between the columns and the architraves is documented in Sahure's and Niuserre's mortuary temples, see: Borchardt, *Sahure* I, 45, Bl. 9; Borchardt, *Neuserre*, 55–56, Abb. 3–36, Bl. 13.

[371] Borchardt, *Sahure*, 43, Bl. 6.

[372] They represented six-stemmed *papyrus* columns – Borchardt, *Neuserre*, Bl. 13; in contrast to them, the columns of the same type that were erected in the king's valley temple were 6.30 m high – Borchardt, *Neuserre*, 10, Bl 5.

[373] Verner, 'Ein entfallener und ein neuen Beleg zur Geschichte der achtstengligen Lotossäule', *BSEG* 9–10 (1984–1985), 333, Abb. 7.

[374] *Cf.* Junker, *Gîza* XI, Abb. 50a: the height of the cavetto cornice in the case of the columned portico of Seshemnefer's IV tomb was 0.86 m.

[375] See Verner, *Realm of Osiris*, fig. on p. 158; Vachala, *Relieffragmente*, 100, Bl. 115.

[376] Borchardt, *Sahure*, 7, Bl. 3; Borchardt, *Neuserre*, 35, Abb. 14.

Coming back to the relief fragment from the Mastaba of Ptahshepses, one cannot relate the building in this sketch with vizier's tomb, the monument which was depicted in it. There is no proof, that the building which was depicted on this relief block presented a view of the actual tomb. Nevertheless, having in mind the elaborate design of the both eight-stemmed lotus columns, we can (hypothetically) suppose that Ptahshepses tried to follow the royal models with his use of more ornate designs. Equally hypothetically, we can speculate that, above the architrave of the portico, a cavetto cornice was placed which protruded not only above the portico, but also above the side walls of portico, overlooking the roofing terraces of the mastaba as well as its outer walls. It does not seem probable that the design which has been supposed in the case of Seshemnefer IV's tomb was used also in the case of Ptahshepses' New Portico.

As we can see in the case of the Old Portico, but also in other instances of the tombs dated to the second half of the Fifth Dynasty and to the Sixth Dynasty, it is very probable, that statues of the tomb owner were displayed in the New Portico. Nevertheless, this hypothesis can not be supported by the excavated remains of the portico's pavement and masonry. No incision in the pavement which has been found in the Old Portico (see the following chapter) have been discovered in the New Portico. On the other hand, seeing that both additions to the Initial Mastaba served for the erection and cult of the tomb owner's statues and also other analogies coming from the Memphite Necropolis,[378] we can suppose that the statues were erected flanking the main entrance to the mastaba. Having in mind the fact that the period of construction was a peak time for the sun cult in Egypt, and the fact that this period was characterised by changes in non-royal tomb architecture, we cannot to rule out the idea that obelisks were erected in the entrance portico as well.[379] We can see such a simultaneous use of statues and obelisks in the case of the entrance to the tomb of Rawer[380] or slightly later dated tomb of Seshemnefer IV[381] in Giza (see also *chapter 5.3.1*).

4.3.4 Room no. 3 – Old Portico

Because of the construction of the New Portico, the space behind this new monumental entrance was also changed. The Old Portico was remodelled into a quite extraordinary "hypostyle hall" with a pair of columns (*pl. 36*). This was done by the simple enlargement of the portico to the east. During these works the whole eastern wall of Room no. 3 and also the eastern parts of its north and south walls came into existence. The room which came into being in this way was 4.40 m wide and 6.32 m long. It was also decorated with reliefs and statues (for a discussion concerning the precise date of decoration for Room nos. 3, 4, 10, see *chapter 4.2.4*). The preservation of the walls of these newly built sections is not good. As was already mentioned, the area of the entrance to this room was badly destroyed.

Another problem is presented by the assessment of the ceiling level above the eastern enlarged part; there are two possibilities:

1) This ceiling was constructed at a higher level. In this case, the ceiling beams would be laid on an architrave above the columns erected during the second building stage (there is no idea, to which extent this masonry should be transformed in order that the new ceiling blocks could be added). The ceiling blocks would be laid in the

---

[377] Despite the fact that the supports for the roof of the entrance to the tomb did not survive, H. Junker in his discussion came to the conclusion that they would have been two plain-shaft columns – *Gîza* XI, 101, Abb. 50.

[378] Seshemnefer IV: Junker, *Gîza* XI, 109–110, Taf. I, XI, XIIb, XIIIc–d.

[379] K. Martin (*Garantsymbol*, 49, 202) dates the usage of tomb obelisks to the late Fifth and to the Sixth Dynasty, *i.e.*, into the period after the proposed date of the construction of the Mastaba of Vizier Ptahshepses. For further discussion on the tomb-obelisks see: Martin, *Garantsymbol*, 48–62.

[380] Hassan, *Gîza* I, 6, fig. 3.

[381] Seshemnefer IV: Junker, *Gîza* XI, 110–111, Abb. 49, Taf. XIVb–c.

east-western direction and no alternation of the masonry (entablature) above the architrave would be needed. Nonetheless, there is a problem with the assessment of the level at which this new ceiling would have been constructed. To ascertain such a height, one would need to know the height of the masonry above the architrave. We can only theorize that it could be 0.52 m, *i.e.* one cubit, high. Therefore, the ceiling in this part of Room no. 3 might have been at a level of ca 5 m above the floor.

2) It is also probable that the ceiling of this new eastern part of the room could have been constructed at the same level as that of the original portico. If this hypothesis would be correct, the masonry lying on the architrave must have been reshaped, otherwise, the architrave could not have been used as a support for the newly added ceiling beams of the room's eastern part. In this case, the height of the ceiling in this part of Room no. 3 would have been about 4.48 m (see p. 85).

In this room we can also see that the tomb of Ptahshepses was built as a *Gesamtkunstwerk* ("synthesis of the arts") mixing architecture, relief decoration[382] and statues into one combined structure. It is possible to document this effect especially

Fig. 4.3.11a–b Old Portico, northern part of the western wall with free space in the relief decoration and with the incision for the erection of a statue; present situation

in the area of the western wall of the room. In front of the western wall, two life-sized statues were very probably erected. Their positions are clearly marked by two shallow incisions in the pavement and by free spaces left in the decoration of the wall (see *pl. 35, figs. 4.3.11a–b*). The third incision is located in the north-east corner of the room. It is not, however, possible to say whether it was also connected to the free space in the relief decoration. It seems that the lower part of a statue made of granite actually was found by de Morgan during the excavation around this space,[383] and this increases the likelihood of the presence of a statue in the original design. Due to the poor quality of de Morgan's documentation, unfortunately, it is not possible to say whether this statue originally stood on this spot or in front of the western wall.

In combination with the architecture of the room, the statues standing in their positions in front of the undecorated parts of the wall created one complete unit which, most probably, came into existence as a result of the overall plan of the

[382] Verner, *Reliefs*, 8–27, pl.1–11, photos 2–24.

[383] De Morgan, 'Découverte du mastaba de Ptah-chepsés dans la nécropole d'Abou-Sir', *RevArch* 24 (1894), fig. 1. Due to the fact that this fragment of the statue was attached to the pavement by means of mortar, B. Patočková does not contradict that this is the original place where the statue was erected (Patočková, *Fragmenty soch*, 140).

Pl.1 Figure of Ptahshepses carved on one of the pillars in the open courtyard

Pl. 2 Cemetery of Nobles in Abusir from the summit of Niuserre's pyramid

Pl. 3 Cemetery of Nobles in Abusir from the summit of Sahure's pyramid

Pl. 4 View of the mastaba from the Nile valley

Pl. 5 The northwest corner of the mastaba with a discernible (whitish) casing block of the Initial Mastaba

Pl. 6 Three-dimensional reconstruction of the Initial Mastaba, bird's view

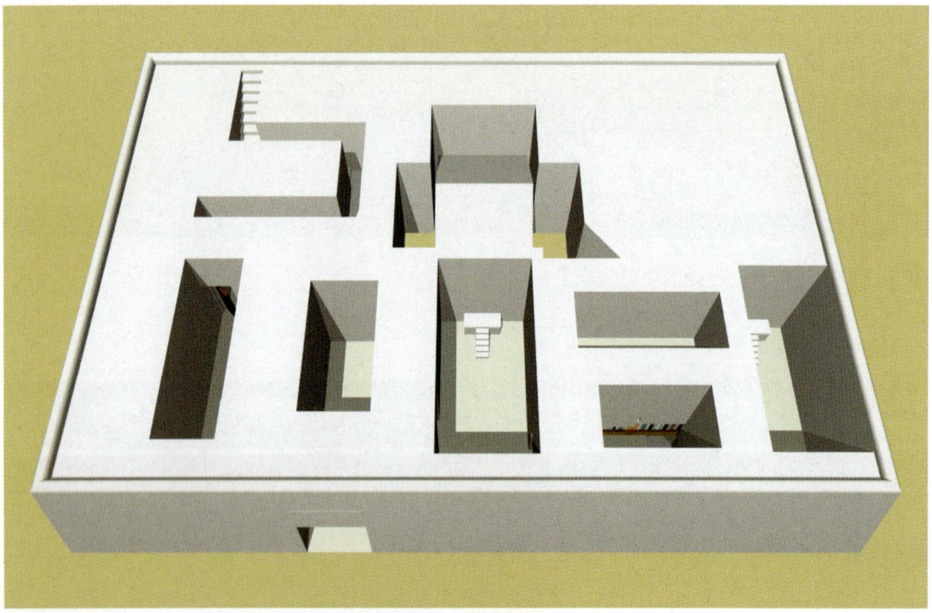

Pl. 7 Three-dimensional reconstruction of the Initial Mastaba, bird's view without the tomb's roof

Pl. 8 Three-dimensional reconstruction of the Initial Mastaba visualised without its roof, view northwards from above

Pl. 9 Room no. 26, remains of the palace façade decoration on the western wall

Pl. 10a–b Room no. 26, details of the remains of the palace façade decoration on the western wall

Pl. 11 Room no. 26, reconstruction of the palace façade decoration

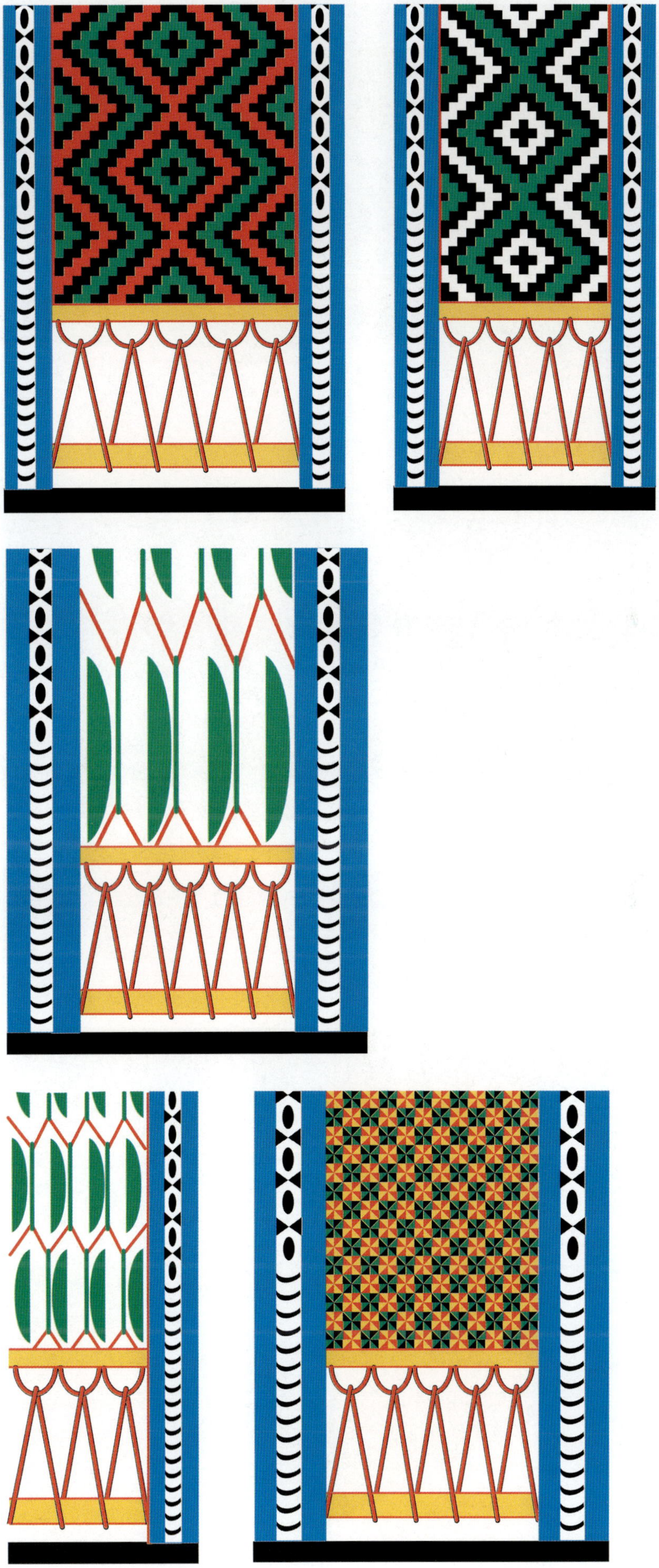

Pl. 12 Room no. 26, reconstruction of the palace façade decoration, details

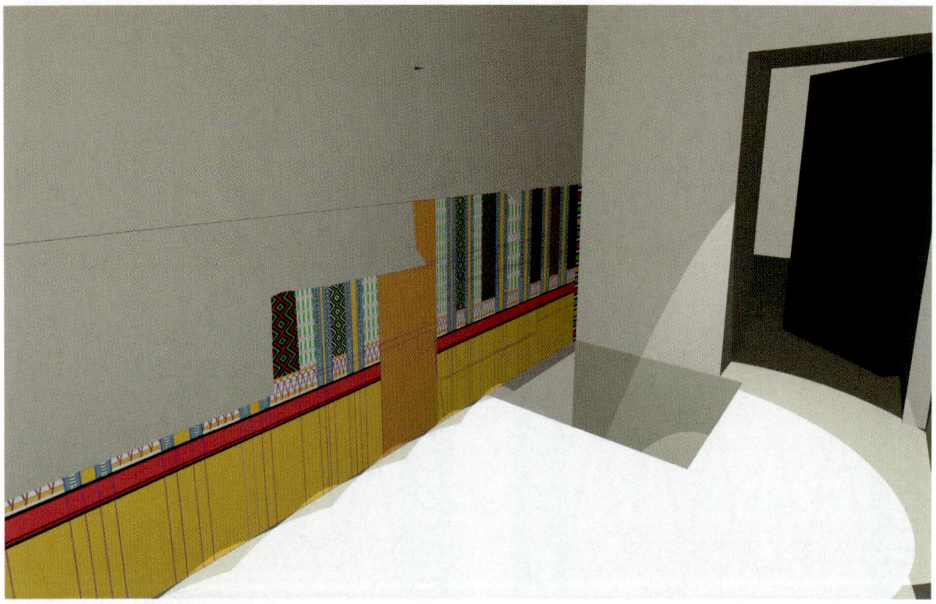

Pl. 13 Three-dimensional reconstruction of the original appearance of the western wall of Room no. 27 with palace façade decoration as viewed from the south-east

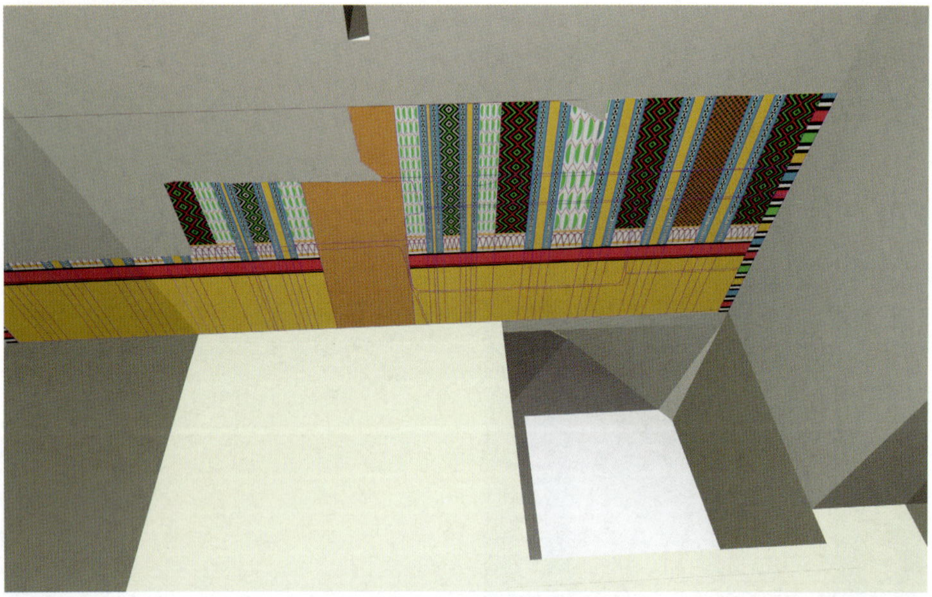

Pl. 14 Three-dimensional reconstruction of the original appearance of the western wall of Room no. 27 with the palace façade decoration and the mouth of the descending corridor

Pl. 15 Three-dimensional reconstruction of the original appearance of the western wall of Room no. 27 with the palace façade decoration and the mouth of the descending corridor

Pl. 16 Western part of the Initial Mastaba, the construction pit for the burial apartment of the tomb owner, as seen from the south

Pl. 17 Burial chamber with two granite sarcophagi, as seen from the east

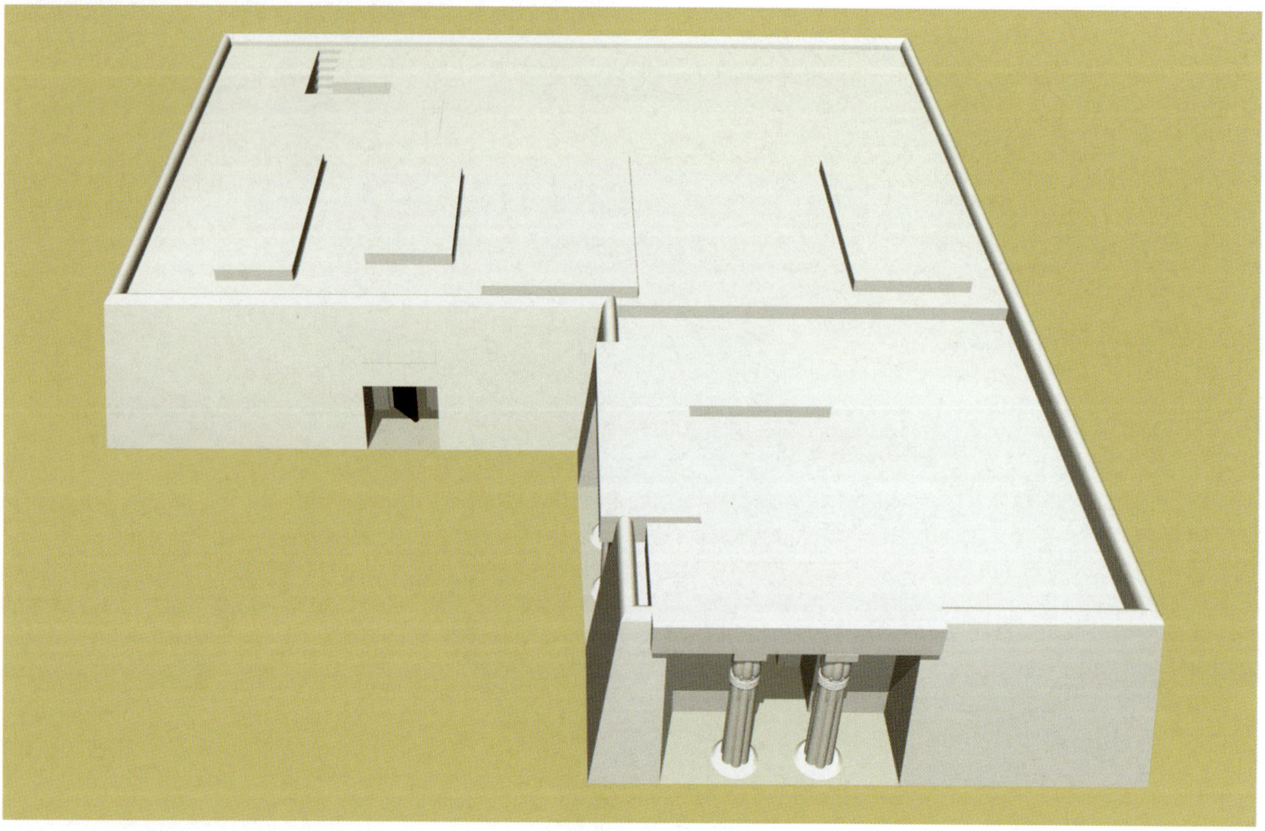

Pl. 18 Three-dimensional reconstruction of the mastaba after the second building stage, view from above

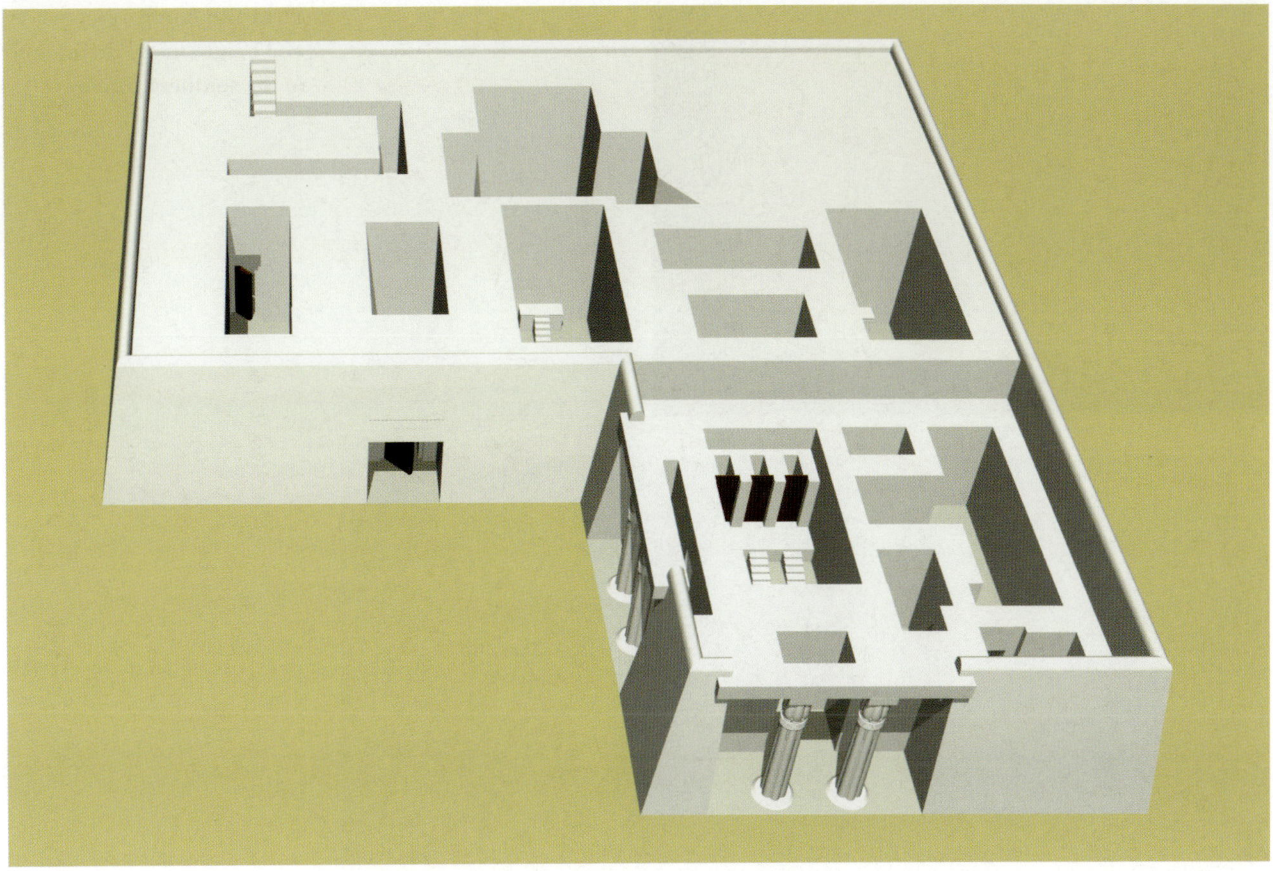

Pl. 19 Three-dimensional reconstruction of the mastaba after the second building stage – without its roof terraces, view from above

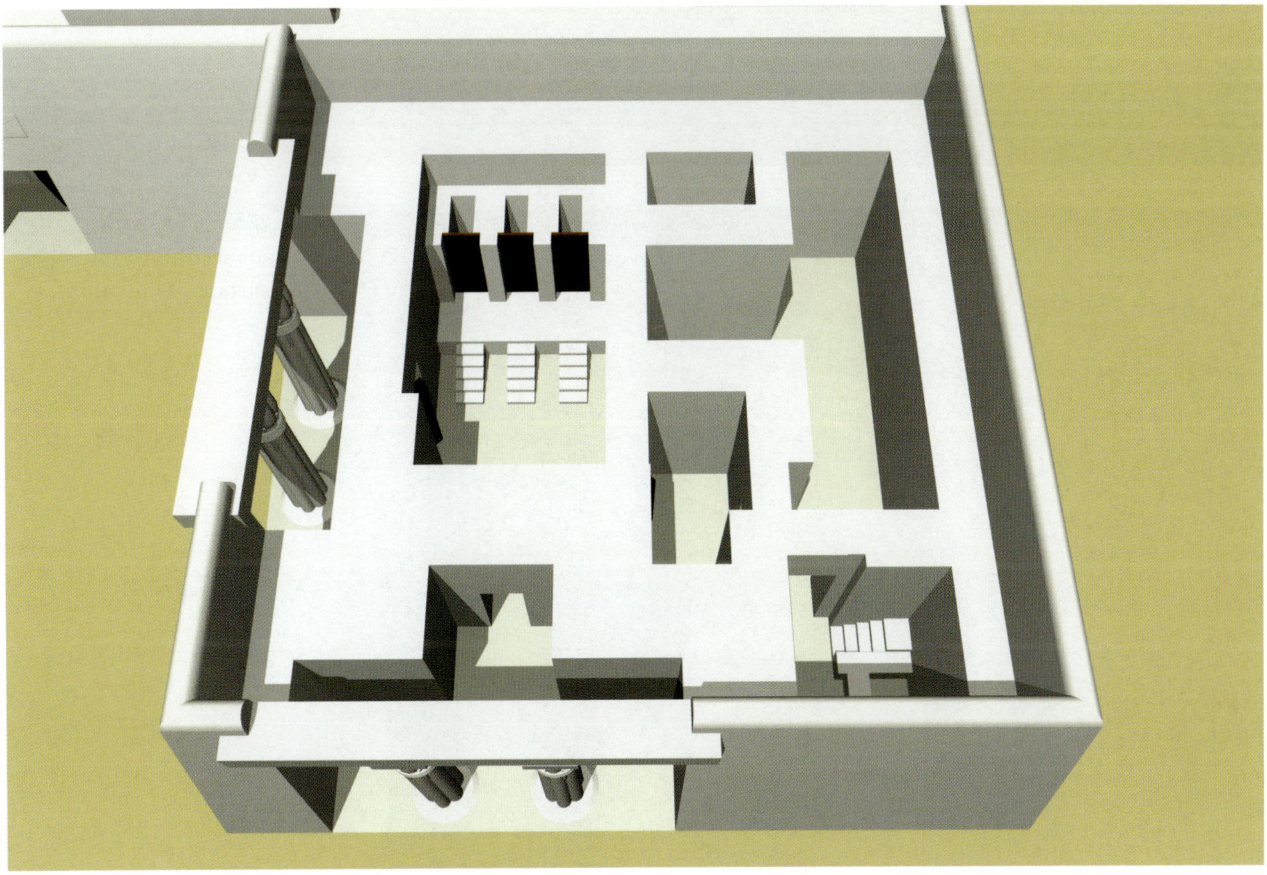

Pl. 20 Annex of the second building stage, view from above

Pl. 21 Old Portico, grey-white and beige simple decoration of the southern column

Pl. 22a–b Old Portico, remnants of the blue colour on surface of the columns

Fig. 23 Room no. 4 (Chapel with Three Niches), western part with niches

Pl. 24 Room no. 4, north-west corner with small staircases leading to the podium in front of the niches constructed in the western wall

Pl. 25 Room no.4, the decorated southern wall of the southernmost niche

Pl. 26 Room no. 4, basalt washer and pivot holder in the mouth of one of the niches

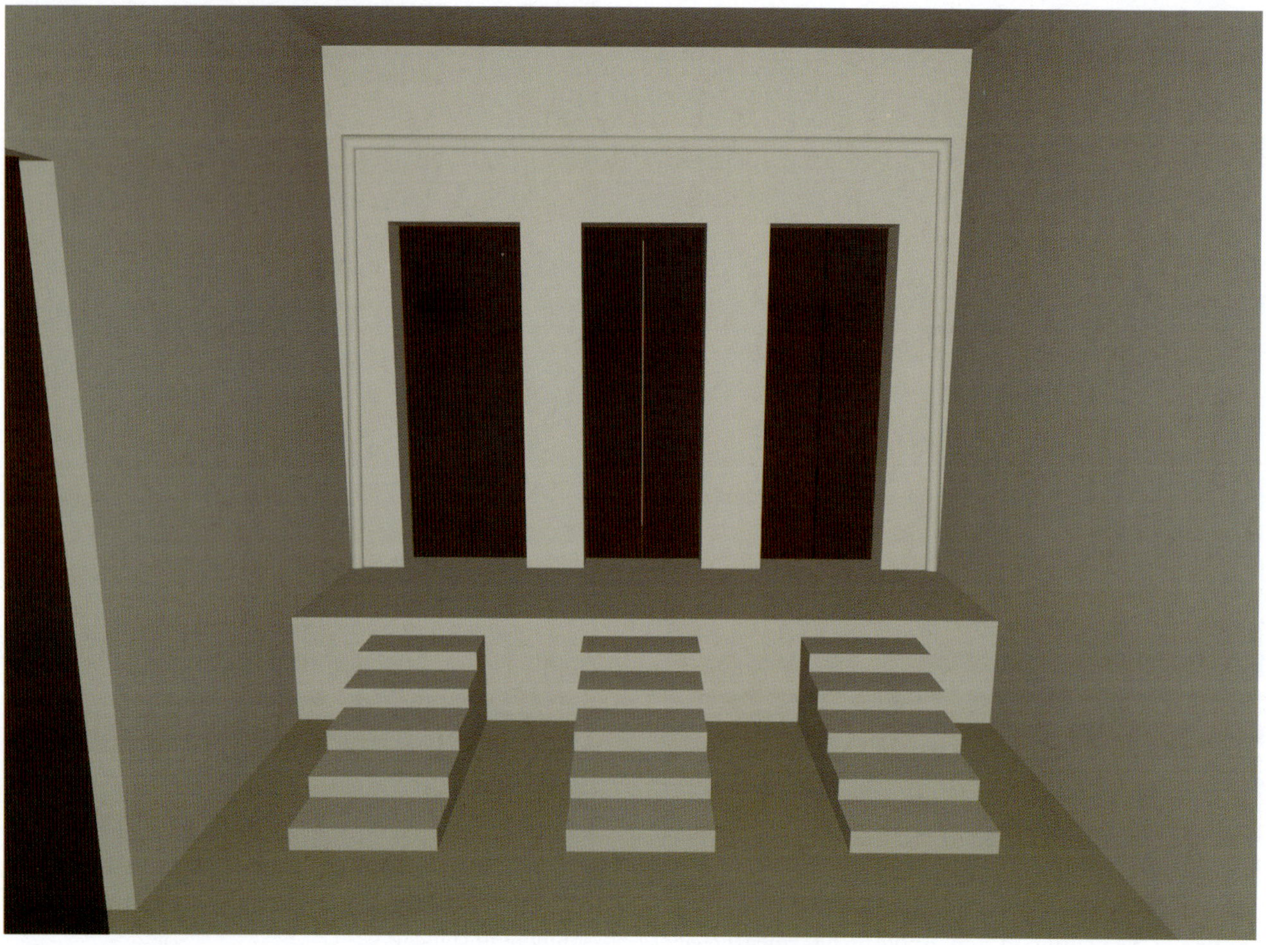

Pl. 27 The schematic computer reconstruction of the form of the western wall in Room no. 4

Pl. 28 Three-dimensional visualisation of the mastaba, view from the south, with the pair of pillars reconstructed in the Southern Portico

Pl. 29 Three-dimensional visualisation of the mastaba, view from the south, with the pair of columns reconstructed in the Southern Portico

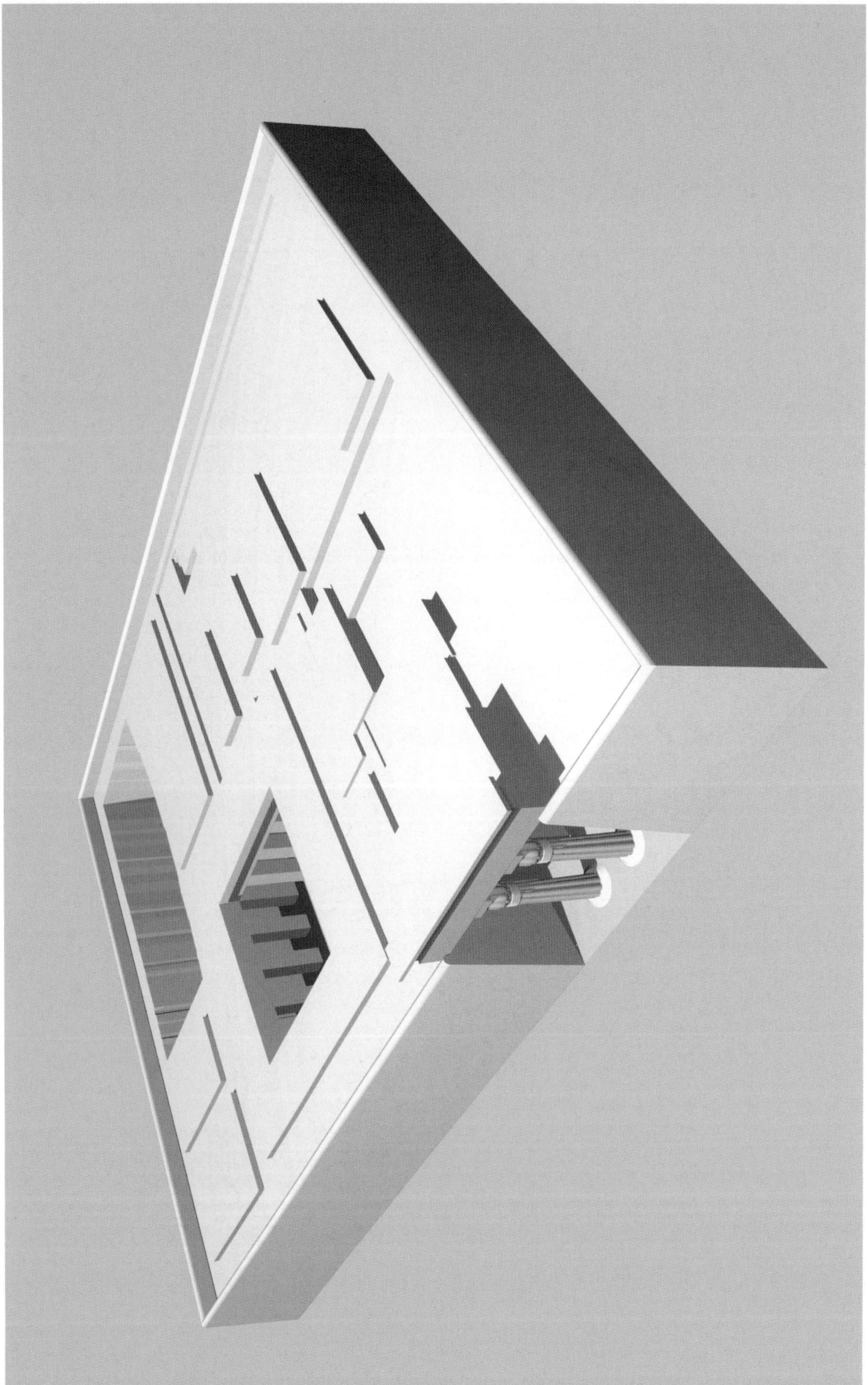

Pl. 30 Three-dimensional visualisation of the mastaba after the third building stage, view from above

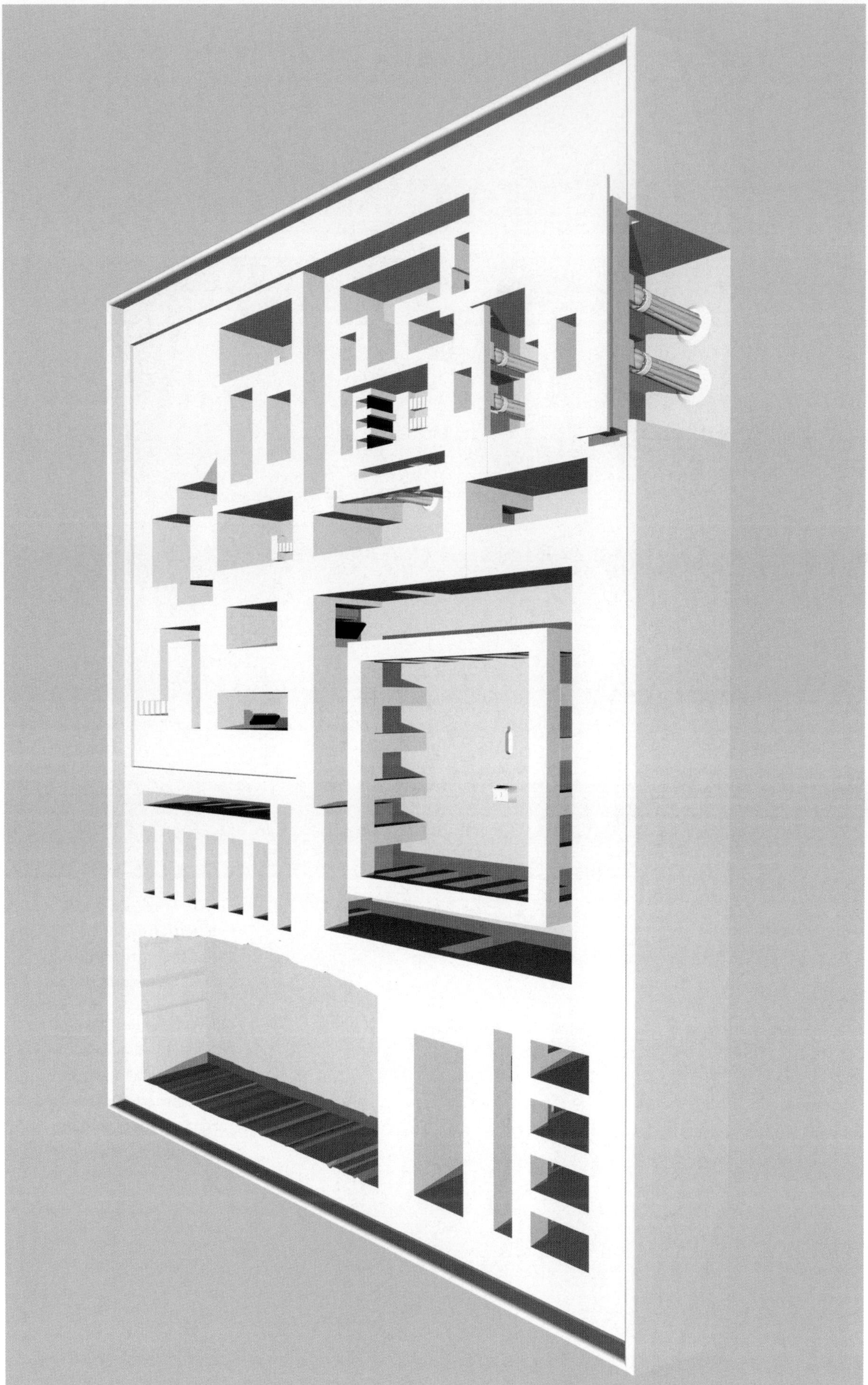

Pl. 31 Three-dimensional visualisation of the mastaba – without its roof terraces – after the third building stage, view from above

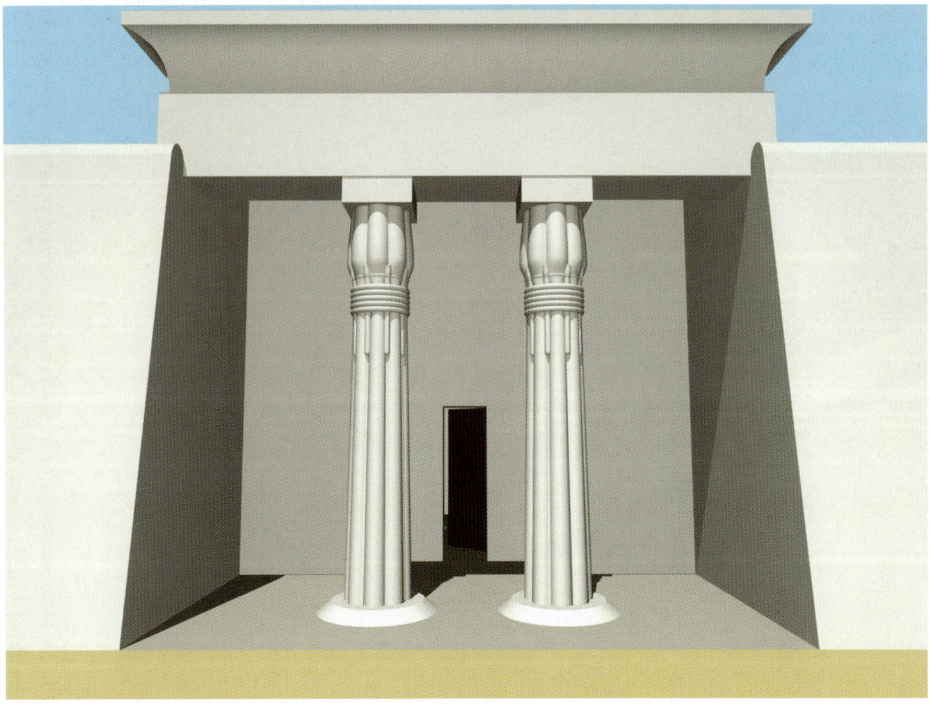

Pl. 32 Three-dimensional visualisation of the mastaba after the third building stage, view from the east

Pl. 33 New Portico and the north-eastern corner of the mastaba; modern reconstruction made by the archaeological mission of the Charles University

Pl. 34 Three-dimensional visualisation of the New Portico

Pl. 35 Old Portico, southern part of the western wall, with a free space left in the relief decoration and remains of colouring in the pavement where the statue had been erected

Pl. 36 Chapel with Three Niches and the Old Portico, with one pair of the six-stemmed lotus columns in the foreground

Pl. 37a Pillared courtyard from the north-east

Pl. 37b Pillared courtyard, ambulatory from the south-west

Pl. 38 Pillared courtyard, western row of pillars

Pl. 39 Pillared courtyard, three-dimensional reconstruction of the western wing of the courtyard's ambulatory

Pl. 40a–b Offering table found in the area of the pillared courtyard

Pl. 41 Pillared courtyard, three-dimensional visualisation with the hypothetical placement of the offering table; view from the north

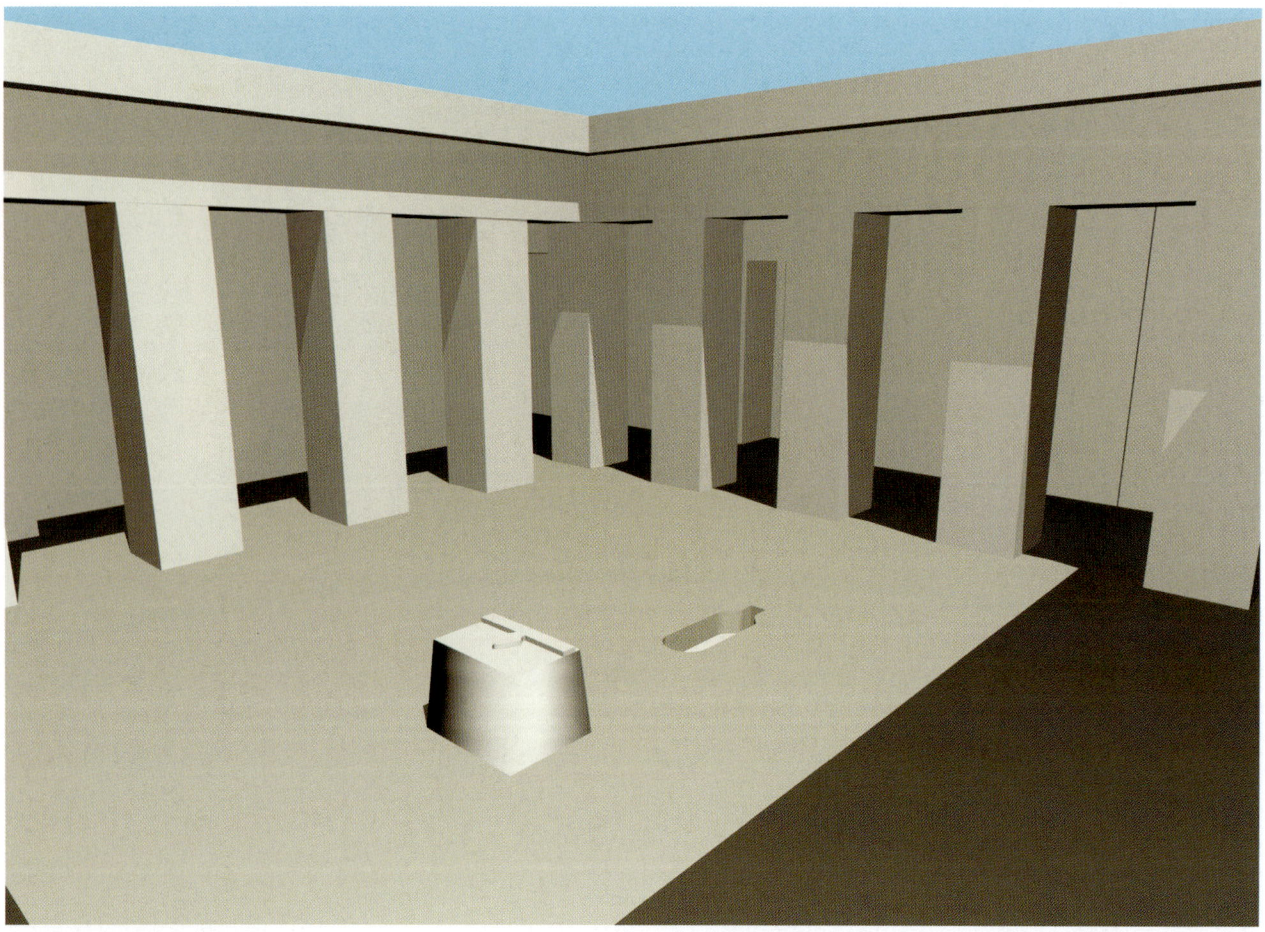

Pl. 42 Pillared courtyard, three-dimensional visualisation with the hypothetical placement of the offering table; view from the south-east

tomb. It is apparent, that this arrangement – mixing the relief and sculptural decoration – did not originate as a matter of chance as was mentioned by de Morgan.[384] Nevertheless, the fact that parts of the walls behind the statues were not decorated shows that the relief decoration was made in respect of the statues. The statues were apparently erected in this place before the creation of the reliefs.[385]

4.3.5 Room nos. 10 and 11 – Southern Portico

One of the most enigmatic parts of the whole Mastaba of Ptahshepses is the space lying to the south of the Southern Portico (Room no. 10). This puzzling space has been marked as Room no. 11. A limited part of the masonry of this room, built during the third building stage, is preserved. It represents a very small part of the core masonry, originally belonging to the room's south wall (see in the background in *fig. 4.3.14*). This core masonry consisted of large blocks of local limestone and of limestone splinters. It ran parallel to the south wall of the annex built during the second building stage, *i.e.* in an east-west direction.

The remains that we do have today enable us to reconstruct the original appearance of the room in only one way: during the third building stage, the Southern

Fig. 4.3.12 Northern wall of Room no. 10–11 with its relief decoration, the "pilaster" and smoothed wall of Room no. 12

Portico was enlarged to the south by the construction of the aforementioned wall. In this way, this enlarged room was transformed into a T shaped layout (see *fig. 4.3.1*). The length of the room was 9.49 m but the precise width of this room is not known. It is quite likely from the archaeological situation that the width of Room no. 11 was the same as that of Room no. 12, *i.e.*, 2.30 m. Therefore, the whole new space connecting the Southern Portico (2.45 m wide) with the newly added Room no. 11 might have been 4.75 m wide.

Another question is whether this new room had a ceiling or not. The relief decoration which survived on the north wall of the room to the left and the right of the Southern Portico plays an important role in solving this problem (see on *fig. 4.3.12*).[386] This decoration preserved *in situ* offers confirmation for our assumption that reliefs also adorned the west, south and east walls of this new room. Leaving aside this supposition, the decoration of the northern wall would not have been used in a place which would not be properly sheltered by a ceiling. Following on from the fact that the preserved decoration represents fine, slightly raised coloured

[384] De Morgan, *RevArch* 24 (1894), 30.
[385] For a discussion concerning the relationship between statues and Egyptian architecture see Arnold, in: *L'art égyptienne*, 64–69.
[386] See Verner, *Reliefs*, 114–115, Pls. 61–62, photos 116–117.

reliefs, whose use is typical for sheltered spaces, we can suppose that some kind of roofing once existed above this decoration. In relation to this there are two possibilities of what this roofing looked like:

1) The whole room could have been roofed and in this way the room would have been a closed room as is the case with the Old Portico.
2) The newly constructed addition to the original Southern Portico might have been a narrow atrium with a coping running along its walls; this coping would then protect the relief decoration.[387] In this case, it is not possible to confirm the existence of supports for this coping in the archaeological material.
3) There is the eventuality that a roof might then have projected over the edges of the northern walls of Room no. 10, and that it ran along the northern wall of the enlarged Room no. 11. As a matter of course, one of the functions of this roofing would have been the protection of the relief decoration.

The second solution layout is attested, *e.g.* in the tombs of the G 6000 Cemetery in Giza. Here we can see in the Mastaba of Neferbauptah that the space with a coping might have represented quite a small area.[388] Despite this fact, to make such a construction in the southern part of the enlarged Southern Portico would be quite a complex task. This solution would be connected with a complicated construction of a roof running along the narrow courtyard. Therefore, it appears more probable that the Southern Portico, enlarged southwards by an east-westerly oriented oblong addition, represented a ceiled room.

The variety of topics in the preserved decoration of the room – including the scenes of dragging of the statues, the piles of offerings, offering bearers and the vizier depicted together with his family and members of the official staff[389] – is so wide that it does not allow us to ascertain the function of the room in any simple way. It does not seem to possess a crucial ritual meaning, apart from the significant function of being the connecting room between the Chapel with Three Niches and the pillared courtyard. Nonetheless, the enlarged Southern Portico was somehow connected with the offerings which were depicted on its side walls. It might have been used to house some of the offerings put to use during the ceremonies in the chapel, as well as in the courtyard. However, one cannot exclude another possibility. Logically, Room no. 10–11 is the exit from the Chapel with Three Niches and it might have been the ritual break between the shrine and the courtyard where, presumably, other rituals took place.

There is also the problem of a doorway between the newly conjoined Room no.10–11 and the pillared courtyard (see *fig. 4.3.13a–b*). Such a doorway certainly existed in the south wall of this room, but the problem is where this doorway was located. There are two possibilities:

1) the entrance could have been located in the axis of the south wall of the room, opposite the entrance to Room no. 4 in the portico,
2) or, it could have been located in the south-east corner of the room, by the entrance to Room no. 12.

ad 1): In this case the entrance to the ambulatory of the pillared courtyard would lead slightly off (to the east) the axis of the space between the pair of the pillars in the north-west corner of the courtyard. We can speculate to what degree such a layout would be convenient for the cultic activities carried out in the mastaba

---

387 In the case of the open courtyard of the Mastaba of Ti we can also see a fine, slightly raised coloured relief decoration. Therefore, the second mentioned possibility, attempting to explain how the ceiling of the enlarged Southern Portico was once designed, cannot be fully ruled out of contention.
388 Weeks, *Cemetery G 6000*, Fig. 3
389 Verner, *Reliefs*, 92–115.

– mainly in connection with the cultic route connecting Room no 4 (the chapel with the niches) with the offering room in the Initial Mastaba (or by taking the route around the courtyard as indicated by the figures incised on the pillars in the courtyard – see hereafter).

ad 2): In this case the entrance to the courtyard would be located on the same axis as the courtyard itself. From an architectural point of view, this layout would make more sense and would be more appropriate as a solution for the same hypothetical situation in royal architecture (which was, above all, axial at its core). On the other hand, we should ask whether it was more convenient for the cultic function of the mastaba if it led the hypothetical cult processions quite a distance from the entrance to the Initial Mastaba. As a matter of course, the courtyard might have been used for some sort of circular processions. Moreover, there is another fact supporting the theory that the entrance from the Southern Portico to the courtyard was in the courtyard's north-west corner. These are the aforementioned relief representations of the tomb owner on the pillars (for the discussion on the these representations, see bellow). These representations seem to show the main cultic route of the courtyard as heading towards its north-west corner and not to the axis of its north wall, where the discussed entranceway might have been located.

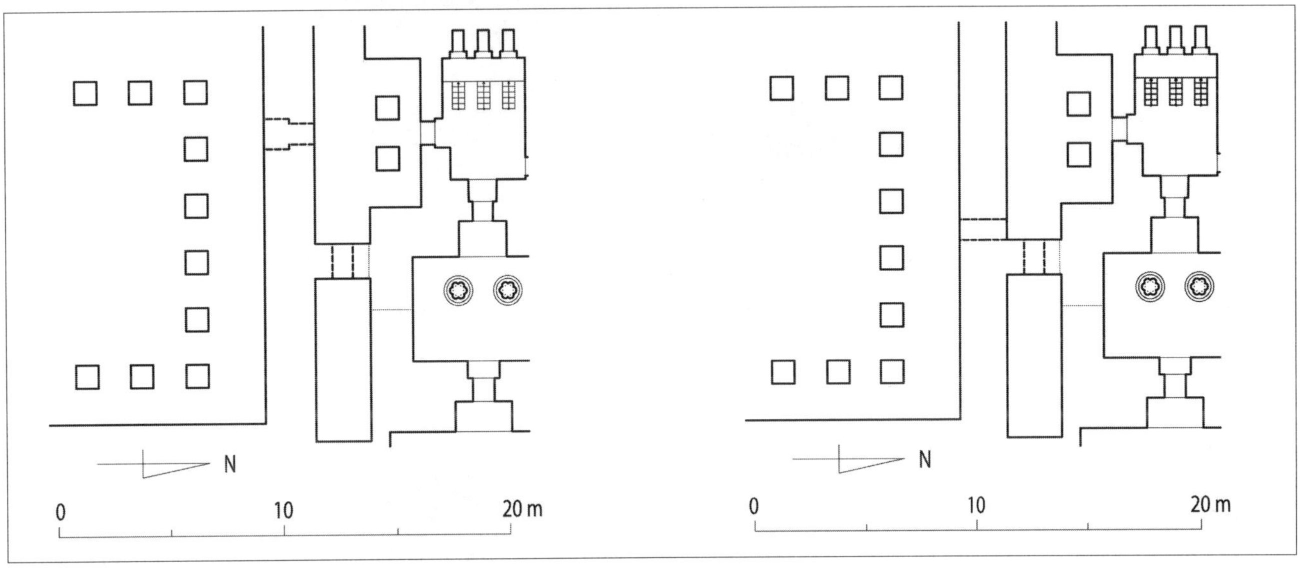

Fig. 4.3.13a–b Two options for the location of the doorway between Room no. 10–11 and the north wing of ambulatory of the pillared courtyard

Therefore it is more probable that the entrance to the Southern Portico was located in the middle of its southern wall, in the general area of the north-western corner of the courtyard.

If the proposed reconstruction of the area to the south of Room no. 4 is right, then the southern wall of the enlarged Southern Portico (Room no. 10–11) and of Room no. 12 was 2.10 m wide. The estimated width is acceptable, on the one hand, because of the fact that this wall had to support the large sized ceiling beams of the ambulatory and, on the other hand, because of the reconstructed width of the ambulatory running along this wall (for further discussion see p. 120–121).

We cannot rule out, that in the western part of the room, a basin was located (see discussion on p. 129). This hypothetical basin would have been connected onto the waste system of the mastaba. Its function is not, as was also the case for the enlarged Southern Portico (no. 10–11), possible to ascertain. In the relief decoration of the northern wall of the enlarged Southern Portico the bringing of offerings is attested. On the other hand, we cannot exclude that this hypothetical basin was placed there during the second building stage and that it was installed in the enlarged Southern Portico. Such rituals cannot be excluded: the bringing of offerings is attested in the decoration of the northern wall of enlarged Room no. 10–11 in the part of its northern wall, where we can suppose the existence of the basin.[390]

[390] *Op. cit.*, 114–115, Pl. 62, Photo 116.

4.3.6 Room no. 12

This room, constructed during the third building stage, is another quite puzzling space. It was built to the east of the Southern Portico and to the north-east of the open pillared courtyard. As is also the case with the Southern Portico, the south wall of Room no. 12 was almost completely destroyed by stone robbers and only small remains of the core of this wall still remain *in situ* (*fig. 4.3.14*). This core masonry has the same character as the core wall creating the south wall of the enlarged Southern Portico. It is therefore possible to suppose that they originally created one unit, together with the northern side wall of the open courtyard. Fortunately, the white limestone casing blocks from the north and east walls of Room no. 12 are preserved.

Fig. 4.3.14 Room no. 12, remaining core masonry of the southern wall

Fig. 4.3.15 Room no. 12 from the east

On the north wall of the room (or more precisely in the space between Room nos. 11 and 12) there is a pilaster which is 1.55 m broad. It could be as a part of a door-jamb as an imprint of a partition wall between both rooms. Together with the clearly perceptible casing of the room's east wall, it provides us with an opportunity of reconstructing the original dimensions of this oblong, east-west oriented space, which was 2.45 m wide and 6.98 m long. Unlike the enlarged Southern Portico, the original floor paving remained *in situ* in the room's eastern part. It was constructed of larger flat blocks of limestone (see *fig. 4.3.15*).

The preserved part of the room's casing and very probably the whole room were not decorated (see *figs. 4.3.12, 4.3.15, 4.3.16*). This fact could be important in relation to our interpretation of the room. As the room lacks relief decoration, it seems that the room did not represent a space in which some cultic rituals were operating.[391] Therefore, two hypotheses concerning the room's function could be

[391] The non-existence of the decoration of this room does not necessarily indicate that it must have been used for the erection of a statue which might have played a role during the rituals.

presented. Firstly, it might have served as a kind of a storeroom. In support of this interpretation of the room's function, it is possible to mention a very close analogy – the Northern Storerooms – which were built during the second building stage. They are also without any decoration (see *chapter 4.2.6*). Secondly, Room no. 12 might have served as a serdab. If this was really the case, then the above mentioned pilaster on the north wall of the Room no. 12 might have originally been a part of a partition wall with a slot connecting the hypothetical statue room no. 12 with the remodelled Southern Portico. Yet another interpretation might see such a serdab connected solely to the pillared courtyard by means of other slots. Such a layout, combining an open courtyard and a serdab is not exceptional in the

Fig. 4.3.16 Room no. 12, eastern wall

tomb architecture of the Fifth and Sixth Dynasties. Here it is possible to mention, among others, two particular examples. The first is found in the Mastaba of Ti in Saqqara.[392] To the north of that tomb's pillared courtyard there is a serdab connected by means of slots not only with the courtyard but also with the entrance portico to the whole tomb. In the case of the Mastaba of Ptahshepses, however, there was no documented direct connection between Room no. 12 and the New Portico (Room no. 1). The same pattern can be found in the tomb of Ptahhotep I in Saqqara.[393] Here, two serdabs flank the walls of the open pillared courtyard; they are connected to the courtyard by means of a series of slots. The above-mentioned examples show that such a solution to the space management was possible.

In other non-royal tombs of the period, in the parts of walls where serdab slots were located, the relief decoration thematically emphasized the existence of these slots and represented a ritual reference for the statue(s) located in the serdab.[394] Unfortunately, the relevant relief decoration, which could help give us a more precise interpretation of the room function, is absent in the case of the Mastaba of Ptahshepses, and the collection of fragments of relief decoration cannot help in this respect.

4.3.7 Room no. 13–14 – pillared courtyard (see *pl. 37a, b*)

The pillared courtyard is the largest space in the mastaba and the key area of the third building stage (see *fig. 4.3.17*). Beside its cultic function, it was also the cross-

---

[392] See Épron, Daumas, *Le tombeau de Ti* I, fig. 1.
[393] Hassan, *Ny-'ankh-Pepy*, 12, pl. XXVIII B, XXX B. A further example is the tomb of Nebkauhor Idu built in Saqqara – Hassan, *Neb-Kaw-Her*, fig. 1, 23.
[394] *Cf.* Wild, *Le tombeau de Ti* III, Pl. CLXXII.

Fig. 4.3.17 Pillared courtyard from the north

roads for the major pathways for the entire mastaba. Nevertheless, the preservation not only of the walls of the ambulatory around the courtyard (especially in the case of its north wing), but also that of the pillars is lamentable. The ambulatory lacks the relief decoration previously removed by stone robbers and the floor pavement is also to a large extent destroyed. Its best preserved parts are located in the area of the south wing of the ambulatory and in between the pillars. As we have seen already in Room no. 12, the floor pavement was made of large flat limestone blocks.

4.3.7.1 Dimensions and layout of the courtyard

Concerning the dimensions, it can be said, that the courtyard itself forms a precise square – its dimensions were: 11.25 × 11.25 m (21.63 × 21.63 cubits). As the casing of the walls of the courtyard has been removed, it was not easy to estimate the width of the ambulatory (Room no. 14) – and therefore the dimensions of the whole courtyard. However, to the north-west of the entrance to Room no. 16, *i.e.*, the niche numbered as no. 15, a smaller limestone block of paving remained *in situ* (for this situation *fig. 4.3.18*). On this block the imprint of a wall facing remains, and therefore it is possible to measure the width of the ambulatory there, which was 2.16 m (between the original face of the ambulatory's side wall and the faces of the pillars). This wall imprint leads us to assume that the courtyard was once cased with white limestone blocks decorated with reliefs. This supposition is also confirmed by a small part of the relief decoration which has been preserved on the south wall of the doorway entrance to Room no. 32 in the south-western corner of the courtyard.[395] The ambulatory, and particularly its casing along the courtyard's northern and eastern side is not so easy to document. It seems very probable that the width of the casing of the ambulatory wall (*i.e.* the distance between the face of the core masonry and of the casing itself) was not identical in the separate parts of the courtyard's ambulatory. The imprint on the pavement of the ambulatory, both in the south, as well as in the west, provides a good guide to the width of this

[395] Verner, *Reliefs*, 117, 119, pl. 82, photo 129.

Fig. 4.3.18 The niche in front of the entrance to Room no. 16; on the pavement block there is an imprint of the casing of the southern wall of the pillared courtyard's ambulatory in Room no. 15

wall. Moreover, it is clear that the casing of a wall that is about 5 m high needs to have some space, so that the core masonry needs quite a thick casing if it is to have the same width in the ambulatory. It is also evident that the width of the casing blocks was not equal in all the instances around the ambulatory's side walls. Moreover, we sometimes have some backing masonry between the core masonry and the casing which was essential for the stability of the casing masonry.

The side wall of the northern wing of the ambulatory has not survived at all. If we take into consideration the width of the side wall of this ambulatory wing, it is very probable that the casing had a width that was close to that of the south wing of the ambulatory (0.53 m). In this way, the north wall of the ambulatory would perfectly fit with the north wall of the entrance recess that had been made in the Initial Mastaba (Room no. 21): there would thus be no irregularity. If this supposition is correct, then the width of the northern ambulatory would be very close to that of the southern wing of the ambulatory – 2.17 m.

More complicated is the situation along the western side of the courtyard. From the plan of the core masonry of the mastaba (see *fig. 4.3.1*), it follows that the masonry and the casing built during the third building stage to the south of the south-east corner of the Initial Mastaba is not in alignment with the eastern face of the Initial Mastaba. In this way, a more complex course of the wall of the western ambulatory can be projected (see *pl. 39*).

The core masonry built in this part of the ambulatory's western wall during the third building stage clearly shows that the width of the ambulatory was not similar to that of the southern or northern wings, but instead much narrower. The problem is that no part of the casing or of its imprint in this part of the ambulatory has survived. If we take into account the width of the casing in the northern part of the same wall (which was built during the first building stage (see *chapter 4.1.1*), *i.e.* ca 0.38 m), the width of the ambulatory here might be inferred to be as little as 1.65 m. For practical reasons it is not possible to assume that the casing here would have been even wider. As we have already implied, it is very probable that the casing of the north part of the wall in the ambulatory western wing was in fact the casing of the Initial Mastaba. Therefore, the ambulatory was wider in this section (which was 8.65 m long) than it was in the case of the southern section, at least 2.45 m. It is probable that the space that resulted was used for the erection of supposed stone *naoi* for the placement of statues (for the hypothetical existence of statue-*naoi* in this area, see further) or the freestanding statues.

The situation along the east wall of the ambulatory is also complex (see *fig. 4.3.19*). In this area, the distance between the face of the core masonry and the faces of the pillars is quite small – only 2.36 m. This could have two explanations. If the casing alone of this wall was equal in its width to the casing of the side walls in the other parts of the ambulatory then the eastern wing of the ambulatory was about 1.7–1.8 m wide here. But if it were the case that the width of the ambulatory would have been equal to those in the southern and northern wings, then the width of the casing would have been much smaller (less than 20 cm). It is apparent that such a width would not be sufficient for the construction of the casing of a wall ca 5 m high and the load of large ceiling blocks from the ambulatory that they would have to bear. Therefore, it is more probable that, as hypothetically was the case with the southern part of the western wing, the eastern wing of the ambulatory was also narrower than the northern and southern wings.

Fig. 4.3.19 Pillared courtyard, core of the eastern wall built of limestone blocks with bossage

4.3.7.2 Pillars

The pillars erected along the sides of the courtyard itself are the most prominent feature of the space.[396] They were made of monolithic blocks of mediocre quality of porous limestone (*fig. 4.3.20*)[397] and their state of preservation, therefore, is not very good. The pillars have squared shafts (1.09 × 1.09 m), but the corner pillars are not squared, but instead slightly oblong (1.09 m width × 1.19 m length), as appeared in the case in the courtyards of Khufu,[398] Userkaf,[399] and Khentkaus II [400]. The pillars (the tallest of them is no more than 3.55 m), have not survived to their original height, which therefore has to be estimated. The inward looking faces of the pillars are decorated with striding figures of the tomb owner in sunk relief (*pl. 38*). The figures of Ptahshepses are 1.39 m high and the base border (marked by a narrow band) was – for all of the pillars – at a level of 1.47 m; the uppermost part of the figures was therefore at a height of 2.86 m (*fig. 4.3.21*).[401] Above the figures, there were incised the hieroglyphic signs which introduced the name of Ptahshepses with his highest titles, among them, the title of King's son (see *fig. 2.2* and discussion on this title on p. 20–21). Lower parts of these texts are still preserved (especially in the case of the western row of the pillars), however, their upper parts are not *in situ*. Despite this fact, Žába was lucky enough to find fragments of these upper parts of inscriptions. If one adds them above the texts surviving *in situ*, one can reconstruct the height of the pillars as 4.10 m.[402]

The pillars once supported architraves on which the ceiling of the ambulatory rested (*fig. 4.3.22* and *fig. 2.1*). The architraves were adorned with sunk relief

---

396 For a discussion concerning the pillar system of the courtyard see: Korecký, in: *Preliminary Report*, 109–115.
397 As with the material which was used for making the columns in the New Portico, it is very probable that the stone from which the pillars were formed was quarried in the area to the west of Lion's Hill, an area to the south of the Abusir necropolis; see also note no. 367.
398 *MRA* IV, 62, Tav. 9, fig. 1, Tav. 10, fig. 7.
399 Labrousse, Lauer, *Ouserkaf*, 48, fig. 51, general plan *in fine*.
400 The oblong pillar, still standing *in situ*, was attested in the courtyard of Queen Khentkaus II in Abusir (see: Jánosi, in: Verner, *Khentkaus*, 152); another pillar, which is also oblong was not found in its original situation. This fact enabled P. Jánosi to reconstruct the original situation in two forms, with oblong pillars erected along the entire periphery of the courtyard, or, as is also the case with the Ptahshepses mastaba, only at its corners (see: Jánosi, in: Verner, *Khentkaus*, 154, fig. 72a–b).
401 Verner, *Reliefs*, 117–119, pls. 79–81, photos 132–134.
402 Korecký, in: *Preliminary Report*, 112–113, figs. 59–61; Balík, Vachala, in: *Abusir and Saqqara 2000*, 320, fig. 6; Balík, *Mastaba*, fig. on p. 73.

Fig. 4.3.20 Pillared courtyard, one of the pillars erected in the western row

Fig. 4.3.21 Pillared courtyard, south-western corner with pillars of the ambulatory in the courtyard

Fig. 4.3.22 Present position of the architraves and the north-eastern corner of the pillared courtyard

decoration comprising hieroglyphic texts mentioning the tomb owner's titulary, his name and his figure.[403] As is the case concerning the pillars, the architraves were of two formats. The "standard" architraves were 2.45 m long, 1.02 m wide and their height was 1.02 m, too (*fig. 4.3.23*). At both ends of the architraves there were grooves for the insertion of dovetail cramps used here for improving the stability of the whole construction (*fig. 4.3.24*).[404] It is not possible to say from which material these cramps were made.[405]

The second group of architraves was used in the corners of the courtyard. Their shape had to be adapted to this use. We can document this type only in the

---

[403] Verner, *Reliefs*, 116–118, pls. 72–78, photos 118–128.

[404] For a discussion concerning these cramps, see Arnold, *Building*, 124–127.

[405] The cramps used in Khaefre's valley temple were made of copper (Hölscher, *Chephren*, 43, Abb. 26,); in the case of the basalt fittings, used in the open courtyard of Sahure's mortuary temple, they were improved by the addition of pins; Borchardt, *Sahure* I, 45, Abb. 47; in Niuserre's open courtyard, the cramps were made of gneiss: Borchardt, *Neuserre*, 56, Abb. 35, 36, Bl. 13. *Cf.* also Labrousse, Lauer, Leclant, *Le temple haute du roi Ounas*, 29, pl. XII B, C.

Fig. 4.3.23 Pillared courtyard, upper surfaces of the standard architraves with grooves for stabilizing cramps

Fig. 4.3.24 Groove for inserting a cramp in the upper face of an architrave

Fig. 4.3.25 Pillared courtyard, corner architrave as seen from above

Fig. 4.3.26 Pillared courtyard, preserved crown of the core masonry belonging to the eastern outer wall

case of one surviving corner architrave found during the excavation of the courtyard. It is now lying in the north-eastern corner of the courtyard (see *fig. 4.3.25*). This rather weathered architrave is now 2.45 m long, its width at least 0.99 m and its height 1.02 m. One side of the architrave is oblique. Regrettably, it is not clear whether both sides of the architrave were oblique or not, or whether its underside ran straight to the end of the block (in which case the block would have been longer). These architrave blocks were joined to the pillars, as was the standard way in this period, by pins.[406] The roof of the ambulatory would then have been at a level of 5.14 m. No data concerning the height of the roofing blocks are available.[407]

Following the above mentioned measurements, the roof terrace of the ambulatory can be pinpointed at a level of about 5.65 m (for the present situation of the outer wall of the courtyard, see *fig. 4.3.26*).[408] The eastern wall of the courtyard could have been crowned at the same level; however, due to the existence of the stairway (see *chapter 4.2.4*) we should assume the existence of a low wall encircling the whole of the newly built part of the mastaba. Such a wall – at least 1 cubit, *i.e.* 0.52 m, high[409] and at least also one cubit thick[410] – was probably topped by a curved crown. In this way, it is possible to estimate the height of the eastern outer wall of the courtyard as around 6.17 m, or 6.69 m (in the event that the encircling wall was 2 cubits – 1.04 m – high).

The sides of the pillars facing the courtyard were adorned by aforementioned standing figures of Ptahshepses, made in sunk relief. The figures are oriented differently on the individual sides (see *fig. 4.3.44*). If we follow the common direction of these images, it seems that Ptahshepses would enter the courtyard through the doorway from Room no. 16, which was located in the north-south axis of the court, then pass through the courtyard along two routes – along the courtyard's south and western sides, or southern, eastern and northern side. The figure then heads towards the north-west corner of the courtyard and approaches the entrance to the Initial Mastaba. It seems very clear that these depictions illustrate a direct connection between Room no. 16 and the cultic rooms of the Initial Mastaba.

It is also apparent, that the decoration of the pillars and architraves – that of the figures of Vizier Ptahshepses and of his titles and epithets – was made in an effort to achieve maximum artistic effect. The line above which the figures of the deceased were portrayed was not a random choice, but made in connection with the level of the visitor's eyes. In this way the visitor's sight is focused on the higher sections of the pillars where the main parts of Ptahshepses' body were to be found.

---

406 Korecký, in: *Preliminary Report*, 109, presumes that the pins were made of wood; *cf.* Borchardt in *Sahure* I, 45, Bl. 9, mentions basalt pins; Borchardt, *Neuserre*, 55–56, Abb. 35–36, Bl. 13.

407 Only hypothetically can one assume that their height was one cubit, *i.e.*, 0.52 m.

408 *Cf.* Balík, Vachala, in: *Abusir and Saqqara 2000*, fig. 6.

409 The estimated reading is the lowest possible. As is well documented, these walls might reach a height of 1.80 m – as we can see in the case of the tomb of Shepseskafankh located in Cemetery G 6000 in Giza (Weeks, *Cemetery G 6000*, fig. 3).

410 To ascertain the thickness as well as the height of this encircling wall is not possible because no part of its masonry as well as no block is preserved.

In this way, it was ensured that neither the figures nor the pillars overall appeared narrow (due to the rules of the viewer's perspective) and the effect on the visitor was even more monumental.[411] The dark, sunk reliefs of the vizier's figures and of the hieroglyphic lines and columns on the sun bathed pillars and architraves made a kind of a frame for dark spaces between the single pillars. The sunlit surfaces interchanged with the dusky rectangles of the ambulatory or *vice versa*: the spaces would be bathed in light, but the side of the pillars not facing the sun would appear dark. Perhaps this effect might have also played some role in the positioning of the proposed *naoi* with statues (see below). As a matter of course, we cannot rule out the notion that in the free spaces between the pillars other statues were erected. However, it should be underlined here, that no trace of any such arrangement was found during the archaeological work; the idea is purely hypothetical.

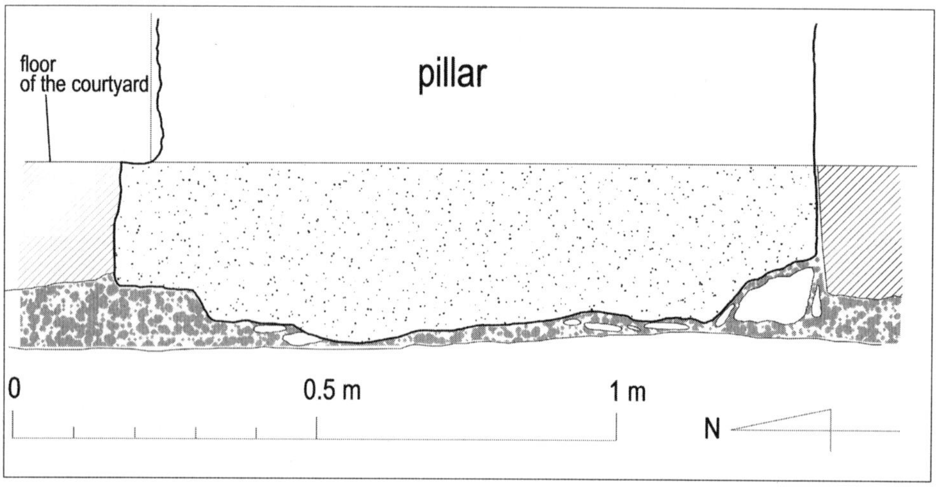

Fig. 4.3.27 Pillared courtyard, section through the embedding of the pillar erected in the south-western corner of the courtyard

Fig. 4.3.28a–b Pillared courtyard, embedding of the pillar in the south-western corner of the courtyard

As is well known, the pillared courtyard in the Mastaba of Ptahshepses is not the only example of its kind known to us from Old Kingdom architecture. The most famous, and chronologically also the closest comparison, is the courtyard built in the Mastaba of Ti.[412] As was the case with the pillars in the Mastaba of Ptahshepses (see *fig. 4.3.27, 4.3.28*), the pillars in Ti's tomb were embedded directly in the pavement, without the use of any kind of base. This way of fixing of pillars predominated in both the Giza and Saqqara necropoleis and we also find it in the Mastaba of Mereruka.[413] For further discussion on this topic, see *chapter 5*.

---

[411] *Cf.* also Balík, *Mastaba*, 44.
[412] See Épron, Daumas, *Le tombeau de Ti* I, fig. 1.
[413] *PM* III, 525; Duell, *Mereruka*, figure opposite to pl. 2.

4.3.7.3 The system of channels in the mastaba

In the north-south axis of the courtyard, its northern half contained a basin. It was connected to the system of waste canals which once began in the major offering room of the Initial Mastaba (see *chapter 4.1.9*). The basin was embedded in the pavement of the courtyard. It is only partially preserved up to the present day, about one third of it having been destroyed (see *figs. 4.3.29, 4.3.30*). The basin was made of fine white limestone and has an elongated shape. Its dimensions were: 1.61 × 0.72 m.

Fig. 4.3.29 Pillared courtyard, basin during the time of its unearthing

Fig. 4.3.30 Pillared courtyard, basin, present situation

The basin was cut out in a rectangular block and also the basin tank (1.31 × 0.43 m) itself has a rectangular shape. In the northern end there is an outfall which served for the overflow of waste liquids. The waste channel comes from the north-west and runs under the basin itself; the outfall was somehow connected with the channel. Nevertheless, this was not possible to confirm during archaeological excavations as this space has been largely destroyed. The channel then runs in a north-easterly direction towards the pillars in the north-east corner of the ambulatory (see *fig.*

4.3.1). It then changes direction and runs directly to the east, below the outer wall of the mastaba (*figs. 4.3.31– 4.3.33*). Whether it ended as a blind drain outside the mastaba (or under the masonry of the mastaba's outer wall) was not possible to ascertain, as the small sondage that was made from outside the outer wall of the mastaba, found no sign of the existence of such a drain.

Fig. 4.3.31 (left) Pillared courtyard, eastern part of the waste canal

Fig. 4.3.32 Pillared courtyard, terminal part of the waste canal running out of the courtyard's ambulatory

The waste system ran from the major offering room below the outer masonry of the Initial Mastaba in an east-west direction (see *figs. 4.3.34, 4.3.35*). The construction of its channels was quite simple. A groove forming the channel itself was cut into the lower blocks made of limestone. The groove was 15 cm wide (12 cm in its bottom) and 13 cm deep; in the part of the channel running below the eastern outer wall of the mastaba, the groove was 14 cm wide and 16 cm deep. The blocks of the channel were not smoothed properly (neither was the groove itself). On the other hand, the separate blocks were joined by high quality mortar. These lower blocks were covered by flat, worked limestone blocks. It seems that these upper blocks were not joined with the lower part of the channel. Due to the activities of stone robbers, the waste system was almost totally destroyed, especially in the north-western part. This fact enabled us to study it in this area. The part of the waste system constructed during the third building stage was connected to the drain of the channel coming from the Initial Mastaba.

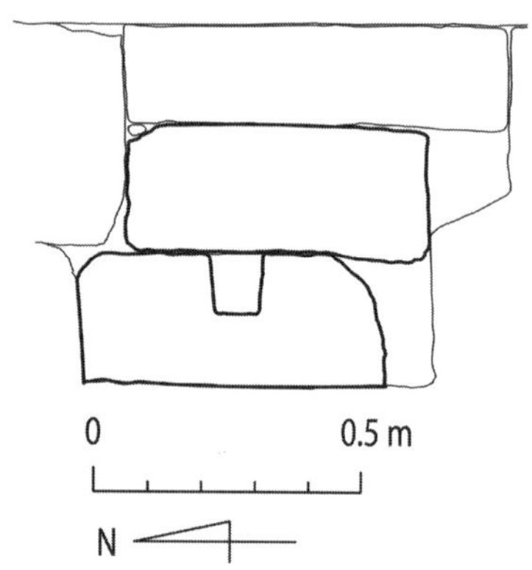

Fig. 4.3.33 Pillared courtyard, section through the waste canal leading under the masonry of the eastern side wall of the courtyard's ambulatory

This part of the mastaba was occupied by the enlarged Southern Portico during the third building stage. Following the archaeological plan of the mastaba made by V. Fiala (see *fig. 1.12*), a block with the forked channel was documented in the western part of the enlarged Southern Portico. The channel in this block on Fiala's plan was traced to its connection with the outlet from the channel built in the eastern outer wall of the Initial Mastaba. However, this situation is not possible to ascertain now. The block with the forked channel no longer exists here (it seems that it was removed for some unrecorded reason since its excavation in the year 1961). If this block had indeed existed in this place, then it would mean that in the western part of the enlarged Southern Portico there was some kind of basin. There is no attestation of a channel in Room no. 4. Therefore, this forked line leading off the "main" channel had to be terminated by a basin. As has been already mentioned on p. 117, an accurate determination of its function (*i.e.* whether it was a libation or a purification basin) cannot now be ascertained.

The hypothetical basin would have been connected with the main channel from the north. In order to reach the basin (which was located in the axis of the newly

Fig. 4.3.34 Pillared courtyard, waste canal running below the masonry of the Initial Mastaba

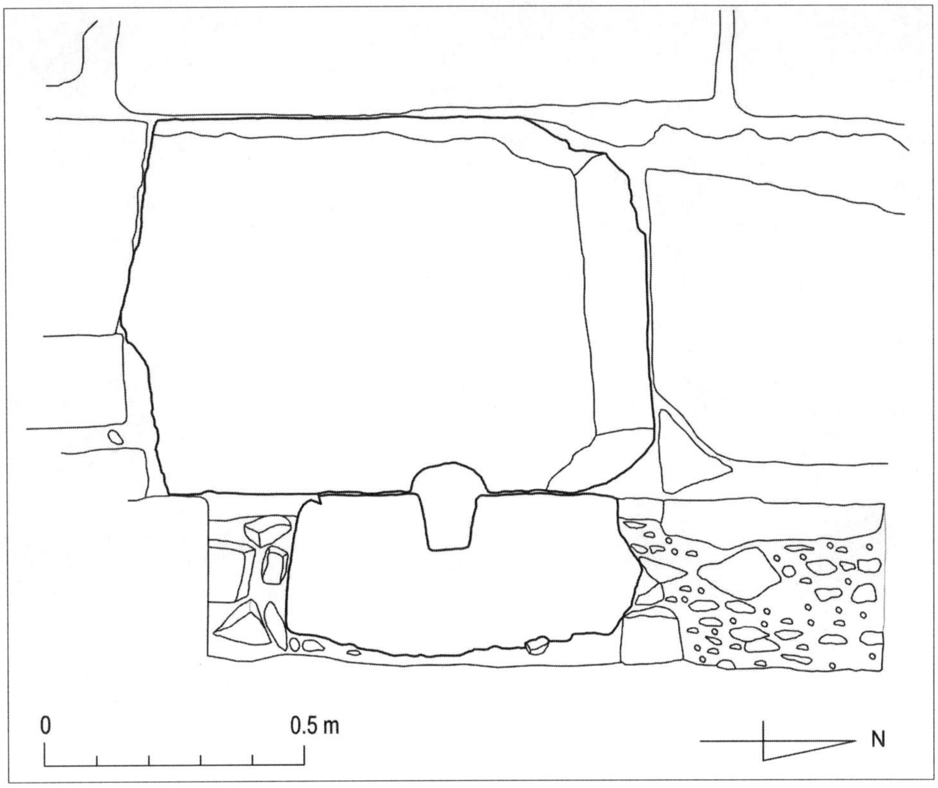

Fig. 4.3.35 (right) Pillared courtyard, section through the waste canal running below the masonry of the Initial Mastaba

constructed courtyard), the direction of the channel had to be changed from an east-west to a northwest-southeast direction. Unfortunately, the precise location of this switch of direction was destroyed by stone robbers. The channel then headed towards the basin placed in the courtyard, *i.e.* in the northwest-southeast direction and from the basin along the southwest-northeast axis outside the mastaba.

It is interesting that the ancient builders did not hesitate to erect pillars above the channel (see *figs. 4.3.36–4.3.39*). This approach was documented by archaeological excavation in two places – in the north-west and north-east corners of the courtyard. This situation shows that, during construction, the waste system of the enlarged mastaba was first laid down and then the pillars were erected.

In the middle of the northern wing of the ambulatory, almost exactly on the north-south axis of the courtyard, another basin was placed (see *fig. 4.3.40, 4.3.41*). It represents a much simpler installation than that of the basin located in the centre of the courtyard – merely a shallow circular hole with an outfall rather than a basin. The hole was cut into a large flat block of the ambulatory pavement (its dimensions were 1.25 × 1.28 m) and has quite small dimensions: depth 0.12 m, diameter 0.17 m. An interesting fact is that the outlet points to the north, *i.e.*, towards the wall of the ambulatory. Evidently, it was not connected to the waste channel crossing the courtyard. It is not clear whether the hole itself was used, or whether a metal (copper?) pot was put into it. The hole could have come into existence during the construction of the mastaba, or shortly after its completion. On the other hand, the walls of the hole were cut and polished – although, with poor craftsmanship. Therefore, it could have represented a secondary activity, made at the time when the original function of the courtyard had already ceased. Whenever the hole was cut, its connection with the north-south axis of the court is apparent. For further discussion on this part of the courtyard, see *chapter 5*.

Fig. 4.3.36 Pillared courtyard, remains of the waste canal running below the pillar and the pavement of the courtyard in its north-western corner

Fig. 4.3.37 Pillared courtyard, intersection of the northern and western row of pillars; in the foreground, remains of the waste canal; view from the north

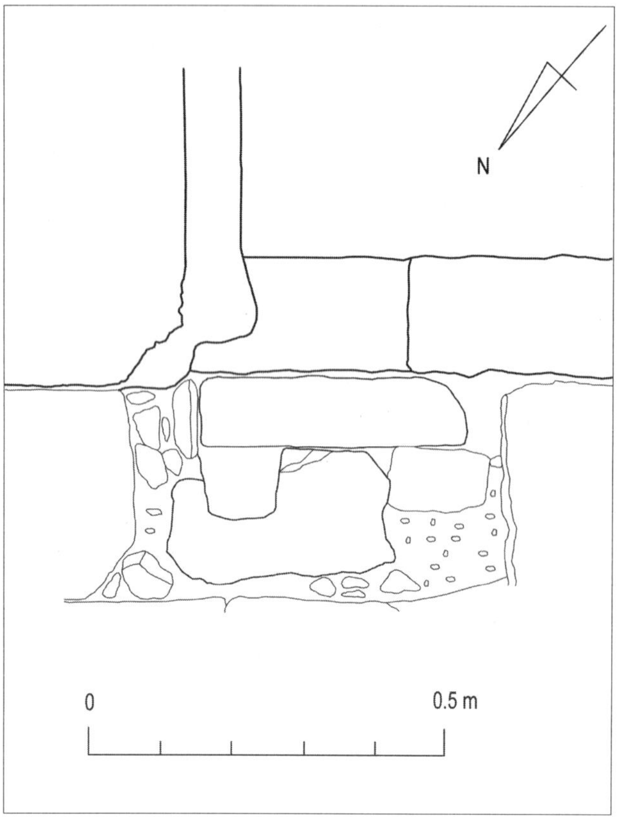

Fig. 4.3.38 Pillared courtyard, section through the waste canal going under the pillar and the pavement of the courtyard in its north-western corner

Fig. 4.3.39 Pillared courtyard, northern wing of the courtyard's ambulatory; remains of the canal system

Fig. 4.3.40 Pillared courtyard, northern wing of the courtyard's ambulatory, and the basin cut into the pavement

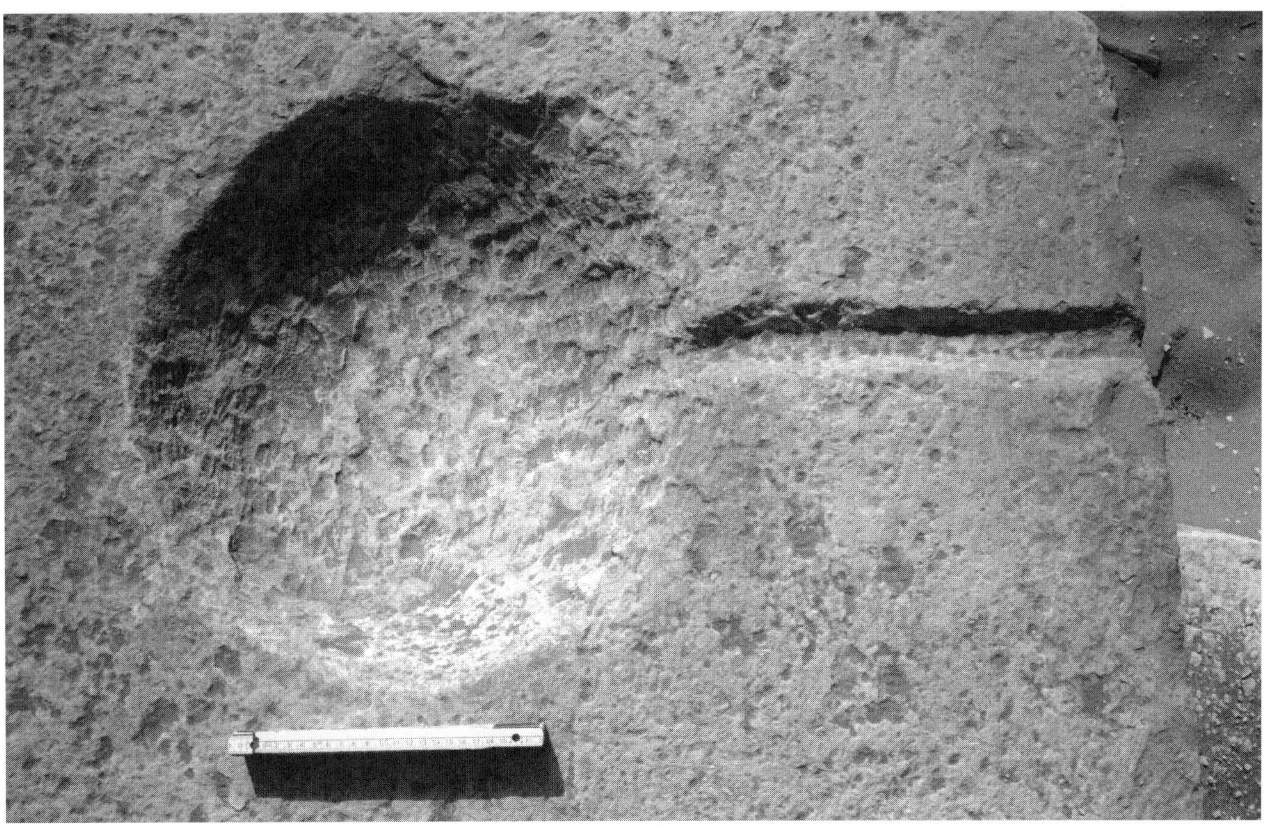

Fig. 4.3.41 Pillared courtyard, close-up of the basin cut into the pavement

4.3.7.4 Other (hypothetical) features of the courtyard

During the archaeological excavation, Zbyněk Žába found in the area to the north of niche (no. 15)[414] a very badly weathered altar with the hieroglyphic sign *ḥtp*.[415] The altar is formed by an irregular block of rather low quality limestone with the following dimensions: upper surface: 0.99 × 0.65 m, the lower surface: 1.03 × 0.84 m. Its height is 0.70–0.72 m. The sign *ḥtp*, which was made by a 4 cm high relief adorning the upper surface of the altar, does not bear any other hieroglyphic inscription (pl. 40).

Because the block was not found *in situ*, it is not possible to locate its original position – either in the court, or elsewhere in the mastaba. Nevertheless, the altar block could have been brought to the area of the mastaba secondarily by stone robbers. It is thus possible to speculate that it was originally located in the neighbouring tombs or in Niuserre's mortuary temple. An older plan of the Mastaba of Ptahshepses places the altar as being in the north-south axis of the courtyard. This hypothesis has been visualised on *pls. 41–42*.[416]

The pillared courtyard in the Mastaba of Ptahshepse might have also served as the place where the tomb owner's statues were venerated. Hypothetically, these would have been placed not only in Rooms no. 4, 16 and 22, but in the courtyard as well. These statues could have been placed in the granite *naos* or *naoi*, whose fragments were found during the archaeological excavation.[417] The *naoi* might have been erected along the northern part of the western wing of the ambulatory. In this part, the ambulatory of the courtyard was broad enough to enable the erection of these naoi and, moreover, there was a recess in the western wall which would allow the naoi to be to some extent protected.

The erection of naoi, or their construction is also recorded in other Old Kingdom tombs. The most important is the example documented in the tomb of Ptahhotep I in Saqqara. Here a stone faced niche was discovered, constructed in the side wall of the courtyard. Apparently, it once housed a statue.[418] Other niches were excavated in the tomb of Rawer.[419]

However, the erection of one or more statues in granite naoi might be possible to connect above all with a practice found in rock-cut tombs of the period. In many cases, these tombs encompass rooms with engaged statues placed in their side walls. The engaged statues were usually framed by lines and columns of hieroglyphic texts.[420] The fragments of naoi found during the excavations of the Mastaba of Ptahshepses also bear hieroglyphic texts, mentioning the names and titles of Ptahshepses. It is, therefore, not improbable to link these finds with the engaged statues from other (mainly rock-cut) tombs of the period. In this connection, we can suppose that the architect of the second enlargement of Ptahshepses' tomb intentionally planned the above-mentioned irregularity of the western wing of the ambulatory. If we assume that the number of the naoi was large, then they might have been erected one beside each other. The analogy of the engaged statues in rock cut tombs is more apparent in this way.

Beside the statues hypothetically erected in the naoi, other statues might have been erected in the courtyard. Whether it might have been the large-sized (about 3.60 m

---

[414] Unfortunately, Žába, even in the relevant excavation notebook, does not give any precise information concerning the situation in which the block was found.

[415] Žába, in: *Preliminary Report*, 18.

[416] *Cf.* plan made by V. Fiala (*fig. 1.11*); Balík, Vachala, in: *Abusir and Saqqara 2000*, fig. 1; Balík, *Mastaba*, figs. on p. 55, 67 and 72.

[417] *Cf.* Patočková, in: *Critères de datation*, 230; however, for further interpretation we should wait for the full publication (now in preparation) of statue fragments found in the Mastaba of Ptahshepses.

[418] Hassan, Iskander, *Ny-ʿnkh-Pepy*, p. 37, fig. 12, Pl. XXIX C.

[419] Hassan, *Gîza* I, Pl. XIII, XIX.

[420] We can document such design in the tomb of Nefer in Saqqara, or the tombs of Qar and of Meresankh III in Giza and in other tombs of the period.

high) granite statue(s) mentioned in the relief decoration of the Southern Portico,[421] is not possible to ascertain. As shown by M. Rochholz, it seems that the inscriptions accompanying the depiction of the statue may have been an exaggeration based on Ptahshepses' endeavour to follow royal models.[422] However, this does not rule out that a large, life-sized or even over life-sized statue – or, possibly more than one – was erected in the courtyard.

4.3.8 Room no. 16

This room, located south of the north-south axis of the courtyard, was accessible from the courtyard by means of a deep passageway ("Room no. 15"). Because there is a difference of 0.60 m between the levels of the floor of the courtyard and of Room no. 16 (*fig. 4.3.42*), the passage was certainly equipped with a short ascending stairway with three or four steps enabling access to the room. However, no direct proof of such stairway was documented during the archaeological excavations. Despite the fact that the space of the deep niche – Room no. 15 – and the actual entrance to Room no. 16 was largely destroyed, it seems, following the layout of the passageway, that the door opened into the courtyard.

Fig. 4.3.42 Pillared courtyard, southern part with the entrance to Room no. 16

Room no. 16 was a rectangular, north-south oriented chamber, 3.25 m wide and at least 8.00 m long. In the north-east corner, there was a doorway leading to the south-eastern complex of storerooms (nos. 17–20). Despite the fact that the area of the doorway is almost completely destroyed, it is possible to assume that it was equipped with one-leafed wooden door, which opened into the corridor of the storerooms.

Room no. 16 was also destroyed to a high degree, as is shown by the almost complete lack of casing on the western, southern and eastern walls. This destruction of the casing enabled the study of the inner masonry of the side walls which were built quite shoddily by rather small blocks of limestone. As is the case of south-eastern storerooms, these two side walls were built after the construction of the outer wall. On the north and the east wall, small parts of the original relief decoration remains *in situ*. In the case of the eastern wall, they depict part of a male figure with a short hieroglyphic inscription, as well as some ships on the northern wall.[423] A large part of the pavement of the room's floor was also removed. The pavement once consisted of large, well worked and carefully smoothed blocks (*fig. 4.3.43*). We can hypothesise that high quality of work done in connection with pavement blocks and also the recorded relief decoration was because of the function of the room. It was apparently different from the function of Room nos. 17–20, located further to

---

[421] Verner, *Reliefs*, 104–105.

[422] This problem has been discussed by M. Rochholz 'Statuen und Statuendarstellungen im Grab des *Ptḥ-šps*', *SÄK* 21 (1994), 267–269, 272–273.

[423] Verner, *Reliefs*, 120, photos 130–131, pl. 83–84.

the east. In Peter Jánosi's opinion it served a similar function to Room no. 22 in the Initial Mastaba, *i.e.*, for the display of a statue.[424] That the room played an important role in the cultic functioning of the whole mastaba is shown by already discussed direction of tomb owner's relief depictions on the pillars at the courtyard (see *fig. 4.3.44*).[425]

Fig. 4.3.43 Room no. 16 from the north

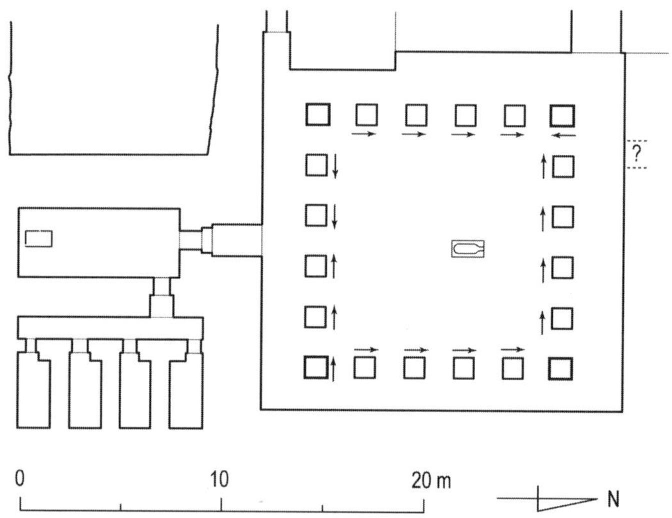

Fig. 4.3.44 Scheme of the orientation of relief figures decorating the pillars erected in the courtyard

4.3.9 Room nos. 17–20

When they constructed these storerooms, the masons who built this south-east group of storerooms, together with Room no. 16, used the perimeter wall as the supporting masonry for the inner rooms of the mastaba, as well as for the outer masonry of the mastaba. The fact that the masonry of the side walls of the storerooms, as of Room no. 16 were not joined with the outer wall of the mastaba clearly shows, that the perimeter wall made of large, roughly made blocks was erected first, and then the walls of the inner rooms of this area. The storerooms were connected to each other and with Room no. 16 by means of a south-north oriented corridor (which opened into Room no. 16 by the already mentioned doorway in its north-western corner). The corridor was 1.53 m wide and 9.15 m long. In its east wall there were entrances to the four storerooms.

The storerooms had almost exactly the same layout. Basically, they were rectangular, east-west oriented rooms with entrances in their west walls. Despite

---

[424] Jánosi, 'Les tombes privées »des maisons d'éternité«', in: *L'art égyptienne*, fig. 37.

[425] A masons' mark in this room has been discussed by D. Magdolen ('Some Notes on One Graffito from the Mastaba of Ptahshepses at Abusir', *GM* 182 [2001], 87–96). In his opinion, the inscription on the southern core wall of the room and the entries which is possible to connect with the overall plan of the mastaba and of the dimensions of the pillared courtyard.

the fact that their layout was nearly identical, it is interesting that the storerooms did not have identical dimensions. Their width varied from 1.64 to 1.67 m and length 3.25 to 3.33 m. This fact was almost certainly caused by mistakes made during the measuring and delimiting of the separate rooms during the preparations for the construction of the storerooms themselves.[426]

Fig. 4.3.45 South-eastern complex of storerooms from the south-east

The walls of the storerooms were cased with finely worked blocks of quality white limestone and their floors were also paved by well worked and smoothed flat limestone blocks (see *fig. 4.3.45*). The partitions between the separate storerooms (0.88–0.89 m) were faced with casing slabs hiding the core masonry of roughly worked stones alternating with well worked limestone blocks.[427] This would have improved the stability of the partitions. It is important to emphasize that the pavement blocks used in the storerooms and in the corridor are smaller than those used in Room no. 16. This fact possibly shows the higher level of importance of the latter room, *i.e.*, the supposed cultic function. The level of the corridor and of the storerooms was the same as that of Room no. 16, in that all were elevated above the level of the courtyard's pavement.

The doorways leading to the separate storerooms were equipped with one leafed doors, as is shown by the pivot frames found *in situ*. In the case of storerooms nos. 18–20, the door pivot was placed to the right when looking into the storerooms (to the east). In storeroom no. 17, the pivot was located on the left side. In relation to the architectural layout of the individual storerooms it seems that they did not incorporate a second floor or any kind of semi-floor. The reason for this supposition is that neither traces of a staircase nor any traces of such floor were found in the masonry still remaining *in situ*.

An important question is that of determining storerooms' function. Following the supposition that Room no. 16 very probably served as a kind of a chapel connected to the cult of the tomb owner's statue, it is very probable that the storerooms functioned in connection with this cult.

---

[426] Compare the similar situation in the case of the niches located in Room no. 4, built during the second building stage – see *chapter 4.2.5*.

[427] For a similar technique see – Arnold, *Building in Egypt*, 148–150, figs. 4.72.3 and 4.76. The same technique was documented in the case of the masonry in the mortuary temple of the Pyramid Lepsius no. 24 in Abusir or, in Niuserre's mortuary temple at the same site.

4.3.10 Room nos. 32–39

In the south-west corner of the pillared courtyard there is a deep door recess which gives access to corridor no. 32. The casing of the doorway has only partially survived in its western part and in the doorframe itself. The rest was destroyed, therefore requiring estimates of its dimensions. If the casing on this part of the western wall of the courtyard had the same width as was the case for its southern wall, then the length of the passageway was 2.25 m. However, if the casing was about 35 cm wide, as was recorded for the northern part of the same courtyard's wall, the length of the passageway would be ca 1.88 m. The width of the door recess was 1.35 m.

The passageway was once equipped with double leafed wooden doors, as is established by the two limestone washers which remained *in situ* in the pivot holders placed on both sides of the doorway to room 32 (see *fig. 4.3.46*). Their position and the layout of the doorway recess show that the doors opened in the direction of the pillared courtyard. The doorway itself is 0.96 m wide and 1.16 m long. It gave access to corridor no. 32, a rectangular, north-south oriented space.

In its southern wall, Room no. 32 had an entrance to Room no. 40 and in the northern end of the west wall, there was an entrance to the corridor, Room no. 33, and the storerooms, nos. 34–39. The walls of the corridor were cased with finely worked white limestone blocks. Its pavement consisted of flat, well-worked, white limestone blocks (see *fig. 4.3.47*).

Fig. 4.3.46 Doorway between the courtyard and Room no. 32

Corridor no. 33, which is connected to passageway no. 32, is an east-west oriented, 1.04 m wide and 13.58 m long room. As was already mentioned in *chapter 4.1.1*, its entire north wall was created by the casing of the Initial Mastaba, and it therefore sloped at an angle of 82° (*fig. 4.3.48*). The doorway between Room no. 32 and 33 was equipped with a one leafed wooden door which opened into the corridor, Room no. 33. The southern boundary of Room no. 33 was broken up by doorways leading to the individual storerooms. It has to be underlined that the area of the south-west storerooms is one of the most badly destroyed areas in the entire mastaba (*fig. 4.3.49*). Almost no part of any single partition between the storerooms still remains *in situ*. However, it is still possible to say that there were six storerooms (Room nos. 34–39). A study of the remaining masonry of the storerooms revealed the fact that their masonry was built at the same time as the masonry of the north wall of Room no. 40. This fact is clearly shown by their interconnecting junctions.

Fig. 4.3.47 Room no. 32 from the north

Fig. 4.3.48 Remains of the northern wall of Room no. 33, which was created by the casing of the southern outer wall of the Initial Mastaba

Fig. 4.3.49a–b Overall views of the South-western complex of storerooms

The lower sections of the southern walls of the storerooms were created by large limestone blocks. These were up to 2 m long, a minimum of 0.70 m wide and 0.75–0.92 m high.[428] These blocks were certainly put in place before the beginning of the construction of other masonry in this area. They delimited the area of the storerooms from that of Room no. 40. The partitions between the separate storerooms were then adjoined to these large blocks. This masonry was built by using the same method as was used for the partitions between the individual south-east storerooms (see *chapter 4.3.9*). On the east face of the core masonry of the mastaba's western outer wall, there are builders' marks clearly establishing the face of the south walls of the storerooms. Due to the poor state of preservation of the storerooms' masonry, it is not possible to say whether the storerooms were equipped with stairways or second floors. However, it does not seem likely that the stairways and second floors were present in the storerooms. As shown by an only partially remaining pivot-holder in Room no. 37, one can suppose that each doorway was equipped with a one leafed wooden door (*fig. 4.3.50*). This fact was also confirmed by the finding of a block of a door jamb with hollows for a latch (see *fig. 4.3.51*) unearthed in the area of these storerooms. Thus, it probably came from the same area. It seems that the door opened into the storeroom (because the layout of the individual storerooms was certainly identical or very similar, we can

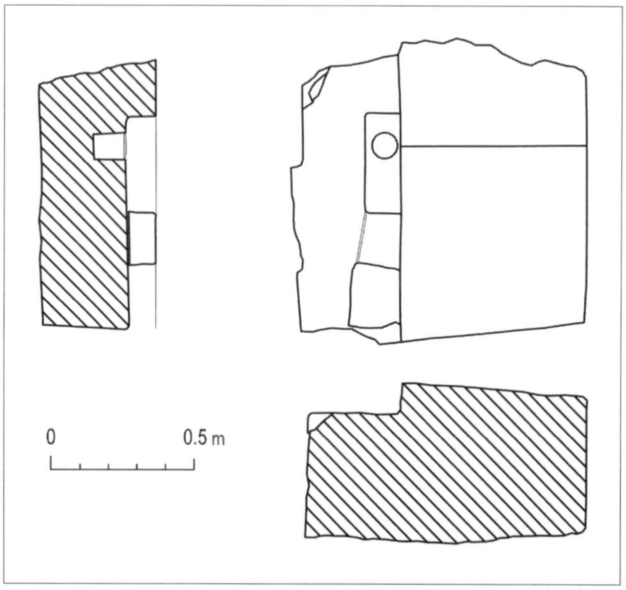

‹ **Fig. 4.3.50 Middle part of the south-western storerooms; in the centre, there are remains of masonry belonging to Room no. 37; view from the north**

Fig. 4.3.51 Block belonging to a door jamb coming from the area of the south-western storerooms

suppose that other doors in the storerooms opened inwards). As shown by the remaining evidence, the storerooms were paved with flat white limestone blocks, as was the case for the south-eastern complex of storerooms.

By the construction of two groups of storerooms, the number of storerooms built during the third building stage, ran to ten. This total is the same as was the number

---

[428] See Verner, *Baugraffiti*, Pl. 8 – E.

of storerooms built in the intimate sector of the royal mortuary temples during the Fifth Dynasty. It is not easy to answer the question why Ptahshepses constructed such a high number of storerooms. As has been suggested, the storerooms in the south-eastern sector were probably intended for equipment that might have been used in the service of the statue in Room no. 16. Contrary to these storage facilities, the storerooms in the area of the south-western sector of the mastaba might have been connected with the statues erected in the naoi placed in the western wing of the courtyard ambulatory. On the other hand, because these storerooms were constructed closed off from the courtyard, they could have also been connected with the originally planed function of Room 40. Alternatively, these storerooms could have been used for both areas, Room no. 40 and the courtyard. Altogether, the Mastaba of Ptahshepses encompassed 14 storerooms (if we accept that the group of the Northern Storerooms was really used for the storage of goods – for the discussion on this problem see *chapter 4.2.6*).

4.3.11 Room no. 40 – Boat-room

Room no. 40, located in the south-west corner of the mastaba, represents one of the most intriguing rooms in the whole tomb. It has an unusual elongated, east-west oriented ground plan with dimensions of 23.80 × 9.72 m; in the broadest spot,

Fig. 4.3.52 Room no. 40 from the east

it is 10.62 m wide. The most striking feature of the room is the curved north wall, which resembles the shape of a hull of a ship (*fig. 4.3.52*). Therefore, the room was given the name the "Boat-room".

The masonry of its side walls was built on a layer of sand and small fragments of limestone (*fig. 4.3.53*). The west and south walls of the room constitute the outer wall of the mastaba and were built of large, monolithic blocks of local limestone (see *figs. 4.3.54, 4.3.55*).[429] The blocks were only cursorily worked and the quality of the joins is also quite unrefined. Unlike the western wall of the room, the south wall was built on a foundation layer that was constructed of large, flat, less well-worked blocks of local limestone. This foundation layer protrudes 0.95–1.05 m into the room. In contrast, the east wall was built of regular, rectangular, well-worked limestone blocks. The second lowest layer was built of larger (ca 1 × 1.2–1.5 m) limestone blocks; in the upper layer the blocks were more elongated. The curved wall was also built by means of quite regular blocks with bossed outer faces

[429] *Cf.* Verner, *Baugraffiti*, pl. E – plan Nr. 8.

Fig. 4.3.53 Room no. 40, north wall from the south-east

Fig. 4.3.54 Room no. 40, west wall from the east

Fig. 4.3.55 Room no. 40, eastern part of the southern wall – view from the north

Fig. 4.3.56 Doorway between Room nos. 40 and 32, east wall

(*fig. 4.3.53*). These two walls are in contrast with the south and west walls whose megalithic blocks do not join regularly. As was the case with the south-eastern complex of storerooms, these two walls were built after the construction of the outer wall of the mastaba.

Near the centre of the northern wall of the room there is a doorway. Despite the fact that most of the casing of the doorway was finished, the part where the northern wall joins Room no. 40 was not smoothed (*fig. 4.3.56*). The doorway is 0.85–1.03 m long and its width is 0.95 m.

After considering the state of preservation of the room's walls, the non-existence of a pavement in the room and also the incomplete condition of the doorway to the room, it is possible to say that the room was not finished as planned.[430] Nevertheless, the layout and the function of the room is one of the most important questions concerning the whole mastaba. Because of the poor documentation made during archaeological excavations of the room, it is not possible to say whether the mud brick masonry in the shape of two hulls was really found there. Such masonry outlining the shape of two boats is shown on the plan in the *Topographical Bibliography*.[431] Only mud brick masonry has been found in the room, supposedly dating to the period of the New Kingdom.[432] At this time, a brick wall was built from the entrance to a small room located in the north-west part of the Boat-room (see *figs. 4.3.57, 4.3.58*).[433] The wall apparently enclosed an area which was used for some unknown purpose during this period. Because of this structure, a quite small, oblong space came into existence along the western part of the northern wall of Room no. 40. From an examination of the existing documentation for the Boat-room as a whole it follows that no part of a wooden ship was ever found here.

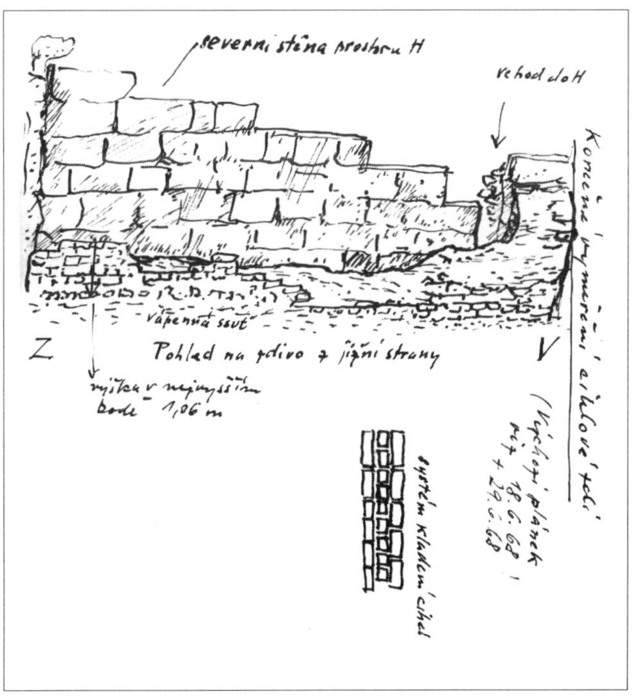

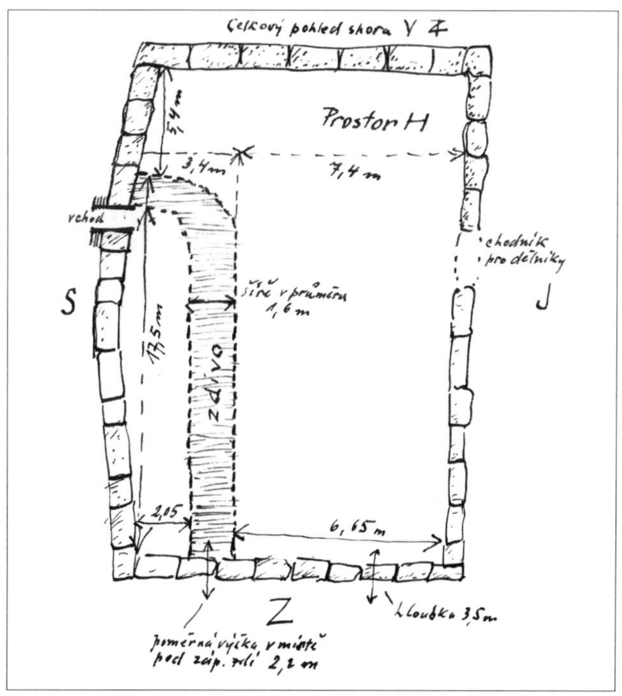

Fig. 4.3.57a–b Room no. 40; J. Midžiak's sketches from the excavation notebook showing the secondary mud brick masonry

In relation to the interpretation of the room's function, the masons' marks have again played an important role. Astonishingly, they bear contradictory testimony to each other. The first one was documented on the eastern half of the south core

[430] See also Fiala, in: *Preliminary Report*, 52.

[431] *PM* III, plan XXIX; *cf.* Jánosi, in: *L'art égyptienne*, fig. 37.

[432] In this period, the secondary use of the mastaba's area began – *cf.* Charvát, in: *Preliminary Report*, 100–105; *idem*, *Pottery*, 197.

[433] J. Midžiak, *Exc. Notebook 1968*. Unfortunately this wall was dismantled without any adequate documentation made during the archaeological excavation.

Fig. 4.3.58a–b Room no. 40, secondary mud brick masonry

wall of the room.[434] Apparently, it records the fact that a stairway along its southern wall leading to a hypothetical second floor of the room, or, more plausibly, to a roof terrace was originally intended for the room. Keeping this fact in mind, it is quite complicated to imagine that behind one or two large wooden ships – such as those outlined on some plans of the mastaba – a staircase could have been located along the southern wall of the room, *i.e.*, along the opposite wall to the entrance to

[434] Verner, *Reliefs*, E – plan Nr. 8.

the room. How could it be possible to get to this stairway on the other side of the room if two boat-shaped structures were in the way? The answer to this question is unfathomable and no proof for such a layout is available. For further discussion on this topic, see *chapter 5*.

The problems connected with the funerary boats of the Old Kingdom were recently discussed by H. Altenmüller.[435] In his opinion, the boats in the Mastaba of Ptahshepses might have been installed on the roof of Room no. 40.[436] Beside the originally published plans of the mastaba, Altenmüller argues on the basis of one close analogy in favour of the supposed function of the room: being that case attested in the tomb of Kagemni in Saqqara.[437] Here in the upper parts of the mastaba's superstructure was encountered a pair of finished boat-shaped spaces, which were blocked out by stone beams, if we accept the description given by the excavator. This indicates that in the case of Ptahshepses' and Kagemni's mastabas, the presence of "ships" represented another symbol of the magnates' efforts to emulate the royal models of their times.[438] However, as the evidence is so limited, it is very hard to ascertain the possible real function of these installations in the framework of the rituals and beliefs connected with the non-royal mortuary cult and tomb. It seems that these two nobles used these features in their tombs only for reasons of prestige and not for the original religious function that has been attested in royal architecture. It is not possible to support with evidence the recent supposition of U. Fritz that these installations can be connected with the sun cult.[439]

From the masons' lines documented on the western core wall of Room no. 40,[440] these marks convey the information that at least the north side was planned to be inclined. It allows us to suspect that the room itself was built as an open space. On the other hand, a ceiling might have been constructed, but it would not have covered the whole extent of the room.

In regard to the southern side wall, the situation is more complicated. Only a short, *vertical* line has been documented on the southern end of the western wall of the room. This piece of information can have two explanations. The southern wall of the room might have been planned as vertical and the southern part of the room could have been roofed. It is not clear, however, whether this roofed part was in this case separated from the northern part of the room by a wall, or whether, along the southern wall of Room no. 40, a kind of a gallery with (wooden) supports (pillars or columns) was intended to be constructed. On the other hand we must keep in our minds the idea that the preservation of the masons' line is not complete and perhaps inclined masons' lines might once have existed there, too.

In bringing up the subject of these masons' lines and marks, the discovery of two masons' marks should be mentioned here. The both of them included the unit of measure known as *ṯbt*. On the reading of this word see M. Verner,[441] who has suggested that this unit might be connected with the curving of the north wall.

In summing up these various pieces of information and to evaluate the appearance of room no. 40 in antiquity, we cannot rule out the proposition that, originally, the room was really planned for the housing of a boat (or two boats?). However, it is apparent, that the room was not finished according to its original plan. It is not thus

---

[435] Altenmüller, 'Funerary Boats and Boat Pits of the Old Kingdom', *ArOr* 70/3 (2002), 269–290.

[436] *Op. cit.*, note 16. Here I would like to correct a piece of information mentioned in the article, that "traces of the stairway" are present on the wall of the room. As has been mentioned in this chapter, only traces of the masons' lines for a staircase were documented in this room.

[437] *PM* III, 521; Firth, Gunn, *TPC* 21, pl. 51.

[438] For the archaeological attestation of the boat burials in the royal mortuary complexes, see Altenmüller, *ArOr* 70/3 (2002), 269–271.

[439] Fritz, *Typologie*, 66.

[440] Verner, *Baugraffiti*, E – plan nr. 8.

[441] Verner, '*Ṯbt* – Ein bisher unbekanntes altägyptisches Maß?', *MDAIK* 49 (1981), 479–481, Taf. 79a–b; *idem*, *Baugraffiti*, 176. *Cf.* Roik, *Längenmaßsystem*, 63, for the discussion on the "*Nbj*-Maßsystem" see Roik, *Längenmaßsystem*, 57–167.

possible to determine whether any boat was ever placed in the room because this supposition is not documented in the archaeological material. Therefore, we cannot rule out, that room remained unfinished and roofless. As the badly documented find of a secondary brick wall documents, the Boat-room was used secondarily during the later periods of the Egyptian history.

4.3.12 Summary of chapter 4.3

The third building stage presents the final major building stage of Ptahshepses mastaba. During it, the tomb owner decided to follow his intention to reconstruct the tomb into a temple-tomb, the transformation of a mastaba-like construction into a vast building in which ground plan and architecture partially followed their royal models – the mortuary temples of kings and queens. Ptahshepses included in his large tomb the monumental portico, the large, pillared courtyard, several cultic rooms and a high number of storerooms. Through the erection of two eight-stemmed lotus in the New Portico, the architects of Ptahshepses' tomb participated in the development of these stone supports in ancient Egyptian architecture: this is the first attestation of this type of column in Egypt. However, some parts of the originally planned tomb's spaces or architectural elements remained unfinished. This is most visible in the case of the Boat-room. There is no supportable hypothesis concerning the originally planned appearance of this room. Despite this fact, the mastaba represents the first example of the temple-tomb for a non-royal tomb owner.

It is evident that during the second half of the Fifth Dynasty and during the Sixth Dynasty several other tombs were built in Saqqara which were characterised by large dimensions and complex ground plan. Among them one can enumerate the tombs of Ti,[442] Mereruka,[443] Kagemni,[444] Khentika[445] and Ankhmahor.[446] In Giza and Saqqara, several other tombs were built with similar features – the pillared spaces and large dimensions; nonetheless, the dimensions of this second group of tombs were smaller than those in the previous group). Among these tombs one can enumerate the cluster of tomb belonging to Senedjemib Inti and other members of his family located to the north-west of Khufu's pyramid in Giza,[447] as well as the family tomb of Ptahhotep I. These tombs were not as voluminous as the previously mentioned tombs.

At the same time, it seems that the Ptahshepses mastaba became a kind of model for some of the above mentioned tombs of other magnates.[448] The builders of these later tombs were evidently strongly influenced by Ptahshepses' efforts as a constructor of an *ideal*, large and complex mastaba.

4.4 Further construction work in the area of the mastaba

4.4.1 The mud brick enclosure wall

The Mastaba of Ptahshepses underwent further development after the death of the tomb owner. As was already mentioned, some of the rooms, were not finished at that time. Significantly, the most important and the most obvious construction of the mastaba's last building stage was the erection of the mud brick enclosure wall around the enlarged mastaba (see *fig. 4.4.1*).[449]

The distance between the enclosure wall and the outer walls of the mastaba was 3.5 m in the north, almost 5.05 m in the west, 3.25 m in the east and 5.40 m to

---

442 Épron, Daumas, *Le tombeau de Ti* I, pl. I.
443 Duell, *Mereruka*, plan on the opposite page to pl. 2.
444 Firth, Gunn, *TPC* II, pl. 51.
445 James, Apted, *Khentika*, pl. III.
446 Badawy, *ᶜAnkhmᶜahor*, fig. 16.
447 Brovarski, *Senedjemib*, figs. 2–3.
448 This supposition has already been suggested by Jánosi, in: *L'art égyptienne*, 63.
449 Žába, in: *Preliminary Report*, 29–30; Verner, in: *Preliminary Report*, 33, fig. 3.

the south. The wall was not of the same width on each of its wings. In the north, the enclosure wall was 2 m wide at its base and it was preserved for only a few decimetres.[450] The situation in the southern wall is different, as it follows from the section of this wall published by Petr Charvát,[451] both faces of the southern wing were inclined.[452] The inclination of its faces was about 78°. At a height of about 2 m above the pavement around the mastaba, the preserved masonry of the wall was 1.27 m wide.[453]

Fig. 4.4.1 South-western sector of the mastaba and the respective part of the mud brick enclosure wall

The western wing of the enclosure wall was 1.54 m broad at the preserved top of the wall.[454] The narrowest part of the enclosure wall was in the east. This wing of the wall was only 0.33 m broad and it seems that it was also lower than other parts of the enclosure wall.[455] In front of the New Portico the enclosure wall was interrupted by a mud brick wall that served as a screen. The wall screening the portico was 2.52 m wide (and therefore also much broader than the other parts of the eastern part of the enclosure wall) and 8.89 m long. It is preserved up to a level of 1.60 – 1.70 m: its original height is not possible to reconstruct. The wall was constructed 3.17 m to the east of the eastern façade.

---

[450] Žába, in: *Preliminary Report*, 30.

[451] Charvát, *Pottery*, Pl. 71.

[452] Whether it was also the case with the western, northern and eastern wings, was not possible to ascertain at the time of the documentation made by this author.

[453] Unfortunately, the already mentioned drawing published in Charvát's account of the pottery found in the Ptahshepses mastaba, is accompanied by two scales, therefore, it is not possible to determine the width of this wing of the enclosure wall at its base. In the archives of the Czech Institute of Egyptology, there is no documentation concerning this part of the enclosure available. Verner, in his report on the season of the year 1974 (*Preliminary Report*, 33) mentions that this wing of the enclosure wall was 1 m broad.

[454] Z. Žába mentions that the northern wall was 2 m wide at the base (*Preliminary Report*, 29), this was reading was not possible to verify during the work on this monograph. The western wing of the enclosure wall is covered by high layers of blown sand.

[455] Žába, in: *Preliminary Report*, 29.

Table 1

Wall/wing	Dimensions (m)	Bonding	Material	Mortar	Notes
western wing	0.26–0.27 × 0.13 × 0.08	A3 (5)[457]	brown-grey mud material with a large addition of sand, small limestone fragments and detritus	brown-grey sandy-mud material with a large addition of limestone detritus and weathered pottery sherds	
southern wing	1) 0.27–0.28 × 0.14–0.15 × 0.08 2) 0.285–0.30 × 0.12.5 × 0.14	A3	1) light brown-grey sandy-mud material with a large addition of sand, small limestone fragments and detritus and a smaller addition of weathered pottery sherds 2) dark-brown mud material with a small addition of sand and a small amount of weathered pottery sherds	1) muddy grey-brown material 2) brown mud material	bricks of group *1* built in parallel with the ascending upper border of the lower part of the wall (bricks of group *2*; fig. 4.3.)
eastern wing	0.34 × 0.16 × 0.09	A3	brown-grey mud material with an addition of limestone splinters and detritus	brown-grey mud material	
screening wall	0.36–0.37 × 0.19–0.20 × 0.11–0.12	A3	brown-grey mud material with a small addition of limestone detritus and large pebbles	brown-grey sandy-mud material with a large addition of limestone detritus and weathered pottery sherds	

The composition of the separate sections of the mud brick enclosure wall and the screening wall in front of the New Portico was not uniform. The description of the brick formats and mortars in the separate wings of the wall[456] and in the screening wall in front of the New Portico are best understood from *table 1*.

From this, we are able to arrive at several conclusions. Apparently, the separate wings of the wall were not built all at once, but section by section. This is shown by the different formats and sizes of the brick used in the individual wings, but also by different materials used for the manufacture of the bricks. Nevertheless, the fact that, during the construction, different brick formats made of different materials were used can also indicate that the separate wings of the enclosure wall were built by different groups of workers. On the other hand, due to the large addition of sand in the brick material, it is very probable that bricks were made on the premises of the constructional site, together with the re-use of bricks from some older building(s). This fact may imply that the construction of the wall was made in relative haste (and therefore by several groups of workers?).

Fig. 4.4.2 Southern wing of the enclosure wall

A very interesting situation exists in the case of the southern wing of the wall. In this instance, the construction of the wall consists of two parts. At least in the middle part of this wing, the section between the lower and upper part of the wall is inclined (see *fig. 4.4.2*). Unfortunately, the wall has been re-buried under blown sand at the present time which inhibits re-excavation. Moreover, there is no documentation concerning this inclined section from the time when the wall was excavated. In order to construct such an slanting plane of a brick layer, there are several irregularities in the brick bond of the lower part of this wall – some bricks were built in as edgers (see *fig. 4.4.3*). The upper part of this wing of the brick-wall was constructed in parallel to this slanting section: its brick layers are also inclined. There is no direct explanation for this slope: the slanting section ascends towards the west, *i.e.* towards the constructional site of Niuserre's pyramid complex, but

---

[456] Unfortunately, the brickwork of the northern wing of the enclosure was not documented at the time of the archaeological excavations at all. The wall is now covered by rather high layers of debris and blown sand. Thus, it has not been possible to re-excavate it and the author was therefore not able to document it during his re-examination of the mastaba at the beginning of the 2000s.

[457] For the description of mud brick bondings, the system created by A. J. Spencer was used see: Spencer, *Brick Architecture in Ancient Egypt*, with special reference to the Corpus of brick bonds on Pls. no. 1–20.

also that of Djadajemankh's mastaba. One can hypothesise that the sloping crown of the lower part of the wall was used as a kind of provisional transport ramp. The width of 1.27 m of the upper part of the wall (see below in this chapter) is not large enough for such a ramp. It seems, therefore, that if the top of the wall had been used for transportation purposes, it might have been used only for transporting smaller amounts of building materials or small elements of architecture or masonry (*e.g.* as was used for the transportation of mud bricks used in the additional masonry erected along the eastern façade of the Mastaba of Djadjaemankh). After some unknown period of time, the upper part of this wing of the enclosure wall was added and the works thus finished.

Fig. 4.4.3 Brick bonding in the southern wing of the enclosure wall

The mud brick enclosure of the Ptahshepses mastaba, together with the screening wall in front of its monumental entrance, had two main functions: the first, and most obvious, was to resist any attack or unauthorised entrance from the outside of the mastaba, and the second purpose was to make a shield against blown sand (as was mentioned in *chapter 3*, the mastaba was built on a slope, which was so steep that it was important to build such a protective construction). In the area to the west of the mastaba, the slope had the character of a retaining wall, rather than a free-standing construction. In the north-west, north, east and south-east, the wall formed a standard enclosure wall. Due to the poor state of preservation of the wall, its height is not possible to reconstruct. The highest preserved part of the wall was in its south-west corner, where it was 3.30 m.[458] Considering its function in this area, the wall might have been quite a tall construction here. The slope along which it is constructed is 5 m high and one can hypothesize that the height of the wall was equal to that. As a consequence of the different width of the individual wings of the enclosure wall, one can suppose that these separate parts of the enclosure wall were not of the same height.

As has been previously mentioned, the courtyard between the outer walls of the mastaba and the enclosure wall was paved with well worked flat blocks of limestone.

In front of the New Portico another mud brick wall was built. A tiny, secondary wall, 0.87 m thick, was constructed in the New Portico.[459] This wall was built in a later period, when the functioning of the mastaba had begun to decline. When this took place precisely it is not possible to reconstruct.

---

[458] Žába, in: *Preliminary Report*, 30.
[459] *Ibid.*, 31 and also fig. 1.11.

It is apparent that the construction of the enclosure wall was the last large task of this building stage. It is not possible to date its construction precisely. Nevertheless, as has been clearly shown by Petr Charvát, the compact layer of clay with high amounts of pottery sherds dated to end of the Old Kingdom came into existence above the already ruined enclosure wall, confining the enclosure wall to a time before that.[460] Between the ruined wall and this clay layer a thin layer of blown sand had accumulated. Therefore, one can suppose that there was some span between the construction of the enclosure wall, its partial destruction and the depositing of the clay layer. Charvát also did not exclude the possibility that the clay layer came into existence prior to the construction of a small, Old Kingdom mastaba excavated by the archaeological team of the Charles University to the south-west of the Ptahshepses mastaba.[461] The clay layer with the Late Old Kingdom pottery sherds clearly shows the date *ante quem*. In this way it is possible to hypothesize that the most fitting time for the construction of the enclosure wall of the Ptahshepses mastaba would have been the period after the death of Ptahshepses and prior to the end of the Sixth Dynasty.[462]

4.4.2 Other constructional changes

One cannot exclude that several smaller changes were made during the functioning of the mastaba, above all in connection with suggested, smaller-scale damage caused by activities that were being conducted in the mastaba and also by the accumulation of rubbish layers, mainly in the outer spaces of the mastaba or in its closest neighbourhood. This was possibly also the case with the previously mentioned narrow wall constructed in the New Portico. One of the reasons for its construction might have been the aggregation of the waste layers in this area.[463] These continued to accumulate till the end of the Sixth Dynasty. As there is no sufficient archaeological documentation of this masonry and the archaeological situation connected with it, it is not possible to date this masonry. Following the personal communication of Miroslav Verner, based on some finds made during the excavations of the Boat-room and dated to the New Kingdom, one can hypothesize that this secondary masonry was constructed during the later periods of the Egyptian history, probably during the New Kingdom.

* * *

Thus it is that, after the masons had finished their work on the Ptahshepses mastaba, other structures were erected in the areas around it. These were all built in mud brick and seem to have been built after the death of the tomb owner. In the main, the walls erected appear to have had the purpose of keeping sand and rubbish at bay, but perhaps the walls were also intended to give a certain seclusion to the magnate's monument.

---

[460] Charvát, *Pottery*, 195, 197, Pl. 71.

[461] Verner, in: *Preliminary Report*, 33–34, fig. 3; Charvát, *Pottery*, 195.

[462] As is quoted by M. Verner (in: *Preliminary Report*, 34), after some period of time, the area between the Mastabas of Ptahshepses, Djadjaemankh and the Mastaba of the Princesses was paved by head-to-head mud bricks. This pavement also covered the above mentioned small mastaba to the south-west of the Ptahshepses mastaba and layers dated to the Fifth and the Sixth Dynasty. This fact enables us to date the construction of this pavement to the time of the very end of the Old Kingdom or the First Intermediate Period. M. Verner adds that this pavement, was destroyed during the New Kingdom.

[463] The same situation one can observe at the entrance to the Raneferef mortuary temple (see Verner, in: Verner *et al.*, *Raneferef*, 78–79).

5. Architectural and functional analysis of the mastaba

5.1 The first building stage

The Initial Mastaba presents us with evidence of the transitional period of Old Kingdom tomb building in regard to non-royal mortuary architecture. Even though this tomb represents in its rectangular shape, its north-south orientation and its sloped outer walls, a typical mastaba construction of the time, its architecture incorporates many interesting and non-standard elements. They will be discussed in the following paragraphs.

As has been shown by Jánosi[464] the reigns of Neferirkare and Niuserre represented a turning point in the development of the superstructure of the mastabas. Until that time, the massifs of the superstructures enclosed only a niche or a chapel. From that time onwards, some mastabas were not built as solid blocks, but contained a number of internal rooms. This innovation was apparently connected with shifts in the function of the tomb's superstructure, reflecting a new emphasis on the cult of the statue[465] and the inclusion of one or more statues in serdabs and in other rooms as free standing statues.[466] An example of this trend appeared early on, in the Initial Mastaba of Ptahshepses. While the cult of the statue had gained a new emphasis in the tomb, however, the inscriptions and two-dimensional decoration still remained important elements of the Initial Mastaba's decoration, securing the identity of Ptahshepses by the display of his titles and his representation in different attitudes, roles and appearance.

Even though the Initial Mastaba was a tomb with a standard layout, it encompasses several innovations and some exceptional features: most importantly, the burial chamber with a saddle roof, the use of the east-west oriented offering chapel and also the use of a staircase should be mentioned as among the more significant elements. These innovations show the endeavour of the tomb owner to approximate royal models as a symbol of his own high social status. In this aspect, Ptahshepses' Initial Mastaba was at the forefront in the development of non-royal tomb architecture.

5.1.1 Vestibule

It seems that the first room of the Initial Mastaba, the vestibule (no. 22) presents confirmation of the fact that the tomb was a house of the deceased, his domicile on earth. As was already mentioned, in the vestibule (Room no. 22) located directly behind the entrance to the Initial Mastaba, a (large-sized) statue of the deceased was very probably erected. Such a layout, with the statue of the tomb owner in its first room, might be connected with the idea of the mastaba as the house of the deceased,[467] who, embodied in the statue, greeted the visitor to the tomb as he

---

[464] See P. Jánosi, '„Im Schatten" der Pyramiden – Die Mastabas in Abusir. Einige Beobachtungen zum Grabbau der 5. Dynastie', in: *Abusir and Saqqara 2000*, 454. *Cf.* Bárta, 'Architectural Innovations in the Development of the Non-Royal Tomb During the Reign of Nyuserra', in: *Structure and Significance*, 105–125.

[465] Statues played an important role in the beliefs connected with the non-royal tombs. Apart from the false door, the statue was the second-most important object of the tomb cult (Bolshakov, *Man and his Double*, 108).

[466] The furnishing of tombs with statues and serdabs as well as two-dimensional decoration was also a matter of luxury.

[467] We cannot to rule out, that the statue, which should have been made of wood, might have been used in the rites conducted on the roof of the mastaba and connected with the staircase (see below). This vestibule room was connected with the corridor-like room (no. 23) leading to the staircase.

would have done in his own domain during his life on earth. One has to suspect that this idea was also present in the design of the entrance to the Initial Mastaba as we can see in other examples of the non-royal tombs of the period, however, no part of the architecture, or inscriptions once decorating the entrance did not survive. Therefore, one cannot to hypothesize in concern of its original appearance.

5.1.2 Offering rooms

The vestibule was connected with the major offering room (no. 25). As a matter of curiosity, there is a question as to why Ptahshepses built in his mastaba two offering rooms, but only one burial chamber. A major offering room can be surely attributed to the tomb owner because of its location in respect to the main burial chamber.[468] This offering room is located to the east of the burial chamber, where certainly Vizier Ptahshepses was buried. But a problem arises connected with the second, smaller offering room located in the Initial Mastaba: for whom was it designed? Contrary to the situation regarding the case of the major offering room and also the standard situation of other tombs, behind the western wall of Room no. 28 there was no burial chamber. This fact was so puzzling for Žába that he undertook quite extensive work in this part of the mastaba's masonry in search of some other burial chamber:[469] his efforts were in vain. As has been shown in *chapter 4.1*, it seems, that at the time when it was decided to put inside the burial chamber the second sarcophagus, the ground plan of that chamber had already been settled and the space to the north of the burial chamber was already filled by the core masonry of the mastaba. To remove this masonry might have been a quite an arduous task;[470] therefore, Ptahshepses might have come to the decision not to construct another pit for a second burial chamber. The circumstances where the burial of his wife was put in the same burial chamber as that of her husband and the tomb owner is not typical within the framework of the Old-Kingdom non-royal tomb architecture. In the majority of cases, the places of burial for the wives of nobles were at least constructionally separated in the same tomb, if not constructed in a different place – as was the case originally for Princess Khamerernebty. The Mastaba of Princesses was constructed for her. It is very probable, that – following the original plan – she probably should not have been buried together with Ptahshepses because, at the time when her own private tomb was first started, she might not have been married to Ptahshepses (see *chapter 2*). Thus, her burial chamber was not incorporated into the original ground plan of the Ptahshepses Initial Mastaba. After her marriage to Ptahshepses, her altered situation was signalled by the inclusion of her sarcophagus within the burial chamber in the noble's own tomb. Despite this fact, the work on the Mastaba of Princesses was not stopped and its construction was continued. In this way it was changed into the conjunct place of the last repose of at least two other members of Ptahshepses' family.[471]

The minor offering room of the Initial Mastaba encompasses several features which determine its function: above all its east-west orientation and a part of the offering table with a short flight of steps located in the axis of the room. The offering table stood at the foot of a false door which did not survive at all. The design of the offering table is so distinct, that it enables us to suppose that the offering cult for another person was being conducted here. This person very probably was the

[468] The relation of the ownership of the burial chambers and of the offering chapels has been discussed by P. Jánosi, 'Aspects of Mastaba Development: The Position of Shafts and the Identification of Tomb Owners', *Abusir and Saqqara 2001*, 337–350.
[469] Žába, in: *Preliminary Report*, 27–28.
[470] However, we know that in some cases the core masonry of the mastaba superstructures were changed and the new approach became incorporated into the already finished masonry of the mastaba. One of these examples is apparent in the tomb of Sekhemkai's usurped mastaba in Giza (Junker, *Gîza* XI, 8–10, Abb. 1, 6, Taf. IIId).
[471] See Borchardt, *Neuserre*, 126–134.

spouse of Ptahshepses. Although one might expect to find a serdab somewhere nearby, following the thorough study of the masonry in this area of the mastaba, it does not seem probable that in the northern, minor offering room (no. 28) a serdab was planned, as was proposed by P. Jánosi.[472]

Despite the fact that the offering room is so largely destroyed, one might, following the presence of the waste system (see p. 54–55), expect the existence of a basin there. In Abusir, we encounter libation basins in the offering rooms of the royal mortuary temples of Sahure,[473] Neferirkare[474] and Niuserre.[475] On the other hand, basins only infrequently became a part of the internal equipment of the offering rooms in the non-royal tombs. One such example is the offering chapel of Senedjemib Inti from Giza.[476] His basin is located in the eastern part of the chapel, in the north-eastern corner of the room. Unfortunately, as the basin in Room no. 25 of the Mastaba of Ptahshepses did not survive, it is not possible either to reconstruct its precise location or its design within this place. Unlike the theoretical basin in Ptahshepses' offering room, the basin located in the tomb of Senedjemib Inti is not connected to a waste canal.

5.1.3 Entrance to the burial apartment, the palace of deceased

Room no. 26, connecting the two offering rooms, had an important practical function, but it also served a religious purpose. The entrance to the burial apartment was located in the pavement of the room. This entrance was carefully sealed and incorporated into the pavement. The descending corridor was blocked by limestone blocks which were designed to prevent the looting of the burial chamber. The palace façade decoration once adorned the western wall of the room (see *fig. 5.1*). Such a façade indicated a distinct border between the world of living and the world of deceased,[477] between the "interior" and the "exterior" worlds,[478] and it presented a clear marker that the palace of the deceased in the afterlife was located in the subterranean region of the tomb.[479] In this way, the deceased might have been taken to be Osiris.[480]

---

472 Jánosi, '„Im Schatten" der Pyramiden – Die Mastabas in Abusir. Einige Beobachtungen zum Grabbau der 5. Dynastie', in: *Abusir and Saqqara 2000*, note 59 on p. 462.

473 Borchardt, *Sahure* I, Bl. 16; *MRA* VII, 64, Tav. 6: the basin was located in the southern wall of the offering room, at its eastern end. The situation in Sahure's mortuary temple is more complicated as basins had also been installed in other rooms of the "inner temple".

474 Borchardt, *Neferirkare*, 31–32, Abb. 34, Bl. 10, *MRA* VII, Tav. 10: a cavity for a basin was inserted in the axis of the east wall of the offering room. The surface of the cavity was only roughly worked. Apparently, a copper basin was inserted into the cavity located in a niche. The niche was not connected with any kind of canal or pipe such as the one documented in Sahure's mortuary temple. A similar situation is to be found in the tomb of Nyankhnesut at Saqqara: it is located on the east wall of the east-west oriented, narrow offering chapel facing Nyankhnesut's false door. There is a rectangular, shelf-like space above the basin made of limestone blocks. The basin itself is set below the shelf and directly in the eastern wall of the offering chapel. Contrary to the example in Neferirkare's temple, the basin is well worked. It is also made of limestone and is rectangular in shape, but the inner faces of the basin slope down to form a smaller rectangular floor.

475 As was discussed by Maragioglio and Rinaldi (*MRA* VIII, 30, Tav. 4), the existence of a basin might be only assumed in the western part of the king's mortuary. The state of preservation of this part of the temple is so bad, that only a surviving part of a canal indicates the existence of the basin.

476 *PM* III, 87–89; Reisner, *Giza Necropolis*, fig. 162; Brovarski, *Senedjemib* II, Pl. 3; or further, *e.g.*, G 4350 – Reisner, *Giza* I, 189, fig. 97.

477 Altenmüller, 'Der Grabherr des Alten Reiches in seinem Palast des Jenseits, Bemerkungen zur sog. Prunkscheintür des Alten Reiches', in: *Homm. Lauer*, 12, 19.

478 Jánosi, in: *Abusir and Saqqara 2000*, 460.

479 Altenmüller, in: *Homm. Lauer*, 17. In the opinion of H. Altenmüller, it was the place where the regeneration of the deceased into "Osiris" took part. As a matter of interest, there is a problem concerning the period when the cult of Osiris became a part of the Egyptian religious system. Apparently, the cult originated in the non-royal sphere at the latest in the middle of the Fifth Dynasty, but was very probably present already during the Fourth »

Fig. 5.1 Giza, the Mastaba of Seshemnefer IV. Palace façade decoration above the entrance to the descending corridor leading to the burial chamber

On the religious level, the deceased were the lords of their palaces in the afterlife. According to Altenmüller's argument, these "palaces" might also have been the place where the rebirth of the tomb owners took place.[481] Again, according to Altenmüller's opinion, the deceased was also reborn as "Horus". In this way, we might create the direct analogy of the deceased, being "Horus" with the king, who was the embodiment of Horus. With this in mind, and seeing the aspiration of Ptahshepses to incorporate architectural forms of the royal pyramid complexes into his own burial cham-ber and elsewhere, one might suppose that behind the construction of the saddle ceiling in his burial chamber might have been the idea of the rebirth of the deceased as "Horus". The same ideas and concepts were also connected with the architecture within the burial chambers of the kings of Ptahshepses' time.[482]

The descending corridor leading to the burial chamber is an important element in the architecture of the mastaba. As was mentioned by Peter Jánosi,[483] it is plausible that the use of the descending corridor instead of the vertical shafts in several Abusir non-royal tombs was based on the shifts within the religi-ous concepts of the time and not on purely technical reasons. These corridors should be connected with the place where their openings were located, *i.e.* below the palace-façade decoration.[484] In this situation, the opening of the descending corridor placed in an *inner* room, as is attested in Ptahshepses' and Djadjaem-ankh's tombs, makes an exception to the general practice, for the majority of the other examples had the mouths of their descending corridors placed outside a tomb room – or else in a courtyard, or even in front of the eastern façade of the tombs.[485] It seems that the examples from Djadjaemankh's tomb and Ptahshepses' Initial Mastaba represent the beginnings of the development of this layout of architecture. It is, therefore, probable that the rules connected with it were not well established in the time of the construction of these two particular tombs. Despite the fact that the corridors were located in the interior of the tombs, the

» Dynasty (Begelsbacher-Fischer, *Götterwelt*, 121–125; Altenmüller, 'Zu Isis und Osiris', in: *Wege öffnen*, 17). One can suppose that, during the construction of the Mastaba of Ptahshepses, some of the Osirian religious aspects might have played a role in the formation of its architectural features, especially in the subterranean part of the tomb.

[480] Griffith, *Osiris*, 21, 67–68; *idem*, *LÄ* IV, 625, Barta, *Opferformel*, 15; Bárta, in: *Structure and Significance*, 120.

[481] Altenmüller, in: *Homm. Lauer*, 18–19, in the opinion of H. Altenmüller, the deceased was reborn as "Horus".

[482] One should be reminded here that the palace façade decoration was, in only a slightly later period, introduced to the decoration of the western part of burial chambers of the kings, where their sarcophagi were placed. The first attestation is in the pyramid of King Unas in Saqqara.

[483] Jánosi, in: *Abusir and Saqqara 2000*, 458

[484] Beside Room no. 26 and the already mentioned example in Djadjaemankh's mastaba in Abusir, this layout is also attested in the tombs of Seshemnefer IV (Junker, *Gîza XI*, 106, Abb. 49, 51, Tf. XIIc, XIII a–b). However, in this case, the palace façade decoration is placed on the outer wall of the mastaba, not in an internal room, as is the case with Room no. 26. The opening to a *vertical* burial shaft is placed below the palace façade in Mereruka's tomb (Duell, *Mereruka*, Pls. 105A, 107.)

[485] Jánosi, in: *Abusir and Saqqara 2000*, 461–465.

entrances to the descending corridors were located outside the "palaces" of both these tomb owners. These "palaces" were represented by the palace façade decorations. Subsequent examples of the mouths of the descending corridors were located in the interior rooms or spaces of these tombs.

The fact that the opening to the corridor is located not outside, but inside the mastaba is of chronological importance. It seems that the period when the Cemetery of Nobles in Abusir was flourishing represents a turning point for the position of the descending corridor. The older tombs – such as the Mastaba of Userkafankh – had the opening of the descending corridor to the burial chamber of the tomb owner located on the *outside* of its superstructure.[486] On the other hand, the tomb of Djadjaemankh included a chronologically very interesting and important form of a descending corridor. The burial chamber of his wife was accessible by means of a vertical shaft, which was connected with a descending corridor with a rather low angle of incline inside the tomb. Contrary to that example, the burial chamber of the tomb owner himself was accessible from a cultic space located *inside* the mastaba. Furthermore, this descending corridor was oriented along a similar axis as was found with the corridor in the Mastaba of Ptahshepses.[487] There is also a question, whether this arrangement represents the deliberate intention of the tomb builder, or whether it came into the existence by chance? The majority of examples of descending corridors (Reisner's type 9) were oriented from the east to the west, (or, as was also the case with Ptahshepses Junior's II tomb,[488] from the north to the south).[489] Therefore, the two mentioned examples from Abusir represent a kind of an exception to the majority.

5.1.4 Serdab

The shifts in religious beliefs and especially the religious practices of the time are also revealed by the introduction of serdabs into the ground plan of the mastabas: this is especially the case with the development of serdabs into spacious rooms which one can see at the end of the Fourth and the beginning of the Fifth Dynasty. The date of the innovation of serdabs in non-royal tombs might still be subject to discussion, but nevertheless, serdabs had already become an integral part of tomb architecture during the Third, but certainly by the Fourth Dynasty.[490] The Fifth Dynasty represented the period when larger and corridor-like serdabs started to be constructed.[491] In large mastabas built in Giza, Saqqara and Abusir, serdabs became a standard part of their architecture after the reign Menkaure.[492]

It seems that Ptahshepses' Initial Mastaba, together with the monument of Djadjaemankh, represented an important turning point in respect to the development of serdabs in the Old Kingdom. Contrary to the situation that existed in other tombs, the serdabs in these two tombs were not located in rela-tion to the offering rooms. Because of the change in the orientation of the offering chapels (Room no. 25) from a north-south to an east-west direction, the serdab could not be positioned behind a false door, but instead had to be located in another part of the mastaba. (In the standard way, the earlier serdabs were located either behind the false door or behind the side walls of the offering chapel). The statues located in these more distant serdabs, therefore, were not as involved in the offering and purification rites that were carried out in front of the false

---

486 In contrast to that example, the burial chamber of his spouse was accessible by means of a vertical shaft inside (?) the tomb. Borchardt, *Neuserre*, 111–112, Abb. 90, Bl. 20.
487 Borchardt, *Neuserre*, Blatt 22, 23.
488 Bárta, *Ä&L* 10 (2000), fig. 2.
489 Reisner, *Giza*, 151.
490 Bárta, 'Serdab and Statue Placement in the Private Tombs down to the Fourth Dynasty', *MDAIK* 54 (1998), 65-75. Lehmann (*Serdab*, 18–19) dates the beginning of the use of serdabs in non-royal tombs to the Third Dynasty.
491 Jánosi, in: *Abusir and Saqqara 2000*, note no. 36 on p. 454.
492 Brescianni, in: *LÄ* V, 876.

doors.[493] Does this mean that rituals carried out in both offering chapels (Room nos. 25 and 28) of the Ptahshepses mastaba were different from those executed in other mastabas? A part of the rituals which were carried out in front of the slots connecting the offering rooms with the serdabs (*e.g.*, fumigating by incenses as we can see in Ti's mastaba)[494] apparently could not be carried out in the offering rooms of the Initial Mastaba. Their execution had to be transferred to the actual place of the serdab(s). On the other hand, the serdab in the Initial Mastaba was not positioned by chance. Its location behind the palace façade decoration of Room no. 26 perfectly fitted the function of the latter room. It represented on the one hand another kind of communication between the world of living and that of the afterlife (the statues were objects of some of rituals) and, on the other hand, a frontier between the world of the living and the dead. In this way the function of the burial chamber as a burial palace occupied by the deceased was reinforced. The deceased owner of the tomb was presented in the serdab in his statues located behind the palace façade, so strengthening the idea of the post mortal domicile of his soul in the tomb. Due to the position of the serdab, the *ka* of Ptahshepses might have communicated directly with those who were in charge of carrying out the rituals connected with his statues.

Beside these aspects already mentioned, serdabs might have also played an important role in the burial rituals. This situation has been discussed by Nicole Alexanian. It seems that the serdabs were left open before these ceremonies.[495] During burials, beside mummies also statues of the deceased were transported to roofing terraces of mastabas in order to be the object of these rites. After the rites concluded, the statues were lowered down to the serdabs through openings in tomb ceilings and then the serdabs were closed. As was already mentioned, the pavement of Room no. 27 was elevated above the floors of other rooms in the Mastaba of Ptahshepses. This was also the case of some other serdabs in the non-royal tombs. Therefore, the roof of this space might also have been constructed at a higher level and the roofing masonry above the room might have been thinner (was it created by "just" one layer of roofing beams?) than was the case in the other rooms in the mastaba. If it really was so, the roof of this room might have been of a simple construction which facilitated the carrying out of this ceremony and the final closing of the serdab.

5.1.5 Staircase

The staircase (Room no. 24) leading to the roofing terrace of the Mastaba of Ptahshepses was a vital element of the architecture of the Initial Mastaba and is one of the first examples of the stairway in a non-royal tomb. It signifies the importance of the tomb owner and his high position in court society as well.

In our research we encountered other stepped approaches to the roof terraces among non-royal tombs. It seems that these approaches had the same character as those built in the tombs and complexes of queens and they represent real staircases (see further) rather than ascending ramps which are documented in the complexes of kings. Staircases were a part of ancient Egyptian architecture from the Predynastic Period.[496] In the framework of royal mortuary architecture, stairways were used from the reign of King Den onwards.[497] The first use of a staircase in an aboveground building is attested in the pyramid complex of Netjerikhet.[498] Staircases disappeared in the construction of the royal complexes

[493] *Cf.* Bolshakov, *Man and his Double*, 108.

[494] Wild, pl. CLXXI.

[495] Alexanian, 'Himmelstreppen und Himmelsaufstieg. Zur Interpretation von Ritualen auf Grabdächern im Alten Reich', in: *Grab und Totenkult*, 32–33.

[496] Badawy, *Egyptian Architecture*, 17–18, fig. 7.

[497] Petrie, *Royal Tombs* II, 9, pls. LVI.5–6, pls. LVIA.3–4, LXII.

[498] *CEAEM*^{2}, 176, fig. 210; Lauer, *Pyr. à degres*, 132–133, pls. LV, LVIII.1, LXIV.1.

from then until the Fourth Dynasty, but was then again attested in Khafre's pyramid complex in Giza (*fig. 5.2*).[499]

Fig. 5.2 Giza, the Pyramid Complex of Khafre. Staircase leading to the roof of the mortuary temple

In the Fifth Dynasty, the use of staircases and ascending ramps leading to the roofing terraces gradually grew more frequent. Thus, we encounter staircases, particularly stepped ramps, in the Abusir royal mortuary complexes built during the first half of the Fifth Dynasty. In the first pyramid complex of the Fifth Dynasty, that of Userkaf, it is likely that a staircase was probably constructed in the south-east sector of the mortuary temple.[500] Leaving aside the famous examples of the staircases in the storerooms of Sahure's mortuary temple, we are also confronted by an ascending ramp leading onto the roofing terrace in the northern part of the temple.[501] Due to the non-standard building development of Neferirkare's complex, the location of a staircase leading to the roofing terrace is not known precisely from the archaeological remains. The use of such a staircase, however, is postulated on the basis of information mentioned in Neferirkare's papyrus archive.[502] Maragioglio and Rinaldi[503] reconstructed staircases in both storerooms located to the south of the stone part of the mortuary temple: unfortunately it is hard to say whether or not this staircase led to the roof terrace. In Niuserre's valley temple,[504] a staircase leading to the roofing terrace is also attested. Another staircase is, more hypothetically, suspected within the mortuary temple itself: following Borchardt's reconstruction, the staircase should be placed in the area to the north of the main entrance to the temple. However, due to the poor state of preservation of the temple's masonry, it is not possible to confirm this hypothesis.[505] The same situation – the poor state of preservation concerning the masonry of Djedkare's mortuary temple – is responsible for the fact that we can only suggest a staircase or ascending ramp's position in his South Saqqara ground plan.[506] Contrary to that situation, though, a staircase in the pyramid temple of Unas has been attested.[507] As it happens, the period of the Sixth Dynasty does not represent a period of retreat in the use of staircases – as is shown by the example in the pyramid complex of Pepy II.[508]

---

499 It was located in the mortuary temple and it led to the roof of the construction from the area of the storerooms – Hölscher, *Chephren*, Bl. XVIII.

500 Labrousse, Lauer, *Ouserkaf*, 43, figs. 43, 45, pl. 17a; *MRA* VII, Tav.1: the construction of this staircase was destroyed by intrusive activities during the Late Period and only the foundations of a stepped ramp were documented.

501 Borchardt, *Sahure* I, p. 66, pl. 16; *MRA* VII, Tav. 6. As in the example from Khafre's valley temple, the stepped ramp in Sahure's temple twice changed the direction of its flights.

502 Posener-Kriéger, *Les papyrus d'Abousir* I, 29–34, II 510–511.

503 *MRA VII*, 134, 172 Tav. 14. In the so-called treasury we encounter a real, stepped staircase built partially of stone and partially of mud bricks – Borchardt, *Neferirkare*, 33–34, Abb. 37–38; *MRA* VII, 134, Tav. 12.

504 Borchardt, *Neuserre*, 12, Bl. 3, 28.

505 Borchardt, *Neuserre*, Bl. 28; *MRA* VIII, Tav. 5. The existence of other staircases was inferred in the cases of both "*Eckbauten*" for Niuserre – Borchardt, *Neuserre*, 98, Bl. 28.

506 Djedkare: *MRA* VIII, Tav. 16 (in the area of the storerooms).

507 Labrousse, Lauer, Leclant, *Le temple haute du roi Ounas*, 40, fig. 12, pl. XV. This staircase apparently led to the roofing terrace. In this case, the staircase did not represent an ascending corridor with notches, but a standard staircase.

508 Jéquier, *Pepi II*, vol. III, 3, pl. 2.

As for the purpose of such staircases, P. Jánosi[509] came to the conclusion that the staircase constructed in the mortuary temples could be used by the guards for access to the roofing terrace. This suggestion was substantiated by P. Posener-Kriéger as a result of evidence coming from Neferirkare's papyrus archive.[510]

One encounters, in due course, staircases leading to roof terraces in the mortuary temples of queens. The oldest attested example of this kind has been documented in the pyramid complex of Menkaure, in the mortuary temple of G IIIa.[511] For our further discussion the staircase constructed in the tomb of Unas' queen Nebet is important.[512] The location of this staircase is extraordinary in relation to the ground plan of the mastaba: the staircase is directly connected to the offering chapel. The other examples of use come from the mortuary temples of queens Wedjebten[513] and Iput II. Also this staircase neighbours the main offering chapel.[514]

The staircases in non-royal tombs have been detected from the Early Dynastic Period.[515] Contrary to the staircase located in the mortuary temples of kings and leading to the roofing terraces, the staircases built in the mortuary temples of queens or in mastabas of officials represented standard staircases. Such staircases one may encounter in the storerooms of the kings' mortuary temples by their pyramids. For access to the roofing terraces of the royal temples, ascending ramps with incised strips in their pavements – or better to say, ascending corridors with incised floors – were used. Why it was so, it is not fully clear. Hypothetically, we can suppose that an important role was played both by the number of persons taking part in the ceremonies and observations being conducted on the roofing terraces from the nature of these actions (guarding, rites connected with the sun cult, or, with some astral aspects of religious beliefs). However, climbing the steps of standard staircases is more strenuous than mounting ascending corridors; in this connection, if standard staircases are used, there could be an accumulation of persons in the quite confined spaces of the staircases, especially when there were large numbers of persons taking part in rituals. An ascending corridor enables a stately procession; a staircase does not. Because of these factors, ascending corridors might have been preferred for practical reasons in the royal mortuary temples. Perhaps the answer for the question why the ascending corridors were not used in the non-royal tombs lies in the cost of making a staircase. The ascending corridors needed larger amounts of masonry in solid foundations to the floor, which construction might have been more arduous.

As for the purpose of such staircases, P. Jánosi[516] came to the conclusion that the staircase constructed in the mortuary temples could be used by the guards for access to the roofing terrace. This suggestion was substantiated by P. Posener-Kriéger as a result of evidence found coming from Neferirkare's papyrus archive.[517] No final word on the solution of this question can be said at this point in time. One may only suppose that the actual staircases/ascending corridors in the royal mortuary temples would have had a combined function: they were the means to reach roof height for those who guarded the vast areas of the temples, as well as for providing access to the roofing terraces of the temples for some of the religious rituals.

Regarding the staircase built in the Initial Mastaba of Ptahshepses, one needs to realise that staircase construction was not an easy exercise for those who built the

---

[509] Jánosi, *Pyramidenanlagen*, 158.
[510] Posener-Kriéger, *Les archives d'Abousir* I, 29–34, II 510–511.
[511] Reisner, *Mycerinus*, 59–60, plan IV, Jánosi, *Pyramidenanlagen*, 158.
[512] Munro, *Unas-Friedhof*, 43–44, Taf. 6.
[513] Jéquier, *Oudjebten*, 12f., fig. 5, pl. I.
[514] As Jéquier himself mentions this is only a reconstruction: *Neit et Apouit*, 44, pl. XXXVI. *Cf.* Jánosi, *Pyramidenanlagen*, Abb. 75.
[515] Saad, *Helwan*, plans 3–17.
[516] Jánosi, *Pyramidenanlagen*, 158.
[517] Posener-Kriéger, *Les archives* I, 29–34, II 510–511.

non-royal tombs of the period,[518] therefore, the construction of them was proof both of the importance of the cults which were conducted on the tomb roofing terraces and the importance of the tomb owners themselves. In general, the majority of examples of staircases in the non-royal tombs listed below came into existence in the period from the second half of the Fifth and remained till the first half of the Sixth Dynasty:

- Ptahshepses (Abusir), staircase leading from a corridor-like room, presumably used as a storeroom,
- Ptahhotep I, staircase leading from a room with two pillars; [519] this tomb is dated to the reign of Djedkare,[520]
- Akhtihotep Hemi (Nebkauhor), staircase leading from the pillared hall;[521] dated to the reign of Unas,[522]
- Niankhba, staircase leading from the pillared hall; dated to the reign of Unas,[523]
- Ihy-Idut, staircase leading from the small room which served as a corridor leading to the storerooms.[524] This tomb was originally built during the reign of Unas and usurped during Teti's reign,[525]
- Neferseshemre, staircase leading from the pillared hall;[526] the tomb being dated to the early Sixth Dynasty,[527]
- Ankhmahor, staircase leading from an open pillared hall;[528] dated to the early Sixth Dynasty,
- Nikauisesi, staircase from an undecorated, L-shaped open courtyard;[529] the tomb is dated to the reign of Teti,[530]
- Kagemni, staircase leading from the large room connected directly with the entrance; this tomb is dated to the early Sixth Dynasty,
- Watetkhethor (Mereruka), staircase leading from the pillared space behind the entrance to the tomb of the vizier's wife;[531] this tomb is also dated to the early Sixth Dynasty,
- Nedjetempet (?).[532]

As follows from the above list, the majority of these staircases were constructed in the tombs located Saqqara. N. Alexanian, who has studied the material associated

---

[518] *Cf.* G. Jéquer, *Manuel*, 144.
[519] Hassan, Iskander, *Ny-ʿnkh-Pepy*, 35, pl. 12.
[520] *PM* III, 596; Baer, *Rank and Title*, 75.
[521] Hassan, Iskander, *Neb-Kaw-Her*, Vol. 1, 44, fig. 1, pl. 46A, Vol. 2, fig. 12.
[522] Strudwick, *Administration*, 56–57.
[523] In Hassan-Iskander, *Hemet-Rʿ*, 43, the respective room is not described as a staircase; for the dating, see: *PM* III, 629 (Sixth Dynasty); Strudwick, *Administration*, 102 (middle reign of Unas).
[524] *PM* III 617; Macramallah, *Idout*, XX, pls. II, III; Kanawati, Abder-Raziq, *Iyneferet*, 38, pls. 14(a), 29.
[525] Abder-Raziq, *Iyneferet*, 36–38.
[526] Capart, *Rue de tombeaux*, I 23, II pl. VIII, Kanawati, Abder-Raziq, *Neferseshemre*, 20, pls. 5(b), 39–41; in the opinion of Capart, the staircase was used during burial ceremonies for transporting the mummy of the deceased to the roof terrace where the opening of the burial shaft was located. An important fact is, that several blocks of the stairway ceiling are preserved, indicating the slope of the stairway as 17.5°. It seems that the stairway incorporated at least one landing.
[527] *PM* III, 511; Kanawati, *Neferseshemre*, 16.
[528] *PM* III, 512, pl. L.; Capart, *Rue de tombeaux*, I, 59, II, pl. XVIII; Badawy, *ʿAnkhmʿahor*, Fig. 16, Fig. 60.
[529] Raziq, Krekeler, *MDAIK* 43 (1986), fig. 1; Kanawati, Abder-Raziq, *Nikauisesi*, 29–30, pls. 39, 40; a part of a sloped roof inclined at the same angle as the stairway, *i.e.* of 30°, with at least one landing.
[530] Abder-Raziq, *Nikauisesi*, 23.
[531] Duel, *Mereruka*, plan on the opposite page to pl. 2.
[532] Despite the fact that Kanawati and Hassan were not fully convinced of the interpretation of the relevant room, which did not show any traces of a staircase, they marked a staircase on a schematised plan of the tomb. (Kanawati, Hassan, *Nedjetempet*, 14, fig. pl. 36; *cf.* Fritz, *Typologie*, 210, plan 139). Unfortunately, such an interpretation cannot be fully documented.

with staircases recently, connects the appearance of the staircases in the non-royal tomb during this particular period to shifts in the religious beliefs.[533]

Another important fact to note is that, in Saqqara, there are two main clusters of tombs which feature staircases: those in the neighbourhood of the Pyramid Complex of Unas (one of these tombs was Niankhba's tomb – *fig. 5.3*) and those which are mainly located in the Teti Pyramid Cemetery. It would seem that the

Fig. 5.3 Saqqara, the Mastaba of Niankhba. View of the area where a staircase was located

tombs with staircases in Teti's cemetery were constructed in an almost identical fashion to each other. One might therefore suggest that they were used for similar ritual needs. In Alexanian's opinion this accumulation of tombs with staircases should be connected with the appearance of the *Pyramid Texts* in the Unas pyramid and then their use in the pyramids of the Sixth Dynasty. She points out that the arrival of the *Pyramid Texts* coincides with the shifts in the texts of offering formulae in tombs which appeared at the same period.[534] The staircase built in Ptahshepses' mastaba, is one of the first, if not the first example of its kind in Old-Kingdom non-royal architecture. One cannot exclude the idea that the same religious beliefs connected with the construction of the staircases built at the very end of the Fifth Dynasty were effectively being circulated in the middle of this period.

N. Alexanian is not alone in her argumentation for the use of the staircases as the transport route of the mummy. A similar theory had already been proposed by A. Badawy in 1970s. He was of the opinion that[535] the staircases located in the mastabas of nobles were used for carrying the mummy of the deceased onto the roof terrace during the funeral, in order to transfer the mummy to the entrance to the burial shaft.[536] For this same purpose, the ramps leading to the roofs of the mastabas were also used. They are attested in the archaeological (see *fig. 5.4*),[537] and epigraphical material (*fig. 5.5*).[538]

With the Mastaba of Ptahshepses, the access to the burial apartment was through a descending corridor (Room no. 29). Construction of a vertical shaft, which is the standard way of connecting the burial chamber with the outer world, was not possible in the Ptahshepses mastaba, due to the construction of the saddle roof

533 Alexanian, 'Himmelstreppen und Himmelsaufstieg. Zur Interpretation von Ritualen auf Grabdächern im Alten Reich', in: *Grab und Totenkult*, 27–40.
534 *Op. cit.*, 35–36.
535 Badawy, *ʿAnkhmʿahor*, 12.
536 *Cf.* Fitzenreiter, *Statue und Kult*, 76–77.
537 Alexanian, *Netjeraperef*, 36–38, Abb. 4, 15, Taf. 7; Alexanian also presents the list of other attestations of such ramps in this place. Rzeuska, in: *Egypt 1999*, 162–164.
538 *PM* III, 235–236; Alexanian, 'Ritualrelikte an Mastabagräbern des Alten Reiches', in: *Stationen*, 8–11, 18; Hassan, *Gîza* IV, 175–179, fig. 122, pl. L.

Fig. 5.4 Dahshur, the Mastaba of Netjeraperef. Mud brick ramp leading to the roof of the tomb

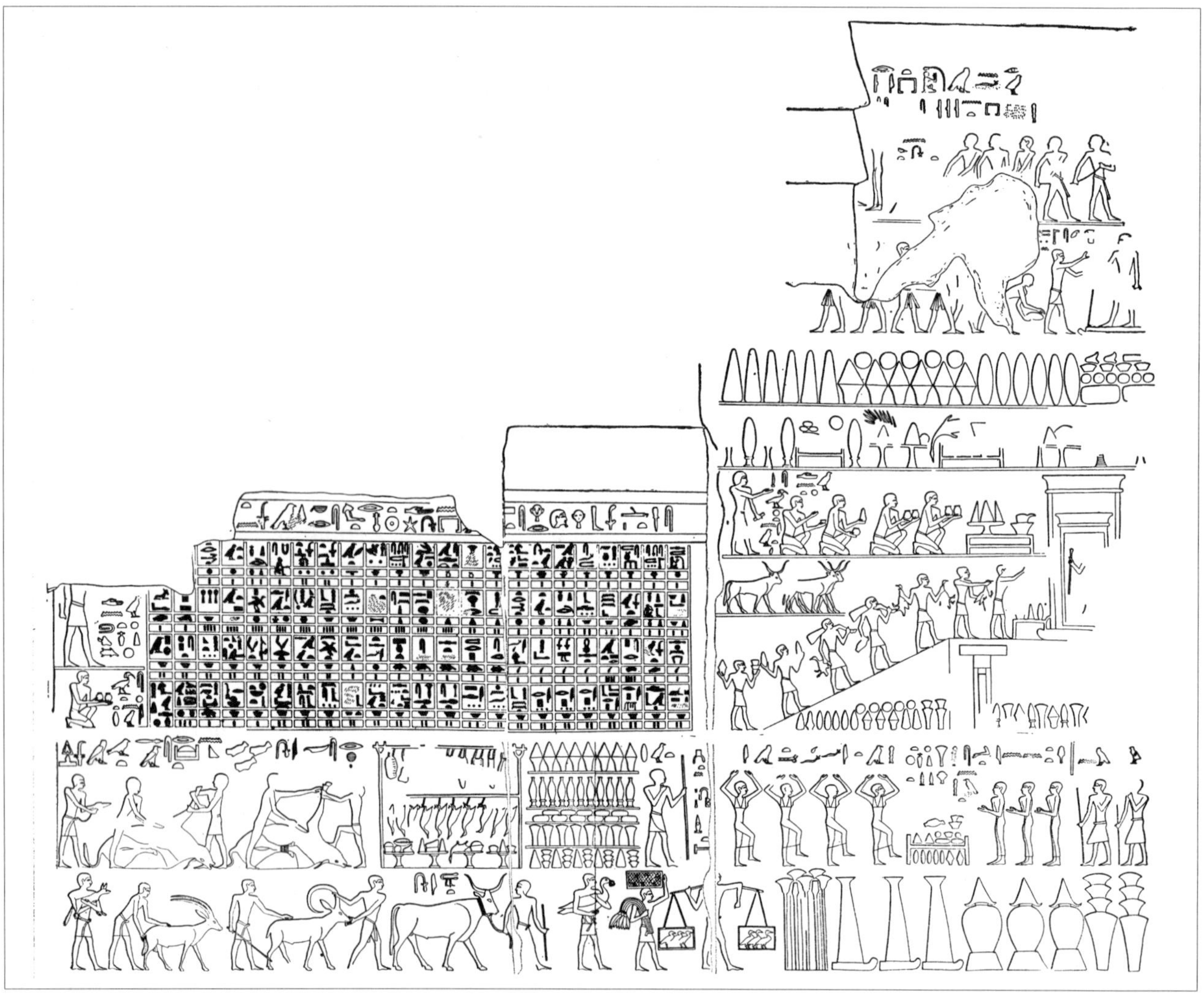

Fig. 5.5 Giza, the rock tomb of Debeheni. Scene of the funeral with the ramp leading to the roof of a tomb

above the burial chamber. It seems that both the use of the saddle roof and the staircase were important from the point of view of religious beliefs at that time. Therefore, despite the fact, that in its layout and architecture the Initial Mastaba is similar to that of Djadjaemankh, it is important to point out that in the tomb of Djadjaemankh no staircase was constructed. In view of this fact one may suppose that this change in the ground plan of the Initial Mastaba was caused by (slightly) different religious beliefs.

To ascertain the function of the staircases constructed in the non-royal tombs is a challenge that has not, as yet, been satisfactorily answered.[539] The main problem is the rather bad state of preservation of staircases in the tombs in which they were constructed and thus, our knowledge about their function is rather hampered. In this connection, we need to examine two areas in ascertaining the function of staircases in non-royal tomb: the practical aspect and the religious aspect.

The practical side of the use of the staircase cannot be lightly dismissed. Like other prestige and large monuments in both royal[540] and non-royal cemeteries, this tomb and its valuable contents would surely have been guarded, and from the vantage point of the roof, a guard could best keep watch for robbers or desecrators. It seems probable, therefore, that guarding this mastaba and its equipment may have been necessary. The use of staircases in tombs was limited to the upper layers of the Egyptian society of the period and none have been documented in the tombs of lower officials.[541]

On the other hand, we should remind ourselves that, in Egyptian culture, the roof of the sacred buildings played an important role in the performance of rituals.[542] Moreover, it seems that the cult of sun god Re "on the roof" was attested for Sahure's and Neferirkare's time.[543] The elite layers of the Egyptian society were much more influenced by the religious beliefs connected with the king and the royal family than the lower social strata were, and it is likely that they wished to imitate their rulers when it came to religious beliefs.

Both the rites carried out in front of the mummy and the transportation of statues of the deceased to the roofing terrace[544] were aimed at securing the successful ascension of the dead. The deceased may have pinned their hopes on their existence in the firmament with the sun god,[545] the "great god" mentioned in the offering formulas.[546] In studying the pictorial documentations of these rituals, we discover that a part of them also represented also the offering ritual.[547] In this connection, it seems to be important that majority of the staircases in the non-royal tombs were entered from those parts of the mastabas, in which storerooms were located.

Nicole Alexanian has indicated that the deceased's free-standing statues might have been transported onto the roof terraces – not only during the burial of the deceased itself, but after the burial as well.[548] As a matter of fact, these statues were the objects of ceremonies. In the case of the Ptahshepses mastaba, the statue, which was presumably erected in Room no. 22 (see p. 45) – a room which was connected via Room no. 23 with the staircase, might have been brought through the staircase to the roof of the mastaba. Moreover, other free standing statues which are thought to be placed in the mastaba (in Room nos. 16 and 4) might have also been the object of the rituals conducted on the tomb's roof.

As is well known, the period when the Mastaba of Ptahshepses was built represents one of the peaks of the sun cult.[549] As Overseer of all the King's Works, Ptahshepses was responsible for the construction of royal buildings, among which

---

[539] Jánosi, 'Les tombes privées »des maisons d'éternité«', in: *L'art égyptienne*, 62.
[540] We should assume that as was already mentioned for Neferirkare's mortuary temple (see p. 157, note 510) it is very probable that the staircase was also used for members of the guards to climb to the roof terrace to maximise the building's protection.
[541] Precious equipment which was kept inside the tombs, together with highly-valued linen supplies, *etc.*, might prove a temptation to thieves, so these issues should be born in mind when thinking about the function of the staircase in Ptahshepses' tomb.
[542] Helck, *LÄ* VI, 755–756.
[543] *Urk* I, 24.3, 247.17–248.1; Begelsbacher-Fischer, *Götterwelt*, 166.
[544] See already mentioned theory of Alexanian, published in: *Grab und Totenkult*, 27–40; the staircase in the Initial Mastaba of Ptahshepses is discussed on pages 33–34.
[545] *Op. cit.*, 38.
[546] Kees, *Totenglauben*, 27–28, 110; Bonnet, *Reallexikon*, 346.
[547] See *fig. 5.5*.
[548] Alexanian, in: *Grab und Totenkult*, 27–40.
[549] *Cf.* notes 588 and 589.

we can also count the sun temples. As a matter of course, he might have been influenced by the concepts and ideas connected with these constructions.

5.2 The second building stage

After an unspecified time, the Initial Mastaba was extended and the second building stage marks a major break in the development of the tomb. This enlargement of the mastaba must certainly be connected with Ptahshepses' promotion to the higher echelons of Egyptian society.

The construction of the annex during the second building stage is clearly demonstrated by a change in the architecture of the mastaba: its concepts were grander and they apparently derived in part from royal models. As was already mentioned, they marked a shift in the function of the tomb. The superstructure of the mastaba was altered into a kind of a private temple built for the display of tomb owner's statues – this concept was then further developed on a vast scale during the third building stage. It was not the only shift in the conception of the tomb. Ptahshepses tried, at least partially, to emulate royal models with the use of floral bundle columns made of stone and the construction of the chapel with niches – all architectural elements used in royal projects. In his appropriation of those royal models it can be seen how powerful his status must have been by this time. His mastaba is the only Old-Kingdom non-royal tomb in which the floral bundle columns have ever been recorded so far.

5.2.1 Vegetal columns

Generally, Old-Kingdom architecture embraced the existence of two forms of supports: columns and pillars, made of both stone and wood. In the framework of profane architecture the development of columns is easily traced[550] and the sacral (or mortuary) architecture took these columns as models for its own development. In some cases, wooden support-columns were also used in the framework of royal architecture. They were a solution for non-standard situations – as we can see in the valley temple of Menkaure's pyramid complex,[551] in Neferirkare's[552] and Raneferef's[553] mortuary complexes. However, wooden columns were used also in the framework of private mortuary architecture, as we can see in the case of Djadjaemankh's tomb, in which a colonnade of plain wooden columns was erected along the eastern façade.[554]

Nevertheless, the supports made of stone are more important for this study. Coming back to the period of the Third Dynasty, we can see the first recorded examples of supports made of limestone which were used in Netjerikhet's pyramid complex in Saqqara. These supports are known as engaged columns, and they include built in, vegetal semi-columns. They were used in this pyramid complex in quite high numbers.[555] From the reigns of Snofru and Khufu onwards, stone supports – this time, in the form of pillars – became an integral part of royal mortuary architecture. However, an important change in the use of supports in royal mortuary architecture, especially in respect to their forms, happened at the end of the Fourth Dynasty and the beginning of the Fifth Dynasty. This change is documented in the existence of columns located in the entrance coridor[556] in the

[550] Plain columns in the "hypostyle hall" of the production centre built to the south of the Wall of the Crow in Giza: Lehner, *Aeragram* 4/1, 2000, 2; plain columns in the governor's palace in Ain Asyl: Soukiassian, *EA* 11 (1997), 15–16.

[551] Plain columns, Reisner, *Mycerinus*, 40–41, plan VIII–IX.

[552] Lotiform columns, Borchardt, *Neferirkare*, 20–22, Abb. 18.

[553] Lotiform and papyrus columns, Verner, *Raneferef* I, 33, 52–53, figs. 1.2.6., 1.2.7., 1.2.32.

[554] Borchardt, *Neuserre*, 118, Bl. 22.

[555] For example the attached columns in the entrance corridor, or the papyrus semi-columns in the court of the North House: Lauer, *Pyr. à degres*, 117–119, 124–126, 155, pls. XXXVIII–XLVIII. *Cf.* Phillips, *Columns*, 37–42.

[556] The columns were used here in a similar context to those in the entrance corridor of »

mortuary temple of Userkaf's queen Neferhetepes.[557] We can suppose that this shift in the architectural forms used might have been connected to modifications within religious concepts and the function of these supports. The transition of the form of stone supports in the royal mortuary complexes from pillars to floral (bundle) columns reached its final stages during the building activities in the Abusir Pyramid Necropolis.

The large construction projects in Abusir contributed greatly to the development of supports in Egyptian architecture, especially with the use of vegetal, free-standing columns made of stone, such as first appeared in the mortuary temple of Sahure. An integral part of this development was also present in the Ptahshepses mastaba. In the Old Portico, the tomb owner was permitted the erection of a pair of columns. It is difficult to elucidate the intention of the tomb builder. One hypothetical reason is evident: the choice of the columns' form could have been a part of Ptahshepses' endeavour to follow the royal models in the pyramid complexes built in Abusir. Nevertheless, the lotiform columns bore a profound meaning connecting them with ideas of resurrection.[558] Thus, we can suppose that this concept might have prompted the introduction of the columns.

One may ask why Ptahshepses was allowed to use lotiform columns in his tomb but not, apparently, papyriform columns. Papyrus plants were depicted in the relief decoration of non-royal tombs[559] and the scenes of papyrus marshes were also very probably part of the decoration of the Mastaba of Ptahshepses as follows from the relief fragments found during the excavation of the mastaba.[560] It is apparent, that, at least in a later, directly subsequent period to that of the construction of the Mastaba of Ptahshepses, the depictions of the papyrus thickets, tomb owners floating through the papyrus marshes and of the *sšš w3ḏ* ritual might have been located as in the vestibules[561] and in those parts of the walls of offering rooms in which their entrances were located.[562] The depiction of the papyrus plants played an important role in the concept of spaces to be crossed between the outer world and the nether world of the tomb. Apparently, the papyrus plant possessed different functions in its two-dimensional and three-dimensional representations. Whilst three-dimensional representations – columns – are attested only in royal architecture, the two-dimensional – reliefs – are attested both in royal and non-royal tombs. We might, thus, suppose that papyrus (and palm) columns were particularly – and perhaps exclusively – connected to the royal cult. These columns might have been connected with the concepts of the king ruling over the riverine, flooded and fertile landscape and for this reason they were not used in the Ptahshepses mastaba.[563]

The newly erected Old Portico with its two lotiform columns represented a point on the border between the world of living and the world of dead in which the deceased awaited his rebirth, a function that might have been underlined by the hypothetical use of lotiform columns in the Southern Portico (see p. 102). This latter portico might have had the same function as the Old Portico, for both of them gave access to the Chapel with Three Niches, an area of the netherworld with Ptahshepses embodied in his statues and awaiting his resurrection, and for this reason it had to be ritually protected.

» Neferirkare's mortuary temple (however, here, as is well known, there were two lines of columns that were used), and as in the columned corridor connecting this mortuary temple with the pyramid court – Borchardt, *Neferirkare*, 37, Bl. 10.

557 Plain or palm columns: see Labrousse, Lauer, *Ouserkaf*, 147–148, fig. 351, pl. 31.

558 *Cf.* Verner, 'The Columns of Abusir', in: *OKAA*, 350–351.

559 Harpur, *Decoration*, *passim.*

560 Vachala, *Relieffragmente*, 158-161.

561 *Cf.* Duell, *Mereruka*, Pls. 11, 15–19.

562 *Cf.* the offering room of Akhtihotep: Davies, *Ptahhetep*, pls. XIII, XIV; the pillared room of Mereruka: Duell, *Mereruka*, Pls. 127–129.

563 In the case of the papyrus columns, one can connect them with the myth on Horus raised in the papyrus marshes. In this case the ruler would be then identified as Horus.

5.2.2 Statue niches of the triple shrine

From the numerous statue remnants we have, it seems evident that Ptahshepses – probably in his most important guises as a functionary – apparently tried to portray himself in the statue niches of this sanctuary as the lord of his "realm". In this way he tried to emulate the chapels with five niches built in the mortuary temples of the Egyptian kings from the time of reign of King Userkaf. The fact that such an architectonic solution was quite unusual in the non-royal tombs of this period shows how extraordinary were the ideas concealed in the elements of architecture in this room. This is confirmed by the fact that there is only one example of a similar kind documented in a non-royal tomb – the offering chapel in the Saqqara tomb of Rashepses.[564] In this tomb we encounter a larger room with three niches in its western wall as well. As in the case of the Chapel with Three Niches in the Mastaba of Ptahshepses, we can suppose that the niches were used for the placement of statues of Rashepses. Nevertheless, as was already mentioned in *chapter 4.2.5*, the niches in Rashepses' mastaba very probably show some different features: the different length/width ratio, the non-existence of pivot-holders for shrine doors, the fact that the niches were not raised above the floor of the chapel and, most importantly, the non-existence of the short staircases in front of the niches. We can only regret that the original documentation of the tomb[565] of Rashepses is not more detailed and that no follow-up analysis could be done. Such follow-up work would perhaps help us to come to a better understanding of the ritual functions of the niches.

Beside the analogies enlisted in *chapter 4.2.4*, another example of a niche with a statue is the well known one in the pillared hall in Mereruka's tomb in Saqqara (no. A 13). This niche was placed in the axis of one of the aisles made by the pairs of pillars erected in the room. It is well elevated above the pavement of the room. In the niche, there is an engaged, but striding statue of Mereruka, dressed in a kilt and with a heavy curly wig on his head. The statue is placed on a base inscribed with his titles and name. As in the niches in Ptahshepses' mastaba, Room no. 4, the side walls of the mouth of the niches are decorated by alternate stripes of green and yellow. The niche was closed by two wooden door leaves.[566] On both sides of the niche, there is a torus moulding, which indicates that once there was a cavetto cornice above the niche. In front of the niche, in its axis there was placed a travertine offering table in the form of the sign *ḥtp*, placed on the limestone base, accessed by a short staircase. As part of the surrounding decorations, there are relief bare depictions of Mereruka, also dressed in kilt, but portrayed without a wig with his bare head shaven. These depictions are located axially on the both sides of the statue niche.[567] There are several features of this assemblage which are very similar to those encountered in Room no. 4 of the Ptahshepses mastaba – the small staircase in the axis of the niche, its elevation above the pavement of the room, the stripped decoration of the niche's mouth and the closing of the niche by the wooden door-leaves as well as the threefold depiction of the tomb owner – of Ptahshepses in the form of three statues, that of Mereruka in the form of one statue and two relief depictions[568] – seems to be of some importance. A major difference between the niches of the two viziers is the absence of stone offering tables in front of the niches of Ptahshepses' chapel. One cannot exclude that the statues erected in the niches

---

[564] *PM* III, 494–496, plan XLIX; *LD* I, Bl. 36, *LD* Text I, 165–167.
[565] *LD* I. Bl. 39, *PM* III, Pl. XLIX.
[566] Duell, *Mereruka*, pls. 147, 148.
[567] *Op. cit.*, pl. 123.
[568] The fact that there was only one niche with a statue in Mereruka's pillared chapel might have been a result of some unknown circumstances which definition is beyond our capabilities (that this layout was not originally planned in the room – for that explanation might one use its location in the northern and not the western wall of the pillared hall –, or perhaps for some financial reasons, the layout was incomplete *etc.*). However, if one would take into account the triple number of depicitions of the noble, then one can see some parallelism between these Mereruka's portrayals and those of Ptahshepses.

of Room no. 4 might have been handled in a similar way to the statues in the royal mortuary temples – *i.e.*, that the regular toilet of the statues was performed on them. Should that be the case, no offering table would have been necessary. As the statue in the niche of Mereruka's pillared hall represents an engaged statue, it is apparent, that rituals of the toilet were not carried out in this case.[569] In this way, the function of this niche was more probably connected with the offering rituals than those of the toilet and it has much more to do with the false door than the statue-niches. Thus, to locate close analogies to the Chapel with Three Niches, one has to seek for parallels in the royal mortuary temples (see the discussion in *chapter 4.2.5*).

The entire western wall of Room no. 4 was designed as one unit: a kind of large false door. This approach to the design of the cultic room decoration one can see in the case of some non-royal tombs. For example, two false doors of almost identical appearance are placed in the western wall of Ti's offering chapel. The false doors stand on a low base, which is moulded in relief (see *fig. 5.6a–b.*). The torus mouldings of both false doors, creating the borders of the doors, are also perched on this base. Thus the wall makes one artistic and functional unit.

The existence of torus moulding which once encircled the whole western wall in Room no. 4 of the Mastaba of Ptahshepses (see p. 92) is indicative of the existence

Fig. 5.6a–b Saqqara, the Mastaba of Ti. Western wall of the offering chapel with two false doors "resting" on a low base

of a cavetto cornice – which itself is not directly attested. The introduction of this architectural feature for false doors may have been dated to the middle of the Fifth Dynasty.[570] This seems to fit with the dating of the construction of the Ptahshepses mastaba and especially of the second building stage to this time, *i.e.*, not before the reigns of Neferirkare/Niuserre.

[569] One cannot to exclude fully that the priests preparing the toilet of the statue of Mereruka might have adorned the nobles' statue with garments and performed their rituals in front of the statue.

[570] Wiebach, *Scheintür*, 18–21; Cherpion, *Mastabas*, 75, criterion 54.

5.3 The third building stage

The third building stage saw Ptahshepses convert his mastaba into a temple tomb. The use of the floral – lotus – columns in both the Old and New Portico gave Ptahshepses an opportunity to use this "new-fashioned" element of architecture in his tomb. The monumental dimensions of the entrance to the mastaba coincide with the fact that the tomb was changed into the temple tomb. The monument now encompassed forty rooms and areas, which created an intricate ground plan of cultic and auxiliary spaces.

As a result of all these alterations, the Mastaba of Ptahshepses joins the group of large tombs belonging to the second half of the Fifth and of the Sixth Dynasty, a group that includes the mastabas of Ti, Rashepses, Ihi, Nebkauhor, Niankhba, Khentika, Nefersekhmet Sheshi, Ankhmahor, Mereruka, Kagemni, Ptahhotep I and Akhtihotep in Saqqara and the tombs of Rawer and Senedjemib Inti in Giza. The majority of them encompassed a pillared room, an east-west oriented room and a staircase. Beside their separate elements, their size is another parameter in which they vary from other non-royal tombs. Together with these features, one may mention the large number of internal rooms.

5.3.1 Columned porticos

Despite the fact, that the tomb in its late form can be compared with these tombs, there is one difference, that has been already discussed: the use of the floral bundle columns in the Mastaba of Ptahshepses. The concept of showing high social rank by the size of the tomb and the complexity of its architecture was certainly emphasized by the erection of two impressive eight-stemmed lotiform columns in the New Portico, which became a new monumental gateway into the vizier's "private realm".[571] The New Portico, an adaptation of the Old Portico, not only copied its function, but also its layout. Nevertheless, the presence of the first eight-stemmed columns in the Egyptian architecture (see *chapter 4.3.3*) highlights the uniqueness of this mastaba. The monumental impact of the entrance – especially as seen from the Nile Valley – undoubtedly went beyond the mere construction of a new gate to Ptahshepses' other world.

As is well known, small obelisks were erected in front of the entrances to the tombs of the nobility (*fig. 5.7*) in the second part of the Old Kingdom as we can see also in the case of the entrances to the mortuary temples of queens.[572] Their connection with the sun cult is apparent, in this connection they were very probably also the symbol of regeneration.

Taking into consideration the impressive height of the New Portico, there might have been some idea to approach as closely as possible to a monument akin to a royal valley temple, a structure which presented a monumental gateway to the pyramid complex of the king. The walls of the portico itself were very probably elevated above the masonry of mastaba's outer walls. This distinguished it from these outer walls and so created a prominent and in a way also independent element of architecture.

With the New Portico in place, the Old Portico (originally the entrance to the mastaba), became a quite strange "hypostyle room" with its two columns and several – at least three – free standing statues and decorated side walls. The relief scenes covering the walls of the portico are connected mainly with the provisioning and transportation of goods and offerings. On the walls of the Southern Portico (which also became either a fully or partially roofed room), one can not only see scenes connected with the provisioning of the offerings and goods, but also the pulling of (colossal) statues and a depiction of employees from the offices under

---

[571] In the opinion of M. Verner, the use of floral bundle columns in the ambulatories of the royal mortuary temples also seems to refer to the solar function of these courtyards (Verner, in: *OKAA*, 354).

[572] Jánosi, *Gräberwelt*, 104; Martin, *Garantsymbol*, 48–62.

Fig. 5.7 Giza, the Mastaba of Seshemnefer IV. Entrance to the tomb from the south-east

Fig. 5.8 Saqqara, the Mastaba of Ti. Pillared courtyard

the control of Ptahshepses, while he and members of his family are also present. Moreover, a (purification) basin was very probably located in the western part of this newly reconstructed room. It is therefore apparent that this room was not without a cultic meaning. There is also a possibility that the room was connected with a serdab. The existence of multiple serdabs in one tomb is one of the features of mastabas which one can find in tombs constructed in those times.[573] In this case the enlarged and covered Southern Portico might have served for rituals connected with the statue(s) placed in the hypothetical serdab in Room no. 12.

5.3.2 Pillared courtyard

The pillared courtyard is the largest and important space not only of the third building stage, but also of the whole Mastaba of Ptahshepses. As was the case with Ti's mastaba (see *fig. 5.8*), the design for Ptahshepses' monument was probably influenced by models in the royal mortuary temples. Nevertheless, it seems that despite the fact that Ptahshepses was able to use some of features which were standard for the royal architecture of his time (saddle ceiling in the burial chamber, niches in Room no. 4), he did not have the right to use columns in this courtyard. The erection of the pillars in the courtyards of the mastabas of Ptahshepses, Ti and in other non-royal tombs has another aspect. As has already been mentioned, Fourth Dynasty kings used pillars in their courtyards, and this idea was transformed into the use of columns in the porticos and open courtyards of their mortuary temples by Fifth Dynasty times.

In Jéquier's opinion, pillars were derived from door jambs transferred into stone.[574] It seems that the pillars were modelled to represent forms and shapes

---

[573] We can encounter such examples, *e.g.*, in tombs of Ti, Rawer and Ptahhotep I.

[574] Jéquier, *Manuel*, 152.

which could be seen in the rocky edges of the deserts along the Nile valley. It is also evident that pillars evolved in function from tree trunks which at the beginnings of Egyptian architecture supported roofs of primordial, prehistoric buildings. Nevertheless, the most important practical reason for the use of pillars was the fact that their production was easier than that of columns. Generally speaking, in the earlier periods of the development of Egyptian architecture, it had been the prerogative of the kings alone to use pillars in their tombs. Their use in the tombs of queens and higher officials came at a later period of time. These officials, living during the Fifth and the Sixth Dynasty, could then, it seems, use the idea of pillars in their own monuments (see *figs. 5.9, 5.10*).

On the other hand, the use of the stone columns was not fully ruled out for important commoners, as we can see in at least two instances of a columned porticos of the Ptahshepses mastaba, where large stone columns were erected. One has to ask why stone (floral) columns were not used in the courtyard. It seems that the explanation may have roots in both economic reasons and those related to religious function; but there is every possibility that there were unbreakable barriers between the social and cultic status of the godlike king and his vizier that prevented certain usurpations of royal prerogatives.

Fig. 5.9 Giza, the Mastaba of Senedjemib. Pillared hall

Fig. 5.10 Saqqara, the Mastaba of Niankhba. Pillared hall

The royal mortuary complexes were regarded as the domicile of the king's soul. Dieter Arnold[575] considered them as constructions provisioning the eternal existence of a king's corpse (by means of the mortuary cult), through a decorative and sculptural program,[576] but they were also seen as a vehicle for commemorating

[575] Arnold, *MDAIK* 33 (1977), 1–14.

[576] Jánosi, 'Die Entwicklung und Deutung des Totenopferraumes in den Pyramidentempeln des Alten Reiches', in: *Ägyptische Tempel*, 153, sees in the decorative program of the mortuary temples the way in which the eternal presence of the ruler in the mortuary temple, residing among the circumpolar stars of the firmament, was confirmed.

triumphs over the enemies of Egypt and ensuring the success of the eternal reign of the king in the afterlife. An important contribution to this discussion is Ricke's opinion, that the mortuary temple was divided (by a transverse corridor) into two parts: the inner part – the "temple of offering" and the outer part – the "temple of worship".[577]

The open courtyards embellished along one or more sides by rows of pillars located in such temples of worship were part of the mortuary temples from the beginning of the Fourth Dynasty.[578] During the reigns of kings from Sahure to Unas the courtyards were equipped with columns bearing plant motifs (palm, lotus and papyrus) supplemented by plain columns. However, we also encounter vegetal columns in the monumental gateways to the pyramid complexes – the valley temples. As was the case with the open courtyards in the mortuary temples, the use of floral columns in the valley temples had a profound meaning connected with the ideas of resurrection. The entire courtyard, and possibly even the ambulatory surrounding it, could present an image of the Nilotic landscape with its black basalt pavement[579] representing the waters of the Nile flood, columns representing the riverine valley vegetation (palm, lotus or papyrus plants) and the starry roof of the ambulatory representing the persistent firmament. The walls of the ambulatory bore relief decoration giving life to this "artificial" world.[580] So, it seems that in the tomb complex of the lord of the entire land, his earthly country would be envisioned.[581]

At this level, there was a distinct demarcation between the roles played by the king and mortals such as Ptahshepses. We do not know why these differences in the architectural appearance of the royal and elite non-royal tombs existed, but we suppose that some religious ideas must have been used only by kings. Evidently, it was not acceptable for Ptahshepses and other high nobles to create such an artificial landscape by the use of selected elements of architecture in their tombs.

As for the economic grounds for the non erection of the floral bundle columns, it is clear that the making of elaborate limestone columns was an expensive and time-consuming task and that the capacity of craftsmen to carry out these tasks was limited by the priority given to the construction of the royal pyramid complexes and sun temples. In view of this argument, the importance of the appearance of the both monumental column pairs in the entrance porticos to the Mastaba of Ptahshepses is even more striking than it would first appear. One can add that the practical or "financial" reasons might have also played some role and they were connected with the importance of the individual queens.[582] From an economic point of view, the use of the "royal" materials, basalt and granite attested in the royal courtyards was also beyond the scope of Ptahshepses.[583]

---

[577] Ricke, *Bemerkungen AR* II, 65; *cf.* Arnold, 'Rituale und Pyramidentempel', *MDAIK* 33 (1977), 8–9. One can only advance the hypothesis, that the vast Ptahshepses mastaba might also have been divided into two parts – that with offering rooms in the Initial Mastaba and those of the later additions which were concentrated on the worship of the deceased (and his family).

[578] As a matter of course these courtyards very probably had their predecessor in the pyramid complex of Netjerikhet.

[579] For the use of basalt in the Old-Kingdom architecture and in open courtyards of the royal mortuary temples see: Hoffmeier, 'The Use of the Basalt in Floors of Old Kingdom Pyramid Temples', *JARCE* 30 (1993), 117–123.

[580] *Cf.* O´Connor, 'The Interpretation of the Old Kingdom Pyramid Complex', in: *Stationen*, 143.

[581] Here the relief scenes from the Seasons' Chapel in the Sun Temple of Niuserre could possibly be mentioned (Edel, Wenig, *Jahreszeitenreliefs*). Some scholars connect this decoration with the interpretation of the sun god as a creator and lord of the universe (Begelsbacher-Fischer, *Götterwelt*, 167). The king, as the son of the sun god, could be brought into this context as the lord of the country.

[582] The tombs of some queens were well made (the tombs of Meretneith, Khamerernebty II, Ankhesenpepy II). On the other hand, there are many examples of poorly made queens' burials (Nimaathap II, Khuit I, Meresankh IV, *etc.*). An important fact is that the tombs of some queens are not known at all, despite the persistent endeavour of researchers.

[583] This is clearly valid for its use on a larger scale and should be compared with the use of granite for the making of sarcophagi.

These considerations appear to be at the root of an explanation for the absence of columns in the pillared court of the Ptahshepses mastaba, but without further evidence from this distant period, our explanation must remain largely hypothetical.

The presence of column bases in the entrance corridor of the mortuary temple of Queen Neferhetepes – and the nature of those columns is restricted to the base alone – is the only instance of columns known for Old Kingdom queens.[584] With this possible exception it is well known that stone floral columns were not used in the pyramid complexes of Old Kingdom queens.[585] When pillars were used in queens' complexes and in the large mastabas of nobles during the second half of the Old Kingdom, they represented the now-abandoned patterns of architecture coming from the pyramid complexes of kings. However, for some unknown reason, chosen people could have the columns in the porticos or covered vestibules, but not in open courtyards, where only the erection of pillars might be acceptable. It is interesting to think about the fact that even though columns were not in wide use in the stone burial buildings of queens and nobles, we do encounter wooden columns in their architecture. Such wooden columns were erected in the courtyard along the eastern façade of Djadjaemankh's mastaba in Abusir.[586] They seem to stand for some important religious function. The columns in Djadjaemankh's tomb were plain columns; they did not present a bundle of plant stems or a palm column. However, floral bundle columns, apparently made of wood, became an integral part of the mundane architecture – as we can infer from the relief decoration in non-royal tombs.

Taking this view into account, we can suppose that the general omission of plant-motif capitals for columns in open courtyards and large roofed halls in the tomb complexes of queens and nobles was, despite the fact that their manufacture was already well mastered, influenced mainly by religious reasons and the different rank of kings and of their queens.

5.3.3 Decoration in the pillared courtyard

The relief decoration in the open courtyard of the Mastaba of Ptahshepses did not survive. In those cases where the decoration of the pillared courtyards and pillared halls is known, it is apparent that the nobles tried to show themselves as the "rulers" of their private realms provisioning themselves with pictorial goods for their mortuary cults. This is most obvious in the decoration of the pillared courtyard of Ti and the pillared halls of some other large mastabas of the second half of the Fifth and of the Sixth Dynasty (see below). Therefore, we can see in the decoration of the courtyard of Ti the scenes presenting a poultry farm belonging to the House of the Eternity, the carrying of the noble in the palanquin, slaughtering of the cattle, bringing of the offerings, delivering of the goods from the Southern Egypt by ships.[587] All these scenes are concentrated on the showing the tomb owner's high social rank and his provisioning for his mortuary cult. There is not a big difference between the relief decoration of Ti's courtyard and that of the pillared halls in other tombs of the period.[588]

---

[584] Unfortunately, the owner of a small pyramid complex which is appended to the mortuary temple of Djedkare in South Saqqara is not known (see discussion with other bibliographical references in Jánosi, *MDAIK*, 45 [1989], 187–202 and Jánosi, *Pyramidenanlagen*, 36–37). The columns once erected had the papyrus bundle form (see Jánosi, *MDAIK* 45 [1989], 192–193, Taf. 21) which would be a one-off attestation in a non-royal tomb complex.

[585] Jánosi, *Pyramidenanlagen*, 179. Nevertheless, wooden columns were used in the case of the mortuary temples of pyramid complexes of Menkaure's queens GIIIa and c (Reisner, *Mycerinus*, 58–59, 67, pls. IV, VI).

[586] See note 554.

[587] Épron, Daumas, *Le tombeau de Ti* I, pls. XIV, XIX, XXII–XXIV, XXVIII, In connection with the fact that the Mastaba of Ptahshepses was not fully completed, it seems to be interesting that the tomb of Ti also lacked completion.

The pillared courtyard in the Mastaba of Ptahshepses had an important communication role. Apparently, it was not only for every-day practical use, but was also significant on the religious, abstract level. One notes that the courtyard was connected to Room no. 16 (hypothetically, with the tomb owner's statue) and with the area of the Initial Mastaba in which the most important cultic places were located. The pillars in the court were adorned with figures of the Vizier and King's Son, Ptahshepses, depicted in sunk relief. We can follow these figures along all the sides of the courtyard. They were so oriented that the noble, incarnated in the statue – which might have been made of wood and was very probably housed in Room no. 16 (see p. 134) – crossed the courtyard from the entrance to Room no. 16 towards the entrance of the Initial Mastaba. This route might have indicated the route of the statue in procession through the courtyard. We cannot rule out that, during this journey, some rituals might have been carried out. Any rituals carried out along the way could have been connected with the sun cult.[589] In the Initial Mastaba, the statue might have taken part in further rituals. As has been mentioned, the statue might have been taken up the staircase (enclosed in a naos?)[590] and made the object of rituals carried out on the roofing terrace of the mastaba.

5.3.4 Basins

The courtyard in the Mastaba of Ptahshepses was equipped with at least one, but more probably two basins. The large basin was located in the middle of the courtyard, in its north-south axis, the second was quite carelessly cut into the pavement of the northern ambulatory of the courtyard.

Generally speaking, one can note that, at the beginning of the Fifth Dynasty, basins became a part of the cultic equipment of the offering rituals in non-royal tombs.[591] In this period, the basins – which were regarded as cult objects at that time – were introduced to chapels, where they were usually found in front of the offering niches. Keeping this fact in mind, there is the question as to what function the basin located in the centre of Ptahshepses' pillared courtyard originally served. No false door was apparent or presumed in the area of the pillared courtyard. Also

---

588 Mereruka: beside the niche (discussed above) and his two accompanying relief representations, there are the following scenes: Mereruka in the palaquin, the feeding of the animals, the display of the offerings, bringing of the offerings, *sšš wꜣḏ* and Mereruka with his spouse and ships. The only major difference lies in the depictions of the burial ceremonies.

589 The openness of the courtyards constructed in some of the large mastabas enables one to hypothesise about their possible relationship to the cult of the sun god (*cf.* Arnold, *Tempel*, 201; Begeslbacher-Fischer, *Götterwelt*, 166). U. Fritz has recently mentioned, that these open pillared spaces were part of a "sun cult complex" and that they represented "sun courtyards" (Fritz, *Typologie*, 26–27, 65; she follows the main division of the tombs as presented by Brinks, in *Grabanlagen, passim.*), these "sun complexes" should had followed their models in royal architecture. In her avenue of arguments, Fritz mentions that the original function of their models in the royal temples was lost by their transfer to non-royal tombs and these sun cult complexes became, in her opinion, "functionless". In this connection quite oddly, she comes to the conclusion that the whole south part of the Mastaba of Ptahshepses, built during the third building stage, presents a sun cult complex. To follow her conclusions one should know more about the religious beliefs which were behind the architecture of the courtyards. In connection with Fritz's hypothesis, we can only mention that the Mastaba of Ptahshepses came into existence during the period of the culmination of the sun cult – a time which had resulted in the construction of the sun temples (Kaiser, *MDAIK* 14 [1956], 104–116, Abb. 1; Winter, *WZKM* 54 [1956], 222–233; Moursi, *Hohenpriester des Sonnengottes*; Rochholz, in: *Ägyptische Tempel*, 255–280). Whilst on the one hand Fritz's supposition cannot be completely ruled out, this conjecture remains problematic because it lacks – in the present state of our knowledge – direct evidence.

590 Alexanian, in: *Grab und Totenkult*, 27–40. Despite the fact sunbeams played an important role in the rituals carried out on the roofing terrace, it has been supposed by N. Alexanian that the statues were placed in the wooden naoi. If her suggestion is correct, this would mean that the sunbeams could touch the statue itself only through the opened door of the naoi.

591 Junker, *Gîza* III, 203; Junker *Gîza* VII, 120–123; Mostafa, *Opfertafeln*, 124–127; Bárta, 'The Mastaba of Ptahshepses Junior II at Abusir', *Ä&L* 10 (2000), 60; Hölzl, in: *L'acqua*, 310. For a general understanding of libation rituals see: Bonnet, *MDAIK* 14 (1956), 11–16.

in connection with this fact and also due to the fact that the basin was connected with the mastaba's waste system, the cultic use[592] should not be assumed.

One of the most important parallels for this discussion is a large basin located in the pavement of the courtyard in Seshemnefer's IV tomb (see *fig. 5.11*).[593] In this example, this large rectangular basin was not joined to a waste canal. Another example of a basin located in an open courtyard is the basin placed in the centre of

Fig. 5. 11. Giza, the Mastaba of Seshemnefer IV. Basin in the courtyard

the court enclosed by the tombs of Senedjemib's Inti's family in Giza. It is obvious for Brovarski[594] that that court functioned as the common place of a cult which could have been centred around the basin. The basin, nevertheless, differs in its form and it was not connected with a waste canal as is the basin in the courtyard of Ptahshepses.[595] Seshemnefer's basin had much larger dimensions (2.00 × 1.20 m) than that of Senedjemib Inti (0.85 × 0.53 m).

In connection with the function of these basins, Junker wondered whether Seshemnefer's basin could be used during the rites connected with purification relating to the embalming of the mummy: certainly its symbolic meaning was mentioned in this connection. These basins dated to the Old Kingdom have been by the Austrian Egyptologist interpreted as a kind of pool,[596] on which the deceased should traverse in his ships.[597] In Reisner's theory, these basins were filled with water during some rituals and used for the ceremonial purification of priests and other visitors.[598] In Junker's opinion, these basins could have had quite small dimensions and his thoughts on this matter were focussed on a purely ritual level.[599]

If one supposes that the basins from the Ptahshepses' courtyard served for purification purposes, one could assume that such a basin would be located in the area of the entrance to a cultic room. We can see this in the case of the entrance to the Mastaba of Ptahshepses Junior II,[600] where the basin was located directly in the

[592] See also further in this chapter.
[593] Junker, *Gîza* IX, 106, fig. 49–50, pls. 12C, 13A. *Cf.* the existence of a large pool in the area of the tomb of Khentkaus I in Giza (Hassan, *Gîza* IV, fig. 32) and a large basin alongside the mortuary temple of Shepseskaf in South Saqqara (Jéquier, *Mastabat Faraoun*, Pl. VI).
[594] Brovarski, *Senedjemib*, 11.
[595] *Cf.* Brovarski, *Senedjemib*, pl. 3.
[596] Junker, *ArOr* 20 (1952), 187–189.
[597] Junker, *Gîza* XI, 106–107.
[598] Reisner, *Giza Necropolis*, 83; Brovarski, *Senedjemib* I, 11, note 15.
[599] Junker, *ArOr* 20 (1952), 187–189.
[600] Bárta, *Ä&L* 10 (2000), 49, 59, pl. 2.

entrance to the mastaba. There are also other examples in which this purification function apparently prevailed.[601] However, there is one exception which seems to be more similar to the basin in the Ptahshepses' mastaba. It is the instance provided by the tomb of Nefer.[602] As follows from the plan published by Hassan, there was a basin connected with a drainage channel which was located in the middle of an open courtyard. In his description, however, he does not mention any basin.[603] An interesting fact is that all the pieces of evidence in this respect come from Giza. As already mentioned by Miroslav Bárta,[604] it is thus possible to document the relationship between the Abusir tombs built during the reign of Niuserre and the contemporary tombs from the Giza necropolis.

The pillared courtyard of Ti's mastaba, which represents the closest analogy to the courtyard of Ptahshepses, does not contain any basin, but the extensive devastation of this area by tomb and stone robbers has made it impossible to predict whether or not there had been one in the first place.[605] Basins attested in the courts of the royal mortuary temples clearly show that they served not in the carrying out of rituals in the courtyards, but that they possessed a clearly practical purpose. Bearing in mind the large open area on which large amounts of water certainly collected during the short, but heavy (winter) rains, the necessity of including such a basin in the courtyard clearly would have had a practical purpose.[606] Due to the profound disturbance of the mortuary temples, though, there are not a lot of well documented examples. This is the case for both Menkaure's[607] and Userkaf's mortuary temples,[608] where the existence of a collecting basin in the courtyard was possible to suppose only on the basis of the remains of waste canals. A collecting basin was also reconstructed by L. Borchardt in Niuserre's open courtyard.[609] Following Borchardt's conclusion, the basin, made of red quartzite, was covered by a lid made of basalt or quartzite with punched holes. Another collecting basin has been attested in the mortuary temple of Pepy II.[610]

Having in mind the analogies from the royal mortuary temples and also the analogy coming from the tomb of Nefer, it is thus very probable that the basin located in the centre of the court of the Mastaba of Ptahshepses was used mainly for the collection of water. We cannot rule out, though, that it was provided with a covering of a flat stone with drilled apertures.

While the basin in the centre of the courtyard very probably served a drainage purpose, a small hollow located in the pavement of the northern wing belonging to the courtyard's ambulatory might have been used for religious purposes. It seems that a (metal) basin was inserted into this globular socket. It should be underlined, however, that it is not possible to document whether its outlet – leading to the

---

[601] For the list of these attestations, see: Bárta, *Ä&L* 10 (2000), 60.

[602] Hassan, *Gîza* III, 202, fig. 167.

[603] Hassan, *Gîza* III, 202: "On the axis of the mud-brick doorway, there is a drain measuring 7,50 × 0,20 × 0,15 m cut in the floor of the court-yard. It begins with a small recess and slopes down to the east, ending just in front of the entrance of the courtyard. The part of this drain (1.50 m in length) adjoining the recess, was found roofed with small slabs of white limestone, and covered with pieces of stone and mud. The part (3.50 m in length) near the doorway of the chapel was found roofed with huge blocks of white limestone; the middle part, however, was found unroofed." It is very probable, that the channel was intended to drain the rain water from the court outside.

[604] Bárta, *Ä&L* 10 (2000), 59–60.

[605] See Épron, Daumas, *Ti*, pl. 1.

[606] Malek, in: *Pyramid studies*, 32.

[607] Reisner, *Mycerinus*, 25.

[608] Labrousse, Lauer, *Ouserkaf*, plan *in folio*.

[609] Borchardt, *Neuserre*, 55, Bl. 5, Bl. 28. Contrary to Maragioglio and Rinaldi, who stressed that the mortuary temple did not incorporate a system of waste channels – see *MRA* VIII, 28–30.

[610] Jéquier, *Pepi II* III, 23, Pl. 29.

north – was connected to the waste system of the mastaba or not (*cf. chapter 4.3.7*). The location of this basin on the north-south axis of the courtyard seems to support the assumption that this hollow was used for religious and most likely sacrificial ceremonies. If so, the basin might have provided a kind of a substitute for the non-existing offering basin in the courtyard.[611] We cannot exclude that a statue (or statues?) might have been erected in this place later and that this basin might have not been a part of the original plan. This seems to explain the inferior quality of workmanship with which the hole was cut out into the pavement of the courtyard's ambulatory in an unknown moment of time (*i.e.*, after the death of Ptahshepses).

5.3.5 Altar

The finding of the weathered altar to the south of the basin in Ptahshepses' courtyard raises several questions, mainly where it was originally located (it was not found *in situ*) and, secondly, which purpose it served. Because there is an altar in the neighbouring tomb of Ptahshepses Junior II,[612] we cannot rule out that the altar found in the courtyard of Ptahshepses Senior was really located in the courtyard. The altar of his son was placed below its southern wall, intentionally above the descending corridor leading to the burial apartment of the deceased. In contrast to the altar found in the courtyard of Ptahshepses Senior, an inscription mentioning the name and titles of the tomb owner was cut into the surface of the altar of Ptahshepses Junior II.[613]

Altars are recorded in the open courtyards of royal mortuary temples from the period of the Fourth Dynasty, namely: Khafre,[614] Sahure,[615] Niuserre,[616] Unas[617] and Teti.[618] In Malek's opinion, in the practical sense, such altars could have represented a place where the offerings were placed before their use within the offering cult.[619]After the intended ceremonies were carried out, the offerings were distributed for use in the non-royal tombs.[620] Following Malek's suggestion for the altars in the royal open courtyards, such an altar, hypothetically located in the courtyard of the Mastaba of Ptahshepses, could have also served for the display of the offerings used in separate parts of the mastaba.[621] Suggestions for ultimate destinations that come to mind are: Room no. 16, located to the south of the courtyard, a room which certainly should be expected to be connected with some cult; the Chapel with Three Niches and, of course, the two offering rooms in the Initial Mastaba.

---

611 These might have been connected with the hypothetical statues erected in the courtyard.

612 Bárta, *Ä&L* 10 (2000), 52. On the upper face of the altar the hieroglyphic sign *ḥtp* was made in relief.

613 The form of both altars with the *ḥtp* signs formed directly on their surfaces is not exceptional. There are further analogical attestations of altars placed in front of false doors in offering rooms, *e.g.*, in the tombs of Hemre (Moussa, Altenmüller, *Nianchchnum und Chnumhotep*, 158, Taf. 80b), Ti's northern false door (Épron, Wild, *Ti*, fig. 1), and Ptahhotep II (below the "real", southern false door).

614 Hölscher, *Chephren*, 56

615 Borchardt, *Sahure* I, Bl. 16, Abb. 51–54; Wartke, *ZÄS* 104 (1977), 145–156.

616 Borchardt, *Neuserre*, 55, 68–69, Bl. 14–15.

617 Labrousse, Lauer, Leclant, *Le temple haute du roi Ounas*, 23, pl. VIII.B.

618 Lauer, Leclant, *Teti*, 19, Pls. VII A, XXXIV, XXXV, and Malek, in: *Pyramid studies*, 23–34.

619 Malek, *op. cit*, 34.

620 P. Posener-Kriéger connected the "royal offering of *wśḫt*" – *ḥtp-nśwt ỉmj wśḫt* – without any hesitation to the courtyard (Posener-Kriéger, *Les archives d'Abousir*, 499–501.). The movable *ḥtp*-altars seem also to be attested in the inventory lists in Neferirkare's temple archive. In the text dated to the end of the reign of Djedkare two *ḥtp*-altars were mentioned – "a big *ḥtp*-altar" – *ḥtp ꜥꜣ* – and a *ḥtp*-altar made of "Asiatic copper" – *śṯt ḥtp*(*t*) – Posener-Kriéger, *Les archives d'Abousir*, 134, fig. 2, 141, fig. 6.

621 These offerings could then be distributed from this location into other parts of the mastaba, or, if someone would follow the general outlines given by J. Malek for the situation of Ptahshepses' family, into the tombs of its other members.

If, originally, the altar had been placed in the courtyard, then there are three possibilities of location within it. The first solution, proposed by some authors who dealt with the Mastaba of Ptahshepses, places the altar in the north-south axis of the courtyard, into the neighbourhood of the collecting basin (see Fiala's plan of the mastaba – *fig. 1.11*).[622] The second possibility suggests it might have been placed in the vicinity of the small hole in the northern wing of the ambulatory (see previous discussion on p. 174). Thirdly, the altar could have been somehow connected with the statues possibly erected in the courtyard. As it happens, there is no possibility of now ascertaining the appearance of these installations, although, the placement of this altar in front of one of the larger statues does not present an impossible proposition. If such a statue were to be placed in between two pillars of the courtyard ambulatory, then (from the point of view of Egyptian architectural rules), it might have represented a conceivable arrangement. As was discussed already in *chapter 4.3*, the courtyard might also have included the statues placed in stone naoi: it has been supposed, that a part of the western ambulatory was used for their erection (see p. 132). Thus, if the altar was connected with their cult, one would expect it to be placed in their vicinity, *i.e.*, in the north-western part of the court.[623]

As was already mentioned, the altar might also have been placed in another space of the mastaba. Among the avenue of possibilities available, one has also to think about the original location of the altar, either in a neighbouring tomb or in Niuserre's pyramid complex. In this case the altar may have been transported from its original place across to the Mastaba of Ptahshepses by stone robbers during some later time. However, due to its massiveness, this possibility does not seem to be plausible (in this case, the altar would have been carried to Ptahshepses' mastaba along quite a long track). It is therefore more probable, that the altar was originally placed in the courtyard or, less probably, in Room no. 16.

5.3.6 Statues in the courtyard

As was already alleged in *chapter 4.3.6*, the courtyard of the Mastaba of Ptahshepses was also very probably adorned by statues. They did not present the only way that Ptahshepses allowed himself to be depicted himself in the courtyard. Along with the relief decoration of the side walls of the court, the figures of Ptahshepses were incised, together with his name and titles, on the pillars and architraves of the courtyard's ambulatory.[624] Ptahshepses certainly might have followed royal models in the mortuary temples by the erection of statues in the courtyard.[625] The statues of the king were probably a part of the decoration program of open courtyards in their mortuary temples.[626] One cannot exclude that statues were also located in the open courtyards in the mortuary temples of queens as has been shown in the case with statue-naoi of Queen Khentkaus II.[627] They might have been located in the open courtyard of the queen's mortuary temple in Abusir.[628]

---

[622] *Cf.* Balík, *Mastaba*, fig. on p. 72.

[623] In this case, the position of the altar would have fitted perfectly the situation in the open courtyard of Niuserre's mortuary temple.

[624] As is well known, no figures depicting kings were found on the columns in the courtyards in the royal mortuary temples in this period, but kings were fully represented by their titulary, during the Fifth Dynasty. They appeared with the re-introduction of pillars in the architecture of the pyramid temples during the Sixth Dynasty (from the reign of King Teti) – *cf.* pillars in the courtyard of Pepy's II mortuary temple in South Saqqara (Jéquier, *Pepi II*, vol. III, 23–24, fig. 9, pl. 45).

[625] Ptahshepses, who had his images incised on his courtyard pillars, might have tried to substitute the royal fashion of placing statues of the king in the courtyard. Carving the image is a cheaper and easier way of imitating the royal fashion, but it might have performed the same function.

[626] *Cf.* Ricke, *Bemerkungen AR* II, 50–55, Abb. 17, 19–20 Tf. 2.

[627] Posener-Kriéger, in: Verner, *Khentkaus*, 134–141.

[628] Jánosi, *Pyramidenanlagen*, 153.

As was already mentioned (in *chapter 4.3.7*), Ptahshepses' statue placed in a naos (or statues in naoi) very probably stood in his pillared courtyard.[629] For B. Patočková it seems to be confirmed by the dragging of the statues placed in the naoi in the relief representations on the walls of the Southern Portico.[630] This naos (or naoi) might have been erected in the north-western part of the court.

Using a naos for a statue can also be documented in other non-royal tombs. A naos located in an open courtyard still standing *in situ* was unearthed in the close vicinity of the Mastaba of Ptahshepses – in the tomb of his son Ptahshepses Junior II.[631] It was located by the entrance to the tomb courtyard; in its south-west corner. The naos is a small construction and it certainly did not contain a large statue (its dimensions are only 0.78 × 0.87 × 1.10 m). As the already mentioned altar was placed not far away from the naos, a direct connection between the statue in the naos, the altar and the opening to the corridor leading to the burial chamber (which was also in the area of the altar) is obvious in the opinion of M. Bárta. Another similar analogy is presented by a deep niche-naos in the open courtyard of Ptahhotep I's tomb in Saqqara.[632] This is one of the large tombs of the Fifth Dynasty[633] which also incorporated an open pillared courtyard and other rooms containing pillars. Unlike the pillars in Ptahshepses's courtyard, those of Ptahhotep did not bear a figure of the deceased, but bore only his titles.[634] As might have been the case with the courtyard in the Ptahshepses mastaba, a serdab was located beside the courtyard. It was connected to the courtyard by means of apertures.[635]

Obviously, the pillared courtyard played an important role in the religious concepts lying behind the architecture of the mastaba. It was, in all likelihood, the place where the ceremonies connected with the statue(s) erected in the courtyard (and in other rooms of the mastaba) were carried out. Every effort had been made to underline the eternal appearance of the vizier in his tomb. Hypothetically, it was also the place where, together with the appointed priests, the broader family of Ptahshepses might have gathered in order to take part in specific rites.

5.3.7 Boat-room

The most puzzling room of the whole mastaba is without doubt Room no. 40, the Boat-room. The planned function of this largely destroyed and very probably never finished room might be connected with religious concepts detected in some Old Kingdom non-royal tombs. The ships, whose insertion into Room 40 might have been planned during the third building stage, played an important role in both the royal and non-royal sphere. Two types of ships – the hedgehog and the rowing ship – are documented in connection with *sšš w3ḏ* [636] associated with beliefs in the resurrection. Following the opinion of H. Altenmüller, the hedgehog ship might be connected with sailing during the night, while the rowing ship represented the daytime use.[637] Therefore, one may suppose that in Room no. 40 not one, but two ships had to be placed. The only other case of including ships in a non-royal tomb is the tomb of Kagemni. Here, two "boat rooms" were located on top of the tomb.[638]

---

629 Patočková, in: *Critères de datation*, 230.

630 Verner, *Reliefs*, 104–112, photo 98–102, 105–106, 110–114.

631 See Bárta, *Ä&L* 10 (2000), 49–52, fig. 2, pls. 5, 6. Another naos-niche was documented in the corridor leading to the offering table, built in the wall – Bárta, *Ä&L* 10 (2000), 52–53, fig. 2, pl. 7.

632 PM III, 596–598, Pl. LX; Hassan, *CdE* 13 (1938), 68–70; Hassan, Iskander, *Ny-ꜥnkh-Pepy*, 25–61; Hassan-Iskander, *Hemet-Rꜥ*, fig. 12.

633 For the dating, see Helck, *Beamtentitel*, 138; Martin-Pardey, in: *LÄ* IV, 1181.

634 Hassan, Iskander, *Hemet-Rꜥ*, 36.

635 Hassan, Iskander, *Hemet-Rꜥ*, 38.

636 Altenmüller, 'Der Himmelsaufstieg des Grabherrn. Zu den Szenen des *zšš w3ḏ* in den Gräbern des Alten Reiches', *SÄK* 30 (2002), 14–23 (the article also includes a discussion of the previous works on the subject).

637 Altenmüller, H., 'Die Nachtfahrt des Grabherrn im Alten Ägypten. Zur Frage der Schiffe mit Igelkopf', *SÄK* 28 (2000), 1–27. See also Bárta, *Abusir-South* I, 81–85.

The original concept of this room seems to have had some function involving the roof. Among the masons' lines documented on the southern wall of Room no. 40 there are lines which were apparently connected with the (planned but not executed) construction of a staircase along this wall.[639]

A major problem in connection with the reconstruction of the planned appearance of Room no. 40 is the existence of the doorway in the northern, keeled wall of the room and the planned staircase along the opposite wall.[640] It is hard to imagine that it was originally planned to put into the Boat-room two (and as it follows from the curve of the wall of the northern wall) *large* boats, together with an entrance from the north and a staircase along the southern wall of the room. Moreover, the masons' marks convey the information that at least the northern wall was planned to be inclined. This fact allows us to suspect that the room was partly built or at least planned as an open space.

In the case of the southern side wall, the situation is more complicated. Only a short, *vertical* line has been documented on the southern end of the western wall of the room. This piece of information can have two explanations. The southern side wall of the room might have been vertical and the southern part of the room could have been roofed (and it is not clear whether this roofed part was in this case separated from the northern part of the room by a wall) or whether along the southern wall of Room no. 40, a kind of gallery with (wooden) supports (pillars or columns) should be constructed. Such a gallery might have been approached by the staircase planned along the southern wall of the room. On the other hand, one must have in mind that the preservation of the masons' line need not be an indication of the final plan, and hypothetical lines showing an inclination could have once existed there – as is the case with the northern wall of Room no. 40. Discussing the masons' lines and marks, the find of two masons' marks should be mentioned here, including readings in the unit of measurement known as *ṯbt*.[641] In the opinion of M. Verner, this unit might be connected with the curving of the north wall.[642]

If the supposition that ship(s) had to be installed in the area of the Boat-room is right, then one can also hypothesize that two boat shaped rooms were constructed, and that they might have incorporated two boats. These boats might have presented the night and the day boat as has been suggested by H. Altenmüller[643] and in this

---

638 *PM* III 521; Firth, Gunn, *TPC*, 26, pl. 51; Hassan, *Gîza* VI, 88. Unfortunately, the documentation made during the archaeological excavation is inadequate. It does not refer to any piece of detailed evidence concerning the level at which these two enigmatic "boat-rooms" were built; neither does it mention the methods of their construction and their appearance.

639 Verner, *Baugraffiti*, E – plan no. 8.

640 *Loc. cit.*

641 Verner, '*Ṯbt* – Ein bisher unbekanntes altägyptisches Maß?', *MDAIK* 49 (1981), 479–481, Taf.79a–b; *idem*, *Baugraffiti*, 176. *Cf.* Roik, *Längenmaßsystem*, 63, for the discussion on the "*Nbj*-Maßsystem", see Roik, *Längenmaßsystem*, 57–167.

642 It can thus be seen that data collected in Room no. 40 present contradictory material and do not offer an easy explanation for the original design and function of this room. But with all these considerations in mind, we can propose another solution as to what the originally planned appearance of Room no. 40 might have been. This reconstruction of Room no. 40 presents quite a complicated structured. On the ground-floor, there would be a kind of a passage leading southwards along the southern wall of Room no. 40 to where the aforementioned staircase might have been located. This staircase then might have ascended to an elevated terrace, where the two boat-shaped rooms would have been erected to the north of the staircase opening onto the terrace. If this is correct, then, the corridor should have been constructed below the boat-shaped rooms and it would have represented only a narrow and quite low passage. As a matter of course, the space below the boat-shaped rooms would be filled with core and low quality masonry. However, one has to underline that this solution is only hypothetical and that it follows from the masons' marks documented on the walls of Room no. 40. If the very complicated and only hypothetical aforementioned construction was really planned (and made), the deceased Ptahshepses would have climbed in the form of his statue to the roofing terrace and he could use his ships for traversing day and night firmament.

643 Altenmüller, 'Funerary Boats an Boat Pits of the Old Kingdom', *ArOr* 70/3 (2002), 284.

way Ptahshepses could have secured his day and night journeys with the sun god. The destination of these journeys were most probably meant for the "field of offerings" and "the beautiful west". In this way, his resurrection and "ascension" (in association with the sun god) might have been guaranteed.

5.3.8 Storerooms

Last, but not at least, the storerooms in the Mastaba of Ptahshepses should be discussed here. Altogether, there were at least thirteen storerooms in the mastaba. This number exceed the number available in other large contemporary non-royal tombs. Those tombs of the Fifth and the Sixth Dynasty incorporated the following numbers of storerooms (internal rooms of the non-royal tombs as well as royal pyramid temples – see later – indicating their function as magazines by their layout):

- Ti: 1,
- Ptahhotep I: 1?,
- Akhtihotep: 1,
- Ihi, Nebkauhor: 5–6,
- Niankhba: 4–5?,
- Khentika Ikhekhi: 4,
- Neferseshemre Sheshi: 2,
- Ankhmahor: at least one,
- Mereruka: 5–7,
- Kagemni: 7.

One has to underline the fact that counting the number of storerooms was not an easy task as, in many cases, the function of the individual rooms is not fully obvious. Despite this fact, the numbers clearly show that the difference between the Mastaba of Ptahshepses and other tombs of the period was significant. However, the number of storerooms in the Ptahshepses mastaba is in a way closer (even though lower) to the number of storerooms in the royal mortuary temples than to the numbers of magazines in other large mastabas. In Abusir pyramid complexes we can ennumerate:

- Sahure: at least 28,
- Neferirkare: at least 13 (the original building project had been changed after the death of the king),
- Raneferef: (the original building project had to be changed after the death of the king; at the end of the building development – without the Ritual Slaughterhouse – it incorporated at least 15 magazines),
- Niuserre: at least 14.

One has to add that, towards the end of the Old Kingdom, the number of magazines in the royal mortuary temples rose:

- Djedkare (at least 29),
- Unas (37),
- Pepi I (51),
- Teti (55),
- Pepi II (52).

The previous list clearly shows that the total number of storerooms in the Ptahshepses mastaba was extraordinary in the repertoire of non-royal tomb architecture. Such a high number, which is comparable to the number of storerooms in some royal mortuary temples, seems to show that rituals conducted in the Mastaba of Ptahshepses were quite complicated and that they demanded construction of a higher number of magazines than was normal for elite commoners. It is interesting that this demand was possibly not so high during the construction of the first building stage. As has been already mentioned on p. 47–48, there is no distinct room to which storage can be ascribed in the Initial Mastaba and one has to suppose that a mud brick addition outside the building might have been at least planned, if not really constructed. The situation changed with the first enlargement of the mastaba. In its annex, one can see five storerooms. Therefore, one can suppose that these storerooms might have been somewhat connected with the statues which were erected in the triple-shrine of Room no. 4. The further increase in the number of storerooms during the third building stage is really remarkable and one has to have in mind the overall change of the mastaba into the temple-tomb where a high number of statues were erected. We note that, beside the Ptahshepses mastaba, the highest numbers of storerooms are in those tombs whose groundplans are also quite complicated and their relief decoration highly developed as well (Mereruka, Kagemni).[644]

It is not easy to determine which magazines were used for storing which goods. As was already discussed elsewhere, one can say, that at least two storerooms, Rooms nos. 6 and 8, were used for some more precious instruments used during the rituals in the Chapel with Three Niches. The remaining three spaces among the Northern Storerooms might have been used for keeping the offerings. As a matter of course, some of other magazines should also be used for storing food offerings. One reason for our lack of specific knowledge about the contents of the storerooms is the bad preservation of the individual areas with storerooms themselves, however, the reconstruction of their original appearance did not bring any notable difference in the layout or in the quality of execution as we can see, *e.g.*, in the mortuary temple of Sahure. One may only hypothesize, that as in the south-east and the south-west complexes of storerooms, at least some of the storerooms might have been used for stocking food offerings, the other for other goods and instruments.

5.4 Conclusion of chapter 5

As was shown in this chapter, one may see the importance of the Ptahshepses mastaba for the development of the ancient Egyptian architecture in the mix of the architectural elements used in the royal and non-royal mortuary constructions. This fact was, evidently, affected by the high social status of the tomb owner. There is a possibility that the use of non-standard elements for a non-royal tomb also show that a part of the rituals conducted in the mastaba might have been different in respect with other non-royal tombs. However, it is not possible to precisely determine in which form this difference in rituals conducted in the mastaba might be demonstrated. On the other hand, the mastaba in its form of the second and especially third building stage, is one of the oldest examples of a group of large mastabas built by the Egyptian nobility. At the same time, it is also a primal example of a temple-tomb, the architectural type which developed significantly in the later periods of Egyptian history.

[644] This fact was also noticed by Bárta, in: *Structure and Significance*, 113. He underlines also that these tombs with the higher number of magazines appeared only in Saqqara.

6. Conclusions

6.1 Dating of the mastaba

There are several important questions connected with the architecture of the Ptahshepses mastaba concerning both the social status of its owner and the dating of the tomb. The first question has been discussed in *chapter 2*. From this debate it follows that, despite the fact that the owner of the mastaba, Vizier Ptahshepses, was – apart from the king – one of the most powerful men in the land, there are not many documents relating to either the date of the construction of his mastaba, or any other dates concerning his official career and personal life. These limitations have presented difficulties among the scientists who were dealing with this noble and his magnificent tomb. The dating of the mastaba was already puzzling for the first excavator of the mastaba, J. J. de Morgan. He thought that Ptahshepses lived during Sahure's reign, and that his mastaba was built in this period.[645] This supposition was demolished by L. Borchardt[646] and N. Strudwick.[647] Following their opinions, the numerous attestations of a certain Ptahshepses in the relief decoration of Sahure's mortuary temple clearly relate to a person other than the owner of the mastaba discussed in this monograph. They therefore date the mastaba to the reign of Niuserre. Contrary to this supposition, it was K. Baer who on the basis of his study of Old Kingdom non-royal titularies at the very beginning of the 1960s proposed to set the life-time of Ptahshepses into the reigns of Djedkare and Unas.[648] In opposition to this standpoint, the dates proposed in the *Topographical Bibliography* shifted the period of the construction of the tomb back to Niuserre's reign (or to the middle of the Fifth Dynasty).[649] M. Verner,[650] M. Baud[651] and M. Bárta[652] also date Ptahshepses' life to the reign of King Niuserre.

6.1.1 Sources for the dating of the mastaba

The main source for dating the construction of the Mastaba of Ptahshepses is found in the material that was recovered from the tomb itself. Since the relief decoration was destroyed to a very large extent, the masons' inscriptions, which have been documented and interpreted on the core masonry of the mastaba,[653] provide the most important source of information concerning the different stages of the construction of the tomb. In contrast to these inscriptions, the relief decoration would only play a minor role in the following discussion on the construction dates of the tomb.

It was Miroslav Verner who showed, beside other aspects important for our understanding of functioning of the ancient Egyptian society, the potential of the masons' marks for the dating of the construction of the mastaba.[654] One of these inscriptions contains a reference mentioning the year of the fifth occasion of counting (the cattle). Unfortunately, this inscription does not include the name of a ruler.[655] Despite the fact that the name of the king is missing, this inscription should

---

645 De Morgan, *RevArch* 24 (3e série) (1894), 27–35.
646 Borchardt, *Sahure* II, 122.
647 Strudwick, *Administration*, 90.
648 Baer, *Rank and Title*, p. 76, N°. 167; Baer's period VD.
649 *PM* III, 340.
650 Verner, *Baugraffiti*, 189–191.
651 Baud, *Famille royale*, 451.
652 Bárta, *Ä&L* 11 (2000), 65.
653 Verner, *Baugraffiti, passim.*
654 Verner, *Baugraffiti*, 189–190.
655 Mason's mark no. 194a: *"Rnpt-śp 5 (?), ꜣbd 3 prt, (św) wpw. Sꜣ wꜣḏt."*, "Year of the fifth counting, third month of winter, first day. Phyle *wꜣḏt*." – Verner, *Baugraffiti*, 110, Taf. XXIV, 194. »

be, in M. Verner's opinion, ascribed to Niuserre.[656] The inscription was unearthed in the oldest part of the mastaba – the Initial Mastaba (in the masonry to the west of the Room no. 27) – and thus might indicate a possible date for the beginning of the tomb construction. The name of the king, during whose rule this counting took place, is unfortunately lost. The inscription is thus missing a vital element of its historical identity for the question of the tomb's dating and its information value is therefore somewhat impaired.[657] One cannot rule out, however, that this masons' inscription might have been ascribed to King Neferirkare. The length of his reign is estimated from 8 to 10 regnal years, therefore, the masons' inscription from the Ptahshepses mastaba might be also connected with his name. If this were so, then it would shift the date of the construction of the Initial Mastaba to the reign of this king.

An important element for obtaining an approximate date for the tomb's construction is to be found in the body of masons' inscriptions that mention the names of members of the royal family. A *Baugraffito* connected with the royal family was found in the northern wall of Room no. 22 (in the Initial Mastaba). It mentions one of "the oldest sons" of Sahure, Netjerienre.[658] This advances the age of Ptahshepses to the generation after Sahure. In addition, the name of Princess Khamerernebty was found on masons' marks during the excavations of the Mastaba of Ptahshepses three times. The first two attestations consist only of the name of the princess.[659] The third inscription also contains her title of King's Daughter.[660] Since the princess became the wife of Ptahshepses, the attestations of her name are very important for the dating of her husband's tomb.

Masons' inscriptions mentioning basilophoric personal names constitute another group of some chronological importance. Among them are those referring to a certain Raneferefankh.[661] All these masons' marks were found in the masonry of the third building stage. M. Verner has shown that these inscriptions do not date from the beginning of Niuserre's reign. Keeping in mind the short period of governance of King Raneferef and that of the ephemeral King Shepseskare, the predecessors of Niuserre, these inscriptions can be dated between the 13th and 15th year after the death of Raneferef. It seems that Raneferefankh was born during the short reign of Raneferef and he could have started his professional career at least at the age of 15–17 years (in M. Verner's opinion this span of time should be about 20 years)[662]. These inscriptions secure our supposition that the third building stage of the mastaba was built during the reign of Niuserre.

» The mason's mark is of a later date than two other mason's marks (Nos. 194b and 194c) on the same block. The first contains a part of the title *imj-r3*, which is also documented elsewhere in the Initial Mastaba (see doc. 6). The other mark is illegible.

[656] Verner, *Baugraffiti*, 110–111; Verner, *ArOr* 69 (2001), 402–404; Verner, 'Once more to Nyuserre's dyad', in: *Egyptian Museum Collection*, 1199.

[657] In M. Verner's opinion, this date should be ascribed to Niuserre. However, the possibility remains that the block on which this graffito is written could have been brought from another building project, *i.e.*, it could be connected with the rule of another pharaoh. During the excavations of the Mastaba of Ptahshepses, another inscription that represented a year of counting was found: *Rnpt ... ?...*, "Year of the ?th counting…". It was an orange-red masons' mark found in the filling between the southern wall of the Initial Mastaba and the northern wall of Room no. 33 (Verner, *Baugraffiti*, 130, Taf., XXXVIII, 280, Foto 31). It was clear to M. Verner (Verner, *Baugraffiti*, 130) that it was older than the graffiti no. 280a, which includes the name of Ptahshepses and his title *śmr-wˁtj*. A red line overlapping this, apparently older mason's mark, is clearly an argument in favour of M. Verner's supposition that the block was originally used in another construction context.

[658] Verner, *Baugraffiti*, p. 101, Taf. XXII, 160; for the attestation of this offspring of Sahure see: Borchardt, *Sahure* II, 112, 115, 119, Bl. 33, 44, 49. For a further discussion concerning Sahure's family see, T. El Awady, in: *Abusir and Saqqar*a *2005*, 191–218.

[659] Verner, *Baugraffiti*, 65–66.

[660] *S3t-nśwt* [*Ḫˁ-mrr-nbtj*], Verner, *Baugraffiti*, 96.

[661] *Śḥḏ pr-ˁ3 Rˁnfr.f-ˁnḫ* – masons' marks nos. 55, 64, 392: Verner, *Baugraffiti*, 79, 80, 154, Taf. IX. 59, 64, 80, LIV, 392, Foto 62.

[662] Verner, 'Once more to Nyuserre's dyad', in: *Egyptian Museum Collection*, 1200.

Beside the masons' marks that contain personal names, a group of inscriptions that incorporates the titles of Ptahshepses are also helpful in establishing the relative chronology of the tomb. The attestations of Ptahshepses' ranking title *śmr-wˁtj*[663] come solely from the area of the Initial Mastaba, while the inscriptions mentioning both the titles *ḥ3tj-ˁ* and *śmr-wˁtj*, together with the name of Ptahshepses, come from the third building stage.[664] The title *ḥ3tj-ˁ* also appears only in the masonry of the third building stage.[665] A large part of the masonry belonging to the second building stage is covered by the casing. Therefore, there is a possibility, that the masons' inscriptions mentioning title *ḥ3tj-ˁ* are covered by the casing. On the other hand, attestations of Ptahshepses' highest titles and epithets, later mentioned in the relief decoration[666] are absent among the masons' inscriptions.[667] It seems probable, that Ptahshepses obtained these titles only during later constructional works, possibly during the second, or more probably the third building stage, in the period when the core masonry was already finished.

Beside the previously mentioned masons' marks, chronologically important inscriptions have also been documented in other buildings elsewhere in the Abusir Pyramid Necropolis. The core masonry of the enclosure wall of Niuserre's pyramid complex contained two masons' marks, both mentioning *śmr-wˁtj Ptḥ-špś*.[668] Another document is a mason's inscription found in the masonry of the Mastaba of Princesses and mentioning Ptahshepses' title of *ḥ3tj-ˁ*.[669] The appearance of this mason's inscription in the Mastaba of Princesses introduces some implications concerning the relative date of the construction of both monuments. However, as it has been already shown, one cannot exclude that the title *ḥ3tj-ˁ* appeared already on the now inaccessible masonry of the second building stage in the Ptahshepses mastaba. Moreover, the block with this *Baugraffito* might have been re-used in the masonry of the Mastaba of Princesses. On the other hand, masons' inscriptions with the name and Ptahshepses' title of *ḥ3tj-ˁ* recorded by Borchardt in the Mastaba of Princesses, represent another document illustrating a close relationship of Khamerernebty and Ptahshepses and also the relatively same date of construction of the Mastaba of Princesses and the Ptahshepses mastaba.

Another recording of Ptahshepses and his titles in masons' marks was found on a block in the core masonry of the pyramid complex of a queen, Lepsius no. 24.[670] In this case, the inscriptions contain not only his title *ḥ3tj-ˁ*, but also the title *irj-nfr-ḥ3t*. These inscriptions indicate that the Mastaba of Ptahshepses (or, more precisely, its second and third building stages) was constructed at the same time as some other monuments in the Abusir necropolis and these monuments can all be dated to the reign of Niuserre.

The remains of the relief decoration of Ptahshepses' mastaba contain basiliphorous names of several persons and also the names of mortuary domains. As a matter of course, these names should be used as dating reference only cautiously.[671] On the other hand, the names do present, at least, a dating criterion *post quem*. In the case of the Mastaba of Ptahshepses, respectively its second, but more probably the third building stage, these names date its construction to a period

---

663 Verner, *Baugraffiti*, 66, 95, 97, 100, 105, 113, 122, 130, 131, 137.
664 *Op. cit.*, 122, 131, 136, 142, 144, 147.
665 *Op. cit.*, 99, 128, 142, 143.
666 *Sš mḏ3t nṯr, t3jtj ṯ3tj n s3b, s3-nśwt, s3-nśwt n ḫt.f.*
667 As previously discussed in *chapter 5.2*, it is highly possible that the preserved relief decoration in the Old Portico, the Chapel with Three Niches and in the Southern Portico did not originate until the third building stage.
668 Borchardt, *Neferirkare*, 53.
669 *"Ḥ3tj-ˁ Ptḥ-špś"* – Borchardt, *Neuserre*, 144, Abb. 125.
670 M. Verner, *Excavations at Abusir, Seasons of 1994/95 and 1995/96*, ZÄS 124 (1997), 71. These masons' marks have not yet been fully published.
671 *Cf.* for example: Reisner, *Giza Necropolis*, 33; Seidlmayer, in: *Archäologie und Korrespondenzanalyse*, 17–51; Jánosi, *Giza*, 44–46.

after the reign of Sahure[672] and Raneferef. The mention of Ptahshepses' son Khafini (see p. 24), is of a great importance[673] since the inscription that accompanies the figure contains the name of Niuserre – Ini – written within the cartouche.[674] This basilophorous name indicates that this son of Ptahshepses was certainly *already born* during the reign of Niuserre. Moreover, in the relief, Khafini was depicted as an adult man, not a child. This fact seems to correspond with our view concerning the personality of Ptahshepses described as an adult man at the time of the commencement of construction of his mastaba (*i.e.* of the Initial Mastaba). The other basiliphorous names mentioned in the relief decoration do not reach beyond the reign of Niuserre, but encompass the names of Sahure and Raneferef.[675] Among the names of the funerary domains only one, including Khafre's name, survived almost entirely;[676] in three other examples, only parts of Niuserre's cartouches are preserved.[677]

The tomb of Ptahshepses' son – Ptahshepses Junior II – does not contain any further information concerning the history of the Ptahshepses family. According to the opinion of M. Bárta,[678] the tomb and the life of Ptahshepses Junior II should be dated to the reign of Niuserre or slightly later. This date, and the horizontal stratigraphy of the area in which the tombs of Ptahshepses Senior and his son were built, creates another dating criterion – *not later than* – for the construction of the tomb of Ptahshepses Senior. It should be mentioned here, that it cannot be fully ruled out that some work connected with the construction and decoration of the Ptahshepses mastaba might have been done after the death of Niuserre (there is no direct proof for the suggestion that Ptahshepses died before the king). However, the mastaba had achieved its final dimensions in its third building stage prior to the end of Niuserre's reign, as is shown by the position of the tomb of Ptahshepses Junior II.

The elements of architecture may also contribute something to the solving of the problems of the mastaba's dating to the middle of the Fifth Dynasty. Unfortunately, due to the large scale destruction of the tomb, many elements of architecture and art which might help one to solve this important question have been lost. Among those which survive, one can enumerate the following characteristics of the mastaba:

- *The orientation of both offering rooms built along their east-west axes.* This type of offering chapel was introduced into the architecture of the non-royal tombs during the reign of Kings Neferirkare and Niuserre. Apparently, the Initial Mastaba was one of the first tombs in which an east-west orientation was used.

- *The use of a descending corridor leading to the burial apartment of Ptahshepses.* While in the Mastaba of Djadjaemankh we encounter an access to the burial chamber of this noble's spouse which has a "mixed" design of a vertical shaft and a descending corridor, the access to the burial chamber of the tomb owner was created *only* by the descending corridor. One can see a similar situation operating between Djadjaemankh's burial apartment and the burial apartment in the Mastaba of Ptahshepses. The fact that the tombs constructed in the Abusir Cemetery of Nobles represent a turning point in respect to the inclusion of descending corridors for non-royal tombs seems also to be documented by the evidence from Userkafankh's

[672] Verner, *Baugraffiti*, 101. In the relief decoration, which still remains *in situ*, three attestations of basilophorous names of persons mentioning Sahure as part of their names, have been discerned: *ḥm-k3 ꜥnḫ-Ś3hw-Rꜥ* (Verner, *Reliefs*, 94, photo 86), *ẖꜥkw Mr-[m3ꜥt-Ś3ḥw-Rꜥ]* (*op. cit.*, 66, 157) and *śḥḏ-pr-ꜥ3 śḥḏ ḥmw-k3 ꜥnḫ-Ꞽsi* (*op. cit.*, 96, photo 87).
[673] *Op. cit.*, 43–45.
[674] *S3.f śmśw, śmr-wꜥtj, ẖrj-ḥbt Ḫꜥ.f-Ꞽni* – *op. cit.*, 44.
[675] *Ꞽm3-Ś3ḥw-Rꜥ* – Vachala, *Relieffragmente*, 54; *Nfr-ḥtp-Ś3ḥw-Rꜥ* – *op. cit.*, 116; *Ḫꜥ.[f]-Ś3ḥw-Rꜥ* – *op. cit.*, 64; *Ś3ḥw-Rꜥ-ḏd(i)* – *op. cit.*, 58; *Nj-wśr-[Rꜥ]-mn-wrrt* – *op. cit.*, 78; *[Nj]-wśr-[Rꜥ]-mrj-Ḥr* – *op. cit.*, 66; *[Nj]-wśr-[Rꜥ]-ḥtp(w)* – *op. cit.*, 66.
[676] *Ḥwt-[Rꜥ]-ẖꜥ.f*, *op. cit.*, 244.
[677] *Op. cit.*, 248.
[678] Bárta, *Ä&L* 10 (2000), 66.

tomb, where his wife has a vertical shaft and Userkafankh has a descending corridor. This type of evidence provides a relative dating for non-royal tomb architecture that lies somewhere in the middle of the Fifth Dynasty.[679]

• Of problematic value concerning the dating of the Ptahshepses mastaba is *the placement of the opening of the descending corridor* leading to the burial chamber: this opening was at first located *inside* the tomb. This location in the case of Ptahshepses suggests an early date for the tomb. However, there is not enough available evidence elsewhere regarding these features for us to make a ruling on this at this time. Previously, there was a group of tombs in Giza Central Field which was dated to the end of the Fourth Dynasty. These tombs were once used as the reference set for the dating of this sloping corridor and the beginning of its usage in the framework of Old Kingdom non-royal architecture.

As was shown recently, however, these tombs, with the opening of their descending corridors placed *outside* the massif of the tombs, should be re-dated to the second half of the Fifth Dynasty.[680] These tombs are thus not possible to use as a reference any more. Together with the Mastaba of Djadjaemankh, the Mastaba of Ptahshepses represented the only examples in the Abusir Cemetery of Nobles where the entrance to the corridor was hidden within one of the rooms in the mastaba. As was mentioned in the previous paragraph, both tombs were among the first examples to use the descending corridor.[681] Therefore, it seems probable that the position of the mouth (*i.e.* either in the interior or in the exterior of the mastaba *massif*) had not been settled at the time when these two tombs were built. This is apparent from the evidence in other tombs – especially that of Ti, where the entrance to the corridor leading to the burial chamber was placed in the pillared courtyard.[682] The same situation one can see in the tomb of Ptahshepses Junior II.[683] The tomb of Ti is one of the oldest examples of tombs with a descending corridor. One of the reasons for hiding the corridor entrances inside the massifs of mastabas built by Djadjaemankh and Ptahshepses seems to have been due to the special status of both nobles, for whom the palace façade decoration was placed above the entrances to these corridors.[684]

• *The use of the torus moulding in the western wall of the Chapel with Three Niches.* Despite the fact that the wall did not contain an actual false door, its design was much influenced by the layout of the standard false door. Thus, it seems to be possible to use this as another dating criterion. Following N. Cherpion's opinion, one can date the inclusion of this element of architecture to the reigns of Neferirkare/Niuserre.[685] This, again documents the hypothesis that the life and the construction of the tomb of Ptahshepses might not have been dated *before* the reign of Neferirkare.

---

679 *Cf.* Reisner, *Tomb Development*, 151–155; Jánosi, in: *Abusir and Saqqara 2000*, 463.
680 Jánosi, in: *Abusir and Saqqara 2000*, note 66 on p. 463–464.
681 In the tomb of Khentkaus I in Giza, one can also see also a short descending corridor leading to the burial chamber (Hassan, *Gîza*, 24, fig. 1). Nevertheless, despite the fact that this tomb did not represent a pyramid (and pyramids have been excluded from our study), this queen' s tomb was not taken into consideration. The main reason for this omission is due to the special social status of Khentkaus I, her role in Egyptian history and also the exceptional nature of her stepped tomb itself.
682 For further discussion see: Jánosi, in: *Abusir and Saqqara 2000*, 460–464.
683 Bárta, *Ä&L* 10 (2000).
684 In this connection it is interesting to mention that the masonry of the Mastaba of Djadjaemankh is very similar to the eastern part of the core masonry of the Initial Mastaba (the second sub-phase built after the construction of the burial chamber). This fact could have two explanations: either, both tombs were built by one crew (at a different time?), or, the tombs were built at the same period of time (it would not be possible to ascertain whether by one, or more crews).
685 Cherpion, *Mastabas*, 75.

6.1.2 The date of the construction of the mastaba

The assessment of the precise dating of the Mastaba of Ptahshepses is one of the most complicated tasks connected with the study of its architecture. However, in providing a *resumé* of the previous paragraphs, it should be evident that the construction of the tomb could not have commenced during the reign of King Sahure. At the very least, the second and the third building stage were built during the reign of King Niuserre. Nevertheless, we cannot rule out the idea that the construction of the Initial Mastaba, the first building stage of the tomb, could have started in the period before Niuserre's accession to the throne.

One may also assume that Ptahshepses was (very probably) a mature man when he commenced the construction of his Initial Mastaba, a construction that was later entirely finished. There is also a distinct possibility that some time passed before the decision was made to enlarge this tomb with the annex of the second building stage.

The second building stage presents an important shift in the total concept of the tomb, for this was a shift from a standard mastaba to a temple tomb intended for the cult connected with the erected, free-standing statues that were such a feature of the mastaba. This alteration might have been based on some fundamental change in the life of Ptahshepses. Having in mind the overall situation concerning the succession on the Egyptian throne, such a change might have been presented by the accession of Niuserre to the throne. Ptahshepses, due to his powerful position, could have played an important role in this event. As a reward for his possible assistance in Niuserre's enthronement, his social rank might have been elevated. Such an elevation might have then influenced the concept and appearance of his expanding tomb.

The third building stage presents a continuation of this new concept, enlarging and completing the intention started in the second building stage. In this connection, one has to underline the fact that the change between the second and third building stage was not conceptually large. With regard to this second extension, it seems very probable that Ptahshepses overestimated his potential, in his decision to enlarge his tomb, for which some dimensions were almost comparable to those of the royal mortuary temples.[686] For this reason, Ptahshepses' tomb was not fully completed by the time of his death and it seems that about that time, the resources – which very probably came partly from the royal administration – must have dried up.

One can sum up the chronological outline of the building by saying that the major construction of the mastaba was carried out during the reign of Niuserre; however, there is a possibility that the Initial Mastaba was at least under construction, if not finished, when that king took over the governing of the Egyptian state. Its construction, thus, might have been started during one of Niuserre's predecessors, either Neferirkare or Raneferef.[687]

---

[686] Sahure's mortuary temple: 45 × 41 m (intimate part), 45 × 80 m (whole temple), Neferirkare: 24.6 × 21.5 m (intimate stone part), 71 × 42–49.6 m (whole temple, the majority of its walls were built of mud bricks); Niuserre: 57 × 13 m (intimate part), 48 × 28.5 m (eastern part or outer temple); Djedkare: 41 × 27 (intimate part), 87 × 41 (whole temple).

[687] The quite considerable distance that lies between the mortuary complexes of these kings and the place where the Initial Mastaba was constructed might not have been an influential factor, particularly if the mastaba were built towards the later part of Neferirkare's reign. As we can see in Giza, mastabas of some courtiers were not automatically placed in the closest vicinity to the royal pyramid complex, but some of them lay at quite a distinct distance (*cf.* the situation in Giza's Western Field, Jánosi, *Giza*, 128–154). Moreover, areas close to the constructional site of the complexes of Neferirkare and Raneferef with workshops, transportation ramps and storerooms and with all the building materials cluttering the site, was not an appropriate place for the construction of the mastaba. The advantage of the place which was chosen by Ptahshepses is presented by its relative proximity to the edge of the lowest terrace of the Libyan Desert. Thus, in the view from the Nile Valley, the mastaba was distinctly visible. As a matter of course, among the rulers during which reign the construction of the Initial Mastaba might have been started should be also included the ephemeral King Shepseskare.

6.2 Mastaba's position within the framework of the Egyptian architecture

The Mastaba of Ptahshepses represents one of the most important examples of Old Kingdom non-royal tombs and one of the most important examples of mortuary architecture for this period. Even in his Initial Mastaba, it is obvious that Ptahshepses tried to display himself as a man with a strong position in the royal court by using unique elements of architecture which were at that time intended to be used only in the mortuary complexes of Egyptian kings. This was, for example, the case with his use of the saddle roof in his burial chamber. Another important element of architecture found in the mastaba was the large staircase, leading to the roof of the tomb. At the time of its construction, it was one of the first instances of a staircase in the large tombs of the nobility of this period. The mastaba also incorporated one of the first east-west oriented offering rooms. On the other hand, it is apparent that, at that time, the Ptahshepses mastaba was still closely linked to the traditions of non-royal tombs, for his mastaba resembles the ground plans of other large tombs built in Abusir, Giza and Saqqara.

Thus, the most striking change which happened during the second building stage was the decision to construct a temple-like annex, incorporating the chapel with statue niches, two porticos (and at least one of them adorned by a pair of columns) and a noticeable group of storerooms. It is the contention of this book to show that the main function of this annex was the erection of the tomb owner's statues and the performance of rituals connected with them (including also the storing of goods). As direct models, one can without doubt see the connection to the royal mortuary temples in Abusir – especially that of Sahure, which was certainly finished in the time of the mastaba's construction.[688] One may, therefore, also suppose that the rituals which were carried out in connection with the statue niches in the Ptahshepses mastaba may have had some degree of parallelism with the royal monuments. Thus it was, that the tomb of Ptahshepses became transformed into a kind of a private mortuary temple. The architectural appearance of the mastaba had altered: from a massive block of masonry into a much more complex building that included a high number of spacious cultic chambers, storerooms and other auxiliary rooms and, dominating the mastaba, a large courtyard. This major change from the closed and tranquil architecture of a standard mastaba into an embellished, temple-like tomb might have been epitomised by the construction of the new large entrance and the erecting of two elaborate lotus bundle columns.

During the third building stage of the mastaba, the tomb owner continued his transformation of the tomb into a temple. It is obvious that Ptahshepses was very influenced during the construction of this building stage, not only by the architecture of the royal mortuary temples but also – at least in some architectural forms – by the predominant sun cult.

The newly built monumental entrance to the whole mastaba complex presented an actual gateway between the world of living and that of the deceased. A pair of high, eight-stemmed, lotus bundle columns which are the oldest yet-known examples of this element in the framework of the ancient Egyptian architecture, helped to establish the atmosphere for the prospect of the never ending resurrection of the deceased.

It is hard to say whether this New Portico was already adorned with free-standing statues, but the visitor could almost certainly see them in the Old Portico, where they were accompanied by relief decoration, delicately interconnected with the statues and another pair of lotus bundle columns into one artistic unit. The same effort to follow the royal models one can also assume for other parts of the mastaba. One of the most striking areas of the new addition to the tomb certainly was the pillared courtyard. In this case, we can document the border between the king on

---

[688] There is a possibility that Niuserre's mortuary temple with the five-niched hall was not yet finished at the time when the annex of the second building stage was under construction.

the one hand and commoners on the other. Despite the fact Ptahshepses could use floral columns in the porticos, this was not the case with the court. In this way, his mastaba did not differ from the tombs of queens and other nobles of the period whose courtyards (or ceilinged halls) might also include pillars. It is also apparent, that this courtyard is, together with the pillared courtyard in Ti's mastaba, one of the earliest examples of pillars in a non-royal courtyard. As such, it became a very important unit in the history of ancient Egyptian architecture.

The exactly calculated proportions and rhythm of the lighter surfaces and darker spaces created by the regularly spaced pillars, however, would have constituted a dignified stage for any rites which went on in the courtyard. When considering the court's architectural forms, mainly the use of pillars, one is reminded of the older examples of the royal pillared architecture dated to the Fourth Dynasty.[689] The court architecture and design is a great achievement for the architect of this tomb.

At the same time, the courtyard had its profound functional importance as an important intersection between several transit routes, serving, *e.g.*, for the transportation of offerings to and from the storerooms. Ptahshepses' depictions decorated the pillars. Beside these images, the hypothetical placement of statues (in naoi?) might have served some important religious function.

The Boat-room (Room no. 40) is one of the most intriguing spaces in the whole mastaba. It is not possible to say definitively whether the Boat-room had originally been planned as the location for one ship or more. In the positive case, this design unit might have also come from the concepts of royal architecture – together with its ideas of sun worship as well. If it had been planned that two ships were to be installed in the Ptahshepses mastaba, the idea may have been connected with the concept of the day and night barques used by the deceased kings and/or the sun god in the afterlife. This idea would have been then transferred into the architecture of the Ptahshepses mastaba. If this plan had been realised, it would have presented only the second instance of burying the ships within the framework of non-royal Old-Kingdom architecture.[690]

The high total number of storerooms built subsequently in the mastaba complex might also have been influenced by royal architecture. As has already been demonstrated (see p. 178–179), the number of storerooms in Ptahshepses' mastaba is higher than that in other large tombs of the Fifth and the Sixth Dynasty. The high number of storerooms in Ptahshepses' tomb can be also taken as indirect evidence of the complexity and the size of the rituals which were carried out in the mastaba.[691]

The Mastaba of Ptahshepses was innovative not only in the size and complexity of the groundplan, but also by its use of some elements from royal architecture. These elements then became a standard part of non-royal architecture, *e.g.*, the east-west oriented offering chambers, the descending corridors to the burial apartment and the use of torus moulding.

Despite its exceptional nature, its size, and its use of non-standard architectural elements – *e.g.* of the lotus columns and of the burial chamber with the saddle

[689] *Cf.* The open courtyard in Khufu's mortuary temple (*MRA* I, 60–62, Tav. 9, fig. 1, Tav. 10, fig. 7), the inner rooms of Khafre's mortuary temple (Hölscher, *Chephren*, Bl. III) and the open courtyard of Userkaf's mortuary temple in Saqqara (Labrousse, Lauer, *Ouserkaf*, 45–51, general plan of the temple *in fine*, fig. 51). In this connection, another case of pillared architecture found in royal architecture of the time should be mentioned – that of the Lower Temple which was Niuserre's sun temple, see Ricke, *SH Userkaf* I, 35–40, Abb. 22, 23, 25, plans 1, 5, 7.

[690] As was already mentioned, the other example is that of the tomb of Kagemni in Saqqara (see p. 143).

[691] Bearing in mind that in the Initial Mastaba there was apparently only one storeroom (Room no. 23), which was moreover used as a corridor leading to the staircase, it is possible to suppose that during the primary building stage the magazines were located (or planned?) in a hypothetical building constructed in front of the mastaba. As previously discussed, both enlargements also included the construction of three groups of storerooms. This fact clearly shows the steady increase in the need for offerings and goods used during the rites performed in the tomb and also hints at the growing complexity of these rituals.

roof – and in the complexity of its ground plan, the Mastaba of Vizier Ptahshepses still remained a non-royal tomb, even though a very large and complex one. This clearly shows the fundamental differences in the society between the king on one level and his subordinates on another; but the architectural conventions also stress the difference relating to these groups connected with the beliefs that were held about the life in the other world. In this respect, the mastaba also documents the trends in the development of non-royal tomb architecture which were profoundly connected with changes in Egyptian society at this time. On the one hand, there was the increasing power of the nobles, on the other hand the endeavour of the Egyptian kings from Niuserre onwards to limit it.[692] As a result of these struggles, the social, economic and cultural development of the Egyptian state began to decline at the end of the Sixth Dynasty.[693] It is apparent that in the second half of the Fifth Dynasty and at the beginning of the Sixth Dynasty there were a quite limited number of persons who were wealthy and also highly privileged by their lords[694] and Ptahshepses was one of these. His mastaba belongs among the largest tombs of the period of the second half of the Fifth and the beginning of the Sixth Dynasty,[695] and his power is revealed by the size and architectural elements of his tomb. Other mastabas of comparable status belong to the most powerful nobles of the Egyptian state and are distinguished both by their size and by their complex ground-plans which, in the case of the Ptahshepses mastaba, could consist of up to forty rooms.

In summing up the evidence outlined above, we can say that Ptahshepses' efforts to show his importance and elevated social rank resulted in the emergence of a new architectural type, the temple tomb.[696] The magnates flourishing at the beginning of the Sixth Dynasty were quick to adopt this form for their own eternal memorials, as we see in the tombs of Kagemni, Mereruka and others. Nevertheless, the impetus did not stop there. The development of this form of architecture continued into the later periods of Egyptian history – as we can see in the case of tombs of the regional magnates in Qaw el-Kebir,[697] in Haremheb's tomb in Saqqara[698] or the large Late Period tombs in Western Thebes.[699]

* * *

It is apparent that Ptahshepses, despite his high social status, ambition and efforts to construct for himself a vast monument, was not able to fulfil his dreams in their entirety. Whatever the reasons were (the death of Ptahshepses, the death of Niuserre, a falling into disfavour with the king?), the tomb was not fully finished. Time saw to it that even this unfinished state would not remain untouched, for the mastaba became a frequent target for the later activities of stone robbers and it was also a popular place for a secondary cemetery in later periods of Egyptian history. All this damage resulted in a rather bad state of preservation for this tomb: these remains are all that are known to us today.

---

[692] *Cf. Bárta*, in: *Structure and Significance*, 117–119.
[693] Müller-Wollermann, *Krisenfaktoren*.
[694] Bárta, *loc. cit.*
[695] The mastabas of Ti, Ptahhotep I, Akhtihotep, Ihy, Nebkauhor, Niankhba, Khentika, Nefersekhmet Sheshi, Ankhmahor, Mereruka, Kagemni, in Saqqara and tombs of Rawer and Senedjemib Inti in Giza. For the basic characteristics of this group of Old Kingdom private tombs see Jánosi, in: *L'art égyptien*, 63.
[696] *Cf.* Arnold, *Baulexikon*, 95.
[697] Petrie, *Antaeopolis*, 1–9; Steckweh, *Qâw* 1–44.
[698] Martin, *Horemheb.*
[699] Eigner, *Grabbauten.*

Indexes

Personal Names

Titles

Sites

Monuments

Varia

ABUSIR XI

THE ARCHITECTURE OF THE MASTABA OF PTAHSHEPSES

Mgr. Jaromír Krejčí, Ph.D.

Vydaly
Český egyptologický ústav Filozofické fakulty Univerzity Karlovy v Praze,
Celetná 20, 110 00 Praha 1
Nakladatelství Academia, Středisko společných činností AV ČR, v. v. i.
Vodičkova 40, 110 00 Praha 1

Kniha vychází s finanční podporou GAČR D404/99/D003 a MŠMT ČR,
granty č. MSM 11210006 a MSM 0021620826.

Odpovědný redaktor: Pavel Zátka

Obálka (s použitím fotografie Jaromíra Krejčího) a grafická úprava:
Jolana Malátková
Fotografie: Archiv Českého egyptologického ústavu Filozofické fakulty
Univerzity Karlovy v Praze, Jaromír Krejčí, Jaroslav Novotný, Sammlung des
Ägyptologischen Instituts der Universität Heidelberg, Kamil Voděra, Milan
Zemina, DigitalGlobe Inc., Laboratoř geoinformatiky UJEP, Data System, s. r. o.
Ilustrace: Jaromír Krejčí, Vladimír Hamata, Jolana Malátková, Luděk Wellner,
Griffith Institute, Oxford

Vydání první, Praha 2009
Ediční číslo 10909

Sazba Český egyptologický ústav Filozofické fakulty Univerzity Karlovy v Praze,
Celetná 20, 110 00 Praha 1
Tisk Serifa s. r. o., Jinonická 80, 150 00 Praha 5

ISBN 978-80-200-1728-4